Lecture Notes in Computer Science 13329

More information about this series at https://link.springer.com/bookseries/558

Panayiotis Zaphiris · Andri Ioannou (Eds.)

Learning and Collaboration Technologies

Novel Technological Environments

9th International Conference, LCT 2022
Held as Part of the 24th HCI International Conference, HCII 2022
Virtual Event, June 26 – July 1, 2022
Proceedings, Part II

 Springer

Editors
Panayiotis Zaphiris (iD)
Department of Multimedia and Graphic Art
Cyprus University of Technology
Limassol, Cyprus

Andri Ioannou (iD)
Research Center on Interactive Media, Smart
Systems and Emerging Technologies
(CYENS)
Cyprus University of Technology
Limassol, Cyprus

ISSN 0302-9743   ISSN 1611-3349 (electronic)
Lecture Notes in Computer Science
ISBN 978-3-031-05674-1   ISBN 978-3-031-05675-8 (eBook)
https://doi.org/10.1007/978-3-031-05675-8

Foreword

Human-computer interaction (HCI) is acquiring an ever-increasing scientific and industrial importance, as well as having more impact on people's everyday life, as an ever-growing number of human activities are progressively moving from the physical to the digital world. This process, which has been ongoing for some time now, has been dramatically accelerated by the COVID-19 pandemic. The HCI International (HCII) conference series, held yearly, aims to respond to the compelling need to advance the exchange of knowledge and research and development efforts on the human aspects of design and use of computing systems.

The 24th International Conference on Human-Computer Interaction, HCI International 2022 (HCII 2022), was planned to be held at the Gothia Towers Hotel and Swedish Exhibition & Congress Centre, Göteborg, Sweden, during June 26 to July 1, 2022. Due to the COVID-19 pandemic and with everyone's health and safety in mind, HCII 2022 was organized and run as a virtual conference. It incorporated the 21 thematic areas and affiliated conferences listed on the following page.

A total of 5583 individuals from academia, research institutes, industry, and governmental agencies from 88 countries submitted contributions, and 1276 papers and 275 posters were included in the proceedings to appear just before the start of the conference. The contributions thoroughly cover the entire field of human-computer interaction, addressing major advances in knowledge and effective use of computers in a variety of application areas. These papers provide academics, researchers, engineers, scientists, practitioners, and students with state-of-the-art information on the most recent advances in HCI. The volumes constituting the set of proceedings to appear before the start of the conference are listed in the following pages.

The HCI International (HCII) conference also offers the option of 'Late Breaking Work' which applies both for papers and posters, and the corresponding volume(s) of the proceedings will appear after the conference. Full papers will be included in the 'HCII 2022 - Late Breaking Papers' volumes of the proceedings to be published in the Springer LNCS series, while 'Poster Extended Abstracts' will be included as short research papers in the 'HCII 2022 - Late Breaking Posters' volumes to be published in the Springer CCIS series.

I would like to thank the Program Board Chairs and the members of the Program Boards of all thematic areas and affiliated conferences for their contribution and support towards the highest scientific quality and overall success of the HCI International 2022 conference; they have helped in so many ways, including session organization, paper reviewing (single-blind review process, with a minimum of two reviews per submission) and, more generally, acting as goodwill ambassadors for the HCII conference.

This conference would not have been possible without the continuous and unwavering support and advice of Gavriel Salvendy, founder, General Chair Emeritus, and Scientific Advisor. For his outstanding efforts, I would like to express my appreciation to Abbas Moallem, Communications Chair and Editor of HCI International News.

June 2022   Constantine Stephanidis

HCI International 2022 Thematic Areas and Affiliated Conferences

Thematic Areas

- HCI: Human-Computer Interaction
- HIMI: Human Interface and the Management of Information

Affiliated Conferences

- EPCE: 19th International Conference on Engineering Psychology and Cognitive Ergonomics
- AC: 16th International Conference on Augmented Cognition
- UAHCI: 16th International Conference on Universal Access in Human-Computer Interaction
- CCD: 14th International Conference on Cross-Cultural Design
- SCSM: 14th International Conference on Social Computing and Social Media
- VAMR: 14th International Conference on Virtual, Augmented and Mixed Reality
- DHM: 13th International Conference on Digital Human Modeling and Applications in Health, Safety, Ergonomics and Risk Management
- DUXU: 11th International Conference on Design, User Experience and Usability
- C&C: 10th International Conference on Culture and Computing
- DAPI: 10th International Conference on Distributed, Ambient and Pervasive Interactions
- HCIBGO: 9th International Conference on HCI in Business, Government and Organizations
- LCT: 9th International Conference on Learning and Collaboration Technologies
- ITAP: 8th International Conference on Human Aspects of IT for the Aged Population
- AIS: 4th International Conference on Adaptive Instructional Systems
- HCI-CPT: 4th International Conference on HCI for Cybersecurity, Privacy and Trust
- HCI-Games: 4th International Conference on HCI in Games
- MobiTAS: 4th International Conference on HCI in Mobility, Transport and Automotive Systems
- AI-HCI: 3rd International Conference on Artificial Intelligence in HCI
- MOBILE: 3rd International Conference on Design, Operation and Evaluation of Mobile Communications

List of Conference Proceedings Volumes Appearing Before the Conference

1. LNCS 13302, Human-Computer Interaction: Theoretical Approaches and Design Methods (Part I), edited by Masaaki Kurosu
2. LNCS 13303, Human-Computer Interaction: Technological Innovation (Part II), edited by Masaaki Kurosu
3. LNCS 13304, Human-Computer Interaction: User Experience and Behavior (Part III), edited by Masaaki Kurosu
4. LNCS 13305, Human Interface and the Management of Information: Visual and Information Design (Part I), edited by Sakae Yamamoto and Hirohiko Mori
5. LNCS 13306, Human Interface and the Management of Information: Applications in Complex Technological Environments (Part II), edited by Sakae Yamamoto and Hirohiko Mori
6. LNAI 13307, Engineering Psychology and Cognitive Ergonomics, edited by Don Harris and Wen-Chin Li
7. LNCS 13308, Universal Access in Human-Computer Interaction: Novel Design Approaches and Technologies (Part I), edited by Margherita Antona and Constantine Stephanidis
8. LNCS 13309, Universal Access in Human-Computer Interaction: User and Context Diversity (Part II), edited by Margherita Antona and Constantine Stephanidis
9. LNAI 13310, Augmented Cognition, edited by Dylan D. Schmorrow and Cali M. Fidopiastis
10. LNCS 13311, Cross-Cultural Design: Interaction Design Across Cultures (Part I), edited by Pei-Luen Patrick Rau
11. LNCS 13312, Cross-Cultural Design: Applications in Learning, Arts, Cultural Heritage, Creative Industries, and Virtual Reality (Part II), edited by Pei-Luen Patrick Rau
12. LNCS 13313, Cross-Cultural Design: Applications in Business, Communication, Health, Well-being, and Inclusiveness (Part III), edited by Pei-Luen Patrick Rau
13. LNCS 13314, Cross-Cultural Design: Product and Service Design, Mobility and Automotive Design, Cities, Urban Areas, and Intelligent Environments Design (Part IV), edited by Pei-Luen Patrick Rau
14. LNCS 13315, Social Computing and Social Media: Design, User Experience and Impact (Part I), edited by Gabriele Meiselwitz
15. LNCS 13316, Social Computing and Social Media: Applications in Education and Commerce (Part II), edited by Gabriele Meiselwitz
16. LNCS 13317, Virtual, Augmented and Mixed Reality: Design and Development (Part I), edited by Jessie Y. C. Chen and Gino Fragomeni
17. LNCS 13318, Virtual, Augmented and Mixed Reality: Applications in Education, Aviation and Industry (Part II), edited by Jessie Y. C. Chen and Gino Fragomeni

39. CCIS 1582, HCI International 2022 Posters - Part III, edited by Constantine Stephanidis, Margherita Antona and Stavroula Ntoa
40. CCIS 1583, HCI International 2022 Posters - Part IV, edited by Constantine Stephanidis, Margherita Antona and Stavroula Ntoa

http://2022.hci.international/proceedings

Preface

In today's knowledge society, learning and collaboration are two fundamental and strictly interrelated aspects of knowledge acquisition and creation. Learning technology is the broad range of communication, information, and related technologies that can be used to support learning, teaching, and assessment, often in a collaborative way. Collaboration technology, on the other hand, is targeted to support individuals working in teams towards a common goal, which may be an educational one, by providing tools that aid communication and the management of activities as well as the process of problem solving. In this context, interactive technologies do not only affect and improve the existing educational system but become a transformative force that can generate radically new ways of knowing, learning, and collaborating.

The 9th Learning and Collaboration Technologies Conference (LCT 2022), affiliated to HCI International 2022, addressed theoretical foundations, design and implementation, and effectiveness and impact issues related to interactive technologies for learning and collaboration, including design methodologies, developments and tools, theoretical models, and learning design or learning experience (LX) design, as well as technology adoption and use in formal, non-formal, and informal educational contexts.

Learning and collaboration technologies are increasingly adopted in K-20 (kindergarten to higher education) classrooms and lifelong learning. Technology can support expansive forms of collaboration; deepened empathy; complex coordination of people, materials, and purposes; and development of skill sets that are increasingly important across workspaces of the 21st century. The general themes of the LCT conference aim to address challenges related to understanding how to design for better learning and collaboration with technology, support learners to develop relevant approaches and skills, and assess or evaluate gains and outcomes. To this end, topics such as extended reality (XR) learning, embodied and immersive learning, mobile learning and ubiquitous technologies, serious games and gamification, learning through design and making, educational robotics, educational chatbots, human-computer interfaces, and computer supported collaborative learning, among others, are elaborated in LCT conference proceedings. Learning (experience) design and user experience design remain a challenge in the arena of learning environments and collaboration technology. LCT aims to serve a continuous dialog while synthesizing current knowledge.

Two volumes of the HCII 2022 proceedings are dedicated to this year's edition of the LCT 2022 conference, entitled Learning and Collaboration Technologies: Designing the Learner and Teacher Experience (Part I) and Learning and Collaboration Technologies: Novel Technological Environments (Part II). The first focuses on topics related to designing and developing learning technologies, learning and teaching online, and diversity in learning as well as practices and experiences of technology in education, while the second focuses on topics related to XR in learning and education, chatbots, robots and virtual teachers, and collaboration technology.

Papers of these volumes are included for publication after a minimum of two single-blind reviews from the members of the LCT Program Board or, in some cases, from members of the Program Boards of other affiliated conferences. We would like to thank all of them for their invaluable contribution, support, and efforts.

June 2022   Panayiotis Zaphiris
                                                                        Andri Ioannou

9th International Conference on Learning and Collaboration Technologies (LCT 2022)

Program Board Chairs: **Panayiotis Zaphiris**, Cyprus University of Technology, Cyprus, and **Andri Ioannou** Cyprus University of Technology and Research Center on Interactive Media, Smart Systems and Emerging Technologies (CYENS), Cyprus

- Fisnik Dalipi, Linnaeus University, Sweden
- Camille Dickson-Deane, University of Technology Sydney, Australia
- David Fonseca, La Salle, Ramon Llull University, Spain
- Francisco Jose García-Peñalvo, University of Salamanca, Spain
- Aleksandar Jevremovic, Singidunum University, Serbia
- Elis Kakoulli Constantinou, Cyprus University of Technology, Cyprus
- Tomaž Klobučar, Jozef Stefan Institute, Slovenia
- Birgy Lorenz, Tallinn University of Technology, Estonia
- Nicholas H. Müller, University of Applied Sciences Würzburg-Schweinfurt, Germany
- Anna Nicolaou, Cyprus University of Technology, Cyprus
- Antigoni Parmaxi, Cyprus University of Technology, Cyprus
- Dijana Plantak Vukovac, University of Zagreb, Croatia
- Maria-Victoria Soulé, Cyprus University of Technology, Cyprus
- Sonia Sousa, Tallinn University, Estonia
- Alicia Takaoka, University of Hawaii at Hilo, USA
- Sara Villagrá-Sobrino, Valladolid University, Spain

The full list with the Program Board Chairs and the members of the Program Boards of all thematic areas and affiliated conferences is available online at

http://www.hci.international/board-members-2022.php

HCI International 2023

The 25th International Conference on Human-Computer Interaction, HCI International 2023, will be held jointly with the affiliated conferences at the AC Bella Sky Hotel and Bella Center, Copenhagen, Denmark, 23–28 July 2023. It will cover a broad spectrum of themes related to human-computer interaction, including theoretical issues, methods, tools, processes, and case studies in HCI design, as well as novel interaction techniques, interfaces, and applications. The proceedings will be published by Springer. More information will be available on the conference website: http://2023.hci.international/.

General Chair
Constantine Stephanidis
University of Crete and ICS-FORTH
Heraklion, Crete, Greece
Email: general_chair@hcii2023.org

http://2023.hci.international/

Contents – Part II

Chatbots, Robots and Virtual Teachers

Collaboration Technology

Contents – Part I

Learning and Teaching Online

Diversity in Learning

Technology in Education: Practices and Experiences

eXtended Reality in Learning and Education

Design Thinking for the Construction of Technological Solutions in a Science Course in a Virtual Environment

Carmen Graciela Arbulú Pérez Vargas[1]([📧]) [ID], Alberto Gómez Fuertes[1] [ID],
Moisés David Reyes Pérez[2] [ID], Danicsa Karina Espino Carrasco[1] [ID],
and Luis Eden Rojas Palacios[1] [ID]

[1] Cesar Vallejo University, Pimentel, Peru
carbulu@ucvvirtual.edu.pe
[2] Mayor de San Marcos National University, Lima, Peru

Abstract. The trend of curricular reforms in recent years has been to promote the scientific learning of students, the Peruvian curriculum, through the curricular area of Science and Technology, poses as one of the skills that must be developed in students is the so-called "Design and build technological solutions to solve problems in your environment", whose products are evaluated at an institutional level for the Eureka Science and Technology Fair contest, however many of these need to be strengthened with aspects of creativity at the design level of the technologies, therefore, we set as an objective, to implement Design Thinking to develop competence in the design and construction of technological solutions to solve problems in their environment in female secondary school students in the Science and Technology course, during remote classes. Applying the intervention based on design thinking from the IDEO proposal, considering functional creativity and various cognitive scaffolds developed in electronic learning, the results were favorable, achieving significant differences in the evaluation scores obtained before and after in the first and second phase of the execution of the intervention achieving a Level of significance = 1%, the students were able to identify an alternative technological solution to the problem presented, design the alternative technological solution, implement it and go through the validation process to comply with the specifications of design and operation and evaluates and communicates the operation and impacts of its technological solution alternative.

Keywords: Design thinking · Technological solution · Creativity · Competition

1 Introduction

1.1 Problematic Reality

The quality of science projects is a concern that students and advisory teachers must assume year after year, creativity and innovation are combined for the generation of technological solutions, which compete to scale phases that take them from the institutional stage to a higher level as the national competition.

P. Zaphiris and A. Ioannou (Eds.): HCII 2022, LNCS 13329, pp. 3–13, 2022.
https://doi.org/10.1007/978-3-031-05675-8_1

Therefore, ensuring that technological solutions respond to solving environmental problems will occur when changes are promoted from the school so that female students can develop in the fields of science and technology. It is important to promote the development of skills to create products that, from functional creativity in courses or curricular areas of Science and Technology, are the ground that with the STEAM approach (science, technology, engineering and mathematics) from school allows girls to live active learning experiences with the integration of various areas of knowledge and digital technologies.

In Peru, developing the new National Educational Curriculum from 2016 became a gradual implementation process, political factors such as the transition from one government to another, paused in some way the curricular policy to be implemented through a new National Educational Curriculum of Basic education (CNEB). With this, a new graduation profile for Basic Education students was intended, favored by the development of various skills.

In particular, the new national educational curriculum design for Regular Basic Education (CNEB), incorporated new transversal skills since 2016: skill 28, called "develops in virtual environments generated by ICT" and skill 29 called "Manages its learning autonomously", with a new perspective of assuming technologies and learning within the framework of a renewed curriculum. Regarding scientific thought, promoted from the CNEB, in the curricular area of Science and Technology, it is supported in addition to the National Science and Technology School Fair "Eureka" that aims at the same objective, however, in the year 2020 the health crisis, due to COVID-19, interrupted the traditional modality and gave way to the virtual modality. That is why, through the scientific and technological inquiry and literacy approach, the Science and Technology curricular area demanded from teachers' new adaptations of their practice to develop in students' skills to: "Design and build technological solutions to solve environmental problems". "Explain the physical world based on knowledge about living beings, matter and energy, biodiversity, Earth and the universe" and "Inquire using scientific methods to build their knowledge" (MINEDU 2016).

The Competence called, "design and build technological solutions to solve problems in your environment", hereinafter C3, is the one that aroused our interest, in this research, during electronic learning in remote classes. It is, refers to the student's ability to build technological objects, processes or systems, based on scientific knowledge, technology and various local practices, to respond to context problems, linked to social needs, putting into play creativity and perseverance (Secondary Education Curricular Program, 2016).

However, on the part of the students, they show difficulties in generating projects that respond to creative designs, many times, proposals for experimental designs are made, but these respond to another competence, the vision they have of science is biased to the fact that it is an extensive practice in for men. Regarding the identification of the problems that need to be solved, they are exclusive of objectivist visions and that the determination of the technological solution must start from the researcher.

Likewise, it has little experience in the design and graphic representation of the technological solution with detailed technical specifications. The same one that once built, must be subjected to tests, if they are close to its technological solution products being evaluated so that those that pass the evaluation can participate in the Institutional Science Fair and external phases for its dissemination.

The analysis carried out so far has allowed us to hypothesize possible misunderstood visions regarding teaching by teachers, who have not managed to overcome the often-distorted traditional vision of what science and technology are.

We pose the following research question: What will be the technique that will improve the competence called design and build technological solutions to solve problems in your environment during remote classes?

For this, the following general objective was proposed, Implement Design Thinking to develop competence in the design and construction of technological solutions to solve problems in their environment in female secondary school students in the Science and Technology course, during remote classes.

1.2 Literature Review

Previous studies from a hermeneutical analysis of the information provided from various sources on substantive theories show that the Oslo Manual, the main reference for measuring innovations, in 2005, expressly eliminated the adjective "technological" that it used to add to the term "innovation", arguing that it meant too different things in different countries and contexts (CONICYT 2011), it is thus that referring to technological innovation is inappropriate.

It is evident that technology is integrated into daily life as diverse technological solutions, such as mobile phones, computers, remote controls, the Internet, automobiles, pacemakers, prostheses, water supply systems, electricity and the Internet for societies to function etc. (Ruki and Wulandari 2021; de Vries 1991). being the common of these that they all have a structure and a function that satisfy a need.

All these solutions exist thanks to a determining factor that is creativity, for the design of the technological solution. If it is a question of generating products oriented to C3, the design and construction of solutions that solve environmental problems, in a pandemic context, having the projection that they compete in the Science and Technology Fair, it is adopting the perspective of creativity in engineering, which clearly differs from creativity in fine arts or the like. Engineering creativity results from creativity with a purpose, this can be called functional creativity (Hassan 2016). The concept of functional creativity leads directly to an evaluation approach based on a hierarchy of four criteria: relevance and effectiveness; novelty; elegance and genesis (Cropley and Cropley 2010).

Consequently, it is relevant to consider the concept of functional creativity with an evaluation approach based on a hierarchy of four criteria: relevance and effectiveness; novelty; elegance and genesis (Cropley and Cropley 2010a).

This leads us to the reflection of understanding creativity as a key element in the field of science curricular areas, but not referring to traditional creativity, divergent thinking, but rather to something more specific related to four criteria of creativity functional to define a creative solution (Hassan 2016):
Diagnostic Scale (CSDS). includes:

1. Relevance and effectiveness (the product solves the problem it was intended to solve).
2. Novelty (the product is "original" and "surprising").

3. Elegance (the product is "beautiful" or "nice")
4. Generalizability or malleability (the product is widely applicable it can be transferred Criteria that very well fit the field of production of technological solutions for products to participate in a Science and Technology Fair

In this sense, it is reasonable to consider the bases of the national contest of the Eureka Science Fair, with its category C called Technology and Engineering, referring to the application of techniques based on scientific principles that require the production of technological solutions in the face of an associated problematic situation to health, food or other artifacts as functional products and the categories are oriented towards the investigative competition (Bases National School Fair of Science and Technology "Eureka" 2019).

Finding ourselves immersed in the fourth industrial revolution or Industry 4.0, which has come into our lives as a product of evolution, extensive digitization has favored transparency, use and profitability of large data mining that is generated (Schwab 2016), just as we have experienced in these last two years of the Pandemic.

Therefore, it is interesting to consider that in the context of the COVID-19 pandemic, the importance of educational environments oriented to STEAM and electronic learning was validated, applying E-science teaching with materials related to technology as a contribution (Soroko et al. 2020; Priscylio et al. 2019), with them, students improved learning, arousing interest, increasing their curiosity and activity, when they experience and associate the subject of science in real life (Nugroho and Surjono 2019, p. 5) (Herianto and Wilujeng 2020, p. 1).

As we can see, it is about implementing a curriculum where students can also promote knowledge to understand the user's problem and build a technological solution in a creative way, from the development of innovative ideas and a solution prototype (Freitas da Silva 2020).

Design Thinking Experiences. Thus, several North American schools use Design Thinking to rethink their curriculum, increase, improve curricular documents, overcome the low performance of students, as a teaching and learning approach for the 21st century. Model that converts the teacher in the designer of his own classroom experience and allows a more valuable and authentic change, driven by the needs of the students instead of an administrative mandate (IDEO 2012).

In the same line of ideas, Design Thinking (DT) is a person-centered innovation model (Macedo et al. 2015; Santos et al. 2018) but also considered as: A discipline based on sensitivity and the designer's methods for empathizing with people's needs and what is technologically feasible and what a viable business strategy can convert into customer value and market opportunity (Aranda et al. 2019).

In this way, the educational practices at the center of this fourth revolution, implies making decisions from the implementation of the curriculum in its last level of concretion, the classroom, understood as the space of virtual or physical interaction for learning from the mobilization of capabilities from the STEAM approach.

The research carried out focused on the competence called "Design and build technological solutions to solve problems in their environments" (C3), hereinafter competence

3. This competency involves the combination and integration of the following capabilities (Fig. 1):

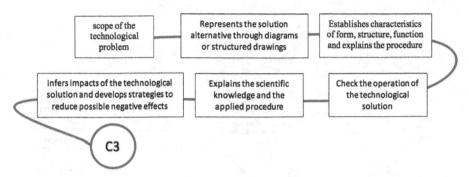

Fig. 1. C3 capabilities path

As evidenced, this curricular area of Science and Technology (hereinafter S&T) is based on technological education, with a critical assessment perspective, where one of the competencies (C3) must put into action functional creativity for design in those products that with nuances of engineering that should contribute to the quality of life of life. In addition, to ensure that these products respond to collaborative creativity, it is based on design thinking, centered on people (IDEO 2015).

In this framework, the importance of technological education in the S&T curricular area is highlighted because it develops students' knowledge of technological solutions in everyday life. They are expected to identify and analyze the structure and function of technological solutions, but also to be able to develop their own technological solutions (Cederqvist 2019).

2   Method

The quantitative method was applied, with the pre-experimental design of a single group (Sampieri 2010), which was subjected to the phases of the Design Thinking methodology.

The research was carried out with a sample of 36 female students between 14 and 16 years of age, who had basic skills in the use of ICT, in the curricular area of Science and Technology, belonging to the fourth year of secondary education, during electronic learning. and the virtualization of the educational service due to COVID-19.

The intervention was carried out for four months and was carried out in two phases, phase I from March to April and phase II from May to June.

3   Study Stages

Curriculum planning of learning experiences with the integration of the Design Thinking methodology, based on a purpose or challenge of interest to the students (Fig. 2).

Characteristics of the didactic solution to develop competence "Design and construction of technological solutions to solve problems in their environment" in secondary school students in the area of Science and Technology within the framework of the Peruvian CNEB discovery.

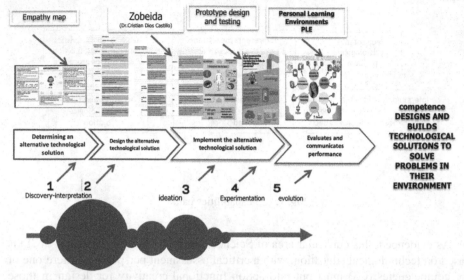

Fig. 2. Route of application of design thinking and applied complementary techniques

March–April Stage. The starting point situation was human-centered. The students assumed the role of designers and for this a key element was the understanding of what it means to empathize.

1. Teamwork and collaborative work were addressed to enrich the design of the solution from the different perspectives. In addition, taking into account not to pose the problem from their own perspective, nor the solution subjectively, but starting from the user's needs, they applied the empathy map technique.
2. The process of empathizing with the subjects of needs involved the design of data collection instruments, for which questionnaires and interviews were constructed to be applied online and physically, the results of which were processed by each team, for which they were given provided cognitive scaffolding for transformation, such as an excel format for them to enter their data and achieve the statistical results that were interpreted, based on these data decision-making was supported
3. Once the problems were identified, they supported each other in parallel using the Zobeida application as a cognitive scaffold for information transformation and the design of their science project. Their general and specific objectives, hypotheses, techniques and instruments were outlined.

May–June Stage

1. The design phase took several days and sessions were mentored by the advisory teacher. In this phase the design was presented in graphics, with data containing dimensions, material specifications and operation.
2. The construction of the prototype, took it to the experimental phase, since it implied the construction under technical specifications to achieve its operation in the testing or validation. All this work demanded in the students search, analysis of the information applying the deductive method. This repetitive experience allowed the results to be contrasted and its functioning to be accepted in an appropriate manner or its rejection to be discarded.

It demanded many hours of work in the students who began this experience that occurred in person in a virtual way.

As well as the difficulties of design and implementation, it evaluates its operation, efficiency and proposes strategies to improve it. Determines an alternative technological solution: when detecting a problem and proposes creative solution alternatives based on scientific and technological knowledge and local practices, evaluating their relevance to select one of them (Table 1).

4 Results

4.1 Normality Tests

Table 1. Test of normality of the evaluation before and after using the Design Thinking methodology normality tests

	Kolmogorov-Smirnova			Shapiro-Wilk		
	Statistics	gl	Sig	Statistics	gl	Sig
Before Phase I	0.337	36	0.000	0.797	36	0.000
Before Phase II	0.424	36	0.000	0.596	36	0.000
After IB	0.379	36	0.000	0.675	36	0.000
After IIB	0.323	36	0.000	0.796	36	0.000

Note: This table shows how much the distribution of the data observed in Phase I (first two months)differs from Phase II (second bimester), (2021).

The attached table shows that the scores before and after in the first and second moments of evaluation using the Design Thinking methodology do not present a normal distribution, that is, Sig. = 0.000 < 0.05, which would indicate that the comparative analysis will use of non-parametric statistical techniques (Table 2).

Table 2. Test of normality of the scores of the difference (After phase I – Before phase I) normality tests

	Kolmogorov-Smirnov[a]			Shapiro–Wilk		
	Statistics	gl	Sig	Statistics	gl	Sig
Difference (After phase I - Before phase I)	0.215	36	0.000	0.873	36	0.001

Note: Data taken in Phase I (first two months), Lilliefors significance correction difference of the evaluation before and after the intervention used to test the null hypothesis (2021).

Shows that the difference scores (After Phase I – Before Phase I) do not tend to a normal distribution (Sig. = 0.004 < 0.05). Consequently, the statistical test of comparison of the scores before and after (Pre and post test) would be within the non-parametric techniques, the Wilcóxon Ranks technique being the appropriate one (Table 3).

Table 3. Normality test of the difference scores (After phase II – Before phase II)

Normality tests						
	Kolmogorov-Smirnova			Shapiro–Wilk		
	Statistics	gl	Sig	Statistics	gl	Sig
Difference (After phase II - Before phase II	0.233	36	0.000	0.902	36	0.004

Note: Data taken in phase II (second two-month period), Lilliefor's significance correction difference of the assessment before and after the intervention (2021).

Shows that the difference scores (After Phase II – Before Phase II) do not tend to a normal distribution (Sig. = 0.004 < 0.05). Consequently, the statistical test of comparison of the scores before and after (Pre and post test) would be within the non-parametric techniques, the Wilcóxon Ranks technique being the appropriate one.

Paired samples T-test				
			Statistic	P
Before phase I	After phase I	Wilcoxon W	45.00	<0.001

P_value <0.001, Ho is rejected at a significance level of 1%

Description:
    If there are significant differences in the evaluation scores obtained before and after at the first moment of application of the Design Thinking methodology (Fig. 3).

Paired samples T-test				
			Statistic	p
Before II	After II	Wilcoxon W	119.00	<0.001

P_value <0.001, Ho is rejected at a significance level of 1%

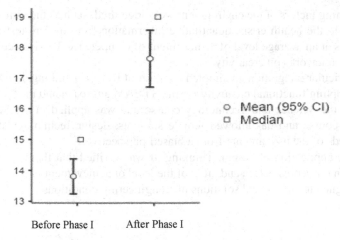

Fig. 3. The figure shows the comparison of the arithmetic mean and the median of the scores before and after phase I of the application of the Design Thinking methodology.

Description:

If there are significant differences in the evaluation scores obtained before and after in the second moment of application of the Design Thinking methodology (Fig. 4).

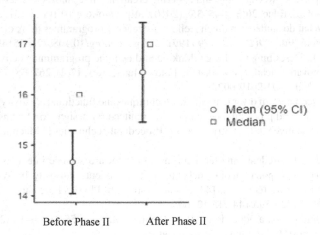

Fig. 4. The figure shows the comparison of the arithmetic mean and the median of the scores before and after phase II of the application of the Design Thinking methodology.

5 Conclusions

Following the objectives of this research, it was shown that the design thinking methodology has promoted specific creativity for the fulfillment of the competence called Design and build technological solutions to solve problems in your environment.

Determining factors of the environment were identified, such as the virtuality of the classes, due to the health crisis, quantitative information from the pre-test that shows qualifications at an average level of achievement of competence 3, existence of various theoretical frameworks on creativity.

The Curricular integration and implementation of Design Thinking, in which it was based on adopting functional creativity for the STEAM approach and the technological approach in the Science and Technology course and was applied in the Science and Technology course and has allowed female students, design technological solutions from the needs of the user and not from a biased perspective.

After the application of Design Thinking, it was verified that there are significant differences in the scores before and after, of the level of achievement of the competition and the designed technological solutions met engineering conditions.

References

Aranda, M.L., Lie, R., Selcen Guzey, S.: Productive thinking in middle school science students' design conversations in a design-based engineering challenge. Int. J. Technol. Design Educ. (2019). https://link.springer.com/article/10.1007/s10798-019-09498-5

Cederqvist, A.-M.: Pupils' ways of understanding programmed technological solutions when analysing structure and function. Educ. Inf. Technol. **25**(2), 1039–1065 (2019). https://link.springer.com/article/10.1007/s10639-019-10006-4

Cropley, D., Cropley, A.: Recognizing and fostering creativity in technological design education. Int. J. Technol. Des. Educ. **20**(3), 345–358 (2010). https://doi.org/10.1007/s10798-009-9089-5

de Vries, M.J.: What do students in dutch technology teacher programmes think of their subject? Res. Sci. Technol. Educ. **9**(2), 173–179 (1991). https://doi.org/10.1080/0263514910090205

Freitas da Silva, I.: Describing the design thinking and extreme programming activities during a technology innovation academic workshop. Innov. Manag. Rev. **17**(3), 267–284 (2020). https://doi.org/10.1108/inmr-03-2019-0039

Hassan, D.K.: Discrepancy of divergent thinking techniques and functional creativity: comparative study of structural and procedural techniques in architectural design. Ain Shams Engineering Magazine Comparative Study of Structural and Procedural Techniques In Machine Translate-ed by Google (2016)

Herianto, Wilujeng, I.: Students and teachers' necessity toward science interactive multimedia e-books based on local potential of gamelan to increase students' curiosity. In: W. A., Pujianto, A. N.A., & D. M.I.B.M. (eds.) vol. 1440, Is-sue Institute of Physics Publishing (2020). https://doi.org/10.1088/1742-6596/1440/1/012100

IDEO: Design thinking para educadores. Res. Technol. Manage. **55**(3), 10–14 (2012). https://www.ideo.com/post/design-thinking-for-educators

IDEO: The Field Guide to Human-Centered Design (2nd ed.). (2015). Retrieved April 20, 2021, https://www.ideo.com/post/design-kit

1MINEDU. Curriculum program for Secondary Education. National Curriculum **259** (2016). https://cutt.ly/TTlBR1F

Macedo, M., Miguel, P.A., Casarotto, F.N.: A characterization of design thinking as a model of innovation. Manag. Innov. Rev. Rai **12**, 157–182 (2015). www.revistas.usp.br/rai/article/view/101357, https://doi.org/10.11606/rai.v12i3.101357

Ministry of Education of Peru. Vice Ministerial Resolution. No. 235-2021-MINEDU. Virtual Educational Contests 2021 General and Specific Rules (2021). https://acortar.link/JyD2Os

National Commission for Scientific and Technological Research, CONICYT. Science and Technology in Chile: What for? vol. 1, no. 1 (2011). https://www.conicyt.cl/wp-content/uploads/2012/07/CyTConicytparaque.pdf. ISBN 978-956-7524-12-9

Nugroho, T.A.T., Surjono, H.D.: The effectiveness of mobile-based interactive learning multimedia in science process skills. J. Phys.: Conf. Ser. **1157**(2), 022024 (2019). https://doi.org/10.1088/1742-6596/1157/2/022024

Priscylio, G., Anwar, S., Salmawati: Need of e-integrated science teaching material developed using 4S TMD model for science learning and teaching in junior high school. In: Proceedings of the 10th International Conference on E-Education, E-Business, E-Management and E-Learning - IC4E (2019). https://dl.acm.org/doi/10.1145/3306500.3306563

Ruki, U.A., Wulandari, A.A.A.: Post covid-19 public space adaptation: a case study of building entrances in Jakarta. **794**(1) (2021). https://doi.org/10.1088/1755-1315/794/1/012243

Schwab, K.: The fourth industrial revolution (2016)

Sampieri, H.: Metodología de la investigación 5ta Edición (5ta ed.) (2010). ISBN 978-9 968-422-931-3, https://acortar.link/JyD2Os

Santos, A., Bianchi, C., Borini, F.: Open innovation and co-creation in new product development: the role of design thinking. Int. J. Innov. **6**, 112–123 (2018). https://doi.org/10.5585/iji.v6i2.203

Soroko, N., Mykhailenko, L., Rokoman, O., y Zaselskiy, V.,: Educational electronic platforms for STEAM-oriented learning environment at general education school (eds.), vol. 2643, pp. 462–473. CEUR-WS (2020). https://lib.iitta.gov.ua/721185/1/cte2019-paper15-final-paper.pdf

Assessement of Assisted Navigation in NUI Virtual Architectural Environments

Viviana Barneche-Naya(iD) and Luis A. Hernández-Ibáñez(✉)(iD)

Universidade da Coruña, 15071 A Coruña, Spain
{viviana.barneche,luis.hernandez}@udc.es

Abstract. This paper describes the results of a case study about how Assisted Navigation and Natural User Interfaces can facilitate user control in virtual architectural walkthroughs and improve the overall experience. This study combines the authors' previous research in these lines, studying the summed effect of both on a UX test scenario. The installation uses a depth camera for NUI interaction and applies an attractor based approach to assisted navigation. The analysis uses the data collected in an experiment with two test groups of participants considering their previous experience and gaming abilities. The experiment was composed of five stages, with three different test sets of increasing complexity. During the test, the system monitored and recorded the user movements to extract relevant data about time to complete the task, number of collisions and time spent in a collision condition. In addition, the users completed specifically questionnaires immediately after completion of tasks. The results indicate the benefits of combining both technologies enhancing the virtual visit experience. It also evaluates the effects of users' previous expertise on 3D video games in the results.

Keywords: Assisted navigation · Natural user interfaces · User experience

1 Introduction

Visiting a digital building, especially for the first time, is an experience of discovery and exploration, just like in the real world. In this regard, the explorative experience of architectural spaces requires visitors to follow their own pace and rhythm, determined by their particular interest in specific elements and parts of the building [1, 2].

However, other specific problems arise when non-technical visitors interactively explore the digital architectural model, such as a museum installation. The model's visual accuracy and realism are not enough to provide a good experience when the act of navigating throughout the virtual building is not easy, pleasurable, intuitive and fruitful.

Navigation in the virtual world and in the natural world share many similarities. For this reason, the most important theoretical contributions come from studies related to navigation in the real world. However, there are many data crossings in both ways [i.e. 3, 4, 5, 6].

The literature related to how people explore spaces introduces two concepts describing the two main strategies humans use to apprehend and understand the environment

P. Zaphiris and A. Ioannou (Eds.): HCII 2022, LNCS 13329, pp. 14–23, 2022.
https://doi.org/10.1007/978-3-031-05675-8_2

and trace trajectories to move along the space. Those strategies are *Navigation* and *Wayfinding*, sometimes considering the former as a kind of the latter [7]. Wayfinding implies developing mental constructions to classify, order and relate spaces and places, creating complex cognitive models of the environment used to plan the route to follow. Previous experiences can also affect this process [8, 9].

In the case of navigation, it uses elements inside the space as references such as landmarks, milestones, reference points and even external aids such as maps. Those reference points are of great importance to attract the user's interest to any given direction due to visual, cognitive and structural factors [10, 11]. Hence, appropriate management of these clues may improve the wayfinding process.

In a previous work [12], the authors proposed an approach based on the field of the Psychology of Perception already pointed by Lewin in his definition of *hodological space* [13] and on Gibson's theory of affordances [14]. The assistance we propose analyses the presence of elements of interest around the user, including objects and architectural features and spaces. The system then weights their importance and capability to attract attention considering their intrinsic interest, distance to the visitor, angle of sight with respect to the user's view direction, and other variables. Finally, considering all this, it will suggest the user a direction to move by smoothly turning the camera to point the visitor to travel to the resultant centre of interest.

Natural user interfaces (NUI) can help obtain more pleasant, user-friendly movement schemes. The emergence of depth cameras technology, pioneered by Kinect systems [15], allows the capture of the user pose and gestures without apparent physical interfaces. Today, many fields, including Architectural Visualization, Virtual Archeology and Virtual Museums, use depth cameras since they are ideal for controlling the user movement inside virtual buildings with minimum or null training and without the need of handling, nor even touching any physical device. This aspect is becoming even more critical in post-COVID times.

In this respect, our previous research [16] tested six gestural schemes. This kind of natural interaction always incorporates a gesture for moving forward and another for turning. Based on the results of this experiment, we selected three of them for the following stage due to their best performance compared to the others.

The study's next phase was intended to determine which of those movement paradigms was best suited for museum visitors, both expert and non-expert users, based on their prior experience with 3D video games. Aspects analysed included navigation performance, interface intuitiveness, efficiency and space awareness, among others [17]. Two movement schemes (Step/Twist, Lean/Twist) were preferred for non-regular and regular gamers, respectively. Although all proposed schemes are functional, the frequent collisions with objects and walls are especially evident when going through doors, turning in corridors, etc. This problem indicates that the user cannot enjoy the experience as it should be, due to issues in movement control.

From the above, this paper will focus on the experience of the architectural walk-through itself in search of better ways to explore digital buildings, using and combining our previous research. On the one hand, using natural user interface schemes for movement and interaction within the digital construction, and on the other hand, using an autonomous agent to assist navigation on such spaces, combined with and taking advantage of those natural interaction schemes.

Another aspect to investigate was to determine if there are differences in the perception of assisted navigation depending on whether the visitor is a frequent user of video games or not.

2   Methodology

The authors took a group of users to study the autonomous agent's effect on navigation in virtual architectural environments. They completed a series of tests comparing the walkthrough experience in two conditions: unassisted and assised by the agent. The authors briefly informed the subjects about the mechanics of the available gestures: Lean or Step Forward to advance, Twist upper body for turning. (See Table 1).

Table 1. Selected movement schemes.

March	Lean forward	Step forward
Turn	Twist upper body	Twist upper body

The authors collected quantitative data, a series of performance-based measures, including task completion times, the number of collisions during navigation tasks, and the number of gestures needed to complete the walkthrough. Furthermore, we used questionnaires to acquire qualitative data related to the users' experience with the navigation system, including notes and responses to open interview questions.

2.1   Test Subjects

Twenty-two participants (54.5% male –45.5% female) took part in this study. Their age ranged from 18 to 57 years (M = 26.9, SD = 11.3). For the most part, they were university students (72.8%), and the remaining 27.2% were faculty and other staff. All people participated voluntarily.

They described their previous experience and gaming abilities. In this study, 54.5% were casual gamers (18.1% played games rarely, 36.4% played video games occasionally), and 45.5% were frequent gamers.

2.2 Session Procedure

Before beginning the test, the moderator explained the session's mechanics to the participants and required them to fill out a brief demographic questionnaire and self-reported gaming experience. Each session took approximately 30 min on average to complete for each individual.

The experiment set consisted of a room with a 65" Ultra HD 4 K TV screen and a Kinect sensor located below it. Some marks on the floor, located at approximately 2.40 m in front of the screen, indicated the experience's starting point. Before starting

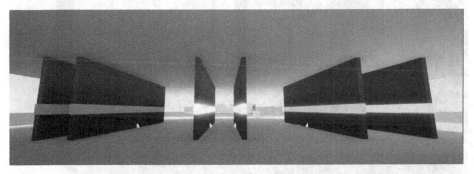

Fig. 1. View of training set for task #0.

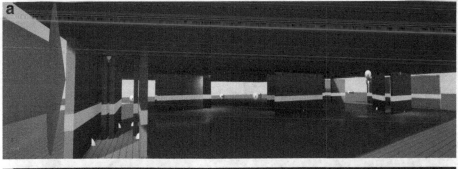

Fig. 2. Set for task #1: (a) User view (b) Attractors, invisible for users, placed in the set.

each task, the system automatically measured each participant's height and idle lean angle for calibration.

The experiment consisted of three different test sets of increasing complexity: training environment (test #0, Fig. 1), simple test environment (test #1, Fig. 2.) with different sizes and open and closed turns at specific points; and complex environment (test #2, Fig. 3) to make a free walkthrough inside the digital model of *Ville Savoye*, a paradigm of the architectural design of the 20th century.

Fig. 3. Ville savoye (a) User view (b) Attractors, invisible for users, placed around the house.

In each scenario, the user performed different navigation tasks. After completing the second and third tasks, the users completed specifically questionnaires.

2.3 Measurement

Each participant fulfilled the same amount of tasks. Performance-based measures were derived from the participants' navigation behaviour without and with assistance. The authors applied a user-centred methodology based on measuring and systematic analysis of the values used to define user experience [18, 19].

In the first one, we measured successful task completion rates (effectiveness) and the mean task #1 completion times in seconds (efficiency). Concerning task #1 time, detecting collisions and determining contact points is of fundamental importance to know its impact on navigation skills.

The system counted the number of collisions (hits) and the number of simulation frames every participant spent colliding with walls or objects. With this data and considering a frame rate of 60 fps, we obtained the percentage of collision time.

The system also measured the number of direction changes and start-stop movements made by the participants during task #1. Finally, we measured user satisfaction for each task through the users' responses to specific questions related to the different aspects of the experience.

3 Results

This study used the IBM SPSS 26 statistics software. The analysis compared several measures obtained from the two navigation systems (unassisted, assisted) obtained from the same user group in two consecutive phases. Since it is a small sample presenting a non-normal distribution, this study used a non-parametric Wilcoxon test ($\alpha = 0.05$).

Task 1. While carrying out the task, especially in those complex spaces, users had more opportunities to collide with narrow passages and tricky turns, making several direction changes and start-stop movements. Comparative analysis of these factors helped determine whether assisted navigation was more effective than unassisted navigation.

In this way, for all participants, the number of collisions in Task #1 is much lower with assistance (2.1, 95% CI 1.4, 2.7) than in the unassisted navigation mode (5.1, 95% CI 3.8, 6.3). However, it is essential to note that collisions did not affect the completion of the task. In general, when using assisted navigation, users made fewer start-stop movements and direction changes for all users independently of their degree of previous experience in video games (See Fig. 4).

After completing Task #1, participants responded how easy it was to perform the task using assisted navigation compared to the unassisted mode. The participants considered that assistance in navigation facilitates movement (Mean 8.4 95% CI 7.6; 9.1), which is why it was easier for them to complete Task #1.

Considering gaming experience, both groups rated the system very positively with very similar ratings, although in this case, frequent gamers rated it better (8.5, 95% CI 7.3, 9.7).

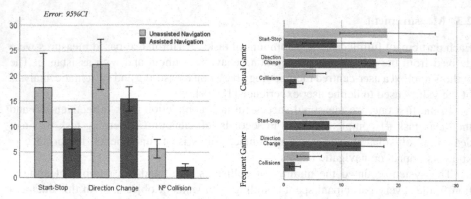

Fig. 4. Left: mean values for the number of start-stops, direction changes and collisions for all users. Right: distribution according to their previous gaming experience.

Subsequently, users rated each aspect of the navigation systems on a 0 to 10-point rating scale. Table 2 summarises the four aspects analysed for all users and considering their gaming experience.

Table 2. Comparative of users' perception of attention share, physical and mental effort, and comfort for assisted (A) and unassisted (U) navigation for all users and according to their previous gaming experience.

☐ Unassisted Navigation
■ Assisted Navigation

0: Worst-10: Best	Variable		All users	Casual gamer	Frequent gamer
0: Motion control 10: Contemplation.	Attention	U	2.4 ± 1.6	2.2 ± 0.7	2.6 ± 2.2
		A	6.6 ± 1.3	6.8 ± 1.1	6.3 ± 1.4
		P Value	0.0044	0.002	0.008
0: Strenuous. 10: Slack.	Physical effort	U	5.0 ± 2.2	3.9 ± 1.8	6.2 ± 2.0
		A	7.6 ± 1.8	7.6 ± 1.8	7.6 ± 1.9
		P Value	0.001	0.006	0.119
0: Complex. 10: Simple.	Mental effort	U	4.9 ± 2.4	4.5 ± 2.6	5.4 ± 2.1
		A	7.8 ± 1.3	8.0 ± 0.9	7.5 ± 1.6
		P Value	0.0025	0.005	0.021
0: Stressed. 10: Relaxed.	Comfort	U	4.0 ± 2.3	3.3 ± 2.4	4.9 ± 1.9
		A	7.7 ± 1.5	8.2 ± 1.4	7.1 ± 1.5
		P Value	0.0008	0.002	0.012

* Data represents the mean ± SD. P values: calculated with the Wilcoxon signed-rank test.

Generally, the assisted navigation system got better assessments compared to the unassisted mode. We detected significant differences ($\alpha = 0.05$) between them in the aspects of attention share, mental effort and comfort for all users and separately for casual and frequent users (See Table 2). Regarding physical effort, we found significant differences in the general group and the casual gamers group, but not for the frequent gamers. $(7.6 \pm 1.9 \ p = 0.119)$.

Task 2. This task's objective is to verify if the navigation assistance helps users understand what they see in one of the most paradigmatic architectural walkthrough experiences: the *Ville Savoye*. Here it is important to note that, although assisted navigation can orient users during their walkthrough, guiding them to the most interesting parts of the building, they never lose the control to modify the current course instantly or choose a different route.

It is interesting to determine if assisted navigation combines well with the movements' naturality and facilitates the contemplation of the spaces. For this reason, after finishing the walkthrough, participants are required to assess the assisted navigation system in aspects related to ease, enhancement, intrusiveness, adaptability, movement assistance and contemplation assistance.

The participants rated the assisted navigation system on a 0 to 10-point rating scale, with 0 being the worst and 10 being the best. Generally, the assessments mean values for task #2 compare both systems favourably to assisted navigation for the five aspects analysed (See Fig. 5).

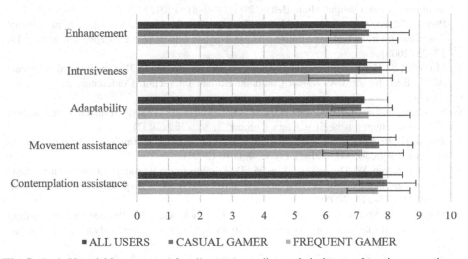

Fig. 5. Task #2 variables measures for all users according to their degree of previous experience.

From these results, one can observe that users with less experience in video games generally appreciate more the assistance for moving and contemplating. However, it seems to be helpful for all users.

4   Conclusions

Natural interaction is an excellent tool for navigation within virtual architectural spaces, which improves with an assistance system with these characteristics.

The effectiveness and efficiency of the user's control system increased with the application of navigation assistance provided by *Paseante*. Times and collisions are reduced, indicating that the assisted trajectories align well with the subjects' intentions.

The user's attention, when assisted, is mainly devoted to contemplating the environment and the enjoyment of the experience instead of controlling the navigation.

Users with less experience in video games perceive the advantages of the assisted navigation system based on NUI more clearly. For all variables analysed, users less experienced in video games gave higher scores than frequent gamers. It suggests that assisted navigation is adequate for installations intended to the general public, such as those present in museums, exhibitions and interpretation centres. People who attend such events can be of any origin, any age and different expertise, including older adults not familiar with the technology.

References

1. Norberg Schultz, C.: Existence, Space & Architecture. Praeger Publishers, London (1974)
2. Holl, S.: Questions of Perception: Phenomenology of Architecture. William Stout Publishers, Richmond, CA (2006)
3. Martensa, J., Antonenko, P.: Narrowing gender-based performance gaps in virtual environment navigation. Comput. Hum. Behav. **28**(3), 809–819 (2012)
4. Parsons, T., Rizzo, A.: Initial validation of a virtual environment for assessment of memory functioning: virtual reality cognitive performance assessment test. Cyberpsychol. Behav. **11**, 17–25 (2008)
5. Minocha, S., Hardy, C.: Designing navigation and wayfinding in 3D virtual learning spaces. ACM (Ed.). In: 23rd Australian Computer-Human Interaction Conference, pp. 211–220. (2011)
6. Pazzaglia, F., Taylor, H.: Perspective, instruction, and cognitive style in spatial representation of a virtual environment. Spat. Cogn. Comput. **7**, 349–364 (2007)
7. Taylor, H., Bruyné, T., Taylor, S.: Spatial mental representation: implications for navigation systems design. Rev. Hum. Fact. Ergon. **4**, 1–40 (2008)
8. Foo, P., Warren, W., Duchon, A., Tarr, M.: Do humans integrate routes into a cognitive map? Map versus landmark-based navigation of novel shortcuts. J. Exp. Psychol. Learn. Mem. Cogn. **31**, 195–215 (2005)
9. Maguire, E., Spiers, H., Good, C., Hartley, T., Frackowiak, R., Burgess, N.: Navigation expertise and the human hippocampus: a structural brain imaging analysis. Hippocampus **13**, 250–259 (2003)
10. Balaban, C.Z., Karimpur, H., Röser, F., Hamburger, K.: Turn left where you felt unhappy: how affect influences landmark-based wayfinding. Cogn. Process. **18**(2), 135–144 (2017)
11. Sorrows, M.E., Hirtle, S.C.: The nature of landmarks for real and electronic spaces. In: Freksa, C., Mark, D.M. (eds.) Spatial Information Theory. Cognitive and Computational Foundations of Geographic Information Science. COSIT 1999. Lecture Notes in Computer Science, vol. 1661, pp. 37–50. Springer, Heidelberg (1999). https://doi.org/10.1007/3-540-48384-5_3
12. Hernández-Ibáñez, L.A., Barneche-Naya, V.: assisted navigation and natural interaction for virtual archaeological heritage: implementation of an attractor-based approach using a game engine. Mediterr. Archaeol. Archaeometry **16**(5), 43–51 (2016)
13. Lewin, K.: The Conceptual Representation and the Measurement of Psychological Forces. Duke University Press, Durham (1938)

14. Gibson, J.: The Ecological Approach to Visual Perception. Lawrence Erlbaum Associates, Hillsdale (1979)
15. Zhang, Z.: Microsoft Kinect sensor and its effect. IEEE Multimedia **19**(2), 4–10 (2012)
16. Hernández-Ibáñez, L.A., Barneche-Naya, V., Mihura-López, R.: A comparative study of walkthrough paradigms for virtual environments using Kinect based natural interaction. In: 22nd International Conference on Virtual System & Multimedia (VSMM), Kuala Lumpur, pp. 1–7 (2016). https://doi.org/10.1109/VSMM.2016.7863168
17. Barneche-Naya, V., Hernández-Ibañez, L.A.: A comparative study on user gestural inputs for navigation in NUI-based 3D virtual environments. Univ. Access Inf. Soc. **20**(3), 513–529 (2020)
18. Sauro, J., Lewis, J.R.: Quantifying the user Experience: Practical Statistics for user Research. Morgan Kaufmann, Burlington (2012)
19. Albert, W., Tullis, T.: Measuring the user Experience: Collecting, Analysing, and Presenting Usability Metrics. Newnes, Oxford (2013)

Evaluation of Mixed Reality Technologies in Remote Teaching

Lea M. Daling[1]([✉]), Samira Khoadei[1], Denis Kalkofen[2], Stefan Thurner[3],
Johannes Sieger[1,4], Taras Shepel[1,5], Anas Abdelrazeq[1], Markus Ebner[4],
Martin Ebner[4], and Ingrid Isenhardt[1]

[1] Information Management in Mechanical Engineering (IMA), RWTH Aachen University,
Aachen, Germany
`lea.daling@ima.rwth-aachen.de`
[2] Institute of Computer Graphics and Vision, Graz University of Technology, Graz, Austria
[3] Educational Technology, Graz University of Technology, Graz, Austria
[4] Institute of Mineral Resources Engineering, RWTH Aachen University, Aachen, Germany
[5] Freiberg University of Mining and Technology, Freiberg, Germany

Abstract. The trend towards remote teaching is steadily increasing and intensified by the current situation of the global pandemic. This is a particular challenge for subjects with a high practical relevance, such as mining engineering education, as practical experiences and on-site excursions are an integral part of the curriculum. In face-to-face teaching settings, mixed reality technologies are already considered a promising medium for the implementation of e.g., virtual field trips. Based on this, the current study addresses the question to what extent the integration of mixed reality technologies is suitable for remote teaching and which strengths and challenges are perceived by students and teachers. For this purpose, two 60-min remote lectures in the field of mining engineering were conducted, in which the use of mixed reality was tested on the basis of shared 360° experiences and 3D models and evaluated by students and teachers. Results reveal that the use of mixed reality in remote teaching was perceived as useful, enabled a realistic experience and improved students' understanding of presented theory compared to traditional teaching methods. In this paper, we discuss possible potentials and risks of using mixed reality in remote teaching and derive directions for further research.

Keywords: Remote teaching · Mixed reality · Virtual excursions · Mining engineering · Education

1 Introduction

1.1 Potentials of Mixed Reality in Mining Engineering Education

The use of Mixed Reality (MR) technologies in teaching brought new opportunities to incorporate the practical experience into theoretical contexts. Particularly in subjects such as mining engineering, which normally rely on excursions and field trips to create

P. Zaphiris and A. Ioannou (Eds.): HCII 2022, LNCS 13329, pp. 24–37, 2022.
https://doi.org/10.1007/978-3-031-05675-8_3

insights into the work area, MR can provide access to high-consequence environments that are difficult to reach. Thus, MR can create a link between theory and practice and thereby improve motivation and learning [1].

Especially in times of the global pandemic, the challenges for teachers to link remote teaching with practical content increased significantly [2]. Despite the limited interaction possibilities in remote teaching, teachers still had to prepare students adequately for their professional life. When applying conventional remote teaching approaches in practical and applied fields of studies such as mining engineering, it is a major challenge to explain the scale and function of machines to students, to give them an orientation and understanding for the (spatial) structure of underground or surface mines, or to illustrate work processes and interfaces in mining [3]. Practical, on-site experience is still an essential component of mining engineering education. However, university resources (e.g., funds, time and personnel) only allow a limited amount of field trips to mine sites for a limited number of students. In addition, the curricular required internships give students only very limited insights into the various facets and disciplines of mining.

MR teaching approaches enable to address those challenges, as they allow to repeatedly conduct virtual excursions to various mine sites all over the world [4]. Making the most of MR's potential for teaching in mining is the goal of the MiReBooks project, which is described below. Subsequently, the research questions derived from the current challenges are described, from which the goal of this study as well as the design and procedure are derived.

1.2   The MiReBooks Project

The MiReBooks project (launched in 2018, funded by EIT Raw Materials) is exploring how teachers in mining education can be optimally supported in preparing for teaching with MR materials and how the use of MR affects students' learning experiences [5]. So far, the project has primarily explored the use of MR experiences in face-to-face teaching and has already revealed promising findings on how MR can enhance students' motivation and provide a better understanding of the teaching content [6]. Thus, MR has already been identified as a powerful medium to enable hands-on experiences in the classroom.

During the course of the project, the requirements for the use of MR in mining education changed drastically. Due to the global pandemic, teaching in presence was largely abandoned, so that practical experiences, field trips and visits became not only costly, but partly impossible. This raised completely new research questions related to the possible use of MR technologies in remote teaching: To what extent can students get hands-on experience remotely? How can instructors ensure that students gain an understanding of procedures and processes? What opportunities are there for interaction with each other and with instructors?

Addressing these changes in teaching due to the pandemic, the current study examines the use of MR in remote teaching. Thus, the current study aimed to make a first contribution to explore this new field of research, focusing on the question where students and teachers see strengths and risks in the use of MR in remote teaching.

1.3   Aim of the Present Study

In order to answer the research question of the perception, usefulness and suitability of MR as remote teaching tool in mining engineering education, we conducted an evaluation study, which is presented below. Two different 60-min remote lectures in the field of mining engineering education were conducted and subsequently evaluated by students (n = 23) and lecturers (n = 2). In order to gain insight into the effectiveness and usefulness of the MR system, we focused on three important aspects: Usability, user experience, and evaluation of the suitability of MR for (remote) teaching.

Following the ISO 9241–11 [7], usability covers the effectiveness, i.e. the ability of users to complete a task using the system, the efficiency, i.e. the level of resource consumed in performing tasks, and satisfaction, i.e. users' subjective reactions to using the system [8]. Moreover, user experience and acceptance of the system provide information about the usefulness that the users see in the system [9].

In order to receive more insight into the reasons for evaluating a system, the strengths and weaknesses as well as potentials and threats from the perspective of students and teachers, the suitability of MR is furthermore directly queried and evaluated.

To obtain statements about these three aspects, the study design and the content and technical design of the remote lectures are presented in the next section. Then, the selection of questionnaires and evaluation questions is presented. Subsequently, the results of the evaluation study are analyzed and discussed. Finally, an outlook on further research is given.

2   Methodological Approach for Evaluating Mixed Reality in Remote Teaching

2.1   Study Design and Procedure

In order to evaluate the use of MR technologies in remote teaching, two different 60-min MR-based remote lectures in the field of mining engineering were conducted and evaluated. Participants were recruited via e-mail and in mining lectures by the lecturers of Freiberg Mining Academy and University of Technology, RWTH Aachen University and Montanuniversität Leoben. Participants were informed in advance that they would be using MR technologies. Participation was voluntary. The required equipment consisted of an internet-enabled laptop or PC with headset and microphone - the VR goggles were provided by the respective research institutions. A total of 13 students attended the first lecture on underground longwall mining and 10 students attended the second lecture on continuous surface mining methods. Four students attended both lectures.

The lectures were delivered via a video conferencing platform and included theoretical inputs as well as several MR-based experiences, such as interactive 360° and 3D environments. Each student was equipped with VR goggles and pre-dialed into a network that all students and the instructor had access to. Before the lectures started, participants received a technical introduction into the VR goggles as well as an introduction into the procedure of the lecture. All participants were asked to imagine this lecture being part of their curriculum. During the use of MR, lecturers had the opportunity to guide students, direct their views, and accompany their explanations with drawings on a 2D desktop version. The lectures were evaluated through an online post-test survey using standardized questionnaires and open questions. Overall, we collected feedback in terms of their usability and in terms of the usefulness of mixed reality in remote teaching by both teachers and students.

In the following, the content and procedures of the two lectures will be explained. After that, we will describe the technical set-up. Finally, the questionnaires and open questions will be presented.

2.2 Description of the Remote Lectures

The lectures conducted covered topics relevant to the actual teaching of mining studies. One lecture was held by a lecturer from RWTH Aachen University, another by a lecturer from TU Freiberg. The lecture design, structure, and content were discussed in advance with didactic experts to ensure that the students were adequately informed about the learning objectives, content and procedure in the lecture. In both lectures, slides were shown via screen sharing to convey theoretical content. Due to the pandemic, the students were asked to participate from home or single work spaces and to behave as they would in a normal remote lecture. In the following, the lectures are described in detail.

Lecture on Longwall Mining. The goal of the test lecture was to convey the concept and key characteristics of the longwall mining method, which is typically applied for the extraction of tabular, flat, and uniform soft rock deposits, such as coal, potash, trona or phosphate rock. During the lecture, the method and involved machine components (shearer, hydraulic shield, armoured face conveyor, beam stageloader, and conveyor belt) and their functionality were introduced and visualized. Learning objectives of this lecture are listed in the following:

At the end of the lecture, …

- the students should understand the key characteristics and fields of application of the longwall mining method.
- the students should be able to explain the function and basic kinematics of the different machine components in longwall mining.
- the students should be able to explain how the different machine components interact with each other to allow for the production and advance of the mining system.
- the students should get an impression for the scale, noise, harshness, and hazards in underground (longwall) mining.

The lecture was structured into three separate sections. The first section was held in a conventional presentation format and introduced the students to the agenda, the lecture's approach, the envisaged learning objectives, and provided instructions on how to use the VR goggles, the controllers and the utilized software.

In the second and main section, the students were introduced to the fundamental concepts and terminology of the longwall mining method, by means of conventional slides including pictures and 3D drawings to illustrate the mining method (15 min). During this section, the lecture shifted to an interactive VR-supported format where the

Fig. 1. Scene of students exploring machine components remotely in VR.

students were asked to explore animated 3D models of the different machine components in VR for 15 min (see Fig. 1).

The students assessed the functionality of the models' different machine components and explored how the machine components interact with each other. After several minutes of individual exploration time, the students shared their observations with the other attendees and discussed them jointly with the lecturer. Subsequently, the lecture shifted to a joint 360° excursion into a realistic underground longwall training mine, where the machinery introduced could be explored in a realistic mining environment. Here, the lecturer guided the students through a series of linked 360°-videos following the route of the mined ore from the mining face to the surface (20 min). The VR-excursion was held in an interactive format. The lecturer explained different concepts to the students and asked questions to the audience. The integrated real-time annotation tool allowed the lecturer to make small live-drawings and annotations in the 360°-scenes to better illustrate certain aspects to the students. Vice-versa, the students were encouraged to ask questions themselves, and could make use of a pointer tool, to indicate points of interest in the 360° section to the remaining audience. In the third section (10 min), the participants were asked to fill out the evaluation questionnaire.

Lecture on Continuous Mining Systems: Bucket Wheel Excavators. The   second lecture topic was continuous mining systems with a special focus on bucket-wheel excavators (BWE). The lecture consisted of introducing the fundamentals, terminology and the key concept on continuous mining systems, as well as presenting the classification of BWE, their main parameters, design and operation principle. Learning objectives of this lecture are listed in the following:

At the end of the lecture, …

- the students understand the design, operation principle and working methods of BWE.
- the students can distinguish between BWE of different size classes and explain their application areas.

- the students can explain the function and kinematics of different machine components.
- the students can explain how BWE is integrated into the mine and how it interacts with other mining equipment.
- the students got an impression of scale and movability of BWE and potential hazards during its operation.

Similar to the first lecture, the second lecture consisted of three main parts. At first, the lecture approach was introduced to the participants, followed by the checklist of equipment required for the lecture (VR-goggles, PC/Laptop with a camera and microphone, etc.), the content of the lecture and learning objectives (15 min).

The main part included the presentation and VR demonstrations, conclusions and a quiz to estimate what participants learned during the lecture. First, a conventional presentation with figures and schemes was held and followed by a demonstration of 3D models (three different BWEs) in VR (10 min). Students were able to ask questions during the lecture. In VR, the lecturer focused the attention of the participants by highlighting machine parts of interest. Subsequently, a slide based presentation showed figures and 2D animations demonstrating different operation modes of BWE (10 min). Then, the students were asked to follow a joint 360° experience (see Fig. 2), where the operation of BWEs in a surface mine was demonstrated (5 min).

Fig. 2. View of the lecturer during a joint 360° experience.

After a short slide presentation demonstrating the operation of BWEs with other equipment in the surface mine (10 min), the students were again asked to join a 360°experience, showing videos of the operation of a belt conveyor, a spreader, and a conveyor bridge (5 min). At the end, students were able to have a discussion with the lecturer; the achievement of the learning objectives was checked based on the quiz results. In the last Section (5 min), participants filled out the evaluation questionnaire.

2.3 Technical Setup

We implemented support for online teaching by connecting the teacher's PC with several Oculus Quest 2 devices over the internet, which provided the students with a shared VR environment. Thus, the system was split into an Android application, which was running on every Oculus Quest, and a single application running on the teacher's PC. The PC application was supporting the teacher with software tools to control the content displayed in the shared VR environment of the students. The implemented set of tools for teaching in MR was based on the design described by Kalkofen et al. [10].

In addition to these tools for teaching in MR, the teacher's environment included the capability for screen sharing, which allowed for an integration with common tools for online-teaching, such as Zoom [11], Cisco WebEx [12], and Microsoft Teams [13]. Therefore, the renote lecture could consist of any kind of traditional teaching material, enhanced by the Mirebooks MR experience. This included images, videos and text, delivered with traditional slide based presentation tools, such as Microsoft PowerPoint. Furthermore, during a remote teaching session, the teacher controlled the content that was shown in VR using common desktop tools for interaction. For example, our systems supported mouse interactions for guiding students' attention, for selecting scene elements, for controlling the video playback, and for sketching on the 360° video during the lecture.

2.4 Questionnaires

In order to be able to make a statement about the effectiveness of MR as a remote teaching tool, criteria for the quality of the technology (e.g. usability), the software and application (e.g., user experience) as well as the suitability of MR in remote teaching were assessed. In the following, we will describe the questionnaires and open questions used to evaluate the MR-based remote lectures.

Perceived Usability and User Experience. Usability was measured using the System Usability Scale (SUS) [8]. SUS items were rated on a five-point Likert scale from "strongly disagree" to "strongly agree". Examples for items are "I thought the system was easy to use." (positively formulated item) and "I thought there was too much inconsistency in this system." (inverse item). In order to calculate the SUS score, ratings were transformed to a range from 0 to 100. A score of 60 to 80 indicates acceptable usability, a score above 80 indicates good to very good usability, and a score of 100 indicates excellent usability [8]. Internal consistency was acceptable with Cronbach's $\alpha = .71$.

User experience was measured to extend and validate the findings of the SUS. Lewis proposed 12 items from the Technology Acceptance Model (TAM) to capture user experience, consisting of the subscales perceived usefulness (PU) and perceived ease of use (PEU) [9]. These items have been slightly adapted to the context of learning. Thus, we used and adjusted the subscales PU (six items, e.g., "using this technology would enable me to learn more quickly.", good reliability, Cronbach's $\alpha = .91$), and PEU (six items, e.g., "learning how to use the technology is easy for me", good reliability, Cronbach's $\alpha = .95$). All items were rated on a seven-point Likert scale ranging from 1 "extremely disagree" to 7 "extremely agree".

Suitability of MR for (Remote) Teaching. Although the usability and user experience scores provided information on the degree to which the factors are assessed, they did not explain why the assessment was made. To capture to what extent and why the participants consider the use of MR as suitable for (remote) teaching, we also included open-ended questions: "What do you see as the particular strengths of using mixed reality in lectures compared to traditional learning materials?; What would have to be changed and improved in order to use Mixed Reality successfully in teaching? What do you think is the biggest opportunity mixed reality offers for learning and teaching? What do you think are the biggest obstacles to successfully using mixed reality for learning and teaching?". Finally, the participants were asked to rate the statement "Mixed reality is well suited for remote learning and teaching." from 1 "strongly disagree" to 5 "strongly agree" and to explain their rating in an open text field.

After reading the material carefully, the interview statements were coded and grouped into categories by meaning following the methodology of qualitative content analysis by Kuckartz [14].

3   Results

All analyses were computed using Microsoft Excel. Since both lectures used the same system, no comparison between the two lectures will be conducted. All data will be described and analyzed on a descriptive level.

3.1   Perceived Usability and User Experience

Usability of the MR system was rated by the participants with an overall score of $M = 83.70$, $SD = 11.70$ indicating a "good" usability. Lecturers rated the usability as "acceptable to good" with $M = 78.75$. Looking at the lectures separately, the first lecture was rated with $M_{SUS} = 84.42$, $SD = 12.64$ by the participants (n = 13) and with $SUS = 72.5$ by the lecturer. The second lecture was rated with $M_{SUS} = 82.75$, $SD = 10.27$ by the participants (n = 10) and with $SUS = 85$ by the lecturer.

User experience was measured with the scales perceived usefulness (PU) and perceived ease of use (PEU). Overall, PU was rated with $M = 5.97$, $SD = 1.32$ and PEU with $M = 6.17$, $SD = 1.10$. On a descriptive level, both ratings were slightly higher in the second lecture (PU$_{L2}$: $M = 6.05$, $SD = .30$; PEU$_{L2}$: $M = 6.23$, $SD = .20$) compared to the first lecture (PU$_{L1}$: $M = 5.88$, $SD = .33$; PEU$_{L1}$: $M = 6.10$, $SD = .28$), as shown in Fig. 1.

3.2   Suitability of MR for (Remote) Teaching

All answers to the open questions of the student evaluation questionnaire were transformed into categories and frequencies were counted. Due to the low number of lecturers, answers of the lecturers were not analyzed by frequency. The categories were clustered using the strength, weaknesses, opportunities and threat (SWOT) scheme. Results are summarized in Fig. 4.

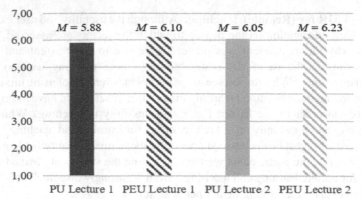

Fig. 3. Average ratings of perceived usefulness (PU) and perceived ease of use (PEU) of the MR system in lecture 1 and lecture 2 on a scale from 1 "extremely disagree" to 7 "extremely agree"

Strengths. Example statements for strengths of MR in lectures emphasize that MR was perceived as a teaching tool and medium that could bridge the gap between theory and practical experience: *"Especially in mining education it's hard to see many machines and environments in presence, MR can solve this problem for students and makes them experience many things."* Another aspect that was reflected in the statements was sustainability, stating that MR *"helps students to understand e.g., mining methods without the need to visit several mining sites around the world personally. It also helps persons who can't imagine components/machines from a 2D picture/plan or animation."* In this regard, the combination of 360° videos and 3D was mentioned to be a helpful aspect: *"A very good thing was the combination of the 3D model and the video."*

From the teachers perspective, *"more realistic impressions and better understanding for scale, size, noise, as well as the functionality of the equipment"* as well as *"much clearer understanding of different objects/processes, particularly in mining, where the operations might be extremely sophisticated"* were mentioned as particular strengths.

Weaknesses. Concerning the weaknesses, however, it was pointed out that low quality of MR content might hinder from enjoying the experience: *"The quality should be high because when the picture is very pixeled or blurred you can easily get a headache"*. From the first lecture we furthermore received the feedback that there is a high need for *"synchronized views. The lecturer should have a function for synchronizing all views before he / she starts to draw in the models"*.

This statement was supported from the lecturer in the first lecture: *"Sometimes I was not sure if everyone is following me."* An overview function of seeing if everyone is looking to the right spot was implemented as a trial function in the second lecture, where we received positive feedback. Another feedback from the lecturers was that it *"is way more exhausting for the lecturer, as he frequently has to test, check, and observe if everything is running smoothly and if the students can follow the lecturer. However, this might change once one gets used to it."*

Opportunities. When asked about general opportunities of MR, the students stated that MR offers *"seeing real mines working or how certain mining procedures are done in real*

Strengths	Weaknesses
Students' feedback (N = 20) • Better understanding and remembering of content (6; 27%) • Better visualization/realistic presentation (6; 27%) • Virtual excursion (5; 23%) • Hands-on experience (3, 14%) • More interesting lectures (; 9%) **Lecturers' feedback (N = 2)** • More realistic impressions • clearer understanding of different objects/processes	**Students' feedback (N = 12)** • Quality of videos and other visuals (6; 50%) • Few interaction possibilities (2; 17%) • Stability of the app and hardware (1; 8%) • Too less guidance in VR (1; 8%) • Content was shown too fast (1, 8%) • Too less introduction into the medium (1; 8%) **Lecturers' feedback (N = 2)** • High workload for the lecturer • Overview of student's view was missing
Opportunities	Threats
Students' feedback (N = 21) • Better understanding/easier to memorize (5; 24%) • Virtual excursion(5; 24%) • Insights into the functionality of machinery and processes (4; 19%) • Realistic experiences in remote learning (4; 19%) • Interactive learning (2; 9%) • Support in classroom teaching (1; 5%) **Lecturers' feedback (N = 2)** • Enforcing explorative learning • demonstration of real cases in mining	**Students' feedback (N = 17)** • Availability of devices/ overall costs (6; 35%) • Effort to create content (3; 18%) • Appropriate visualizations and explanations (3; 17%) • Quality of content (2; 12%) • Assuring students can follow the lecture (2; 12%) • Motion Sickness (1; 6%) **Lecturers' feedback (N = 2)** • High effort to prepare a lecture

Fig. 4. Summarized answers to open question in SWOT categories. N indicates the total number of statements.

scenarios", which seems to be a particular strength with regard to the current pandemic: *"Especially in situations such as the current pandemic, when students cannot be present in a classroom or go on field trips, this still enables a better visualization of reality."*

From the lecturer perspective, opportunities mentioned were *"being able to show realistic 360° videos instead of conventional videos. Enforcing the explorative learning, and giving students the chance to look around in their own pace"*. The lecturers also mentioned that they MR is particularly suitable *"for some introduction sessions on various mining methods. Specific contents and calculations still require more classic tools, but for a good realistic introduction it can be really helpful."*

Threats. Finally, we asked about the biggest obstacles to successfully use MR for learning and teaching. On the one hand, the students stated that the overall costs and availability of VR devices in university teaching might be a risk factor: *"The price of the VR sets, setting everything up, building high quality models"*. On the other hand, *"the creation of good models and videos"* as well as *"capturing and recording the information from mines"* was seen as a threat when using MR in teaching.

The lecturers mentioned that *"the preparation of this test lecture was quite some effort, but that is mostly due to the current status where it is not fully finished. Thereby, I must say that not only the 360° videos, but also the classic slides required more thoughtful preparation."* Moreover, they said that during the MR lecture, *"more questions [were] devoted to dynamic processes, which were not easy to explain with pictures/schemes."*

Suitability of MR for Remote Teaching. As already indicated by the statements above, students "strongly agreed" with $M = 4.65$, $SD = .63$ to the suitability of MR as remote teaching tool. Open comments underline this rating, emphasizing that usually *"remote lectures are less engaging and more boring - VR makes it more interesting"* and that MR offers the *"opportunity to see far away places and machinery without long travel distances"*. Nevertheless, students stated that even if *"MR can support the lecturer to make it more understandable, [...] it doesn't solve the general problems of remote learning."*

The lecturers stated that in comparison to other remote lectures, MR allows *"much more interaction possibilities such as drawing and pointing to convey the content form the real perspective, demonstration of real cases in mining."*

4   Discussion and Outlook

The present study aimed to provide initial findings on the suitability and quality of mixed reality (MR) technologies for the use in remote teaching in the field of mining engineering. For this purpose, two different remote lectures were conducted, in which interactive 360 videos as well as 3D models were presented with the help of VR goggles. The lectures were evaluated with a posttest only design by both students and teachers.

The results show promising results for the suitability of MR in remote teaching as well as some challenges that still need to be addressed in order to use MR widely and successfully. In the following, the limitations of the study are discussed, followed by a discussion of the results with regard to technical aspects as well as content- and didactic-related findings.

4.1   Limitations of the Study

This study provides initial insights into how MR tools are perceived in remote teaching by both students and instructors. Due to the current pandemic situation, these are important findings to investigate further. However, some limitations should also be considered when interpreting the results. One of these limitations relates to the sample. Participation in the study was voluntary and thus attracted mainly students who were interested in the topic and in trying out new technologies anyway. The teachers already had previous experience with the technology. The sample size was based on a realistic lecture in mining engineering. However, the results should still be validated using a larger and more divergent sample.

Another limitation relates to the posttest-only study design. Two different lectures were tested, which are not easily comparable. Furthermore, there was no comparative lecture that was performed without MR, for example. Also, the technology was minimally modified and adapted between the lectures in order to directly incorporate feedback, e.g. on interaction possibilities.

With these limitations in mind, some exciting findings can nevertheless be derived and discussed in the context of this study, which will be addressed in the next section. Furthermore, indications for further research are suggested.

4.2 Opportunities and Challenges of using MR in (Remote) Teaching

Technical Aspects. Overall, our evaluations reveal that the perceived usability and acceptance of the used applications is already pretty high. Most of the students did not experience any problems. At this point it has to be mentioned that technical support was present before and during the lecture, which supported both teachers in preparing the lecture and students in setting it up and operating it. If possible, this should be ensured during the first use of the technology in a normal or remote lecture in order to reduce the workload of the teachers.

Nevertheless, there is still potential for improvement in the quality and editing of the MR content. Since not all lecturers have the possibility to create their own high-quality content, possibilities for sharing and making available 360° recordings, 3D models, etc. must be established. The availability of devices as well as the overall costs of preparing and conducting MR lectures are seen as a barrier. Possibilities for lending and cooperation of universities should be considered here in order to be able to use the technology broadly.

Since keeping track of the students and the software tools used at the same time was initially difficult for the lecturers, functionalities for directing and monitoring the attention of students should be further evaluated. The lecturer reported to have a high workload during the lecture, making it harder to only concentrate on conveying the information and knowledge. We therefore suggest to at least have a technical support present or even to include one of the more experienced students as a tutor and facilitator between technology, students, and the lecturer.

Content Related Aspects. As a main result, we can conclude that MR was considered helpful and beneficial for learning within the course of our study. Both 3D models and 360° videos were considered as useful teaching tool, especially when combined. While 360° videos were reported to provide a realistic impression of situations and processes similar to field trips, schematic 3D models were mentioned to help illustrating complex processes and machinery. Especially with regard to remote teaching and learning, MR allows for more interactive, hands-on learning. Lecturers emphasized that drawing and pointing functions were helpful to react to questions and explain functions and processes in more detail.

Both Students and lecturers saw the creation of high quality content as one of the biggest challenges of using MR in (remote) teaching. This applies not only to the creation of 360° or 3D content, but also to the content of the lecture itself. The lecturers emphasized that it took a lot more effort to create a sophisticated lecture, where slides and MR content is combined in a didactic well thought out way. All in all, it became apparent, that teaching and learning with MR is currently associated with a high effort and task load, but at the same time also leads to a more intensive consideration of learning objectives and media selection, which in turn increases the quality of teaching.

5 Conclusion and Outlook

The present study shows that MR technologies are a promising teaching medium for remote teaching settings. The evaluation of two MR-based remote lectures in the field of mining engineering reveals that the strengths and opportunities of using MR for university teaching argue for overcoming current challenges, especially with regard to availability, cost, and effort of using MR. From the perspective of the learners, the use of MR in remote teaching was perceived as useful, since it enabled a realistic experience and improved the understanding of presented theory compared to traditional teaching methods. From the teachers perspective, the lecturers agreed that they were able to convey the knowledge better than in remote teaching without MR. At the same time, the lecturers reported that they were much more intensively occupied in the preparation and during the lecture, because in addition to the preparation of the content, they also needed to provide technical support. Moreover, it becomes evident that the success of mixed reality technologies in teaching does not only depend on the technical design. The didactic integration into the teaching concept as well as the individual preparation of the teachers for technology-based and interactive teaching and learning also play a decisive role.

The results suggest that MR is able to bridge the gap between theory and practice, which should be verified in further studies. Thus, future research should validate the initial, mainly qualitative results with larger sample sizes. Moreover, the effectiveness of MR in remote teaching should be investigated within an experimental design in direct comparison to traditional remote teaching as a control group. This analysis could, through the addition of objective criteria for measuring learning success, provide substantial information about the quality in relation to the achievement of learning objectives As outlook, further research should relate to the question how teachers can be enabled to prepare their own MR-based teaching and how this workflow can be evaluated.

Acknowledgements. This work is part of the project "Mixed Reality Books (MiReBooks)" and was funded by the EIT RAW Materials. The author is responsible for the contents of this publication.

References

1. Dede, C. J., Jacobson, J., Richards, J.: Introduction: virtual, augmented, and mixed realities in education. In: Liu, D., Dede, C., Huang, R. et al. (eds.) Virtual, Augmented, and Mixed Realities in Education, vol. 59, pp 1–16. Springer, Singapore (2017). https://doi.org/10.1007/978-981-10-5490-7_1
2. Hughes, M.C., Henry, B.W., Kushnick, M.R.: Teaching during the pandemic? An opportunity to enhance curriculum. Pedagogy Health Promot. **6**(4), 235–238 (2020)
3. Scoble, M., Laurence, D.: Future mining engineers – educational development strategy. In: Proceedings of the First International Future Mining Conference, pp. 237–242. Sydney (2008)
4. Daling, L., Eck, C., Abdelrazeq, A., Hees, F.: Potentials and challenges of using mixed reality in mining education: a Europe-wide interview study. In: Lloret Mauri, J., Saplacan, D., Çarçani, K., Ardiansyah Prima, O.D., Vasilache, S. (eds.) Thirteenth International Conference on Advances in Computer-Human Interactions, ACHI 2020, pp. 229–235. IARIA (2020)
5. Bertignoll, H., Ortega, M.L., Feiel, S.: MiReBooks – mixed reality Lehrbücher für das Bergbau-Studium (MiReBooks—mixed reality handbooks for mining education). Berg Huettenmaenn Monatshefte **164**(4), 178–182 (2019)

6. Daling, L., Kommetter, C., Abdelrazeq, A., Ebner, M., Ebner, M.: Mixed reality books: applying augmented and virtual reality in mining engineering education. In: Geroimenko, V. (ed.) Augmented reality in education, Springer Series on Cultural Computing, pp. 185–195. Springer, Cham (2020). https://doi.org/10.1007/978-3-030-42156-4_10

7. International Organization for Standardization: ISO 9241–11:2018 Ergonomics of human-system interaction — Part 11: Usability: Definitions and concepts. International Organization for Standardization (2018)

8. Brooke, J.: SUS-A Quick and Dirty Usability Scale. Usability Evaluation in Industry. CRC Press, Boca Raton (1996)

9. Lewis, J.R.: Comparison of four TAM item formats: effect of response option labels and order. J. Usability Stud. **14**(4), 224–236 (2019)

10. Kalkofen, D., et al.: Tools for teaching mining students in virtual reality based on 360° video experiences. In: 2020 IEEE Conference on Virtual Reality and 3D User Interfaces Abstracts and Workshops (VRW), pp. 455–459. IEEE (2020)

11. Zoom Video Communications Inc: Zoom. https://zoom.us/

12. Cisco Webex: Cisco Webex. https://www.webex.com/

13. Microsoft Corporation: Microsoft Teams. https://www.microsoft.com/

14. Kuckartz, U.: Qualitative Inhaltsanalyse: Methoden, Praxis, Computerunterstützung (Qualitative content analysis: methods, practice, computer support). 3rd. edn. Beltz, Weinheim Basel (2016)

Design of a Virtual Reality based Pedagogical Framework

Doga Demirel(✉) and Abdelwahab Hamam

Florida Polytechnic University, Lakeland, FL 33805, USA
{ddemirel,ahamam}@floridapoly.edu

Abstract. In this study, we designed and implemented a virtual reality-based pedagogical framework. The framework can be altered to be used for any laboratory-based class such as biology, chemistry, and physics. The framework has four main modules: Interface, Companion, Virtual Reality Scene, and Online Dashboard. The "Interface" module allows for the human computer interaction. The "Companion" module is based on voice recognition and replaces a laboratory assistant. The Online Dashboard acts as a user interface for teachers to create virtual laboratory scenes and upload them to the Virtual Reality Scene. We carried out a usability study and asked five faculty members with different backgrounds to carry out five tasks. The results showed that all the subjects had a positive experience with the virtual reality based pedagogical framework. The subjects mentioned that they expect virtual reality to be part of education in the near feature, especially for laboratory classes and that the pandemic has proved that VR is the future.

Keywords: Virtual reality · Education · Framework

1 Introduction

In schools, laboratories are utilized as tools to get the students more involved in the scientific process [1]. The hands-on experience learned from laboratories compliments the material learned in the class and enhances problem-solving and critical thinking skills [2, 3]. Even though in-person laboratories have their merits, the laboratories are often expensive [4], they can only be conducted during laboratories hours, and the outcomes of the laboratories were arguable [5, 6]. If a student missed a laboratory, it was almost impossible to make up the work as it needed a physical laboratory environment with specific tools to carry out the experiment. After the disruption of traditional education due to the spread of COVID-19, classes that included laboratories were the ones affected the most. The students weren't allowed to participate in the labs in person. Alternately, the students were watching videos and carrying-out experiments at home.

We believe with the integration of Virtual Reality (VR) in education [7], we can overcome the mentioned problems of in-person laboratories and enhance student learning [8–10]. Due to the increase in technology and other distractions in classrooms, students start to lose interest in the subject 15 min into the lecture/laboratory [11, 12]. VR headsets immerse the user by placing them in a non-physical world and cutting their connection

P. Zaphiris and A. Ioannou (Eds.): HCII 2022, LNCS 13329, pp. 38–47, 2022.
https://doi.org/10.1007/978-3-031-05675-8_4

with the real world. The utilization of VR in education allows for (a) students to be immersed in an environment where they can learn without distractions, (b) a low-cost, one-time purchase, and (c) an available and accessible 24/7 platform. In our previous study [7], we showed a 6-min video demonstration of our VR chemistry lab and asked 109 General Chemistry students questions. Out of the 109 students, 42.7% of the students strongly agreed and 37.3% agreed that learning general chemistry with VR will be more engaging.

Virtual Reality (VR) simulation is used as a teaching methodology in several domains. The multitude of hand-skill training benefits from VR applications since VR tackles several challenges facing traditional training methods. For instance, conventional surgical training for prospective medical students and medical residents relies on cadavers and animal parts, which are expensive, messy, and hard to repeat frequently [13, 14]. As a consequence, VR training for surgical training received attention from the research community, such as cataract surgery simulation [13], hepatic surgery simulation [15], cricothyroidotomy simulation [16], and gallbladder surgery simulation [17].

In certain domains, virtual reality education and training have surpassed traditional methods in terms of efficiency and quality of learning [18–21]. Welding and painting are two such domains. In hands-on skills education and training domains such as those, traditionally, the students need to practice with actual equipment to gain hands-on expertise and learn the subtleties of the trade. With the introduction of accessible VR headsets, hands-on training has moved gradually from using real tools to using a VR setup. The student is equipped with a headset and mock tools that resemble the real tools. The student movement and tools movement are virtually represented and tracked in VR. The instructor is supplied with an external screen to see what the student is doing in the virtual world. The results of the virtual reality simulators for core skills education such as welding, and painting were significant statistically and demonstrably. For example, the VR training adoption in welding was spread into over 140 countries with curricula available in 16 languages. The rate of training certificates completed has risen by 41.6%. This significant rise can be attributed to the rate of VR simulation training [20].

Physical science classes have also been considered in VR education. VR has already been in use to teach organic chemistry [22], physical chemistry [23], and biochemistry [24, 25]. In addition, we have implemented a chemistry lab simulation that is designed to allow students to access the lab in a safe and comfortable setting to give students confidence for the time that they first approach the actual chemistry lab. The simulation will allow students to "touch," "feel," and "handle" the chemicals and lab equipment with the use of haptic gloves. Our initial study [7] introduced the students to the notion of attending a VR chemistry lab, and the response from the students was primarily positive.

The notion of a VR learning framework is slightly mentioned in the literature [24, 26–29]. A VR framework could refer to a learning framework applied to VR technology to enhance the pedagogy of the system. One such framework incorporates ACE teaching framework into an interactive spherical video-based virtual reality [26]. Another paper describes an immersive virtual reality application in a teaching environment. But rather than focusing on the technology, the paper describes a framework adapted from the cognitive theory of multimedia learning. The result outlines how VR teaching should be designed based on knowledge of multimedia learning [27]. A classroom Framework for training teachers is described in [28].

Some references refer to the learning framework as the ability to customize the VR for teaching purposes [24, 29]. The authors in [24] developed a customized VR to intervene with children with a neurodevelopment disorder. The application includes functionality to monitor children's interaction with the therapist. The authors in [29] developed an open-source interactive molecular dynamics VR network for students to perform short tasks on enzymes. The open source allows multiple participants to cohabit the same VR environments as well as touch and feel the response of dynamic molecules.

Our system that we are proposing is a complete VR learning framework that allows the instructor to create their lessons. The framework provides customization by the instructor through a web-based dashboard. The customized settings can be loaded to the VR application where students can receive lessons while feeling and viewing their surroundings in the VR environment.

2 Methods

2.1 Framework

Our framework is designed to work with different laboratory types such as biology, chemistry, physics, mathematics, etc. The framework created in this study has four main modules: (a) interface, (b) companion, (c) dashboard, and (d) VR scene, as seen in Fig. 1.

We decided to integrate Oculus Quest 2 [30] as the VR headset for this framework due to its low-cost and untethered nature. The interaction with the seen is carried out with the VR controllers, while the other integrated human computer devices include: keyboard, mouse, and Touch haptic device [31]. In our framework, VR headset and controllers have direct access to the VR scene module, and they are used to manipulate 3D models and navigate in the scene. The final component of the "Interface" module is voice recognition. The voice recognition captures the voice input and sends it as an input to the "Companion" module. "Companion" module replicates a laboratory assistant during laboratory work and helps the student by listening to and addressing commands from the student during the simulation. We use speech recognition to track the voice commands to the companion requested by the student. Due to its high accuracy, we used Google's API to convert speech to text. The word error rate of Google API is the lowest, with 9% compared to other speech recognition systems [32]. Students use concise commands rather than continuous speech throughout the simulation, which causes speech recognition to stop listening. Thus, we force the companion to continuously listen for speech starting at the beginning of the simulation and ending when the simulation is complete.

Once the speech is converted to text, the command is mapped to the appropriate function. Every student has their own unique way of expressing the commands. To properly identify the commands, the simulation maps the commands to the appropriate function by using entity linking [33], which is achieved by using spaCy [34]. Entity linking allows words of interest to link to functions for the companion to carry out the commands. During the recording, there is a lot of distortion and ambient noise that can affect speech recognition from a microphone. To avoid this issue, we calibrated the energy threshold for ambient noise levels. The algorithm relies on the energy and spectral

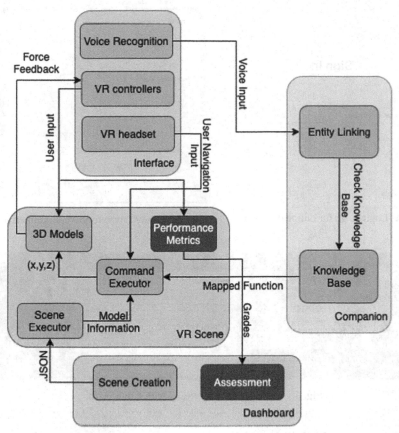

Fig. 1. Overall architecture of the virtual reality based pedagogical framework. The purple components are the implemented components, while the green components are future work (assessment and performance metrics).

characteristics of the signal and applies a three-level two-dimensional thresholding to determine whether the input is speech or non-speech [35].

The online dashboard, accessible through a web browser, for teachers to create laboratories and track and evaluate student performance. Each teacher/supervisor can create a log in to save their laboratories/scenes as seen in Fig. 2. Each task and module's settings are stored as .JSON files in an online database. The settings for each task can be altered by a teacher/supervisor using a simple web browser user interface as seen in Fig. 3. Once the settings are set, a unique identifier will be provided to share with the students which can be seen in Fig. 4. Using the unique identifier, students will be able to load the settings and metrics stored on the online database. Our preliminary tests show that the .JSON file that will hold a scene's settings is <2 MB. The data transfer rate of Firebase is 10 MB per second which will allow the new scene to be downloaded in <1 s [36].

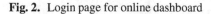

Sign In

Email *

test@test.com

Password *

......

Sign up   Login

Create a scene

Scene Name *

H-bond

Scene Description

This scene will be used to demonstrate hydrogen bonding...

☐ Fire Extinguisher ☐ Interactive Periodic Table
☐ Broom ☐ Eye Washing Station ☐ Scales
☐ Fume Hood ☐ Flask ☐ Chemistry Set

Close   Add Scene

Fig. 2. Login page for online dashboard

Fig. 3. Scene/Laboratory creation interface

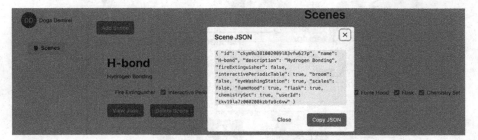

Fig. 4. Scene/Laboratory JSON with a unique id.

After the scene JSON is loaded into the scene through the scene executor, model information from the JSON is passed to the command executor, and the 3D models in the scene are updated. Also, the command executor is responsible for fulfilling the mapped functions received from the "Companion" module.

3 Results

To evaluate our framework, we conducted a usability study. Our goal was to evaluate the framework through the web-based dashboard since it will be the resource available to instructors to customize their VR lessons. Five instructors from Florida Polytechnic University performed the usability study. They are in Computer Science, Electrical and Computer Engineering, Applied Mathematics, and Data Science and Business Analytics departments. The subjects varied in their experience as instructors and their previous exposure to VR technology. Two of the subjects had experience with VR education in terms of surgery simulation, and the rest didn't have any experience with VR education.

The subjects were given a description of the VR learning framework and what we intend to do with the web-based dashboard. The subjects read the instructions on the usability form and filled out the background questionnaire (Fig. 5). The subjects then experienced a VR chemistry lab application that we have implemented using the Oculus

Quest 2. Although they were not evaluating the application itself, they experienced the virtual lab to understand the importance of VR teaching, especially for applicants who did not have a lot of VR exposure, this was important. The applicants were then introduced to the dashboard and were given a series of tasks to do with no guidance:

- Task 1: please create a login name and password
- Task 2: Use your credentials to log in
- Task 3: Add a new scene and select the following elements into the scene: fire extinguisher, the interactive periodic table, eye washing station, and fume hood
- Task 4: View the JSON file of the scene you added
- Task 5: Delete the scene

Usability Study – Virtual Reality Learning Framework

This usability study is intended to evaluate a framework for a learning environment where students can experience classes in a virtual reality (VR) setup. The instructors have the ability to customize the scene according to their preferences through a web portal. The web portal generates a file that can be loaded into the virtual scene with the instructor's customized settings.

We currently have a chemistry class implemented in VR. The web portal is located at the URL below. The web portal can be accessed by first creating credentials. The web portal is intended to provide customization aspects of the chemistry lab. But will be extended for other types of classes.

https://professor-dashboard.vercel.app/dashboard/home

For e.g., an instructor might choose to load the fire extinguisher (as well as the accompanying scenario of putting out fire into the VR chemistry lab)

This study aims to evaluate the learning framework and look into how we can improve on it.

Part 1- Background Questions

Q1- How long have you been an instructor:

   a) 1 to 3 years
   b) 4 to 10 years
   c) 10+ years

Q2- Do you have any experience with online learning:

   a) Experienced
   b) Moderate experience
   c) Never taught online

Q3- Do you have any Virtual Reality Experience:

   a) Experienced VR user
   b) Moderate Experienced
   c) I have tried it a few times
   d) Novice to VR

Do you have any experience in VR education (yes/no)? If yes, please explain:

In which department/area do you teach:

Fig. 5. First page of the usability study instructions provided to the participants of the study. The page contains an introduction, purpose as well as background questionnaire.

The subjects evaluated the tasks based on perceived difficulty on a Likert scale (1 being the hardest and 5 being the easiest). Four of the subjects found all tasks to be straightforward to do. The fifth subject found the tasks easy to do but ranked task 2 and task 3 lower (the subject ranked them at 4). The average values are given in Table 1.

Table 1. Mean values for the perceived tasks difficulties

Task	Mean
Task 1	5
Task 2	4.8
Task 3	4.8
Task 4	5
Task 5	5

The reset of the questionnaire contained the following questions

– How would you like the JSON file to be loaded in the VR lesson:

a) Automatically
b) Having a load button.
c) Copying the JSON file and pasting it to another software before loading the VR application

– How secure did you feel the system is in terms of entering credentials
    (not safe) (very safe)
    1 2 3 4 5
– Do you expect VR classes to become available in the future? (Please explain your answer):
– Would you prefer the website to be simplistic (current version) or have more features?
– Did you find any negative experiences while doing the tasks?
– Any additional comments for improvement?

Except for one subject who chose 'automatically', the subjects prefer a load button to transfer what they have customized on the website to the VR teaching environment. One of the subjects mentioned that the load button is preferable to not load the wrong settings by mistake.

Two out of five subjects did not find the website's features sufficient to promote safety in terms of creating and storing credentials, but three out of five felt that it was safe. The mean value for safety from the questionnaire was 3.8. This area is not directly related to the VR framework but would enhance the overall experience.

The subjects do expect VR to be part of education in the future, especially for laboratory classes, as one of the subjects commented. Another comment on the future of VR classes was "VR allows for users to immerse and carry out tasks without distractions". One user said, "The pandemic has proved that VR is the future."

The simplicity of the website's user interface and features was welcomed by three out of the five subjects, while the other two subjects suggested adding more features and making the features more personable. In the additional comments section, one of the subjects suggested adding a diagram depicting what will be loaded into the VR scene. Two subjects suggested using 'Enter' as a way of navigating (e.g., entering credentials) rather than relying on the mouse. Overall, there was no negative experience, and the prospect of a virtual framework was positive.

4 Conclusion

This paper presents a learning framework for VR based teaching. The framework consists of a VR application for teaching, such as the chemistry laboratory that we implemented, that can be experienced through a virtual reality headset. The application provides haptic feedback to the users to feel the objects surrounding them and thus providing a rich learning environment. In addition, there are various commands that can be issued by the user through a voice user interface. The classes can be customized through a dashboard that can be viewed on a web browser. Typically, the instructor would tweak the course according to their preference and load those custom settings to the VR application. The instructors can save their VR scene settings for future access and can create multiple scene settings and store them under their username.

A usability study was conducted to get the feedback from instructors. Five instructors with various background participated in the study and provided comments on the web-based dashboard. They performed various tasks with minimum guidance and were able to successfully complete the tasks. Their outlook to the future of VR learning was very positive.

For future work, we want to implement the assessment and performance metrics components to our framework and to move our online database that holds scene information to the cloud. Adding assessment, will allow teachers to evaluate student performance through a simple UI. Also, we want to create the ability to share scenes among different instructors. Some UI elements as well as personalized features will be added according to the user's comments in the usability study. Finally, safety web features such as authentication methods will be added to make the instructors' experience more relaxed and pleasant.

References

1. Rowe, R.J., Koban, L., Davidoff, A.J., Thompson, K.H.: Efficacy of online laboratory science courses. J. Form. Des. Learn. **2**(1), 56–67 (2018). https://doi.org/10.1007/s41686-017-0014-0
2. N. S. T. Association, NSTA position statement: the integral role of laboratory investigations in science instruction. NSTA Handb. 2010 **11**, 201–204 2007 (2010)
3. N. Council, "Inquiry and the national science education standards (2000)
4. Jones, N.: Simulated labs are booming. Nature **562**(7725), S5–S5 (2018)
5. Bretz, S.L.: Evidence for the importance of laboratory courses. J. Chem. Educ. **96**(2), 193–195 (2019)
6. Walker, J.P.: Questioning the value of general chemistry labs. Chem. Eng. News **98**(18), 17–19 (2020)

7. Demirel, D., Hamam, A., Scott, C., Karaman, B., Toker, O., Pena, L.: Towards a new chemistry learning platform with virtual reality and haptics. In: Zaphiris, P., Ioannou, A. (eds.) Learning and Collaboration Technologies: Games and Virtual Environments for Learning: 8th International Conference, LCT 2021, Held as Part of the 23rd HCI International Conference, HCII 2021, Virtual Event, July 24–29, 2021, Proceedings, Part II, pp. 253–267. Springer, Cham (2021). https://doi.org/10.1007/978-3-030-77943-6_16
8. Merchant, Z., Goetz, E.T., Cifuentes, L., Keeney-Kennicutt, W., Davis, T.J.: Effectiveness of virtual reality-based instruction on students' learning outcomes in K-12 and higher education: a meta-analysis. Comput. Educ. **70**, 29–40 (2014)
9. Liou, W.-K., Chang, C.-Y.: Virtual reality classroom applied to science education. In: 2018 23rd International Scientific-Professional Conference on Information Technology (IT), pp. 1–4 (2018)
10. Hussein, M., Nätterdal, C.: The benefits of virtual reality in education-a comparision study (2015)
11. Bradbury, N.A.: Attention span during lectures: 8 seconds, 10 minutes, or more? Adv. Physiol. Educ. **40**(4), 509–513 (2016)
12. Wilson, K., Korn, J.H.: Attention during lectures: beyond ten minutes. Teach. Psychol. **34**(2), 85–89 (2007)
13. Shen, X., et al.: Haptic-enabled telementoring surgery simulation. IEEE Multimed. **15**(1), 64–76 (2008)
14. Krummel, T.M.: Surgical simulation and virtual reality: the coming revolution. Ann. Surg. **228**(5), 635–637 (1998)
15. Marescaux, J., et al.: Virtual reality applied to hepatic surgery simulation: the next revolution. Ann. Surg. **228**(5), 627–634 (1998)
16. Demirel, D., et al.: Virtual airway skills trainer (VAST) simulator. Med. Meets Virtual Real. 22 NextMedMMVR22 **220**, 91 (2016)
17. Seymour, N.E., et al.: Virtual reality training improves operating room performance: results of a randomized, double-blinded study. Ann. Surg. **236**(4), 458–464 (2002)
18. Stone, R., Watts, K., Zhong, P.: Virtual Reality Integrated Welder Training. Weld. J. **90**(7), 136s–141s (2011)
19. Stone, R., McLaurin, E., Zhong, P., Watts, K.: Full virtual reality vs. integrated virtual reality training in welding. Weld. J. **92**(6), 167S-174S (2013)
20. Stone, R.T., Watts, K.P., Zhong, P., Wei, C.-S.: Physical and cognitive effects of virtual reality integrated training. Hum. Factors **53**(5), 558–572 (2011)
21. SimSpray | Virtual Reality Paint Training Tools and Technology, SimSpray. https://simspray.net/. Accessed 13 Jul 2021
22. Dunnagan, C.L., Dannenberg, D.A., Cuales, M.P., Earnest, A.D., Gurnsey, R.M., Gallardo-Williams, M.T.: Production and evaluation of a realistic immersive virtual reality organic chemistry laboratory experience: infrared spectroscopy. J. Chem. Educ. **97**(1), 258–262 (2019)
23. Barrett, R., et al.: Social and tactile mixed reality increases student engagement in undergraduate lab activities. J. Chem. Educ. **95**(10), 1755–1762 (2018)
24. Bennie, S.J., et al.: Teaching enzyme catalysis using interactive molecular dynamics in virtual reality. J. Chem. Educ. **96**(11), 2488–2496 (2019)
25. Bibic, L., Druskis, J., Walpole, S., Angulo, J., Stokes, L.: Bug Off Pain: an educational virtual reality game on spider venoms and chronic pain for public engagement. J. Chem. Educ. **96**(7), 1486–1490 (2019)
26. Geng, J., Chai, C.-S., Jong, M.S.-Y., Luk, E.T.-H.: Understanding the pedagogical potential of Interactive Spherical Video-based Virtual Reality from the teachers' perspective through the ACE framework. Interact. Learn. Environ. **29**(4), 618–633 (2021)

27. Mulders, M., Buchner, J., Kerres, M.: A framework for the use of immersive virtual reality in learning environments. Int. J. Emerg. Technol. Learn. IJET **15**(24), 208–224 (2020)

28. K. E. Stavroulia and A. Lanitis, "Enhancing reflection and empathy skills via using a virtual reality based learning framework," *Int. J. Emerg. Technol. Learn.*, 2019.

29. Gelsomini, M.: An affordable virtual reality learning framework for children with neuro-developmental disorder. In: Proceedings of the 18th International ACM SIGACCESS Conference on Computers and Accessibility, pp. 343–344 (2016)

30. Oculus Quest 2: Our Most Advanced New All-in-One VR Headset, Oculus. https://www.oculus.com/quest-2/. Accessed 18 Jan 2022

31. Touch, 3D Systems, 09 Jun 2016. https://www.3dsystems.com/haptics-devices/touch. Accessed 18 Jan 2022

32. Këpuska, V., Bohouta, G.: Comparing speech recognition systems (Microsoft API, Google API and CMU Sphinx). Int J. Eng. Res. Appl. **7**(3), 20–24 (2017)

33. Shen, W., Wang, J., Han, J.: Entity linking with a knowledge base: Issues, techniques, and solutions. IEEE Trans. Knowl. Data Eng. **27**(2), 443–460 (2014)

34. Honnibal, M., Montani, I.: spacy 2: natural language understanding with bloom embeddings, convolutional neural networks and incremental parsing. Appear **7**(1), 411–420 (2017)

35. Bou-Ghazale, S.E., Assaleh, K.: A robust endpoint detection of speech for noisy environments with application to automatic speech recognition. In: 2002 IEEE International Conference on Acoustics, Speech, and Signal Processing, vol. 4, p. IV–3808 (2002)

36. Realtime Database Limits, Firebase Realtime Database, Firebase. https://firebase.google.com/docs/database/usage/limits. Accessed 13 Jul 2021

HCI Issues, Design and Development for a First Responders VR Training System on Dangerous Goods Transportation Incidents

Bruno Emond(✉)[ID], Jean-François Lapointe[ID], Max Kinateder[ID], Eric DeMarbre[ID], Maxine Berthiaume[ID], Irina Kondratova[ID], Natalia Cooper[ID], Noureddine Bénichou[ID], and Stephen Downes[ID]

National Research Council Canada, Ottawa, Canada
{bruno.emond,jean-francois.lapointe,max.kinateder,eric.demarbre,
maxine.berthiaume,irina.kondratova,natalia.cooper,noureddine.benichou,
stephen.downes}@nrc-cnrc.gc.ca
https://nrc-cnrc.canada.ca

Abstract. This paper reports on our progress in the development of a virtual reality (VR) training environment where novice first responders in remote areas are acquiring situational awareness and procedural knowledge for the management of dangerous goods transportation incidents. Our research and development efforts aim to address the problem of providing engaging, realistic, safe, and cost-effective means to train first responders. The adopted process includes conducting requirements analysis in partnership with key stakeholders, as well as the design, development and empirical evaluation of the VR system with sufficient autonomy to support multiple use cases, realistic scenario variations, and real-time feedback during scenario execution.

Keywords: Virtual reality · Dangerous goods incidents training · First responders · Adaptive instructions

1 Introduction

This paper reports on our progress in the development of a virtual reality (VR) training environment where novice first responders are acquiring situational awareness and procedural knowledge for the management of dangerous goods transportation incidents [4]. The system is being developed with off-the-shelf components including commercial untethered Head Mounted Displays (HMD) and widely used cross-platform game engine. Scene 3D models and scripts are added to the off-the-shelf software to provide a realistic training environment and adaptive instructions to allow learning by doing in a self-paced manner.

The paper contains seven sections: problem statement, requirements analysis in partnership with stakeholders, human-computer interaction (HCI) issues, system design, evaluation plan, and summary and conclusions. The problem statement outlines some of the problems/issues the training system is addressing. The requirements section briefly describes how the development team has partnered with subject matter experts and stakeholders to determine key requirements. The HCI issues section presents current challenges faced during the development of the VR training environment, followed by a section on design solutions to overcome issues. An evaluation plan section presents the empirical methods put in place for characterizing learning processes and evaluating the effectiveness of the training environment. The paper concludes with a discussion of the next steps in the system development and evaluation.

2   Problem Statement

Fire emergencies affecting transportation of dangerous goods in remote areas are low-probability but high-consequence events. Training first responders to manage such incidents poses unique challenges given that training resources are often limited (both in budget and time), on-the-job training is unlikely to happen, and safely simulating high-impact training scenarios in the real world is next to impossible. Conventional training methods for dangerous goods incidents for first responders are also limited in terms how engaging, realistic, safe, and costly they are [5,8,10]. Furthermore, the training expertise is often located in urban areas, whereas trainees may be located in remote areas. This suggests that a technology-based approach could offer an essential element to increase first responders' awareness, operation, including procedural knowledge and skills.

Previous research literature points to the a lack of studies assessing training and knowledge gaps of first responders with regards to on-scene decision making, including problems with response tactics, improper assessment and handling of suspicious material, and improper use of personal protective equipment [6]. Our research and development (R&D) efforts aim to address the problem of providing engaging, realistic, safe, and cost-effective means to train first responders in remote areas on the management of dangerous goods incidents. This process includes conducting a requirements analysis in partnership with key stakeholders, as well as the design, development and empirical evaluation of a VR system that has sufficient autonomy to support multiple use cases, realistic scenario variations, and real-time feedback during scenario execution. VR offers a potential alternative to live training methods or web-based e-learning solutions, allowing for realistic and safe simulation of a wide range of dangerous goods incident scenarios. VR training allows the implementation of behavioural training with real-time feedback in complex multi-user simulations. When deployed at scale, VR training quickly becomes more cost-efficient than comparable training alternatives (e.g., physical training) [5,11]. In addition, the effectiveness, credibility and validity of VR training needs to be assessed and compared to existing training methods.

3   Requirements Analysis with Stakeholders

A technical advisory group (TAG) of subject matter experts was established to provide timely information and feedback to ensure that the VR training proof of concept meets the stakeholders' needs and their experience. The information and feedback are obtained through regular meetings and back and forth discussions with the TAG, which led to defining the major requirements. The requirement analysis has enabled to identify a set of specifications related to the context of use, training objectives, and scenario configurations. Requirements were based on the problem description, recommendations from the TAG members, and relevant emergency response guides.

3.1 Technical Advisory Group

A technical advisory group of subject matter experts was established to provide timely information and feedback to ensure that the VR training proof of concept meets the stakeholders' needs. Membership in the TAG team was done by invitation with participants selected to ensure a broad geographical representation and direct experience with emergencies affecting transportation of dangerous goods in remote areas. The TAG included members from the Canadian Association of Fire Chiefs, the Canadian Transport Emergency Centre operated by the Transportation of Dangerous Goods (TDG) Directorate of Transport Canada, a community fire and emergency services, a community hazardous materials section, a provincial firefighter school, a provincial fire Marshall, and the National Fire Protection Association. Project members served as observers but did not participate in the group decisions.

TAG members provided information and expert advice on the training needed by first responders who may be exposed to the threat of fires from the transportation of dangerous goods. Topics examined included scientific, environmental, health, and safety issues. Members were asked to provide comments on the overall research work, comments on a survey to be submitted to stakeholders, input to the development and assessment of the VR tool, and input to help answer any unresolved issues that may arise during the project. The main research team met with TAG members four times by videoconference over the first year of the project. The main efforts were focused on clarifying the training objectives, identifying authoritative legislation, manuals and guides, and offer general comments on iterative versions of the VR scenario as it was being developed.

3.2 Context of Use

Through consultation with domain experts, the following requirements were identified regarding the context of use.

1. Given that the target user group is potentially located in areas without broadly available internet, a training tool needs to have relatively autonomous (offline) processing capabilities. This means that a standalone application for learning and skill maintenance is needed;
2. Given the wide range of potential scenarios and associated required skill levels, a flexible software development paradigm (flexibility in scenario design, in deployment of measurements, assessments, and tutoring strategies) is needed.

This also requires identification of key software elements to capture learners' behaviour and performance;

3. Given that training may also occur supervised, in both, group or individual sessions, capabilities for group usage and/or screencasting are required.

3.3 Training Objectives

First responders can generally be grouped into three skill level categories (with increasing levels of competencies and responsibilities): Awareness level, Operations level, and Incident Command level [15]. The proof of concept VR training tool described in this paper will target trainees at the *Awareness Level* category. First responders who are trained and certified to the Awareness level are individuals who may be the first to arrive at or witness a hazardous material or chemicals incident. They are expected to assume certain responsibilities when faced with an incident involving hazardous material. These responsibilities can be associated with high-level training objectives and include these main steps:

1. Recognize and identify hazardous materials;
2. Protect themselves and others from hazards;
3. Isolate the hazard area and deny entry;
4. Communicate information to an appropriate authority and calls for appropriate assistance.

In addition to the advice from the technical advisory group (TAG) of experts, the Emergency Response Guide [15], NFPA 470: Hazardous Materials/Weapons of Mass Destruction (WMD) Standard for Responders [13], and Transport Canada Competency guidelines [16] were used to identified training requirements.

The main training objectives for the first version of the VR training tool focuses on a first responder being able to safely gather and communicate information about the observed incident. The training objectives do not include actions needed to secure and isolate the hazard area. The following specific learning goals were defined:

1. Approach and safe positioning: This requires the trainee to "not rush in", and recognize information provided by the environment. To safely approach the scene, a responder should seek an upwind and uphill position to start investigation and stay at a safe distance from the hazardous materials location (i.e., outside the initial isolation distance);
2. Hazard identification: This requires using provided inventory tools (e.g., binoculars, a copy of the Emergency Response Guidebook (ERG) [15]) to retrieve information from, for example, placards attached to the transporter (e.g., UN number), and then to recognize associated hazards;
3. Situation assessment and communication: A responder needs to communicate the incident to emergency services and, if needed, to Canadian Transport Emergency Centre (CANUTEC). In this step, the trainee is able to use a cellphone which is provided as inventory tool in VR environment.

3.4 Scenario Configuration

Based on the context of use and training objectives and following the TAG advice and input, a simple proof of concept scenario was developed, in which a trainee would need to diagnose a hazardous material incident and communicate their findings (note that isolating the scene/denying entry was not included in the training goals defined for this scenario).

The scenario is intended to be a relatively simple and relatively common occurrence. The trainee is faced with the following scenario:

- A truck with a cabin and a trailer is jackknifed close to a road;
- The truck is transporting an (initially) unknown (potentially) hazardous material;
- It is unclear whether any or how much material has spilled;
- There are no obvious signs of fire (e.g., smoke);
- There are no buildings or people in the immediate vicinity of the incident;
- It is daytime and overall visibility is good;
- The environment contains vegetation on the side of the road, a small river/brook/ and there is a point of elevation not too far away;
- Continuous wind from one direction;
- Daytime temperatures are below 30C and above 0C;
- No dynamic changes in the scenario (i.e., no fire development, no change in wind direction, etc.).

4   HCI Issues

In order to support training and performance in the VR environment it is necessary to provide appropriate, task relevant cues that can be represented as design features in the simulation. The presence of these instructional design feature within the simulation is important not only for initial training but also for training transfer. Some of the examples of this feature include on screen feedback during simulation or additional sensory cuing in VR. Even though some of these features can reduce the overall fidelity of the simulation, research has shown that the informational content of these features, even if they disrupt fidelity, can enhances not only performance but also overall user experience in virtual environments [2,3].

When considering the elements that must be simulated in a virtual environment to provide an adequate level of training efficiency, several issues emerged. For example, browsing and reading a book in VR, by using solely an HMD and hand controllers is a different experience than in real life (IRL). Other aspects, such as simulating wind, smell and heat using only audio-visual displays technologies asks for some creativity in order to communicate this information in a way that makes sense to users without the possibility of simulating them by using other communication channels. The sections below describe in more details which HCI issues were encountered and subsequently addressed during software development.

4.1   User Boundaries

A VR technology that is proposed to be used in this study is the Oculus head-mounted display. All Oculus VR systems first require to determine the user boundaries, i.e., whether the user will be able to walk in the whole room (a.k.a. room scale boundary) to indicate a safe place to move whilst using VR headset, as well as determine standing or sitting boundary (stationary boundary). These boundaries serve as guidance for the user and they appear when the user approaches too close to boundary edges as a user warning of the possible unsafe actions. In this study, sitting stationary boundary is chosen for the testing to protect novice users of possible injuries that could be caused by falls on the ground as well as reduce possible discomfort (motion sickness) that the user might experience during the movement in VR environment.

4.2   Available Input Devices

In our proposed VR set-up, the hand controllers with ray casting can be used to select, deselect, move or turn the objects or used them to re-locate oneself within the VR environment. The user can also change the position of the head whilst wearing the headset to enable some additional locomotion. The only way to act in the VR environment is by either using the hand controllers or by changing the pose of the head with the headset on. Gesture and speech recognition have been turned off because of interference with the hand controllers and noise in the environment, as well as their limited options in terms of tasks input.

4.3   Locomotion

Locomotion is the motor component of the navigation (which also integrates wayfinding) that allows for virtual walkthroughs in the scene. These walk-throughs are enabled by using the thumb stick located on the left-hand controller combined with the orientation of the headset (which indicates the direction of fore/aft axis). This allows for 3°C of freedom, namely fore/aft and sideways (left thumb stick), as well as the rotation of the head according to the vertical axis.

4.4   Gaze

Since we use a sitting stationary boundary, the viewpoint of the user is controlled mainly by the orientation of the head (pan/tilt/roll) with a quasi-fixed location in space.

4.5   Menu Selection

Selecting items on the menus presented by the headset is done by a vector-based pointing technique called ray-casting in the 3D space [12]. Each hand controllers cast such a ray and menu selection is done by pointing at it with one of the rays and by pulling the trigger of the hand controller related to that ray. Ray-casting selection is used both to start the application and to select the scenario to be used in the application itself. Ray-casting selection is illustrated in Fig. 1 below.

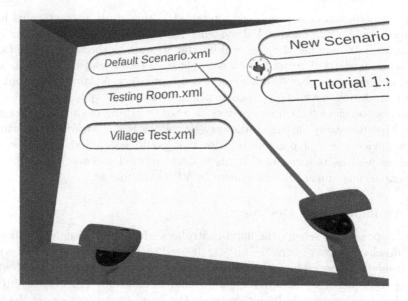

Fig. 1. Ray-casting menu selection of the scenario

Fig. 2. Illustration of the dangerous good transportation incident scene. Compass (red circle) indicates user's orientation and the wind direction is indicated by a small blue triangle.

4.6 Wind Simulation

Given that our user interface is only audio-visual and contains no somatic display, we relied on the use of a visual icon of a compass to illustrate both orientation in space and wind direction. This compass (in red) is illustrated in Fig. 2. It shows the silhouette of a person viewed from above (orientation in space), coupled with a cursor that indicates wind direction.

4.7 Dialogue Interaction

In a 3D desktop application, during a dialogue interaction, the system can halt all movement and require the user to interact with the dialogue before returning to the simulation. This process does not work in a VR environment since stopping head movement whilst immersed in a virtual environment could give rise to some undesirable effects, including motion sickness or disorientation. When in VR environment, user's eyes and head will track towards the interface element they want to select. If the user interface element is attached to the head movement, the element is able to move in space. At the same time, the user simultaneously tries to follow with the controller's ray casting, creating a situation where the pointing line will be chasing the user interface element. The solution to this issue consisted of halting the player's lateral movement but leaving all rotational movements associated with the head active. A dialogue interface fixed in space would then appear in front of the user's current forward-facing direction so that they could interact with it while still looking around. Once the dialogue is ended, the system restores lateral movements.

4.8 Heat and Smell Simulation

Given similar constraints as for wind simulation, i.e., no somatic or olfactory displays, we used simple text messages in a floating dialog box to indicate the detection of heat or smells by the avatar in the VR simulation.

4.9 Inventory Management

In order to complete a task correctly, the learner has to use several tools that are available to them in the inventory. The inventory includes following tools: the Emergency Response Guidebook [15], binoculars and a cellphone. All of these inventory items can be accessed sequentially by pushing the Y Button on the left-hand controller few times, or pushing the B button on the right-hand controller in the similar way.

Book Reading. Since the learners have to consult a book (The Emergency Response Guidebook or ERG, see Fig. 3a) as part of their training, we had to design a usable way to display, browse and read it within the virtual scene. The book itself is part of the inventory for the learner.

Cellphone. Once called from the inventory, the cellphone can be activated by pulling the index trigger of the left hand controller. A floating dialog box then appear (see Fig. 3b) that allows to report the important information to an emergency call centre (a.k.a. as 9–1–1 centre) for assistance.

(a) Emergency Response Guidebook.   (b) Simulation of a phone conversation with a single or multiple choices selection.

Fig. 3. Inventory items (ERG and Phone).

Binoculars. Once called from the inventory, the binoculars are activated by pushing the index trigger of the left hand controller and then pointed to the scene by changing the orientation of same (left) hand controller. They then display a telescopic view of the part of the scene they are pointed to as illustrated in Figs. 4a and 4b.

(a) Binoculars inventory item.   (b) Binoculars in use.

Fig. 4. Inventory items (Binoculars).

5   System Design

The training scenario consists of a VR simulation of a scene involving a dangerous goods transportation incident. The learner is immersed into VR environment using an HMD and views the environment from a first person perspective as illustrated in Fig. 2. The learner can navigate and explore the scene using handheld input devices (hand controllers). The learner can also access inventory items that can be used during task execution such as ERG reference guide book [15] (see Fig. 3a), binoculars (see Figs. 4a and 4b), and a communication device (cell phone, Fig. 3b).

A formative tutoring system is running at the background to provide the learner with feedback as they navigate the virtual environment. The main task for the initial investigation of the incident scene consists of collecting information about the incident while minimizing risks. As the learner moves in the VR scene, he/she needs to maintain a safe distance from the incident location while remaining uphill and downwind to avoid exposure to fluid or gas leaks. A system of spatial zones monitors entries and exits of areas of relevance for the task. The zones to track and provide instructions include zones for proximity danger, down wind, low ground, and safe viewing distance. The zones can be configured to reflect scenario variations such as the nature of the dangerous material and wind direction. For example, if the learner were to move too close to the incident in the virtual scenario they will receive a warning message shown in their display (see Fig. 5). Formative tutoring system can be used to assess how much support a person needs to complete the scenario; the less support one needs the more autonomous is the learner.

Fig. 5. Warning message displayed.

6   Evaluation Plan

As part of this project, a series of studies will be conducted to evaluate and assess whether the VR training tool increases participants' knowledge of the procedures at the Awareness-level training following a hazardous materials incident. Participants will also be encouraged to provide feedback about any possible improvements that can be made to the VR training tool, its overall design as well as the study protocol. The National Research Council Canada's (NRC) Research Ethics Board has reviewed and approved the project protocol (REB#2021/157). The results of each study will undergo a variety of qualitative and quantitative data analyses. The overall findings from this project will be disseminated as peer-reviewed research articles.

In the first study, we will adopt an exploratory approach where participants' preferences will be examined and their feedback about the VR training tool and VR environment will be obtained through online surveys. The results from the first study will be used to provide guidance on possible improvements of the VR environment that will be adopted in the follow-up studies. The second study will focus on comparing the performance of two different types of users a) novices - people with no former Awareness-level training) and b) experts -people with former Awareness-level training) prior to and following training in VR environment. The third study will focus on comparing two different learning set-ups a) a traditional training scenario (e.g., classroom learning) and b) VR training scenario in virtual environment. Both of these studies will collect feedback on a set of metrics and assess the participants' pre- and post-training performance.

In all studies, participants will complete a set of surveys that will be administered to them during the pre-training, post-training, and at the end of the session. The surveys will collect participants' demographics, as well as the data that will capture their individual differences in terms of immersive tendencies (i.e., the propensity to feel immersed) [17], sense of presence (i.e., the feeling of "being there" in the VR scenario) [14,17], overall workload levels (i.e., the amount of mental and physical effort exerted to complete the scenario) [7], cybersickness (i.e., discomfort or unwanted negative side effects induced by VR) [9], and overall system usability (i.e., the ease-of-use of the system and technology) [1]. Additional performance metrics to assess the participants' performance (such as the overall time to complete the task, number of errors, etc.) will be used specifically in the second and third study. All participants will be asked to provide open-ended feedback about the VR training tool as well as their overall experience at the end of the session.

7 Summary and Conclusions

This paper describes the development of a VR training tool for first responders to enable them to increase their situational awareness and knowledge level for the management of dangerous goods transportation incidents. The requirements analysis conducted with our key stakeholders enabled us to develop a VR system that can adapt and support a variety of use cases and scenarios. The training tool has a formative tutoring system that provides learner with an instant feedback during the navigation in VR. During the next phase of the project, we will focus on developing a robust evaluation plan in which we will conduct the usability evaluation from the user's perspective, as well as the overall software validation in terms of data collection. In addition, we plan to continue with the validation of needs assessments with our key stakeholders. The continuous evaluations during the various stages of development will allow us to propose evidence-based VR guidelines and potential solutions for VR training tools to improve training of first responders in a variety of emergency situations.

References

1. Brooke, J.: SUS-a quick and dirty usability scale. Usability evaluation in industry. CRC Press, Boca Raton, May 1996. https://www.crcpress.com/product/isbn/9780748404605. ISBN: 9780748404605
2. Cook, D.A., et al.: Comparative effectiveness of technology-enhanced simulation versus other instructional methods. Simul. Healthc. J. Soc. Simul. Healthc. 7(5), 308–320 (2012). https://doi.org/10.1097/SIH.0b013e3182614f95, https://journals.lww.com/01266021-201210000-00006
3. Cooper, N., Millela, F., Cant, I., White, M.D., Meyer, G.: Transfer of training-virtual reality training with augmented multisensory cues improves user experience during training and task performance in the real world. PLOS ONE 16(3), e0248225 (2021). https://doi.org/10.1371/journal.pone.0248225, https://dx.plos.org/10.1371/journal.pone.0248225
4. Emond, B., Kinateder, M., Cooper, N., Kondratova, I.: Virtual reality for transportation incident management training of first responders in remote areas. In: Interservice/Industry Training, Simulation, and Education Conference, pp. 1–11. National Training and Simulation Association, Orlando, FL (2020)
5. Engelbrecht, H., Lindeman, R.W., Hoermann, S.: A SWOT analysis of the field of virtual reality for firefighter training. Front. Robot. AI 6, 101 (2019). https://doi.org/10.3389/frobt.2019.00101, https://www.frontiersin.org/article/10.3389/frobt.2019.00101/full
6. Galada, H.C., Gurian, P.L., Hong, T.: First responder knowledge and training needs for bioterrorism. J. Homel. Secur. Emerg. Manag. 10(2) (2013). https://doi.org/10.1515/jhsem-2012-0064, https://www.degruyter.com/document/doi/10.1515/jhsem-2012-0064/html
7. Hart, S.G.: Nasa-task load index (NASA-TLX); 20 years later. In: Proceedings of the Human Factors and Ergonomics Society Annual Meeting, vol. 50, no. 9, pp. 904–908, October 2006. https://doi.org/10.1177/154193120605000909, http://journals.sagepub.com/doi/10.1177/154193120605000909
8. Kanazawa, A., Hayashi, H.: The analysis of training effects with virtual reality in simple task. In: 2017 6th IIAI International Congress on Advanced Applied Informatics (IIAI-AAI), pp. 345–350. IEEE, July 2017. https://doi.org/10.1109/IIAI-AAI.2017.201
9. Kennedy, R.S., Lane, N.E., Berbaum, K.S., Lilienthal, M.G.: Simulator sickness questionnaire: an enhanced method for quantifying simulator sickness. Int. J. Aviat. Psychol. 3(3), 203–220 (1993). https://doi.org/10.1207/s15327108ijap0303, http://www.tandfonline.com/doi/abs/10.1207/s15327108ijap0303
10. Kinateder, M., et al.: The effect of dangerous goods transporters on hazard perception and evacuation behavior - a virtual reality experiment on tunnel emergencies. Fire Saf. J. 78, 24–30 (2015). https://doi.org/10.1016/j.firesaf.2015.07.002

11. Kinateder, M., et al.: Virtual reality for fire evacuation research. In: 2014 Federated Conference on Computer Science and Information Systems, pp. 313–321. IEEE (2014)
12. LaViola, J.J., Krujiff, E., McMahan, R.P., Bowman, D.A., Poupyrev, I.: 3D User Interfaces - Theory and Practice, 2nd Edn. Addison-Wesley, Boston (2017)
13. National Fire Protection Association: Competency Guidelines for Responders to Incidents of Flammable Liquids in Transport, High-harzard Flammable Trains (2016). https://publications.gc.ca/site/eng/9.812478/publication.html
14. Slater, M., Usoh, M., Steed, A.: Depth of presence in virtual environments. Presence Teleoperators Virtual Environ. **3**(2), 130–144 (1994). https://doi.org/10.1162/pres.1994.3.2.130, https://direct.mit.edu/pvar/article/3/2/130-144/58820
15. Transport Canada: Emergency Response Guidebook (2020). https://tc.canada.ca/en/dangerous-goods/canutec/2020-emergency-response-guidebook
16. Transport Canada: NFPA470: Hazardous Materials/Weapons of Mass Destruction (WMD) Standard for Responders (2022). https://www.nfpa.org/codes-and-standards/all-codes-and-standards/list-of-codes-and-standards/detail?code=470
17. Witmer, B.G., Singer, M.J.: Measuring presence in virtual environments: a presence questionnaire. Presence Teleoperators Virtual Environ. **7**(3), 225–240 (1998). https://doi.org/10.1162/105474698565686, https://direct.mit.edu/pvar/article/7/3/225-240/92643

An Approach of Holographic Technology for the Practical Distance Education

Chi-Fu Hsiao[1]([✉]), Ching-Han Lee[2], Chun-Yen Chen[3], and Teng-Wen Chang[3]

[1] Department of Architecture, Tamkang University, No. 151, Yingzhuan Road, Tamsui District, New Taipei City 251301, Taiwan R.O.C.
chifu.research@gmail.com
[2] Collage of Future, National Yunlin University of Science and Technology, Douliu, Taiwan R.O.C.
[3] Department of Digital Media Design, National Yunlin University of Science and Technology, Douliu, Taiwan (R.O.C.)

Abstract. In order to face the requirement of distant education after covid-19, this paper has presented a cyber-physical co-existence environment for practical distance learning events, we called it as a "Co-existing Practical Environment, CPE". CPE includes: "Holographic Wearable Device, HWD" for behavior sensing and vision sharing mechanism, cloud "Digital Twin Model, DTM" database for expert correcting variables real time, and collaborative fabrication discussion interface. We built an immersive HoloLens interface to help distance learning participators, understanding the concept of structural mechanics form morphs with mix-reality sensing, communicating the augmented information of parts of models for collaborative fabrication, and sharing the views of operation process for lecturers to solve the technical problems instantly. Furthermore, users are able to make their own custom digital twin project in CPE and optimize their fabricating process by adding more realistic material factors, operation callbacks, or analyzing their practice results in parameters relationships. This paper revised an application of holographic technology with a practical distance learning workshop as example, and discover CPE as a new kind of co-creation, cross-field, and remotely prepared cooperation mechanism. While the epidemic is still ragging, we are looking further researchers of more immersive methods for distance education.

Keywords: Holographic · Digital twin · Distance education · Immersive · Fabrication

1 Introduction

The "cyber-physics Co-existing Environment (CE)" and "Digital Twin (DT)" are important concepts of the "Internet of Things (IoT)", which are newly created by integrating physical feedback data with artificial intelligence, machine learning and software analysis to create a digital simulation of the feedback of the current situation in an information

P. Zaphiris and A. Ioannou (Eds.): HCII 2022, LNCS 13329, pp. 61–70, 2022.
https://doi.org/10.1007/978-3-031-05675-8_6

platform. The concept of IoT is important for digital simulated feedback in the information platform. Through DT, it is possible to perform rapid deep learning and accurate simulation of real phenomena and research objects based on massive information feedback [1].

Besides, Under CE system, "Holo-" technology allows users to apply "Augmented-Reality (AR)" interface through portable devices such as portable smartphones, VR glasses or HoloLens to achieve "Cross-Reality (XR)" immersive experiences. These immersive experiences require not only a high quality and easy-to-use infrastructure platform, but also a large amount of off-site data collection and a sufficient database of samples for different conditions to provide cloud computing mechanisms for analysis, computation, and optimization, and then effectively apply them to the actual teaching field [2].

This paper proposes a "Co-existing Practical Environment (CPE)" to aid participants to communicate with the mechanical equipment through more intuitive physical activities, and then acquire prototypes that allow participants to communicate each other within different professional fields quickly.

Thus, we built an immersive HoloLens interface to help distance learning participators, understanding the concept of structural mechanics form morphs with mix-reality sensing, communicating the augmented information of parts of models for collaborative fabrication, and sharing the views of operation process for lecturers to solve the technical problems instantly. Furthermore, users are able to make their own custom digital twin project in CPE, and optimize their fabricating process by adding more realistic material factors, operation callbacks, or analyzing their practice results in parameters relationships.

2   Precedents

Spatial information in the contemporary environment can be fed back in real time through "ubiquitous" information streaming, so that computing devices can not only sense changes in the surrounding environment, but can also perform the desired or set behaviors of users in real time according to the changing patterns of the environment [3]. This concept of "ubiquitous computing" can be described through three aspects: the process of perception and communication, the activities of the users in the field, and the overall environment that includes the digital space of spatial information and the sensor field [4].

The main purpose of early research on CE is to try to combine the physical environment with virtual information to present it as a physical operation. For example, Lu combines the real environment and virtual information through spatial algorithms and represents the user's environmental operation information through the screen. When a user needs to execute a platform that interacts with the real environment, the interface designer needs to construct the corresponding physical attributes and feedback mechanisms in the virtual space. For example, when users use objects of different materials to interact with the space, such as dropping, flowing, pushing, ejecting, etc., CE needs to further construct a database of the association between various activities and the objects; and immediately render the physical properties of these materials in terms of shape, density, surface touch, etc. through algorithms. The CE needs to further build up a database of the association between various activities and the actor; and through the calculation, it can immediately render the response of these materials with different characteristics such as shape, density, and surface touch to simulate the expected processing effect after planning [5].

However, in the CE that operates everywhere, the spatial-body interactions that were previously only imagined can be fed back to the real environment interface in real time through the digital information flow from various environmental devices and sensors. To effectively respond to real-time changes in environmental information, the CE needs to ensure that feedback information is continuously recorded and applied for future evaluation and optimization during the execution of continuous activities. In other words, a complete set of CE itself is a spatial information model with a complete behavior history of activity, recording, evaluation, and correction process, which is co-constructed by physical and virtual signals in the spatial environment [6].

Under CE, users need to manipulate both virtual and physical objects to transmit signals to the virtual space and perform virtual space browsing or morphing actions. Although virtual space has almost unlimited freedom of generation, how to effectively collect, interpret, integrate, and communicate with user information depends entirely on the constructor's interpretation of the specific information in the environment itself. For learners, how to classify information for classification, and then reproduce the physical and virtual environment through digital media, can be said to be the core issue of contemporary design thinking and industrial practice through narrative power integration.

2.1 Robotrack

Weissenböck of Graz University of Technology presented a series of workshops in 2017. They try to develop a design process for the interaction between spatial environments, human movement and robotic arms. Through the technique of "motion capture system (MCS)", he used ambient body prototypes as design materials and transformed them into parametric path forms based on the information material of these body activities.

A series of tactile experiments were developed to record the hand movements and velocities of the subjects into a database and to convert this information into a GCode to drive the robotic arm. In terms of device setup, Weissenböck's MCS system is equipped with six infrared cameras in a spatial environment and reflective markers on the spatial frame for the cameras to record coordinates of point displacement data [7] (Fig. 1).

During the tracing process of dynamic motion, the trainees encountered many manual forming problems, mainly in the visual motion trajectory which is difficult to provide a stable and accurate motion path. Therefore, the processing parameters of the robotic arm, including heating time, movement speed, direction, and force, need to be optimized by providing a matching continuous algorithm to achieve reasonable forming results.

Weissenböck's new approach of considering machines as design development, however, is not a new approach to human activity. However, the material properties of the cloth of human activity make the overall workflow still need to be corrected by algorithms to correlate detailed movements and real paths, and the experiment itself still has much room for optimization.

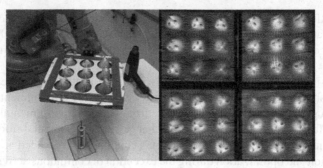

Fig. 1. Weissenböck of Graz University of technology presented a series of workshops to record the hand movements and velocities of the subjects into a database and to convert this information into a GCode to drive the robotic arm [7].

2.2 Immersive Tracking Environment

In 2015, Sci-Arc uses the motion sensor of Microsoft Kinect to track the user's behavioral movements, continuously translates the coordinates of the movers in the space, and activates the robotic arm's activity program through the controller platform. "Immersive Tracking Environment (IMT)" is designed to perform without delays as much as possible, hoping to show the dance behavior between the movers and the robotic arm, just like two performers leading each other.

However, because of the real-time operation of the program, the performance of the sensing and feedback is not synchronized according to the activity mechanism of the arm, and the difference in response time can always be visually detected by the operator of the braking sensor. Since each operator's movement varies from person to person, the interface needs to be developed in such a way that it is easy for the user to learn and to provide real-time feedback on the user's behavioral data in order to facilitate the reconfiguration of the activity parameters between the operator and the robotic arm's control platform [8] (Fig. 2).

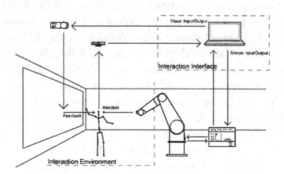

Fig. 2. IMT user and robotic arm environment [8].

Batliner and Newsum found that when the IMT interface can provide information about the robotic arm such as the relative positions of the user and the environment, the relative positions of the robotic arm and the user, the coordinate parameters, and even the robotic arm speed, the axis-damping parameters, etc., and provide real-time adjustment to the participant, it can effectively span the differences in the motion mechanism between the robotic arm and the user, thus optimizing the user's learning of the robotic arm operation.

2.3 Preliminary Study of Human-Computer Interaction

We has been committed to developing a real-time human-computer interaction mechanism and trying to develop a behavior-space model, which use virtual-real integration interface for human-computer collaboration at different times. Through the application of CPE technology, the research team constructs a new direction of recursive collaboration model between designers and digital signals: recording the user's reflective behavior patterns into the spatial-behavior model in the cloud and analyzing the behavior model by changing the visual and auditory reflection patterns (Fig. 3).

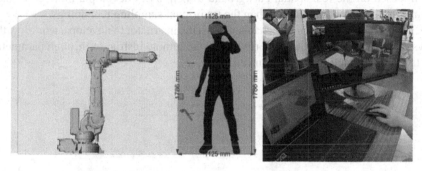

Fig. 3. IMT user and robotic arm environment [8].

We first focused on the interactive feedback mechanism of the VR system, using GUI for the designers to control the robotic arm remotely. Through this series of CE-based hardware and interface software solutions, it is possible to start implementing a digital architecture workflow for human-machine interfacing and communication.

Secondly, ABB's "multi-move" mechanism is applied to command two robotic arms to work together remotely and further develop a psychological "human-machine synergy" working mode based on the synchronization of posture or action records.

Hsiao points out that the designer constructs his own cognitive system from his own conscious feedback to the sensors in the physical space and confirms the effect of his own behavior on environmental changes through the feedback of the digital model. The strategy proposed by the team of WUST attempts to synchronize the physical activity with the robot arm's synergistic mechanism, which in turn allows human cognitive behavioral feedback and environmental data to produce synergy [10].

This study suggests that the main reason why this virtual-real interaction mode can be implemented is that the operator can effectively develop his own recognition of the mapping mechanism between the digital model and the real situation through the synchronization effect of behavioral and visual feedback during the learning process and can then apply the recognition mechanism to achieve the design task.

3   Methodology

This paper propose CPE corresponds to real physical objects and digital models in real time and applied to a distance international workshop "Ourobors" as a practical task. Through a series of processing, analysis, and judgment, feedback is generated on the digital data to optimize the prototyping process and add value to it, and even to optimize the process implementation. In addition to the DTP work structure, CPE environment in this base further enables users to use the immersive wearable device HoloLens for prototyping and calibration to assist design development and manufacturing back testing through the XR mechanism. This workshop is mainly to explore the possibility of construction assisted by Holoimage technology with two main objectives.

Firstly, through CPE, the results of complex shapes and computer algorithms are superimposed on the real spatial background to help users develop a more convenient and intuitive construction method than the traditional sampling technology.

Secondly, the back-testing mechanism helps the instructor to develop a workflow that allows the digital prototype to be corrected by the remote instructor through parameters to optimize the digital twin platform (Fig. 4).

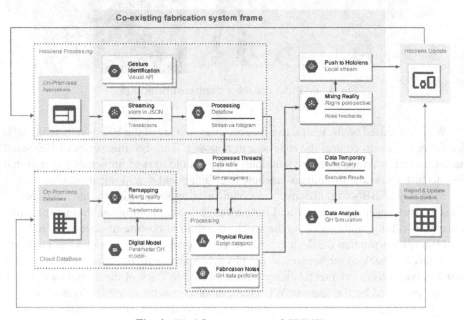

Fig. 4. Workflow structures of CPE [9].

3.1 Subjects and Schedule

The purpose of this international workshop is to explore how MR technology can be used remotely and immersive environment to assist in construction.

First, to project complex shapes and grammars onto the real spatial background through MR technology, and to develop a more convenient and intuitive construction method than traditional sampling techniques.

Secondly, through the back testing mechanism, we will develop a DTP that allows the instructors and trainees to discuss and correct the prototype construction field remotely, even if they are in a different place.

This workshop is divided into two teams, one team to explore the theory of mechanistic patterns and the other team to think about the rules of shape grammar, with about 10 people in each team. The workshop lasted for five days:

1. The first day: we will have a two-hour opening session in the morning, followed by a lecture on the theory of shape and rule manipulation in the afternoon.
2. Second day: the theories were further validated through prototype equipment, and several 40 cm × 40 cm × 40 cm three-dimensional configurations or grammatical shape models were presented.
3. In the morning of the third day, we will have a preliminary exchange on the content of shape and rule design, and in the afternoon, we will integrate the theory of shape and rule into the prototype.
4. From the fourth to the fifth day, the prototype of the shape structure was made through the CPE environment, and a 3 m × 3 m × 3 m structure was completed together, and the exterior was covered with a folded sheet by shape calculation.
5. Finally, a four-hour presentation and discussion will be held in the afternoon of the fifth day, with the following schedule (Fig. 5).

Time			Day 1 8/10(Mon)	Day 2 8/11(Tue)	Day 3 8/12(Wed)	Day 4 8/13(Thu)	Day 5 8/14(Fri)
	9:00-9:30	30	Registration				
Moring 9:00~12:00	9:30-10:00	30	Registration (postponed)	Tutorial: SGI	Midterm Presentation	Design & Prototype MeshFaced Model	Production 300 X 300 X 300
	10:00-10:30	30	Opening Lecturer & Schedule Introduction				
	10:30-10:50	30	Icebreaker				
	10min for break and moving classroom			Break	Break		
	11:00-12:00	60	Course Introduction: Shape Grammar (Andrew)	Design & Concept: SGI pattern	Tutorial: Pattern in Boundary		
Lunch	12:00-13:00	60	Lunch				
Afternoon 13:00~17:30	13:00-14:00	60	Tutorial: Shape Grammar rules (Andrew)	Design & Prototype 40 X 40	Tutorial: Pattern Layout 2D to 3D	Production 300 X 300 X 300	13:30-14:00 Final Presentation
	14:00-15:00	60					14:00-15:00 Panel Discussion
	15:00-16:00	60	Tutorial: GH (Chi-Fu)			Production 300 X 300 X 300	15:00-15:30 Q&A
	16:00-16:20		Teatime(flexible breaktime)				15:30 Awards&Closing Ceremony
	16:20-17:30	30	Tutorial: SGI (Rudi)	Design & Prototype 40 X 40	Design & Prototype MeshFaced Model		
		40					Teatime

Fig. 5. Workshop schedule.

3.2   Instructional Equipments

The teaching and communication during each day were conducted mainly through tele-conferencing equipment and the virtual-reality integration environment developed by our team. The main three-dimensional teaching program used is the visual programming software Grasshopper, and the wearable mixed reality device Hololens for immersive experience of physical and real communication. In addition, the instructors and the students work together with the Self-Maker Center's rapid prototyping equipment such as laser cutters or 3D printers to develop models and assemble prototypes with hardware components (Fig. 6).

Fig. 6. Teaching instruction with teleconferencing equipment and parametric programs, prototype assembly by means of auxiliary tools and hardware components.

3.3   Workshop Process

This paper proposes a distance education workshop into three phases:

1. Starting with simple geometry and mathematical rules, and further creating a variety of complex morphological textures from discrete geometric forms by interfering computer algorithms. Then uploading these preliminary prototypes to a cloud data sets for foreigner instructors.
2. Find specific material and prototyping the DTM in "Holographic Wearable Device, HWD". Due to the material characteristics of unit pieces in the physical space, it is not possible to perform shaping calculations in the digital space without pre-experiment. Thus, we develop the possible prototype states both in physical space, and DTM. After comparing the prototypes in virtual and physical, participating members can obtain reasonable parameters to simulates, and optimize the difference between design approaches. At the same time, the foreigner instructors can correct the deformation parameters and computational algorithm of digital prototype.
3. After the participants have obtained the identification of the unitary components and have been able to construct reasonable rules for the evolution of the digital prototype material parameters from cloud DTM. This phase discusses the result via DTM online and built real constructions physically. As the foreigner instructors review and provide the suggestion via the sharing views from HWD interface on the

one hand, participants reshape the design consequence with gesture pose and real material construction process on the other hand (Fig. 7).

Fig. 7. Assist participants to develop narrative power of quantitative material constructions through CPE mechanism.

4   Conclusions

The CPE mechanism in this study is more than just a one-time production process, but must be able to evolve, regress, and practice agilely with the design phase. On the other hand, the R&D student team needs to be able to provide an accurate and equitable description of the implementation status so that the instructors can quickly and accurately grasp the communication needs and problems that should be solved. The following is a summary of the issues related to the implementation of this CPE workshop for subsequent study.

1. A parametric model of real-time interaction should be established to facilitate a common real and virtual CPE environment for the instructor and the participants.
2. It is necessary to integrate the mechanism of mutual perception between reality and reality and to strengthen the connection between real materials and digital models through effective implementation tools.
3. Although cloud computing allows instructors and students to share the same feedback results, there are still differences in transmission and operation time, which makes the implementation less efficient than comparing the results after each of them has executed locally.
4. There should be a high degree of overlap in the expertise of the instructors, and the development of more complex synergies requires technical staff with long-term experience in cooperation, so that the team can have sufficient systematic process planning when communicating internally.
5. Through parametric operations, it is possible to reproduce prototypes with efficient recording of accurate quality, but the accuracy of the algorithm of the material itself often affects the gap between real and digital prototypes to the maximum extent.

6. The analysis and prediction of the CPE model in terms of intelligent interaction mechanism needs to be further optimized through the setting of key factors to ensure the cumulative evolutionary benefits of each iteration of the design team's update.

This research aims to promote innovative self-creation education, emphasizing the spirit of innovation and creativity in the middle school, and to develop design thinking from the narrative power, applying CPE technology to inject a new mechanism of co-creation, cross-discipline, and even cross-space practice for international exchange and cooperation.

In addition, the project expects to achieve the effect of agile practice through the integration of virtual and real technologies, so that users in different campuses can communicate with the mechanical equipment in different places through more intuitive physical activities and get the ability to communicate with users in different professional fields more quickly and accurately. Secondly, through autonomous sensing and intelligent recognition technology, we can optimize the traditional automatic equipment and expand the possibility of intelligence of the equipment according to the location and material.

References

1. Grieves, M., Vickers, J.: Digital twin: mitigating unpredictable, undesirable emergent behavior in complex systems. In: Kahlen, J., Flumerfelt, S., Alves, A. (eds.) Transdisciplinary Perspectives on Complex Systems, pp. 85–113. Springer, Cham (2017). https://doi.org/10.1007/978-3-319-38756-7_4
2. Chen, C.-Y., Chang, T.-W., Hsiao, C.-F., Huang, H.-Y.: Developing an interactive fabrication process of maker based on "seeing-moving-seeing" model. In: Yuan, P.F., Xie, Y.M.(, Yao, J., Yan, C. (eds.) CDRF 2019, pp. 312–321. Springer, Singapore (2020). https://doi.org/10.1007/978-981-13-8153-9_28
3. Weiser, M.: The computer for the 21st century. SIGMOBILE Mob. Comput. Commun. Rev. 3(3), 3–11 (1999)
4. Jeng, T.: Designing a ubiquitous smart space of the future: the principle of mapping. In: Gero, J.S. (ed.) Design Computing and Cognition '04, pp. 579–592. Springer, Dordrecht (2004). https://doi.org/10.1007/978-1-4020-2393-4_30
5. Lu, K.-T., Chang, T.-W.: Experience montage in virtual space. In: Computer-Aided Architectural Design Research in Asia. TVB School of Habitat Studies, New Delhi, India (2005)
6. Yu, G.-J., Chang, T.-W.: Reacting with care: the hybrid interaction types in a sensible space. In: Jacko, J.A. (ed.) HCI 2011. LNCS, vol. 6763, pp. 250–258. Springer, Heidelberg (2011). https://doi.org/10.1007/978-3-642-21616-9_28
7. Weissenböck, R.: ROBOTRACK: linking manual and robotic design processes by motion-tracking Renate. In: ECAADe 2017, Education and Research in Computer Aided Architectural Design in Europe, 35th, eCAADe (2017)
8. Batliner, C., Newsum, M.J., Rehm, M.C.: Live: real-time platform for robot design interfaces. In: ECAADe 2015, Education and Research in Computer Aided Architectural Design in Europe, 33th, eCAADe, Vienna, Austria (2015)
9. Hsiao, C.-F., et al.: A co-existing interactive approach to digital fabrication workflow. In: CAADRIA 2020, CAADRIA, Thailand, Bangkok (2020)

The Use of Augmented Reality to Motivate Scientific Learning for Preschool Children by Fostering Curiosity

Ruiheng Lan[1] ![ID], Xu Sun[1,2](✉) ![ID], and Bingjian Liu[1,2]

[1] Faculty of Science and Engineering, University of Nottingham Ningbo China, Ningbo, China
{ruiheng.lan,xu.sun,bingjian.liu}@nottingham.edu.cn
[2] Nottingham Ningbo China Beacons of Excellence, Research and Innovation Institute, Ningbo, China

Abstract. Traditionally, scientific knowledge is considered too early for preschoolers to learn and handle. However, recent studies have revealed that preschool children have the ability to learn this knowledge, and it is important for their future development, but a typical kindergarten environment does not have staff with relevant experience, nor the methodology to conduct science lessons. To raise children's interest in scientific content, it is important to appeal to their innate curiosity. Emerging technologies, such as augmented reality (AR) are promising to raise the level of children's curiosity and, therefore, motivate scientific learning. However, it remains unclear how preschool children would make use of AR technology as a learning medium for exploring and gaining scientific knowledge. In this study, a product design called "P-dia" is being proposed, which employed a co-design method to gain insight into preschoolers' preferences and learning behavior. The design contains two parts: an AR magnifier and a learning hub. The AR magnifier makes use of AR as a tool to stimulate curiosity and to encourage free exploration, while the learning hub encloses the learning cycle through interactive learning courses and testing sessions. The preliminary results demonstrate that the design may improve the scientific learning of preschoolers, and the product itself is promising to act as a test platform for research related to AR and children's learning.

Keywords: Curiosity · Interface for children · Augmented Reality · Preschool education · Scientific learning

1 Introduction

Science learning during early childhood has been regarded as a method to strengthen pre-school education [1]. Currently, science education is underestimated in preschool, and little time is spent on this subject because of a limited knowledge of science and the pedagogy of educators [2]. Morgan found that there is always a learning gap when comparing science to literacy and mathematics in kindergarten, which is often difficult

P. Zaphiris and A. Ioannou (Eds.): HCII 2022, LNCS 13329, pp. 71–80, 2022.
https://doi.org/10.1007/978-3-031-05675-8_7

for children to close in the future [3]. Therefore, it is important to determine a method with which to improve preschoolers' scientific learning.

Traditionally, kindergarten teachers teach young children by imparting knowledge in person [4]. However, this method does not conform to the nature of young children because of their short attention span [5]. Under these circumstances, inquiry-based learning has become popular in children's education practice. This is also known as discovery learning. It means that children will perform and construct their knowledge through exploration in an environment with abundant information [6]. This learning approach is highly related to curiosity, an innate and natural phenomenon for children which will lead to exploratory behavior [7]. Children use their curiosity to explore and understand the world around them, and such curiosity is highly related to their acquisition of knowledge [6]. In addition, children's curious nature is positively related to scientific content, and scholars have also begun to emphasize the benefit of beginning science learning at a young age [1]. Such learning is also beneficial to children's future individual development in other domains, including language and literacy [1]. However, there are very few studies concerning a holistic design solution for children's proactive science learning. Therefore, a new design approach is required for science education based on curiosity.

Augmented Reality (AR) is an emerging technology that could create a more intuitive and realistic environment, and it could be used as a novel tool to enhance learning [8]. Recently, as AR technology has begun to mature, it has been widely used for educational purposes in universities, high-schools, and elementary schools [9]. An early example of the application of AR in learning is an AR book created by Billinghurst in 2001 [10]. This design later inspired a greater number of researchers to adopt AR for various educational activities. In the field of scientific learning, for instance, the potential of AR has been explored in supporting spatial learning. By comparing this with traditional role play, the results showed that AR was positively related to students' understanding of spatial concepts within the solar system [11]. However, few studies have explored its use in preschool science learning [8]. Unlike the traditional methods of observation and recording during science courses, an AR interface could superimpose additional information on real objects, which will draw children's attention more naturally [5]. Thus, this study aims to design a product with unique features of AR technology for preschoolers as an educational tool to stimulate their curiosity and encourage proactive learning.

This study demonstrates the development and evaluation of an AR-based exploration and learning product for preschoolers in the context of scientific learning. Section 2 introduces the research background and related work, while Sect. 3 describes the design methodology and design findings, and the product and its evaluation are presented in Sect. 4. The final section concludes the discussion and provides suggestions for future work.

2 Background to the Study

2.1 Preschool Science and Children's Curiosity

Early science learning has been identified as having benefits for personal development [12]. In addition to improving the ability to understand science, this kind of knowledge also supports other domains, especially with regard to language and literacy [13]. Although early science education seems promising in schools, any such benefits can only be maintained on the basis of regular learning. To implement science education into children's regular lives, their natural curiosity should be considered to encourage children to learn proactively. It is suggested that there is a need to provide children with additional opportunities to explore the natural phenomena around them, thereby stimulating their curiosity in their daily lives [1].

"Children are born scientists." Curiosity is an innate characteristic in children [7]. Kindergarten teachers regard this as a more important factor for school readiness compared to the handling of the alphabet, which is commonly considered as the best predictor of children's reading skills [5, 7]. Among all types of inquisitiveness, curiosity is of particular interest because it is highly relevant to information seeking behaviors [7]. The design of this paper will focus on curiosity, which motivates children to gain information proactively and to learn from the natural world.

2.2 Augmented Reality in Early Education

AR technology provides a new interaction method for preschool children. Different from traditional screen learning, which is restricted to reality, AR can be used to build a bridge between the digital world and the real world. This unique characteristic has been suggested to have the ability to enhance learning efficiency by merging real and virtual representations at the same time and in the same space [8]. Additionally, AR is regarded as a form of "magic" which presents fantastical content to children. Although some studies [14] have argued that children may prefer to learn from realistic settings, fantastical technologies can attract children's attention and thereby foster learning.

To ensure the effectiveness of AR learning outcomes, the design of learning content or material is crucial. For example, research has found that elaborate content could strengthen children's memories when it is applied in the relevant content [15]. To guide and encourage children's learning through AR, there are a lot of design elements needed to be explored and specified. Oranç and Küntay have proposed design guidelines and recommendations to be implemented in the user system designs of AR products [8]. For instance, it is suggested that designers assist children to explore their daily lives by encouraging social interaction.

3 Co-design Activity

According to the review of related studies on encouraging children with active learning, there is a need to design a product based on AR technology to raise their level of curiosity and learning through play [9]. During the design process, the co-design method is used to explore the best product form with the target users (preschool children). The following presents the design methodology, the design process, and the final prototype for both the hardware and the software.

3.1 Co-design Methodology

Co-design, sometimes referred to as participatory design, is a human-centered design approach that actively involves both users and stakeholders in the design process [16]. Generally, the design activities will go through the cycles of exploration, generation, and evaluation. Owing to the age characteristics of the participants, it is difficult for preschool children to present their ideas logically and clearly, so the co-design activities have been adjusted accordingly.

3.2 Participants

Six preschool children participated in this study (3 males, 3 females, with ages ranging from 50 months to 72 months, $M = 58.83$, $SD = 7.80$). All of the children were invited from a public kindergarten in Lishui, China. They all received formal kindergarten education systematically and chose to participate in the design activities of their own free will. During the co-design workshop and individual evaluations, all children were accompanied by at least one guardian.

3.3 The Design Process

The design process for this project has four main stages: idea generation, concept generation, form design and demonstration design. During the first and second stages, the participants were firstly asked to join a brainstorming session to gather ideas related to curiosity and the fun of playing. Because of the active nature of preschool children, the session was simplified and organized informally. For example, during the idea generation stage, children were asked to bring their favorite toys and share them with each other. Thereafter, paper and pencils were distributed for them to draw the toys they most wanted. All materials were collected and coded as a reference to the design concepts. At the end of concept generation stage, the synthetized concepts were presented to each child individually to gather their feedback.

For the form design evaluation, three sketch models were presented together to the children and they were allowed to play freely with the prototypes. The interactions between participants and objects were observed and recorded on paper for reference during the final design decision making process. Finally, a 3D-printed appearance model and AR demonstration were presented to the participants for final evaluation. The co-designed outcomes are shown below.

3.4 Design Finding

Based on the findings of the co-design workshop, the final concept focused on designing a product that contains two main functions: encouraging exploration and enhancing learning outcomes. Corresponding to these two functions, the design concept also consists of two separate parts with dedicated functions. In Fig. 1, the design logic and design findings are demonstrated. For the encouraging exploration function, the design idea originated from a magnifier. The AR function was added to foster children's curiosity. To ensure that the learning content would be feasible, a children-centered knowledge database has been proposed to guide the AR content, since there are no existing AR applications in the field of "Early childhood education" [9]. As for the enhancing learning outcome function, a learning procedure for children has been proposed to guide software design. The procedure begins with a free choice of the topics that interest the children. Thereafter, a short interactive learning course from the database will be activated. Following the learning section is an evaluation session to test the learning outcomes, and finally, there will be a digital medal issued on completion of the course.

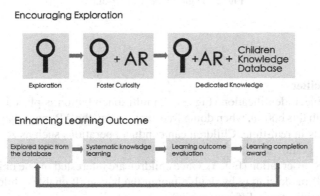

Fig. 1. Design logic and design findings.

4 Prototyping and Testing

4.1 Product Definition and the 3D-Printed Model

The final design is named "P-dia" (Fig. 2). It is designed to encourage preschool children to actively explore their natural environment and learn by themselves. The design consists of two sub-products: the AR magnifier and the learning hub.

The AR magnifier is used as an exploration tool. It includes an AR camera to capture the real scene and displays the augmented images on a circular screen. Once the object is detected, the AR exploration guidance will pop up on the screen to encourage children to investigate further. For example, when the child is observing ants, the guide will ask children to pay attention to what kind of food they are carrying. Explored objects will be transferred wirelessly to the learning hub for further learning and review. The learning sessions include "immediate learning", "reviewing" and "testing". Children go through this process repeatedly until they have handled the related knowledge. The screen of the learning hub is made with a multi-colored e-ink material, which is beneficial for their eyes and provides the feeling of a physical book for young children [17].

Fig. 2. Digital render of "P-dia".

4.2   User Flow

The AR Magnifier

Scenario 1. Object identification (Fig. 3). A multi-touch button is placed on the top of the handle. With this button, when doing free exploration, the AR magnifier will identify different objects in real-time. Children can conduct operations such as zooming in and out with finger gestures.

Scenario 2. AR observation (Fig. 3). Once children are interested in one object, they can activate the AR mode simply by double-taping the button. It enables children to make further observations from different perspectives.

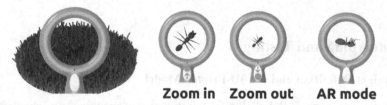

Zoom in   Zoom out   AR mode

Fig. 3. User flow for the AR magnifier.

The Learning Hub

Scenario 1. Identifying topics (Fig. 4). After exploration, the product will record topics automatically based on the database, and all the latest topics will be shown on the homepage. Children may choose the topic in which they are most interested to begin learning.

Scenario 2. Learning and reviewing (Fig. 4). In this section, children will be guided to learn knowledge about the chosen topic. There will be 5 to 10 interactive introduction and question pages for children to work through. They are expected to learn knowledge that meets the standards for preschool children.

Scenario 3. Evaluation and award (Fig. 4). After the learning and review sections, children can choose to take a quick quiz about a specific topic to win a digital medal. This element of the design is expected to encourage children to actively review what they have learned.

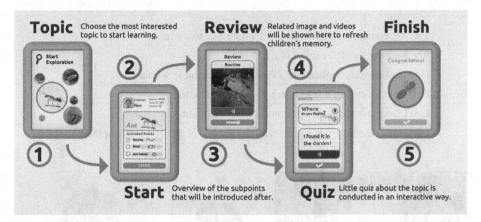

Fig. 4. User flow for the learning hub.

4.3 Usability Test

An informal evaluation (demonstration experience session) was carried out at a preschool in Lishui City in China to investigate users' perceptions of "P-dia". The evaluation contained three parts: appearance model evaluation, AR demonstration experience, and the learning hub user interface experience on an iPad. The same group of children who joined the co-design workshop was gathered for the evaluation. They were first asked to try the appearance model and give comments according to their own experience with toys (Fig. 5). Next, an AR demonstration was presented on a smartphone (Fig. 6). The children could use the smartphone to explore an encyclopedia. For example, when the children focused on an image of a butterfly, an AR butterfly would appear on the screen and then fly away. Finally, the UI of the user flow mentioned above was presented, and the participants were asked to try a specific course to test its content and the consistency between pages. The preliminary results indicated that the children reacted positively to the product, and they all reported that the AR demonstration was attractive. It was observed that the children's curiosity was stimulated, and they all wanted to explore further with the AR mode. Feedback was collected for the purpose of making improvements and iteration (see Table 1).

It should be noted, however, that during the observation, we found that children had a low level of awareness of electronic products, which means the current design of the AR magnifier is prone to breaking without having any external protection material. Design refinement with regard to materials and a protective cover is needed in any future product iteration. Currently, this work is continuing to create a working prototyping for formal assessment, through which to measure both the learning efficiency and the engagement level of young children.

Table 1. User comments.

No	Comments
1	The AR content seems like magic. I would like to try more
2	The learning hub feels soft. I like it
3	How do I use this application? I don't recognize these words
4	I like this magnifier. It is very comfortable to handle
5	Can I see more about the AR content? It is too short
6	Can I share details of the medal with my parents and friends? I want them to see it

Fig. 5. Appearance model and evaluation.

Fig. 6. AR demonstration.

5   Discussion and Conclusion

In this study, a new learning method is proposed to facilitate preschool children's scientific learning through the implementation of AR technology. By inviting the target users to join the co-design workshop, the design outcome is centered on the user needs. The preliminary evaluation demonstrated satisfying results. However, in this study, children's curiosity has not been evaluated in a quantitative manner, which may serve as an evaluation standard for children's learning outcomes. In future study, a method for the measurement of children's curiosity levels should be designed to improve the evaluation accuracy. This could be based on the curiosity measurement method designed by Jirout on the basis of his information gap theory [7]. The measurement method could be integrated into the software design, and the product in turn could serve as a test platform on which to collect and analyze curiosity levels and learning outcomes. Meanwhile, although the pilot evaluation revealed positive feedback, because the participants have joined the co-design workshop, the content may have met their expectations during the design phase. Therefore, a formal evaluation containing children who are not already familiar with the product is needed. Additionally, the current testing method evaluated separately the appearance model and the software. To provide a more integrated experience, a working prototype should be developed in the next experiment.

To conclude, previous design concepts combining AR technology have been limited mainly to software design, and there is a lack of a unified testing platform for preschool children [5]. In this study, the integrated handheld product (P-dia) with a focus on preschool children has been proposed to provide a proper testing platform for similar research topics. Furthermore, P-dia explores the use of AR technology to foster scientific learning in kindergartens by stimulating children's natural curiosity. The design includes a concise framework of its usage flow and a pilot test with six preschool children. We hope that designers and researchers, who are interested in incorporating AR technology into early education, will continue to design suitable products based on natural curiosity and other innate characteristics of children.

References

1. Larimore, R.A.: Preschool science education: a vision for the future. Early Childhood Educ. J. **48**(6), 703–714 (2020)
2. Tu, T.: Preschool science environment: what is available in a preschool classroom? Early Childhood Educ. J. **33**(4), 245–251 (2006)
3. Morgan, P.L., Farkas, G., Hillemeier, M.M., Maczuga, S.: Science achievement gaps begin very early, persist, and are largely explained by modifiable factors. Educ. Res. **45**(1), 18–35 (2016)
4. Spektor-Levy, O., Baruch, Y.K., Mevarech, Z.: Science and scientific curiosity in pre-school— the teacher's point of view. Int. J. Sci. Educ. **35**(13), 2226–2253 (2013)
5. Rambli, D.R.A., Matcha, W., Sulaiman, S.: Fun learning with AR alphabet book for preschool children. Procedia Comput. Sci. **25**, 211–219 (2013)
6. van Schijndel, T.J.P., Jansen, B.R.J., Raijmakers, M.E.J.: Do individual differences in children's curiosity relate to their inquiry-based learning? Int. J. Sci. Educ. **40**(9), 996–1015 (2018)
7. Jirout, J., Klahr, D.: Children's scientific curiosity: in search of an operational definition of an elusive concept. Dev. Rev. **32**(2), 125–160 (2012)
8. Oranç, C., Küntay, A.C.: Learning from the real and the virtual worlds: educational use of augmented reality in early childhood. Int. J. Child-Comput. Interact. **21**, 104–111 (2019)

9. Bacca Acosta, J.L., Baldiris Navarro, S.M., Fabregat Gesa, R., Graf, S.: Augmented reality trends in education: a systematic review of research and applications. J. Educ. Technol. Soc. **17**(4), 133–149 (2014)

10. Billinghurst, M., Kato, H., Poupyrev, I.: The MagicBook: a transitional AR interface. Comput. Graph. **25**(5), 745–753 (2001)

11. Kerawalla, L., Luckin, R., Seljeflot, S., Woolard, A.: Making it real: exploring the potential of augmented reality for teaching primary school science. Virtual Reality **10**(3), 163–174 (2006)

12. Bishop-Josef, S., Zigler, E.: The cognitive/academic emphasis versus the whole child approach: the 50-year debate. The Pre-K debates: Current controversies and issues, pp. 83–88 (2011)

13. Guo, Y., Wang, S., Hall, A.H., Breit-Smith, A., Busch, J.: The effects of science instruction on young children's vocabulary learning: a research synthesis. Early Childhood Educ. J. **44**(4), 359–367 (2015)

14. Walker, C.M., Gopnik, A., Ganea, P.A.: Learning to learn from stories: children's developing sensitivity to the causal structure of fictional worlds. Child Dev **86**(1), 310–318 (2015)

15. Richert, R.A., Schlesinger, M.A.: The role of fantasy-reality distinctions in preschoolers learning from educational video. Infant Child Dev. **26**(4), e2009 (2017)

16. Bella, M., Hanington, B.: Universal Methods of Design. Rockport Publishers, Beverly, p. 204 (2012)

17. Desmarais, N.: E ink and digital paper. Library Faculty and Staff papers, p. 17 (2003)

The Distance Learning Framework for Design-Related Didactic Based on Cognitive Immersive Experience

Yuan Liu[1]([✉]), Hang Su[2], Qian Nie[1], and Yao Song[3]

[1] Beijing Institute of Fashion Technology, Beijing 100029, China
yuan.liu@polimi.it
[2] Central Saint Martins, London, UK
[3] Central Academy of Fine Arts, Beijing, China

Abstract. This research is considered as the transformation of cognitive immersion based on the theory by Liu et al. (2021), to describe the possibilities of immersive learning by distance teaching tools. It provides insights among the importance of distance learning for design education, especially under specific situations such as COVID-19 pandemic. The tools to support distance learning are categorized and discussed, degrees of immersion are compared among formal learning, informal learning and social learning courseware.

The methods rely on an extensive secondary research and literature review, aims to transform the theoretical framework of cognitive immersive learning by online-based tools, also provide new thoughts for innovatively teaching design in the future. As the output, we establish a theoretical model based on online tools, also a design framework to help with course design or idea visualization for instructors.

Keywords: E-learning and distant learning · Immersive experience · Design didactic

1 Online Tools to Support Immersive Learning for Design

1.1 Literature Review: Transformation of Education from No-Distance to Long-Distance

The methods, forms and tools of education are undergoing a worldwide transformation. The innovative pedagogy by Open University UK[1] describes several important directions of teaching with digital technologies, and specifically outlines future methods of learning by harnessing cooperative learning, social learning and constructive learning. One learning theory, connectivism, which differs from the three main theories, is identified by Goldie (2016) as the rebirth of teaching theory under the pressures of technology[2],

---

[1] Download here: https://iet.open.ac.uk/file/innovating_pedagogy_2016.pdf Namely behaviorism, cognitivism, and constructivism.

[2] Namely behaviorism, cognitivism, and constructivism.

© The Author(s), under exclusive license to Springer Nature Switzerland AG 2022
P. Zaphiris and A. Ioannou (Eds.): HCII 2022, LNCS 13329, pp. 81–96, 2022.
https://doi.org/10.1007/978-3-031-05675-8_8

the three old learning theories attempt to define how one individual learns, while connectivism "is the integration of principles explored by chaos, network, complexity and self-organization theories". This trend reflects the impact of technology – not only the application of tools, but also the exploration and understanding of knowledge itself.

Typically, social media engagement helps to get students involved from outside the learning context, to learn through a connected database and related crowd of social groups (Conole 2017; Stella and Gnanam 2004). Technology has reorganized much of human ways of living, communication and learning (Goldie 2016), but one beneficial of engaging technology in education is the free flow and accessibility of knowledge. Students are not only exposed to all aspects of knowledge, but they also have the opportunity to teach. The rich tools of multimedia learning have pushed transformation of education into a new area, both from the content of teaching and the new possibilities of technological characteristics of the medium. Among them, five types of online courses contribute to the transformation. Massive Open Online Courses (MOOCs) and the engagement of social media are supporting a wide range of distance learning. MOOC appeared in 2008 to support connectivist learning through social media engagement (Siemens 2005). XMOOCs are also designed to fulfill the needs of a more didactic and individual-focused teaching tool. Other pedagogical experiments including SPOCs, DOCCs and SOOCs are making this service more personalized and flexible (Yuan et al. 2014).[3]

Based on the above characters, we consider virtual learning tools has potential to transform immersive methods, given its dissemination, open source, and involvement of rich media. Exploring the pedagogy of subjective immersion is a relatively new field (Liu et al. 2021; Liu et al. 2019; Liu 2020; Liu et al. 2018), we hope to provide more possibilities for innovative education by discussing the possibility of online tools.

1.2 Distance Learning

There are many similar expressions related to virtual learning, among them distance learning, e-learning, and online learning (Moore et al. 2011). Clarifying the difference in between is important, as they have different focus under similar terminology. Distance learning has a history of almost two centuries (Merrill et al. 2008), and it has been identified as "the effort of providing access to learning for those who are geographically distant". The most obvious feature of distance learning is the limitations associated with "distance", a subset of distributed learning according to the engaging of media and associated experience (Stella and Gnanam 2004; Moore et al. 2011). Three features are identified from the research of distance learning: the form of instruction between the learner and instructor; the distinguishing of different times or places; and the use of different instructional materials.

Why we select this concept to solve the regional problems in special periods, distance learning still maintains the integrity of the education process (Usluel and Mazman 2009), rather than simply ingesting knowledge through online tools. It still involves key elements from a traditional teaching model, including an instructional environment

---

[3] These abbreviations refer to: SPOCs (Small Private Open Courses); DOCCs (Distributed Open Collaborative Course); SOOCs (Social Online Open Course or Small Open Online Course).

for learners, instructors and institutions (Belanger and Jordan 1999). It is very important, especially for spatial immersive learning, to have an open space for interactions between participants. Interaction between instructor and learner is different in a distance learning classroom, mostly because they are always physically separate. It's the key to consider how to stimulate communications between students, usually under the form of group discussion and problem-solving, thereby effectively enhancing the learning experience. The evolution of navigation also helps support the instructional materials, including hierarchical, sequential, and hypertext. When it comes to intervening through communication technology, synchronous learning is achievable through the engagement of communication media including audio, video, graphics, and text (Fig. 1).

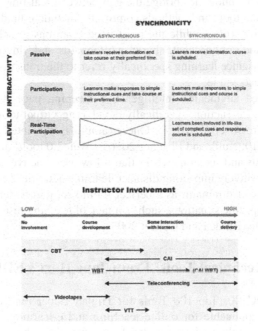

Fig. 1. Up: the interactivity and synchronicity in distance learning by Belanger and Jordan (1999). Down: the instructor involvement in distance learning instructional technologies by Belanger and Jordan (1999).

1.3 Tools to Support Distance Learning: Categories and Typologies

There are six types of technologies to support distance learning, namely: computer-based training; computer-aided instruction; web-based training; teleconferencing; videotape; video tele-training and summary of instructional technologies. Bonk (2000) further identifies the tools to help achieve distance learning as: e-learning tools, collaborative tools, educational websites and evaluation tools. Generally speaking, even students must face problems such as low satisfaction and losing motivation to learn; distance learning still shows outstanding advantages, including learning flexibility, broader knowledge coverage, higher participatory, and superior mastery of course material (Bonk 2000).

From the study of pedagogy, there are two available methods for distance learning, including synchronous learning and asynchronous learning. Synchronous learning refers to the in-time delivery of knowledge between student and instructor, while asynchronous learning allows participants to access knowledge through different timelines and schedules. Most teaching practices combine these two teaching methods regardless of their pros and cons.

To ensure distance learning quality, 24 benchmarks within seven aspects are identified by the Institute for Higher Education Policy of USA. Four types of materials appear in distance learning to support learning activity, including print, audio (voice), computer (data) and video (Bušelić 2012). Printing materials remain as the basic material carrier, while audio or voice technologies bridge the gap between real-time communication in class. Computer based tools and methods commonly include e-mail, online collaboration, and web-based learning, while the most used functions to achieve synchronous communication include online chat, shared whiteboards and video conferences. The videos engaged in distance learning specifically refer to the transmissive media, which is cheap and easily accessible.

Knowledge based augmented intelligence is keeping pace with the increasing demands of distance instruction, specifically developing virtual tools that support any curriculum area (Crowe et al. 2017). One example is the intelligent tutor system (Rodrigues et al. 2010; Kulik and Fletcher 2016). "Web 2.0 tools" usually refers to the blogs, wikis, podcasts and social networks that allow users' active participation in creating content and positively impacting distance learning activities (Usluel and Mazman 2009). Virtual reality also remains as a perfect tool to support distance learning, especially while facing specific situations, such as a lack of teaching resources or physically disadvantaged people (Burdea and Coiffet 2003).

2   Analysis of Technical Tools: From Jane Hart's EDU100

The ranking of EDU100 (Top 100 Tools for Higher Education 2019) provides 100 virtual tools voted applicable for online teaching and e-learning. A 4 D's model is applied to address how the tools can be used for education. This model includes four main categories: Didactic (being taught); Discovery (finding out oneself); Discourse (interacting with others) and Doing (engaging in activities)[4]. The description of tools is under the specific use of learning styles and focus, such as the Google browser, which is described as a web & blogging tool under the "Didactics", while under "Discovery" it is termed a search engine. Since the focus of this research is to provide guidance for immersive learning with distance, we aim to clarify the appropriate tool (or combination of tools) that support a certain level of immersive learning according to the framework we established. We therefore further consider the EDU100, and have determined that the selected tools should meet at least one condition:

a) Support real-time synchronous learning. b) Support asynchronous learning. c) Allow multiple participants and social learning, such as one-to-one communication tool, messaging tool, video meeting platform or collaboration platform. d) Basic transmission

---

[4] The 4 D's model is addressed within the website: https://www.toptools4learning.com/ppl100/.

media is available, such as shared whiteboards, file uploading, videoconference, etc. e) Allow key presentation and course authoring tool. f) Allow access to evaluation or assessment (Fig. 2).

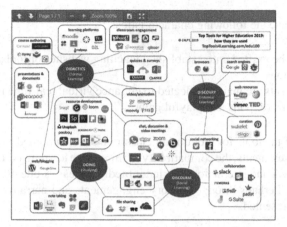

Fig. 2. Screen cut: the 4 key learning areas and classification of EDU100 tools (2019) by Jane Hart. Web address: https://www.toptools4learning.com/about/

We re-analyzed this model, and concluded four typologies based on the online tools given:

2.1 Learning Platforms for Didactic

Learning Platform for Didactic (Formal Learning)
Within the formal learning category, which is typically designed for learning, there are seven tools selected to meet the needs of higher education. They usually have good support for virtual communication and curriculum integrity, which is mainly reflected in component functions including design, delivery and management. Compared with chat and video meeting tools, online learning platforms prefer the traditional curriculum model: one-way information loop for student and teacher. PebblePad claims to be a learning journey platform, as it supports the full learning process including plan, reflect and curate. It could be used as a personal learning platform to support building e-portfolios, e-assessment, and individual tutoring spaces. Mahara functions as a fully featured web application, including 8 features that support learning: personalization, collaboration, smart evidence, open source, customizable, mobile, integration and scalable.

Classroom Engagement for Didactic (Formal Learning)
The tools to help with classroom engagement engage students in distance learning activities for better results. The means to attract students through distance teaching include:

a) learning with light games (Kahoot; Socrative).
b) quizzes and polls for in-class evaluation (Socrative; Poll Everywhere; Mentimeter).
c) data analysis and monitoring (Glisser).
d) formative assessment (Plickers).

These tools have the following characteristics:

1. They need to be grafted onto established teaching websites or tools, such as videos and presentations.
2. The engagements are mainly reflected to enhance virtual real-time interaction, such as in-class quizzes, polls and playful games.

Since most of the tools for monitoring classrooms are embodied in real-time forms and classroom assessments, the compatibility of immersive learning is not shown clearly, but instant feedback and interaction can undoubtedly increase students' integration into teaching content. Perhaps through sensory engagements and narrative, the immersive learning can be presented.

Chat, Discussion and Video Meeting (Web Conferencing)
The web conferencing tool is the most supportive of synchronous learning among existing tools, as it contains in-time delivery of knowledge. The course will strictly follow the syllabus, though the teacher is able to control the classroom and get student feedback through real-time video and message. Most web conferencing tools have been fully developed as a teaching or conferencing platform (BigBlueButton, Adobe Connect, Zoom, Flipgrid, StarLeaf, Slack), while some tools still remain simple video chatting platforms (Skype, WhatsApp, Google Meet).

2.2   Learning Platforms for Doing

Note Taking (Doing)
Immersive Reader is a web-based free reader designed by Microsoft, to enhance the reading experience by engaging immersive factors. The office website noted beneficials including: it improves text creativity; increases reading speed; improves understanding and maintain concentration; and finally but not exclusively, improves writing quality. While using the software to help with reading, the system marks different parts of speech with different colors, at the same time highlighting the words where readers read and guide their vision. It also allows personalized customization for readers to become more immersed.

2.3   Learning Platforms for Discovery (Informal Learning)

Collaboration
The tools categorized in "collaboration" do not limit themselves according to the type of

tool (video chatting, file creating, knowledge organizing), but they all maintain obvious characteristics in multi-threading and multi-terminal cooperation, and they consciously amplify these functions.

Social Networking
Twitter and *Facebook* are the most commonly used social tools, gathering similar interest groups and supporting individual interaction. In terms of education, they may not include many functions to carry knowledge, but they work as virtual platforms for introducing learning topics and guiding directions. As Jane Hart (2019) identified, "social learning" appears to be more valuable than ever, due to the advantages of social platforms, so *Twitter* and *Facebook* also could be functional to enhance social presence (Bronack et al. 2008).

2.4   Learning Platforms for Discourse

Curation
Newer curation tools support informal learning by supporting no-limit summarizing of information, as well as providing the ability to divide and organize them according to learning topics. Normally, the information organized are cross-platformed, including links, articles, videos and tweets. In *Diigo* and *Wakelet*, the user can annotate online information for personal use, creating an organized research base through *Outliner*.

These individual learning tools have several specifics:

a) They account for self-learning need, so that the interface is simplified for easy operating.
b) It has certain community functions for sharing personal understanding of knowledge.

3   Transformation of Immersion: Formal Learning, Informal Learning and Social Learning Courseware

3.1   Selected Learning Tools

Considering that the learning methods and materials remain virtual within online distance learning, we share the same definition based on sensory engagements, and further discuss the transformation of immersion based on two evaluations: the factors of sensory modalities and the narrative to support teaching. Since most network environments do not support senses such as touch and taste, we narrow the sensory participation based on the online platforms to the richness of media materials, that is, immersive interaction through multi-media. We also combined related research to understand what kind of virtual platform and materials better supports learning activities.

We therefore form two comparison groups to define the immersive potential of the tools:

a) Social communication-closed community; synchronous learning-asynchronous learning;
b) The level of multi-media engagement; The level of narrative;

It is worth noting that our goal is not to select a tool with the most immersive learning potential, but to comprehensively consider the advantages of the tool and produce a set of recommendations to achieve sensory engagement (Figs. 3 and 4).

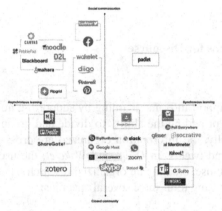

Fig. 3. The cross-coordinate system of the "social communication-closed community" and the "synchronous learning-asynchronous learning".

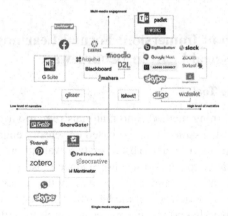

Fig. 4. The cross-coordinate system of the "level of multi-media engagement" and the "level of narrative".

We observed, only the web-conferencing tools and the classroom engagement tools meet the needs of "synchronous learning", "multi-media engagement" and "high level of narrative". The web-conferencing tools could support synchronous and asynchronous learning, as well as engage rich media content to provide an in-depth narrative such as online web chatting, external links and message boards. The classroom engagement tools are used as a means to promote attendance in the classroom, improve students' sense of participation, and allow teachers to better grasp the teaching situation in virtual learning. These tools focus on visualizing data, though there might be other sensory engagements to achieve immersive learning.

The web-conferencing tools remain in a closed community, which means the students are only able to access selected classrooms rather than choosing their own courses through the public platform (like Coursera). Thus, social tools (Facebook, Twitter) do not offer the opportunity to form a certain cultural community for sharing information. Social presence within the virtual classroom mainly relies on the interaction between instructor and student. As for the asynchronous learning, social communication tools play an essential role to connect the certain user interest groups together.

Multi-media engagements seem to better support a higher level of narrative, as the rich media would support better substitution. The best performer still remains the web-conferencing tool, while the second belongs to learning platform. The classroom engagement tools are categorized into the "low narrative, single media" group since their educational function is incomplete and used as an auxiliary.

We therefore hypothesize that the tools under the category "Chat, discussion & video meeting" and "Collaboration" are the main carriers of distance immersive learning, as they are able to support higher levels of immersion. By integrating the classroom engagement tools, we can also enhance the immersive experience to a certain extent.

For web-conferencing tools, we compare the analyzed results with 2 public ranking, the Top 10 Free Virtual Classroom Software in 2019, and the Magic Quadrant for Meeting Solutions 2019.[5]

We finally narrow the focus down to Zoom, Microsoft Teams and Webex Teams through cross-comparing the similarities and differences of functions. We aim to summarize the online framework suitable for immersive learning, also browse other tools that may enhance immersive experience including Socrative and Padlet, to provide practical and applicable suggestions.

3.2 Web-Conferencing Tools: Zoom, Microsoft Teams and Webex Teams

Firdyiwek (1999) identified online pedagogy as the "effective use of the electronic learning environments for the development of cognitive skills through access to information, interactivity with tools, and communication." We divide the analysis of network tools into "access to information", "interactivity with tools", and "communication" to discuss their respective immersive methods under specific functions.

Access to Information
Access to information specifically refers to the process of obtaining knowledge or experience through distance learning. All three web-conferencing platforms do not deviate

---

[5] https://www.gartner.com/doc/reprints?id=1-1OH1GWOA&ct=190909&st=sb.

from the traditional teaching mode, thereby mainly transferring knowledge through synchronous learning. We compare the types of knowledge transmitted on the platforms to explore the application of immersive teaching elements, along with summarizing the method of centralizing assessment information.

The functionality of Zoom is relatively flat, since it only supports single group content rather than switching between different levels of information. That means Zoom can support specific meetings, but cannot obtain multi-level information, such as group discussions after a big class. The difference is that the chat column of Microsoft Teams and Webex Teams can display all the ongoing or history meetings under a flat layer. Although users can only participate in one video chat, they can follow up and update the content in real time through the sidebar. In addition, Microsoft Teams and Webex Teams have independently divided columns called "File" and "Link", which contains all the files and links shared during the course, including materials, assessments and external links. This allows students to have a more intuitive view of the course materials, especially while taking multiple courses at the same time.

The whiteboard and note functions from both Microsoft Teams and Webex Teams as built-in sharing tools supports the process of the discussion, but also provides a more vivid opportunity for students to share their ideas.

For the realization of immersive learning, the intervention of multi-media is inevitable. Multimedia technologies can support design works and allow various participants from different cultural backgrounds access at the same time. Multimedia teaching is a method for long-distance learning, which often refers to the combination of various media information. The two characteristics of multimedia teaching, especially to bring people "immersive" experience, are significant for design activities (Gao 2013).

Considering the above three tools, we summarize two sets of templates for information transmission, both for synchronous learning and asynchronous learning. As in the professional online education tools these two templates do not conflict, we consider them in parallel (Fig. 5).

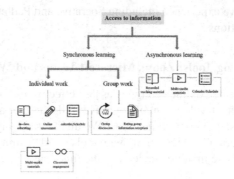

Fig. 5. The access to information based on distance learning.

Interaction with Tools

The interactivity within the web-conferencing tools contains three kinds: interaction between human-content, instructor-student, and students. A calendar allows users to browse monthly meetings and arrangements, as well as access more detailed information by clicking the arrangements. As mentioned before, the whiteboard allows multiple users to create their own sketches or storyboards. With the support of built-in programs, more function is possible: storytelling and narration, visual-audible synaesthesia, classroom engagement tools and educational games. For educational activities, especially which related to design, homework and group reviews require in-depth discussion compared to in-class exams or questionnaires. This provides new ideas for online assessment tools, which provide avenues to develop more in-depth clipboard functions for brainstorming and corporation.

Socrative makes it possible to participate in real-time voting through the mobile phone and the Pad. Cisco Webex also has offline equipment including Cisco Webex Board, Cisco Webex Room Devices and Cisco Webex Desk Devices. As almost all the current mobile terminals have gyroscopes, a wide range of interactive functions may be realized, such as: motion sensing, co-design, online interaction of synaesthetic studies (audible-visual, audible-motion, etc.) (Fig. 6).

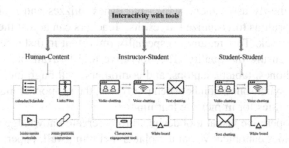

Fig. 6. The interactivity with tools within distance learning.

Communication

All the web-conferencing tools can realize barrier-free video calls. Within Microsoft Teams and Webex Teams, students can make group discussions in small rooms, and the instructors can open new rooms for answering questions if necessary. In general, all participants have the same permissions for the built-in functions, where both teachers and students have the chance to share screens and demonstrate their ideas. Unfortunately, the physical expression of students barely affects course content, the communication between instructors and students only includes facial expressions and voice chatting. Some web software can offer cartoon characters based on facial technologies. This offers some inspiration for providing a personalized experience to enhance immersive experience.

The multi-terminal platform can also enrich the ways of communication, such as implementing different functions through mobile phones and computers (Fig. 7).

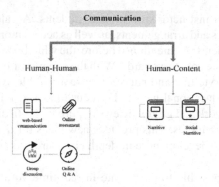

Fig. 7. The ways of communications within distance learning.

3.3 Classroom Engagement Tools: Slack, Socrative and Padlet

Socrative and Padlet do not belong to the same kind of classroom engagement tools, yet all show feasibility worthy of digging in several aspects. Socrative remains as a tool that supports on-the-fly assessment, which publishes quizzes and topics in real time and uses data algorithms to visualize the results. Teachers can adjust the course in-time related to the feedback. This feature is especially important in distance learning, since it can intuitively ensure the quality. The Socrative tool is available in all platforms, including smartphones, tablets, laptops, and computers. Although the current function only stays in data synchronization between platforms, the support of multiple platforms offers new possibilities for immersive learning.

Padlet is a cooperative visual tool designed to co-create knowledge and build social networks. It provides canonical visual templates including wall, paper, storyboard etc., wherein the creator can choose the template needed and display rich multimedia information on the same platform. Within, the "dialogue" and "map" templates allow the creator to simulate a narrative environment that supports specific content, such as telling a story. This feature has significant inspiration for immersive learning, and is remarkably similar to the social communication achieved by Twitter and Facebook. It has the potential to obtain social presence, which can help establish social content outside the classroom.

4 Discussion: Frame Immersive Learning by Distance Learning Tools

In summary, the following suggestions are proposed to help achieve or enhance immersive distance learning. Our purpose is to give guidance to help define a set of course formats and explore the possibility of immersion through existing tools.

1. Multi-platforms to support sensory simulation
   The most substantial difference between online and spatial virtual environments is the somatosensory element, which limits the usage of interactions. Due to the

characteristics of online platforms, some sensory simulations are difficult to perform, which may reduce immersion. By connecting various platforms (smartphones, tablets, laptops, and computers) and performing different in-class duties can enrich human-content interaction and realize more sensory simulation.

2. Multi-media presentation

    Within a limited interface, the network platform displays rich media information, including but not limited to the image, in-time painting, video, document, table, pdf and audio. Multimedia display creates a certain environmental narrative, such as providing audio or video support based on the course content. Meanwhile, multimedia content can be engaged through intervention of online games and interactive videos, and the sense of substitution of classroom content can also be enhanced.

3. Social engagement and interest group

    Social presence is realized within the spatial immersive space by cooperation and user-contribution. It remains similar for distance learning. Social communication can be realized through video chatting with web-conferencing tools, while user-contribution can be established through existing social channels, including Twitter and Facebook. By establishing interest groups and sharing materials outside the classroom, one can enhance students' sense of substitution on the virtual platform. In addition, many online content creation platforms support social network sharing, such as Padlet.

4. Virtual narrative environment

    Narrative remains essential to achieve cognitive immersion. The "textual narrative" is related to the content and method which instructors teach, and the "sensory narrative" can enhance immersion by sensory simulation, much rely on synaesthetic design and scene simulation. What remains important is the intervention of multi-media and suitable classroom guidance. How to achieve a balance between narrative and limited online resources is a further question that requires consideration.

5. Instant classroom effect evaluation

    The classroom engagement tool greatly enriches the interactive experience in the classroom. At each stage during the learning activity, it may confirm the students' mastery and keep them concentrated. Tools like Socrative and Poll Everywhere can play a role in monitoring the progress of the classroom and add fun through playful games. This is a method of encouraging students to create and share content together through co-creating tools, which may become a future direction of distance learning.

5   Project: Design Tool to Frame Immersive Learning

This part of research describes a design tool that helps with course design or idea visualization for instructors to frame and establish an immersive online course. This online platform is a practical guide for idea framing and gathering, the applicable field is not limited to design but includes a wide range of art practice that requires cognitive immersive experience.

The content of the online tool exists in three main categories: the introduction page; the case browsing page; and the "mind board" collected related to different course design. The introduction page contains the literal contributions related to cognitive immersion,

94 Y. Liu et al.

degrees of immersion, and typologies to produce a knowledge basis for the overall theoretical framework. Combined with the diagram, typical cases are assisted by both video and text, and external links are provided for in-depth observation. The case browsing page is based on the typologies of immersion, along with the individual factors involved (Liu et al. 2021). The user can choose the type of immersion according to their interest, then browse the factors under the framework of "personal factor", "social factor" and "environmental factor". It is worth noting that the cases provided within are usually fragmented as a means to explain the accessibility of each factor. This requires the contributor to clearly classify in the first place, and an editorial committee is also needed for evaluating. While browsing the website, users can "collect" the cases of their interest as materials for designing the course structure.

The third part includes a mind "board" that gathers together the user's selections, regardless of each selection's categorization. The collecting page draws on the graphic design of Pinterest to make the visualization more flexible. Users can choose a course format based on the virtual scene and tasks needed, then fill in the media materials as a mode board for course design. The numbers of tasks can be added freely, and notes can help to collect ideas and thoughts. Although the web page provides the basic framework, the specific curriculum design should still rely on users' subjective understanding. If necessary, users can expand the introduction page any time to browse through the definitions of each factor.

Since this online tool remains in the developing stage, we visualize the key pages to help understanding the layout (Figs. 8 and 9).

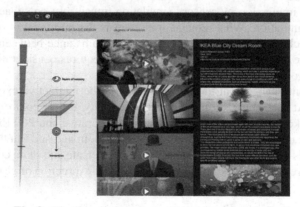

Fig. 8. The introduction page of "degrees of immersion".

Through this webpage, we made a bold attempt, that is trying to integrate offline immersive learning with online teaching tools. This project is still in the initial trial stage, and we continue to explore its applicability and the actual use of online classrooms in subsequent research.

Fig. 9. The introduction page of "factors of presence" under four types of immersion.

References

Belanger, F., Jordan, D.H. (eds.): Evaluation and Implementation of Distance Learning: Technologies, Tools and Techniques: Technologies, Tools and Techniques. IGI Global, Pennsylvania (1999)

Bonk, C.J.: Applying collaborative and e-learning tools to military distance learning: a research framework (Vol. 1107). US Army Research Institute for the Behavioral and Social Sciences (2000)

Bušelić, M.: Distance Learning–concepts and contributions. Oeconomica Jadertina 2(1), 23–34 (2012)

Burdea, G.C., Coiffet, P.: Virtual Reality Technology. Wiley, Hoboken (2003)

Bronack, S., Sanders, R., Cheney, A., Riedl, R., Tashner, J., Matzen, N.: Presence pedagogy: teaching and learning in a 3D virtual immersive world. Int. J. Teach. Learn. Higher Educ. 20(1), 59–69 (2008)

Conole, G.: Research through the generations: Reflecting on the past, present and future. Irish J. Technol. Enhanced Learn. 2(1) (2017)

Crowe, D., LaPierre, M., Kebritchi, M.: Knowledge based artificial augmentation intelligence technology: next step in academic instructional tools for distance learning. TechTrends 61(5), 494–506 (2017)

Firdyiwek, Y.: Web-based courseware tools: where is the pedagogy? Educ. Technol. 39, 29–34 (1999)

Gao, B.: From Long-distance to no distance: performance-based long-distance education in art and design. In: 2nd International Conference for Design Education Researchers Oslo, pp. 2251–2264 (2013)

Goldie, J.G.S.: Connectivism: a knowledge learning theory for the digital age? Med. Teach. 38(10), 1064–1069 (2016)

Kulik, J.A., Fletcher, D.: Effectiveness of intelligent tutoring. Rev. Educ. Res. 86(1), 42–78 (2016)

Liu, Y., Riccò, D., Calabi, D.A.: Immersive learning. from basic design for communication design: a theoretical framework. In: 6th International Conference for Design Education Researchers DRS LEARNxDESIGN 2021. Engaging with Challenges in Design Education, Design Research Society, pp. 756–771 (2021)

Liu, Y., Calabi, D.A., Riccò, D.: A synaesthetic learning approach to cave (2019)

Liu, Y.: Future step of basic design: between synaesthesia didactic and virtual learning. Ergonomia Des. **311**, 311–318 (2020)

Liu, Y., Calabi, D.A., Riccò, D.: Synaesthetic and haptic experiences for design educating an international framework. In: VI International Conference Synesthesia: Science and Art, Editorial Fundación Internacional Artecittà, pp. 1–7 (2018)

Moore, J.L., Dickson-Deane, C., Galyen, K.: e-Learning, online learning, and distance learning environments: are they the same? Internet High. Educ. **14**(2), 129–135 (2011)

Merrill, M. D., Van Merrienboer, J. J., & Driscoll, M. P.: Handbook of research on educational communications and technology (Vol. 3). J. M. Spector (Ed.). New York: Lawrence Erlbaum Associates (2008)

Rodrigues, J.J., Joao, P.F., Vaidya, B.: EduTutor: an intelligent tutor system for a learning management system. Int. J. Distance Educ. Technol. (IJDET) **8**(4), 66–80 (2010)

Siemens, G.: Connectivism: a learning theory for the digital age. http://www.elearnspace.org.Art icles/connectivism.Htm. Accessed 03 Jan 2007

Stella, A., Gnanam, A.: Quality assurance in distance education: the challenges to be addressed. High. Educ. **47**(2), 143–160 (2004)

Usluel, Y.K., Mazman, S.G.: Adoption of web 2.0 tools in distance education. Procedia-Soc. Behav. Sci. **1**(1), 818–823 (2009)

Yuan, L., Powell, S.J., Olivier, B.: Beyond MOOCs: sustainable online learning in institutions (2014)

Developing a VR Tool to Support Repeat Pattern Design Learning

Francisco Queiroz$^{(\boxtimes)}$ 🄳, Maria dos Santos Lonsdale🄳, and Phillip Henry🄳

School of Design, University of Leeds, Leeds LS2 9JT, UK
{f.queiroz,m.lonsdale,p.m.henry}@leeds.ac.uk

Abstract. Virtual Reality (VR) applications have been progressively adopted in design industry and education, and are often associated with increased engagement, creativity, and spatial awareness skills. This study investigates the development and use of a bespoke VR application in textiles and fashion design education, designed to support the teaching and learning of repeat pattern design principles and techniques, transposing the limitations of traditional monitor displays and image editor software. Aiming at identifying potential benefits for students and educators, we have surveyed and observed students who explored the application to visualize their design outputs, applying their pattern designs onto real-size virtual objects and environments. Our findings suggests that VR tools have a positive effect in both learning and design process, allowing students to identify design shortcomings and technical issues, as well as fostering self-evaluation and reflection on their work. Moreover, although findings on spatial awareness are inconclusive, they indicate that the use of the VR application to estimate final dimensions of repeat patterns allows students to identify and correct patterns that have been inaccurately designed.

Keywords: XR and Immersive learning · Textiles design · Virtual reality · Higher education

1 Introduction

Immersive technologies such as Virtual Reality (VR) and Augmented Reality (AR) are increasingly being applied to education, training, research, and industry. Potential benefits of visual and spatial capabilities of VR for presenting, representing and simulating have been anticipated for decades as a major transformation in teaching [1]. More recently, the adoption of such technologies in educational settings has been facilitated by a decrease in prices of VR equipment [2], providing benefits such as lower risk levels, lower costs, and accelerated learning within a safe environment where it is possible to experiment and learn through simulation.

The original version of this chapter was previously published non-open access. A Correction to this chapter is available at https://doi.org/10.1007/978-3-031-05675-8_25

P. Zaphiris and A. Ioannou (Eds.): HCII 2022, LNCS 13329, pp. 97–111, 2022.
https://doi.org/10.1007/978-3-031-05675-8_9

The use of Virtual Reality (VR) in education has been associated with higher level of engagement from students in both STEM and humanities subjects [3,4]. In the case of the School of Design at the University of Leeds, we have identified textile design for interiors and fashion as a potential field of application in which to support students. Although a confident engagement can be readily recognized with Computer Aided Design (CAD), students' understanding of technical space, scale and physical dimensions is often confused by seemingly infinite digital options, particularly for the design challenge of creating repeat pattern. VR is successfully used in diverse sectors of textile and fashion industry [5–7]. With that in mind, this study aims at improving the learning of repeat pattern design through the design and development of a VR tool (Fig. 1) that allows students to preview and apply design outcomes to virtual canvases, objects, and environments before physical prototyping, supporting decision-making in the digital design domain. Our research questions are:

Q1: How does VR visualization impact students' understanding of repeat pattern design principles and technical challenges?
Q2: How do students, educator, and researchers perceive the VR tool in terms of its functionalities and usefulness?
Q3: What are the challenges associated with the in-house development of a VR tool to support pattern design learning?

The remaining of this article is structured as follows: *Background* contextualizes the development and application of the study; *Experiment* describes methods, participants, and stimuli; *Findings and discussion* presents findings and data collected, reflecting on how they addresses our research questions. Finally, *Conclusion* summarizes the study and presents suggestions for further research.

Fig. 1. VR tool in use.

2   Background

Despite the relatively recent emergence of VR as consumer products and increased adoption in the classroom, the exploration of such technologies in textiles and fashion design can be traced back to almost three decades ago [8], and has since then approached a variety of applications, ranging from haptics for sensing textiles textures [9], to cloth simulation for virtual fitting [10], e-commerce and retail [11], and real-size visualization [12]. In architectural design education, VR tools have been associated with better performance and enjoyment from students solving architectural design problems [13]. In fashion design education, they have been used in collaborative creative processes, leading to design outcomes that differ from those obtained from traditional processes [14]. A distinguishing ability for textile designers, and hence a focus of the teaching for the module for which the VR tool was developed, is the ability to create original pattern layouts that work in-repeat for continuous fabric printing. A desirable characteristic for textile products, be they for fashion apparel or Interior soft-furnishing and wallcovering, are that they are designed so the visual effect of the collective pattern elements flow seamlessly without any obvious disruption that might cause an undesired blocky effect, disrupting the intended balance and harmony of the overall composition. Whilst there are numerous textiles design *genera* and infinite aesthetic styles the important taught design principles for repeat layout are primarily locate in scale and color manipulation. A consistent theme in the design-led VR research [15–17] is a positive relationship between immersive technologies and creativity and imagination. Bourdot et al. [18] specifically relate the spatial-awareness students experience in VR with a greater attention to functional appropriateness, while Joundi et al. [19] identify the value Fashion students found in using VR interactive characters compared to real-life static mannequins, as well as an opportunity for an accurate assessment of scale. Lee et al. [20] provide further research to support the advantages of VR design tools in better activating greater physical and perceptual understanding, when compared with 2-D design spaces. Digital design is well-established as an environment for accelerating student experiential learning, the collective aims of the questions in this work are to balance the creative opportunities in VR with purposeful design decision-making. An initial motivation for the present study is, then, providing a tool for students to preview their creations in VR, in a similar way to architectural visualizations VR solutions, aiming at improving their sense of scale and spatial awareness. Regardless of the fact that design patterns are often applied in dimensions as large as 64 cm^2, students often generate image files of their patterns using image editors such as Adobe Photoshop and specialized software such as Nedgraphics, visualized in monitors as small as 13-inch display laptops, therefore usually lacking the means to see them in real size before print. Traditionally, students would produce mock-ups using image editor Adobe Photoshop to preview the application of the patterns they create. In that case, our study aims at providing practice and learning experiences similar to those described by the literature of reference, but having in mind the particular challenges of repeat pattern design.

3   Experiment

Throughout a semester, we invited students from Levels 2 and 3 to preview their design outcomes in a custom-made VR application, collecting information via observation and questionnaires about their interaction with the application, their design outcomes, as well as their attitudes and perceptions towards the application and their own work. Participation was optional and completely voluntary. Results were also informed by the observations from two of the investigators, respectively the instructor for the module and the developer of the application, on their own perceptions about the experiment. The study proposal was approved by the University's Ethics Committee (Ethics reference LTDESN-121). In total, 17 students (Level 2 = 7, Level 3 = 10) out of a total of 24 (Level 2 = 13, Level 3 = 11) participated in at least one of five VR sessions. Methods for data collection included:

1. Pre-visualization questionnaire for collecting students' image files (for patterns and mock-ups); students' satisfaction with mock-ups; verbal description of pattern; suggestions for features in VR tool.
2. Post-visualization questionnaire for collecting dimensions applied to pattern by student in VR visualization; students' satisfaction with pattern; confidence in estimating size and meeting of expectations; reflection on visualized outcome and ideas for improvement; VR tool's comfort, ease of use and learning;
3. Observation on students' use of, and attitudes on, the VR tool; participation in class.

As the experiment took place during the Covid-19 pandemic, all participants received individual silicon face covers for use with the VR headset. Controllers were sanitized with antibacterial wipes before each use.

3.1   The VR Tool

The *VR Patterns* application was developed by one of the researchers, who had previous experience developing games and VR applications, with games engine Unreal Engine 4 (UE4), supported by development sample files provided by Epic Games and Oculus VR headset manufacturer. The tool was compiled as a Windows executable file, and run on a PC linked by USB cable to an Oculus Quest 2 headset.

The application consists of a virtual environment designed as a room measuring 5.2 m × 8 m, featuring the following elements on which students could apply pattern designs: (a) 5.2 m w × 2.6 m h wall; (b) lamp shade; (c) short-sleeved t-shirt; (d) curtains; (e) double bed cover. Those were included to allow students to see their patterns applied to a variety of possible applications (Fig. 2).

Furniture items were created with 3D modeling software Blender, taking in consideration dimensions from real-world products; the t-shirt was exported from fashion modeling software Clo3D; and the wall was created directly in UE4, as part of the virtual environment. All items were texture mapped, either

Fig. 2. Objects and surfaces for pattern application.

manually or programmatically, taking in consideration industry's standard size of patterns for application in textiles. 3D materials were collected or adapted from materials library Quixel and UE4's sample files. Aiming at a natural setting and at minimizing interference with pattern's colors and brightness, the virtual environment's lighting was set to simulate daylight, and to be as uniform as possible across the room.

Interaction with the virtual environment is done through Oculus Quest 2 controller, allowing users to perform the following actions: (a) navigating through the environment using the thumb stick to teleport; (b) opening and closing menu for pattern selection and adjustment using the 'A' button; (c) selecting and applying pattern onto objects, as well as adjusting its dimensions, using the front trigger button to interact with user interface components; (d) capturing high-resolution screenshots using the 'B' button (a functionality added to the prototype throughout the experiment).

Finally, the selection of student-created image files has been facilitated by the use of a repository hosted at Github, where to storage image files, retrievable from within the VR environment through a web browser embedded into the user interface. Image files (in either .jpg or .png format) were collected through the same online forms used for the pre-visualization questionnaire, through which students could upload up to ten image files. Those files were checked, re-formatted if needed, and uploaded to the repository by one of the researchers. Image dimensions were kept at 2048 × 2048 pixels to increase the efficiency of the application, should it be deployed as a stand-alone Android-based application for the Oculus platform.

3.2 Teaching Space and Schedule

On the days when *VR Pattern* was used in class, teaching sessions were structured as follows: one hour for use of the VR tool in the morning, followed by two hours of studio practice. In the afternoon, the VR tool would be available for an additional hour. VR equipment and computer running the application were located in a room adjacent to the studio where studio practice took place.

4 Findings and Discussion

Despite limited scope and duration of the experiment, study findings provided valuable insight on research questions proposed. Throughout the next subsections, we present and reflect on those findings, and how they might inform subsequent studies, experiments, and further development of the VR tool.

4.1 Impact on Learning

Three main aspects of the learning experience seemed to have been supported and reinforced by the use of the VR tool. First, educators have noticed an *increased awareness of design principles*, as students who had used the VR tool have later demonstrated a higher degree of awareness regarding repeat and scale in class, actively asking about design principles and industry standards for repeat pattern design. Post-evaluation questionnaires and ad-hoc discussions in the VR studio also reflected an acquired sense of attention to those principles, particularly the need for seamless borders in a repeat design image file. A Level 2 student (P17) noticed that her design was, in her words, 'not a repeat', as seams could be seen in the application of her pattern onto a VR object (Fig. 3). In that sense, we observe that the VR tool would have worked as a safety net for students who failed to identify such issues when using image editors, before sending it for evaluation or production.

Fig. 3. Incorrect application of pattern caused by non-matching edges

Second, the VR tool has fostered the *identification of technical issues*. Unlike the previous case, those were not related to a lack of awareness to design principles, but glitches accidentally originated from a lack of precision when the creating the image, or artifacts generated when the image file is exported. Identifying those issues allowed students to correct them. '[In] design 1, the scale was off leaving an obvious line after each repeat, this has now hopefully been fixed', wrote P9, a Level 3 student, prompted by the questionnaire to describe improvements made to an image file previously visualized in VR. (Fig. 4). As in the previous case, learners would benefit from the VR tool as an environment where to detect those issues.

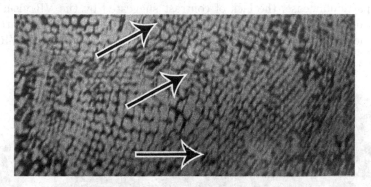

Fig. 4. Visible glitch in repeat pattern design, unnoticed during design in image editor, made evident through VR visualization.

Finally, the VR tool seemed to have a positive impact on students' *evaluation and reflection on their own design outcomes*. Indeed, previewing their design outcomes has allowed them to consider changes in both appearance and applications of the patterns they create. Take, for instance, this answer from a Level 3 student, on whether they considered changing their design after seeing it applied in VR:

> I think i will add more motifs to the design so that it has more movement, using VR helped me to see that the use of colour and composition isn't very balanced - which is something i will improve on. (P5)

Two weeks later, the participant had created a new pattern that attempted to address those points, resulting in a more balanced composition (Fig. 5). In some cases, insights gained from interaction with VR resulted in better fabric print samples. Questioned about their thoughts on their design and possible further modifications, a Level 3 student wrote:

> Applying my design to VR has led me to think i want to increase the scale of my design, I also want to increase the contrast between hues for a more striking design. (P7)

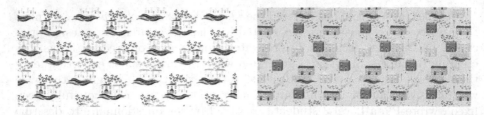

Fig. 5. Original pattern (left) and a second version (right) - an attempt at increasing a sense of balance and movement.

In that particular case, the lack of contrast suggested by the VR visualization was later observed in a fabric print sample of that same pattern. The participant, then, made changes to the design, before visualizing it in a subsequent VR session (Fig. 6).

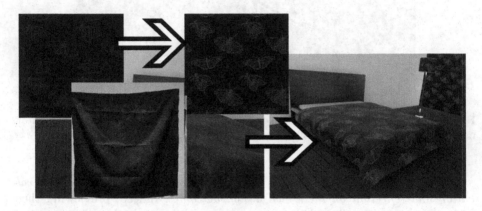

Fig. 6. Changes following VR preview: increase in image/background contrast. Initial lack of contrast was also noticeable in print output.

4.2 Considerations on Scale and Spatial Awareness

Given the initial motivation for this study —and the role physical dimensions plays in repeat pattern design —we proposed the following challenge to students using the application: *Apply the pattern you have designed in the scale you believe to be correct.* Participants would then use a slider in the user interface to scale the pattern to any dimension between 20 cm^2 to 200 cm^2, ideally aiming at the standard 64 cm^2. During the operation, students were able to see the pattern being re-sized in real time on VR objects and surfaces, but would not know the actual measurement until after confirming their choices. At the point, they would be able to revert its size to 64 cm^2. Data collected from 16 participants indicates that, out of 33 attempts, only 6 were scaled within a 25% margin of the standard size. On the other hand, 10 attempts were scaled at 200% or higher (Fig. 7). Although, at first sight, those results suggest a general lack of scale awareness from students, a closer look might reveal other possible explanations.

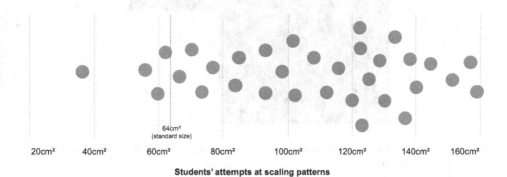

Fig. 7. Dimensions of pattern applied by participants, usually much larger than 64 × 64 cm industry standard.

First, the over-sized application of patters could reflect a desire to see details made imperceptible by *technical limitations* such as the headset's displays resolution (1832 × 1920 pixels), or recommended texture image resolution (2048 × 2048 pixels), and which could be possibly addressed by either the increase of texture image files' resolution or, if needed, the acquisition of higher-end headsets. However, only one participant expressed an opinion suggesting that 'the texture is unclear' (P17). Indeed, in that particular case, the texture looked blurry. However, that could be partially attributed to (a) image compression artifacts over fine line drawing, and (b) sub-optimal use of the image's area (Fig. 8), which suggests a second reason for the number of over-sized applications: the *unintended and/or unnecessary repetition of patterns within the image file*, when students include more than one instance of the repeat tile in their image files. In those cases, a single repeat would be more adequate for the design they have envisioned (Fig. 9).

Cases like the aforementioned ones suggest that students often need to see the repetition taking place within their image files, in order to visualize its application. In that case, other strategies for previewing the repetition (using image editor or otherwise) should be reinforced. It also suggests some students were expecting their patterns to look bigger when applied in the standard size. Indeed some students expressed that verbally, when asked of changes they would like to make to their designs, post-VR experience:

Increasing the scale - my intention was to have larger motifs. (P4)

As the VR mocked up my design in such a small scale, this made me want my final outcome to have a larger scale. (P8)

Fig. 8. Actual repeat pattern (right) would occupy approximately 16% of the area of the original image file

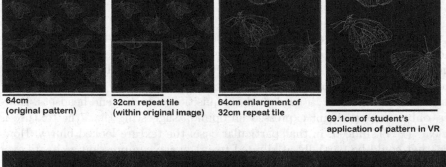

64cm
(original pattern)

32cm repeat tile
(within original image)

64cm enlargment of
32cm repeat tile

69.1cm of student's
application of pattern in VR

Fig. 9. Top: almost twice the standard size of 64 cm², student's size estimation would be closer to accurate if considering a single repeat tile only. Bottom: mock-up created by student before application in VR suggests a single repeat tile would have been the best approach to achieve the student's vision.

In fact, repeat tile for the patterns created by P4 and P8 occupied 70% and 50% of their respective image files. Moreover, as we observe a high concentration of attempts between 120 and 140 cm^2, i.e., roughly twice the standard size, we are drawn to the fact that 10 out of 11 of those attempts used image files where repeat tile appears twice horizontally and vertically (Fig. 10). In those cases, students' estimate would have been very close to accurate, as repeat tiles actually occupy an area close to 64 cm^2.

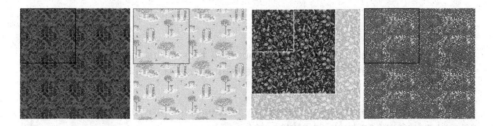

Fig. 10. Sample of image files that have been applied by participants at roughly twice the standard size. Inner squares highlight repeat tile within image.

Whereas enlarging patterns usually suggest an attempt to decrease the number of repeat tiles, making repetition less evident, in cases where there is a considerable amount of variation and detail, larger sizes would make those details more visible. Although more research on size estimation and awareness would be necessary to elucidate the points raised, this study suggests that students are often successful estimating the area their patterns would cover, but not so successful in understanding how their image files should be prepared to achieve that result.

4.3   Perceptions on the VR Tool

Students generally had an enthusiastic attitude towards the VR tool. Regarding its *usability*, the majority of surveyed participants (p = 12) perceived it as easy to use, easy to learn, and comfortable to use (Fig. 11). That assessment, however, contrasts with their frequent need to be remembered how to operate it, as well as with individual remarks. This suggests their previous lack of familiarity with VR tools has (a) prevented them to compare the tool to better realized VR applications, and (b) their enthusiasm has compensated for the tool's deficiencies. Moreover, it could suggest that students might have retrained themselves, holding back negative comments on the researchers and educators' work. In any case, an evaluative usability testing of the tool would be better suited for future iterations of the tool, rather than the initial prototype described in this study.

Students have also expressed their views on the *usefulness* of the VR tool, which mostly reflected the benefits previously discussed on their learning. In that sense, identifying technical problems and design shortcomings seemed useful.

How much would you agree with the following sentence: the VR tool is...

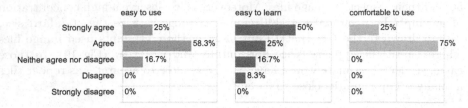

Fig. 11. Users' perceptions of tool's ease of use, learning, and comfort.

I found that using the VR tool helped me to see the design in a bigger context which highlighted some of the faults with the repeat that i hadn't noticed before (P5).

The tool was also considered useful by students for providing a way of observing and reflecting on their creative work:

(The VR experience) made me think about scale when i design on Photoshop and the impact of colors in a room. (P9)

In some cases, students also emphasized creative possibilities and a sense of experimentation and new insights.

I designed (this pattern) originally for wallpaper, but i think it looks better on an object such as the lamp. (P17)

The use of the VR tool to preview the application of patterns was favorably compared by students to the production of mock-ups using image editor Adobe Photoshop (Fig. 12). In fact, some of the students used high-resolution screen captures taken from the VR tool to include in their portfolios for the module's assessment.

I am satisfied with how my pattern looks when applied on...

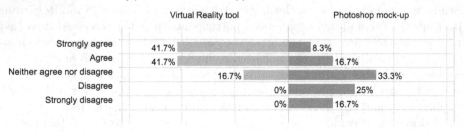

Fig. 12. Comparison of students' satisfaction with the application of their pattern using photoshop and VR environment.

Invited to express their opinions and give suggestions, students pointed out features and functionalities they would like to see implemented, many of which we plan to incorporate in subsequent versions of the tool. Those are: greater variety of objects and garments; greater variety of materials and textiles; testing multiple patterns at once; cloth simulation; better visualization for fashion items; additional environments and improved lighting and shading.

Finally, regarding the perspective of educators and researchers, it is fair to say the focus was shifted from improving students' spatial awareness —this study's initial motivation —to gaining clearer insight on how students understand, plan and execute, their repeat pattern designs. In that sense, the observation of students in their use of the VR tool was valuable, allowing educators to evaluate which aspects of repeat pattern design, from principles to techniques, might need to be reinforced in class.

4.4 Development Challenges and Opportunities

In recent years, the development of Virtual Reality application has been facilitated by real-time 3D game engines with VR capabilities that allow small teams, or even individuals, to engage in the production of this type of software. The in-house development of *VR Patterns*, prototyped by one of the authors, faced challenges that could be described as specific to work in higher-education institutions. Those were:

- **Limited time and flexibility for development and testing:** given the limited number of classes in a semester, and lack of flexibility in rescheduling them, significant modifications to a prototype could need to wait for a subsequent semester to be implemented.
- **Additional technical constraints:** in the case of *VR Patterns*, restrictions in wireless connectivity, possibly related to increased security settings, prevented the wireless connection between the VR headset and PC, in which case a USB cable had to be used.

On the other hand, we have identified opportunities within the academic environment that might help addressing those issues:

- **Close integration between teaching and tool development:** Continuous access to students and educators provide an excellent environment for a continuous development process informed by actual users, having in mind the improvement of current features, as well as the identification of desirable functionalities.
- **Expansion to other modules and programmes:** Outcomes from this study could help attracting new partners and collaborators across the department to help develop and test the application further, particularly those involved in fashion, graphics, product, graphic, and digital and interaction design.

5   Conclusion

This paper described the development and exploration of a Virtual Reality tool to support the teaching and learning of repeat pattern design in higher education. Overall, the use of the VR tool has influenced design outcomes in positive ways, accelerating student awareness on matters of repeat and scale. Initial results suggest students become more focused on the production of outcomes after interacting with the tool, occasionally diagnosing technical problems as well as identifying points for improvement in their design, such as balance, contrast, and use of color in their compositions. As an additional benefit, the tool made possible the identification of issues before print, allowing for corrections to take place before final execution. The VR tool was, overall, well-received by students. Although there was no conclusive evidence on benefits to increased spatial awareness, findings suggest that students can estimate the dimensions of design patterns more accurately and intuitively through the VR tool than through canvases of image editors, in which case the former could be used to support and inform the student's work on the latter.

The outcome and application of students' work in VR was helpful informing educators on design principles and technical information that needed to be reinforced, providing an overview of students' understanding of those. In that sense, having the VR application to inform and support those discussions had a positive, unexpected impact, beyond its use for real-size representation of student work and the training of their abilities in accurately estimating design output dimensions. Further development is recommended for implementation of features such as new virtual materials, objects and environments, ideally being informed by a co-design process involving students, developers, and educators.

Despite limitations in application and sampling, and challenges in development caused by time and infrastructure constraints, results of this study could be useful for educators involved with in-house production of VR tools for education and industry, particularly those related to textiles, fashion, and graphic design.

Acknowledgement. This research was supported by Epic Games through the Epic MegaGrants funding. We would like to thank Design postgraduate students who have previously helped investigating VR tools for pattern design: Dan Yang, Wenwen Wang, Hanyu Zheng, Liantong Lu, Liting Li, Shiyi Xu, Chien-Yu Yeh, Dabang Geng, Yulin Su, Ximing Wang, Zixuan Xie, Haiyi Liu.

References

1. Hoffman, H., Vu, D.: Virtual reality: teaching tool of the twenty-first century? Acad. Med. **72**, 1076–1081 (1997). https://doi.org/10.1097/00001888-199712000-00018
2. Holly, M., Pirker, J., Resch, S., Brettschuh, S., Gütl, C.: Designing VR experiences-expectations for teaching and learning in VR. Educ. Technol. Soc. **24**(2), 107–119 (2021)
3. Garcia, S., Laesker, D., Caprio, D., Kauer, R., Nguyen, J., Andujar, M.: An immersive virtual reality experience for learning Spanish. In: Zaphiris, P., Ioannou, A. (eds.) HCII 2019. LNCS, vol. 11591, pp. 151–161. Springer, Cham (2019). https://doi.org/10.1007/978-3-030-21817-1_12

4. Demirel, D., Hamam, A., Scott, C., Karaman, B., Toker, O., Pena, L.: Towards a new chemistry learning platform with virtual reality and haptics. In: Zaphiris, P., Ioannou, A. (eds.) HCII 2021. LNCS, vol. 12785, pp. 253–267. Springer, Cham (2021). https://doi.org/10.1007/978-3-030-77943-6_16

5. Park, M., Im, H., Kim, D.Y.: Feasibility and user experience of virtual reality fashion stores. Fashion Text. **5**(1), 1–17 (2018). https://doi.org/10.1186/s40691-018-0149-x

6. Liu, K., et al.: 3D interactive garment pattern-making technology. Comput. Aided Des. **104**, 113–124 (2018). https://doi.org/10.1016/j.cad.2018.07.003

7. Adanur, S., Vakalapudi, J.S.: Woven fabric design and analysis in 3D virtual reality. Part 1: computer aided design and modeling of interlaced structures. J. Text. Inst. **104**(7), 715–723 (2013). https://doi.org/10.1080/00405000.2012.753698

8. Gray, S.: IT reaches clothing production. Textile Asia **8**(26), 103–108 (1995)

9. Magnenat-Thalmann, N., Bonanni, U.: Haptic sensing of virtual textiles. In: Grunwald M. (ed.) Human Haptic Perception: Basics and Applications, pp. 513–523 (2008). https://doi.org/10.1007/978-3-7643-7612-3_43

10. Sarakatsanos, O., et al.: A VR application for the virtual fitting of fashion garments on avatars. In: 2021 IEEE International Symposium on Mixed and Augmented Reality Adjunct (ISMAR-Adjunct) (2021). https://doi.org/10.1109/ismar-adjunct54149.2021.00018

11. Lau, O., Ki, C.-W.C.: Can consumers' gamified, personalized, and engaging experiences with VR fashion apps increase in-app purchase intention by fulfilling needs? Fashion Text. **8**(1), 1–22 (2021). https://doi.org/10.1186/s40691-021-00270-9

12. Joundi, J., Conradie, P., Saldien, J., De Marez, L.: Exploring the potential and challenges of VR prototyping in fashion design. In: Proceedings of the Symposium on Spatial User Interaction (2018). https://doi.org/10.1145/3267782.3274768

13. Özgen, D.S., Afacan, Y., Sürer, E.: Usability of virtual reality for basic design education: a comparative study with paper-based design. Int. J. Technol. Des. Educ. **31**(2), 357–377 (2019). https://doi.org/10.1007/s10798-019-09554-0

14. Lee, J., et al.: The use of VR for collaborative exploration and enhancing creativity in fashion design education. Int. J. Fashion Des. Technol. Educ. **14**(1), 48–57 (2020). https://doi.org/10.1080/17543266.2020.1858350

15. Chang, Y.: 3D-CAD effects on creative design performance of different spatial abilities students (2014). https://doi.org/10.1111/jcal.12051

16. Chang, Y.-S., Chou, C.-H., Chuang, M.-J., Li, W.-H., Tsai, I.-F.: Effects of virtual reality on creative design performance and creative experiential learning (2020). https://doi.org/10.1080/10494820.2020.1821717

17. Starkey, S., Alotaibi, S., Striebel, H., Tejeda, J., Francisco, K., Rudolph, N.: Fashion inspiration and technology: virtual reality in an experimental apparel design classroom (2020). https://doi.org/10.1080/17543266.2020.1844807

18. Bourdot, P., Convard, T., Picon, F., Ammi, M., Touraine, D., Vézien, J.-M.: VR-CAD integration: multimodal immersive interaction and advanced haptic paradigms for implicit edition of CAD models (2010). https://doi.org/10.1016/j.cad.2008.10.014

19. Joundi, J., Conradie, P., Saldien, J., De Marez, L.: Exploring the potential and challenges of VR prototyping in fashion design (2018). https://doi.org/10.1145/3267782.3274768

20. Lee, J.H., Yang, E., Sun, Z.Y.: Using an immersive virtual reality design tool to support cognitive action and creativity: educational insights from fashion designers (2021). https://doi.org/10.1080/14606925.2021.1912902

Learning Spatial Transformations and their Math Representations through Embodied Learning in Augmented Reality

Zohreh Shaghaghian⬛, Heather Burte⬛, Dezhen Song⬛, and Wei Yan⁽⌧⁾⬛

Texas A&M University, College Station, TX 77840, USA
{zohreh-sh,heather.burte,wyan}@tamu.edu, dzsong@cs.tamu.edu

Abstract. In Computer Aided Design, Computer Graphics, Robotics, etc., students suffer from inefficient and non-proficient use of the 3D modeling software due to a lack of mathematical knowledge. Deficient knowledge and skills may lead students to use the modeling software through trial-and-error without understanding the algorithms and mathematics. Spatial/geometric transformation is recognized as one of the key factors in learning 3D modeling software. This paper presents a newly developed educational Augmented Reality (AR) mobile application to help students intuitively learn the geometric reasoning of transformation matrices and the corresponding trigonometric equations through play. The application, developed in primary and advanced levels, intends to facilitate the understanding of fundamentals of spatial transformations and their mathematical representations in a self-learning approach. The results of a pilot user study conducted on 7 undergraduate students for the primary level reveal that students' math scores improved after playing with the application.

Keywords: Augmented Reality · Educational application · Spatial transformations · Matrices · Trigonometry

1 Introduction

Despite the development of Computer Aided Design (CAD) software in learning geometry, spatial transformations, and related mathematics, many students still face challenges in solving geometric problems and rely on a trial-and-error process [20]. About 20% of students experience difficulty in problems dealing with spatial skills, such as manipulating figures in space and analyzing complex shapes [1, 2]. Specifically, using the trial-and-error technique in learning modeling software may result in understanding geometric transformations as only motions over an object rather than mapping functions on geometry's variables [3]. Computers can shape and re-mold our mathematical knowledge [4], hence students may adopt their understanding of geometric transformation concepts consistently with the strategies represented by modeling software.

The reciprocal relation between spatial reasoning and math skills [5], and the significance of math and spatial skills in Science, Technology, Engineering, and Mathematics (STEM) education and further professional career is well acknowledged in literature

© The Author(s), under exclusive license to Springer Nature Switzerland AG 2022
P. Zaphiris and A. Ioannou (Eds.): HCII 2022, LNCS 13329, pp. 112–128, 2022.
https://doi.org/10.1007/978-3-031-05675-8_10

[6, 7]. Studying geometric transformations and the associated mathematical concepts is significant for students to consider mathematics as an interconnected discipline and eventually helps students in higher-level reasoning activities [3]. However, the difficulty of learning/teaching geometric transformations and the associated mathematics is acknowledged in the literature [3, 8].

Trigonometry as the mathematical concept inherently involved in transformation matrices is also a subject of interest in many studies. The relevance of trigonometric ideas in linking algebraic and geometric thinking is emphasized by National Council of Teachers of Mathematics (NCTM) [9]. Although learning trigonometry serves as an important prerequisite course for many college-level courses in different fields of STEM [10], students still face difficulty in solving trigonometry problems [11]. Researchers believe that students mostly memorize the formulas without understanding the concepts and the spatial reasoning behind the mathematical equations [11]. The reason may be rooted in the educational system that teaches mathematics in a number sense - as a collection of formulae - rather than emphasizing on the spatial reasonings [5]. On the other hand, researchers found that imagery skill (especially schematic imagery) is directly associated with high spatial visualization skills, meaning that students with high imagery skills outscore their peers in solving geometric-based problems [12].

Augmented Reality (AR) technology as a mediator tool with the ability to augment the physical reality with virtual information may boost learning abstract subject and facilitate understanding the spatial reasoning behind the mathematics of transformation matrices. The augmentation of abstract information besides the inherent capability of AR in perspective matching [13–15] may help students in improving imagery skills which could later help them solve geometry problems.

This paper demonstrates BRICKxAR/T, an educational AR mobile application developed by the authors, to facilitate learning spatial/geometric transformations and their corresponding mathematics in a "Learn through Play" environment. BRICKxAR/T intends to help students better understand the mathematical logics behind geometric modeling through playing with the parameters of transformation matrices. Employing AR features to display the dynamic relationship between physical motion and the corresponding abstract information, the authors attempt to increase the application's ability for self-learning in an intuitive way. Using the AR environment to support embodied learning in a 3D spatial environment, we have contextualized mathematical concepts through synching them to the physical motions in real-time.

The registration of the virtual-physical models enables real-time interaction of physical and virtual objects in AR. The goal of the study is to provide a spatiotemporal experiment where students learn and apply knowledge in the same place, at the same time [16, 17].

This prototype is in the continuation of a previous research project on AR instruction for LEGO® assembly [18], using the same LEGO model as a physical manipulative for the user to interact in the AR environment.

2 Literature Review

The close interrelation between math problem solving and spatial thinking has been reported in studies [5, 19, 20]. Although the textbooks in literature provide essential information to learn the mathematics behind spatial transformations they do not support a practical context to learn and apply the gained knowledge concurrently. Since the advent of CAD methods in the early 1980s, most US engineering schools shifted to CAD systems to teach geometry-related courses [21]. Studies show the superiority of Computer-Assisted Learning compared to the conventional text-books and lectures [2, 21, 22]. However, many studies, including longitudinal research, reveal that mere 3D modeling software may not improve students' spatial skills by itself, and hands-on experiences are still a matter of significance [1, 21, 23]. Theoretical studies in cognitive neuroscience demonstrate that STEM pedagogy specifically benefits from hands-on activities for learning abstract information where there is a lack of real-world referent [24]. Furthermore, the perspective view in 3D desktop software is not the natural user's view; imposing inevitable mental load to interpret any transformation into one's natural perspective view. Finally, CAD workshops may not be interesting enough for students as they often drop the course before ending [25].

2.1 Related Work

AR has been studied in the educational fields like physics, mathematics, chemistry, and biomedical sciences, especially when students cannot feasibly achieve real-world experiences on certain subjects. In these studies, AR is used as a tool to help students embody the real-world perception of objects or abstractions to ease the learning process [26–29]. The results of the studies on the application of AR in education reveal that students' learning efficacy increase when the relevant information is spatially/temporally attached to the real-world experiments [28, 30]. This technology can provide a context in which the learners get involved in the experiment physically/interactively, which could benefit the learners in embodied learning [31]. Supporting a physical learning environment, AR technology helps students better integrate new subjects with prior knowledge and experience [32]. Appropriate integration of body movements with the learning content can significantly improve memory retrieval and knowledge retention [33].

Several AR applications have been developed for learning descriptive geometry and mathematics [34–38] which demonstrate positive impacts of AR intervention in geometry perception. A couple of studies used AR applications as visualization tools, displaying 3D geometries and different representations (for example, images of unfolded geometry) in a spatial environment, to help students' spatial visualization skills in an engineering graphic course [36, 37]. Their studies showed significant Improvement of experimental group over the students who used traditional textbooks in understanding geometry and geometric relations.

In a quasi-experimental study, Dünser et al. (2006) have developed and evaluated an AR application as a geometric construction tool, Construct3D, to improve students' spatial skills of 3D perception and enhance learning mathematical concepts [26, 34]. In their study they compared the AR intervention with a 2D CAD software tool through a user study. Assessing the learning effect through multiple spatial ability tests, they found positive but insignificant differences between the treatment and the control groups [34]. In their experiment student's interaction with the virtual model is realized through a pencil and a panel and no direct physical/virtual model interaction is provided. Furthermore, their application does not display the relation between algebraic equations and the corresponding geometric transformations.

GeoGebra AR is one of the recent AR applications in learning geometry and algebra [35]. It has been explored in a couple of studies [39–41] demonstrating positive and significant impact of the application in spatial visualization and learning mathematics. However, GeoGebra AR, which can display created virtual objects in a physical environment, does not provide a physical interaction/interplay of physical and virtual objects through tracking the physical objects and visualizing the spatial relationship between the physical and virtual objects. This lack of physical – virtual object interplay limits the application's capability of allowing learners' physical manipulation and embodied learning in AR.

With the aim to enhance AR-based learning and overcome the found limitations of existing AR tools used in learning, BRICKxAR/T is designed to facilitate the physical-virtual object interplay and to strengthen AR's unique power of integrating embodied learning and visualization of abstract information.

3 Methodology

BRICKxAR/T app consists of two prototypes for learning geometric transformations and the corresponding mathematics in primary and advanced levels. The prototypes have been developed based on the progressive learning method introduced in literature for learning spatial transformations [42] in three levels of 'motions, mappings and functions' [42]. We have leveraged the AR technology to realize this process for spatiotemporal experiments as follows:

● Motions: AR supports physical motions, physical/virtual models interplay, and embodied learning.
● Mappings: AR supports visualizing graphics to illustrate spatial mapping operations.
● Functions: AR supports synchronized visualization of mathematical functions and their relations with physical motions.

The current app is programmed in C# and developed for iOS devices using the Unity game engine. AR Foundation and Apple's ARKit image tracking method are adopted to register the models. This paper includes: 1) a brief description of prototype 1 and the corresponding result of a pilot user study which can be found in detail in our previous publications [43, 44], 2) a detailed description of prototype 2 development, and 3) the design of future user study corresponding to prototype 2.

3.1 Prototype 1

The preliminary prototype is an RTS (Rotation, Translation, and Scale) game that helps students understand mathematical notions of spatial transformations along with the mathematical components of transformations, such as variables, parameters, and functions. The spatial visualization of graphical representations (distance lines with dimensions and rotation arcs with angles) that are matched with physical motions in real-time, assists students to perceive the geometric reasonings underlying transformation matrices. In the AR device (iPad) user interface, the first- and second-row matrices correspond to the transformations of the physical LEGO model and the virtual model, respectively. Students can play with the models, i.e., translate, rotate, and scale (for the virtual model only) in x-, y-, and z-axes, and follow these matrices to observe the synchronized mathematical functions of the geometric transformations in real-time (Fig. 1).

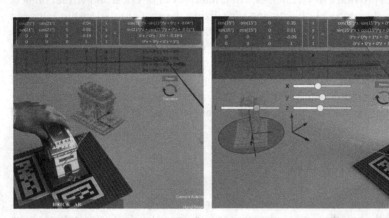

Fig. 1. Left: student playing with the physical model in AR; Right: student playing with the matrix parameters to apply transformations to the virtual model.

User Study

We conducted a pilot user study (TAMU IRB2020-1213M) on a group of 7 undergraduate students (3 females and 4 males; 6 from the College of Engineering and 1 from the College of Architecture). The students had at least college-level knowledge in algebra and geometry and were somehow familiar with AR technology. The students who participated were a convenience sample as they previously worked with the researchers for a related research project, however, spatial transformations and their mathematical representations (matrices) were not learned or used in the students' project tasks.

In the pre-sessions students took online tests, including PVRT (Purdue Visualization of Rotations Test) [45] and a math test on transformation matrices, design based on learning materials of Khan Academy [46], using their own computing devices. Tests answers were not disclosed after the pre-session tests. Due to the COVID-19 pandemic, we hosted the post-sessions and workshops virtually through Zoom meetings with a guidance and Q&A in a 1- to 5-week time interval between the pre- and post-sessions. In the post-sessions, each student was provided with a LEGO set and an iPad with the prototype installed. The students played with the prototype for 30 to 40 min and took the PVRT and math tests afterward. During the play we asked students to follow the step-by-step instructions provided in the prototype and record their screens during the play for our further behavior-based analysis. We evaluated the effectiveness of our application through measuring the learning gain of students in pre- and post-sessions. The results, analyzed using a non-parametric statistical method, show that students' scores improved in the post-sessions in most samples. The mean scores of the students in the PVRT (mean$_{\text{pre-test}}$ = 75.7, mean$_{\text{post-test}}$ = 77.9) and math test (mean$_{\text{pre-test}}$ = 63.74, mean$_{\text{post-test}}$ = 81.32) increased after playing with the app, and more substantially in the math tests (27.59%) than PVRT (2.8%).

We measured the prototype task load using NASA_TLX survey [47]. The results showed that students on average rated the prototype a low demanding task for learning the targeted material. Also, the results from a motivation questionnaire, adopted from MSLQ [48], revealed that students were interested in playing with the prototype and thought that the app was useful for learning transformation matrices. Specifically, all students agreed that what they learned in the workshop helped them in answering the tests in the post sessions and 5 out of the 7 students claimed that they used visual imagery, visualizing what they learned in the workshop, to answer the math tests.

3.2 Prototype 2

The second prototype covers more advanced concepts and applications of geometric transformations such as trigonometric equations behind transformation matrices. In this prototype students will get introduced to the conception of object detection as an example application of geometric transformations in practice, applied in many recent studies [49–51]. Besides physical and virtual interaction and augmentation of abstract information, this prototype intends to leverage AR features to enhance embodied learning by encouraging students to move and rotate physically around the physical model and explore the transformations of virtual camera objects through the physical camera view observing the physical model. The authors are practically adopting this methodology through simulations in parametric modeling to generate the training data of machine learning for brick detection in the LEGO set assembly process in the future development of the application. In this prototype, abstract information and spatial graphics, such as coordinate systems, rotation arcs, distance and projection lines, and notations are displayed in the AR environment and synchronized with physical motions to visualize the geometric reasoning of transformations and the corresponding trigonometry equations behind the transformations.

App Development. Opening the corresponding scene of prototype 2, the physical LEGO model (with image marker attached) get registered in the AR environment and a digital coordinate system will be superimposed on the center pivot point of the model, representing the world coordinate system (WCS) in this experiment. The real-time registration allows students to move or rotate the LEGO model in any step of the experiment. Then, virtual models and spatial graphics (axes, distance lines with dimensions, arcs with angles, etc. drawn in the 3D space of AR for annotations) will be updated seamlessly according to the new position and rotation of the registered model.

Clicking on the "Circle of Altitude", a hemisphere wireframe model is displayed embracing the LEGO model with a highlighted circle drawn by default on the largest circle of the hemisphere perimeter. The mathematical equations corresponding to the calculations of circle radius and height will be displayed on a 2D panel on the screen (Fig. 2).

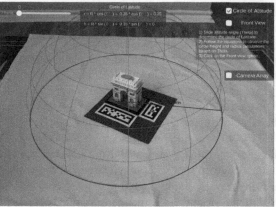

Fig. 2. Left: the physical model attached to the image marker get registered; Right: a circle will be highlighted (in pink color) on a hemisphere embracing the LEGO model.

Then, students can play with the altitude angle parameter of the equations to update the circle, with a new height and radius, that is continuously placed on the hemisphere. Changing from 0° to 90° altitude angles, the circle will be re-drawn seamlessly in the space from maximum radius and minimum height to the maximum height and minimum radius on the hemisphere. The spatial graphics representing the height, base, and hypotenuse of the associated right triangle used in the calculations of the circle height and radius will be drawn in real-time. The corresponding measure notations matched with the numbers in the equations are also spatially adjusted in the AR environment respecting the associated lines (Fig. 3).

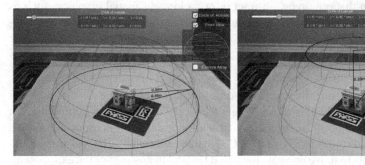

Fig. 3. Using angle parameter, a student can parametrically update the circle of the hemisphere, with different altitudes, heights, and radius.

Students can turn on the front view option to visualize the parametric changes of altitude angle in a sub-window. The optional sub-windows (top- and front-views) are designed in this experiment as those views are common features in desktop modeling software; however, the necessity and impact of those features in the spatial AR environment need to be investigated through user studies in the future.

In the next step, students can parametrically generate a spherical array of virtual camera objects on the drawn circle, using a slider that determines the number of the objects from 1 to 15. Each generated virtual camera object contains a coordinate system which demonstrates its position and orientation respecting the LEGO model with the WCS in this experiment (Fig. 4).

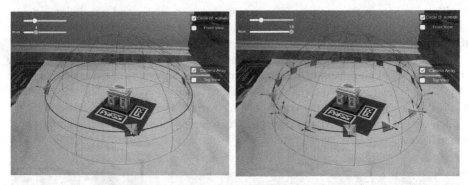

Fig. 4. Parametrically generating virtual camera objects on the drawn circle (pink color) in a polar array fashion.

In this prototype, students can play with the sliders in any step to explore a new scenario. The relative positions and the distances between the generated camera objects get updated seamlessly when the student parametrically changes the circle through the altitude angle parameter. Also, the rotations of the camera objects adjust dynamically so they continuously point to the LEGO model's pivot. Figure 5 shows the automatic transformations of virtual camera objects updated with the new re-drawn circle in real-time.

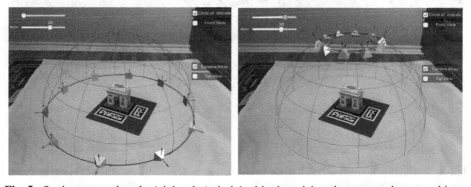

Fig. 5. Student can update the (pink color) circle's altitude and then the generated camera objects get transformed accordingly.

In the next step, as shown in Fig. 6, the student can select any virtual camera object by touching the screen. The selected virtual camera gets highlighted and its corresponding transformation matrices along with the associated trigonometry functions will be displayed on the AR screen. The matrices include three 4 × 4 matrices of rotations, representing rotations around x-, y-, and z-axes, and one 4 × 4 matrix of translation along x-, y-, and z-axes (Fig. 6 bottom). The vector represents a point variable on the camera object that will be multiplied by the translation and rotation matrices for transforming the point from the WCS (the LEGO model's pivot) to a new position (the current position of the selected camera object).

The numbers in the matrices (for example, rotation angles and translations in x, y, and z) match in color with the graphics and notations in the AR environment to catch the student's visual attention in exploring the geometric relations of math functions.

The other sets of mathematical statements placed on top of the matrices show the trigonometry equations behind the calculation of the new position of the selected camera object and in relation to the elements in the transformation matrices. The lines and arcs (with colors matched with the corresponding variables) visualized in AR could help students intuitively perceive the geometric reasoning of the trigonometry equations in the matrices.

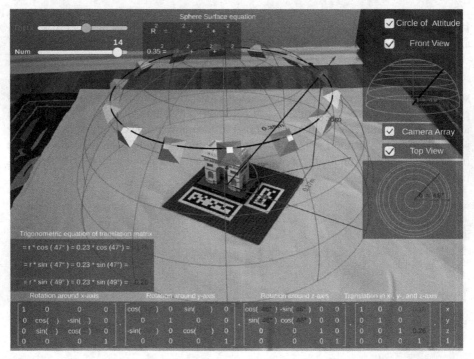

Fig. 6. Students can select any virtual camera object to visualize its transformation matrices and trigonometry equations along with the graphics of dimensions and angles.

The real-time model registration allows students to interact with the physical LEGO at any step of the experiment while all spatial graphics and mathematical representations update seamlessly respecting the WCS (Fig. 7).

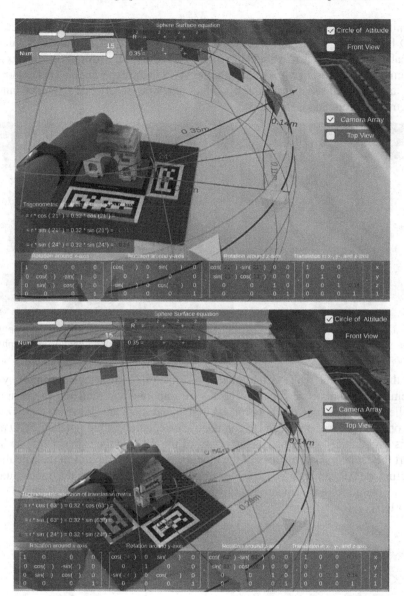

Fig. 7. While student transforms the physical LEGO model from pre-image on the top to image on bottom, the spatial graphics and math representations update in real time accordingly.

Finally, one of the major intentions of this prototype is to encourage students to learn the targeted subject through embodied learning using body gestures. In this experiment, students can practically experience the view of the selected virtual camera through the physical camera of the AR device by physically tracking and aligning the physical camera with the selected virtual camera and taking a screenshot, which can be compared with the renderings from the corresponding virtual camera (Fig. 8). As mentioned before, the renderings taken from different angles by simulated virtual cameras can be used as training data for a separate machine learning project on object detection – detecting LEGO bricks using Convolutional Neural Network (CNN). Aligning the virtual and physical cameras, the matrices could be representative of the transformation matrix of the real camera, i.e., the user's view relative to the WCS in the experiment. This exploration offers an embodied learning through a spatiotemporal experience to understand the geometric transformations in practice.

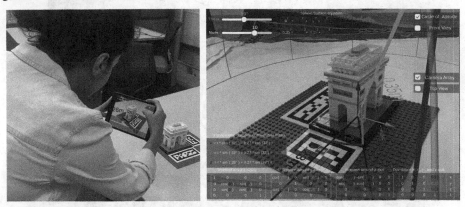

Fig. 8. Left: A student tracking the selected virtual camera object physically using the physical camera on the AR device (iPad); Right: Screenshots showing the camera view from the physical camera/student's view.

In this experiment, while virtual model information (such as the coordinate system, the hemisphere and virtual camera objects) are imported and rendered in the application, the spatial graphics (such as lines, circles, and arcs) are drawn in the 3D space based on the registered model and trigonometric calculation. Although the LEGO model pivot is hypothetically assumed as the origin of the WCS in the experiment, we had to convert the actual transformations of the models and spatial graphics in the calculations respecting the AR camera's WCS. For example, Fig. 9-right depicts the conceptual calculation conducted in the equations of finding P_3 to draw the green line in the 3D space (Fig. 9-left).

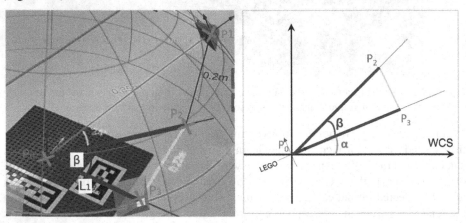

Fig. 9. Left: screenshot from the application (some graphics and notations are added manually for explanation in this paper); Right: conceptual geometric representations to calculate the spatial position of P_3 in the AR environment respecting AR camera WCS.

In Fig. 9, P0 and P1 are the WCS origin and the pivot point of the selected virtual camera object, respectively. However, other points need to be calculated respecting the AR camera's WCS. The notations and calculations corresponding to P_3 are as follows:

$$L_1 = P_0P_2 \cdot \cos(\beta) \tag{1}$$

$$x = L_1 \cdot \cos(\alpha + \gamma) \tag{2}$$

$$y = L_1 \cdot \sin(\alpha + \gamma) \tag{3}$$

$$P_2 = P_0 + (x, y, P_0.z) \tag{4}$$

where: P_0 is the LEGO pivot; P_1 is the selected virtual camera pivot; P_2 is P_1 projected; α is the angle between the registered model in the very beginning (pre-image) and the AR camera WCS; and γ is the angle between the transformed LEGO model (image) and the primary registered model (pre-image).

User Study Design

We will measure the effectiveness of our application through a user study on undergraduate students between control (non-AR) and experimental (AR intervention) groups. The non-AR control group will play the same app with similar learning functions and graphics, but with the AR registration and tracking turned off. The study includes pre- and post-sessions as follows:

- Pre-session:

  o Demographic questionnaire
  o The Purdue Visualization of Rotations Test (PVRT) [45]
  o A Math Test (MT) on transformation matrices and trigonometry equations, designed based on [46, 52]

- Post-session:

  o Workshop of playing with the prototype (AR and non-AR by the experimental and control groups, respectively)
  o PVRT
  o MT
  o NASA TLX survey [47]
  o Motivation questionnaire, adopted from MSLQ [48]

Figure 10 shows two examples of the MT.

Without disclosure of the tests' answers, students are going to participate in the pre- and post-sessions with a 1- to 5-week time interval to avoid Testing and History Threat [53]. We will evaluate students learning gains in the visualization of rotation and math skills through pre- and post-tests and compare students' scores in the non-AR versus AR groups to assess the effectiveness of BRICKxAR/T with AR intervention.

Answer questions 1 to 4 based on the bellow diagrams of a right triangle:

angle	0°	30°	45°	60°	90°	120°	135°	150°	180°
	0	$\pi/6$	$\pi/4$	$\pi/3$	$\pi/2$	$2\pi/3$	$3\pi/4$	$5\pi/6$	π
sin	0	$\frac{1}{2}$	$\frac{\sqrt{2}}{2}$	$\frac{\sqrt{3}}{2}$	$\frac{\sqrt{4}}{2}$	$\frac{\sqrt{3}}{2}$	$\frac{\sqrt{2}}{2}$	$\frac{1}{2}$	0
cos	1	$\frac{\sqrt{3}}{2}$	$\frac{\sqrt{2}}{2}$	$\frac{1}{2}$	0	$-\frac{1}{2}$	$-\frac{\sqrt{2}}{2}$	$-\frac{\sqrt{3}}{2}$	-1

4. If hypotenuse=10, α =60°, what will be the base?

a) We need to know β

b) We need to know the height

c) base = 5

d) base = $\frac{10 \times \sqrt{3}}{2}$

12. Which is the best description for the transformation given by the following matrix
$$\begin{pmatrix} 1 & 0 & 0 & 2 \\ 0 & \cos(t) & -\sin(t) & 2 \\ 0 & \sin(t) & \cos(t) & 2 \\ 0 & 0 & 0 & 1 \end{pmatrix}?$$

a) Combined matrix of rotation and move in 3D space

b) Combined matrix of rotation and reflection in 3D space

c) Combined matrix of scale and move in 3D space

d) Combined matrix of scale and rotation in 3D space

Fig. 10. Two example questions of the MT, designed by the authors

We will measure the task load of our application using the NASA-TLX survey. The survey assesses the application task load based on six dimensions (mental demand, physical demand, temporal demand, effort, frustration, and performance) through rating and pair-wise questions [47]. The result of the survey will demonstrate how tense/uncomfortable vs. light/convenient our application is for students to play. The motivation questionnaire will measure students motivations based on three categories of intrinsic-value, task-anxiety, and self-efficacy [48]. The results will help us infer how confusing versus easy/user-friendly BRICKxAR/T is to play and learn the targeted subject for students.

4 Conclusion and Future Work

In this paper, we have presented an AR educational application, named BRICKxAR/T, which is developed in two levels of primary and advanced, to help students learn the transformation matrices and the incorporated trigonometry equations behind geometric transformations through spatiotemporal experiments. The primary level (prototype 1) involves learning the fundamentals of spatial transformations and their corresponding matrices along with understanding the components of a geometric transformations in 3D modeling software. The advanced level (prototype 2) involves learning spatial transformation matrices and the corresponding trigonometry equations. BRICKxAR/T has the potential to enable (1) embodied learning through hand and body movements based on students' interaction with the physical manipulative in the immersive AR environment and (2) integrated visualization of geometric and algebraic concepts, synchronized with the movements.

As prior literature suggested improvement of the memory retrieval and knowledge retention through the use of AR, this project specifically aims to enhance students learning geometric transformations and their mathematical representations (matrices and vectors) leveraging AR. The completed pilot user study for prototype 1 is promising, and a new user study for prototype 2 is designed to be conducted with undergraduate students from different fields.

Acknowledgements. . This material is based upon work supported by the National Science Foundation under Grant No. 2119549 and Texas A&M University's grants.

References

1. Sorby, S.A.: Educational research in developing 3-D spatial skills for engineering students. Int. J. Sci. Educ. **31**(3), 459–480 (2009). https://doi.org/10.1080/09500690802595839
2. Garmendia, M., Guisasola, J., Sierra, E.: First-year engineering students' difficulties in visualization and drawing tasks. Eur. J. Eng. Educ. **32**(3), 315–323 (2007). https://doi.org/10.1080/03043790701276874
3. Hollebrands, K.F.: High school student's understanding of geometric transformation in the context of a technological environment. J. Math. Behav. **22**(1), 55–72 (2003). https://doi.org/10.1016/S0732-3123(03)00004-X
4. Noss, R., Hoyles, C.: Windows on Mathematical Meanings. Springer, Dordrecht, no. 1984 (1996). https://doi.org/10.1007/978-94-009-1696-8
5. Wheatley, G.H.: Spatial sense and mathematics learning. Natl. Counc. Teach. Math. **37**(6), 10–11 (1990)
6. Stieff, M., Uttal, D.: How much can spatial training improve STEM achievement? Educ. Psychol. Rev. **27**(4), 607–615 (2015). https://doi.org/10.1007/s10648-015-9304-8
7. Blotnicky, K.A., Franz-Odendaal, T., French, F., Joy, P.: A study of the correlation between STEM career knowledge, mathematics self-efficacy, career interests, and career activities on the likelihood of pursuing a STEM career among middle school students. Int. J. STEM Educ. **5**(1), 1–15 (2018). https://doi.org/10.1186/s40594-018-0118-3
8. Gülkılıka, H., Uğurlub, H.H., Yürükc, N.: Examining students' mathematical understanding of geometric transformations using the pirie-kieren model. Kuram ve Uygulamada Egit. Bilim. **15**(6), 1531–1548 (2015). https://doi.org/10.12738/estp.2015.6.0056
9. Yi, M.: International journal of mathematical education in mathematics education graduate students' understanding of trigonometric ratios. Int. J. Math. Educ. Sci. Technol. **47**(7), 1028–1047 (2016). https://doi.org/10.1080/0020739X.2016.1155774
10. Weber, K.: Connecting research to teaching: teaching trigonometric functions: lessons learned from research. Math. Teach. **102**(2), 144–150 (2008)
11. Rohimah, S.M., Prabawanto, S.: Student' s difficulty identification in completing the problem of equation and trigonometry identities. Int. J. Trends Math. Educ. Res. **2**(1), 34–36 (2019)
12. Kozhevnikov, M., et al.: Revising the visualizer-verbalizer dimension: evidence for two types of visualizers revising the visualizer – verbalizer dimension: evidence for two types of visualizers. Cogn. Instr. **20**(1), 47–77 (2002). https://doi.org/10.1207/S1532690XCI2001
13. Ashour, Z., Yan, W.: BIM-powered augmented reality for advancing human-building interaction. In: Proceedings of the 38th eCAADe Conference, TU Berlin, Berlin, Germany, vol. 1, pp. 169–178 (2020). http://papers.cumincad.org/data/works/att/ecaade2020_499.pdf

14. Shaghaghian, Z., Yan, W., Song, D.: Towards learning geometric transformations through play: an AR-powered approach. In: Proceedings of 2021 5th International Conference Virtual Augmented Simulations (2021).https://doi.org/10.1145/3463914.3463915
15. Keshavarzi, M., Parikh, A., Zhai, X., Caldas, L.: SceneGen: generative contextual scene augmentation using scene graph priors, arXiv Prepr. arXiv2009.12395, September 2020. https://doi.org/10.1145/nnnnnnn.nnnnnnn
16. Maghool, S.A.H., Moeini, S.H.I., Arefazar, Y.: An educational application based on virtual reality technology for learning architectural details: challenges and benefits. ArchNet-IJAR Int. J. Archit. Res. 12(3), 246 (2018)
17. Anifowose, H., Yan, W., Dixit, M.: BIM LOD + Virtual Reality, ACADIA (2022)
18. Yan, W.: Augmented reality instructions for construction toys enabled by accurate model registration and realistic object/hand occlusions. Virtual Real. 1–14 (2021). https://doi.org/10.1007/s10055-021-00582-7
19. van Garderen, D.: Spatial visualization, visual imager, and mathematical problem solving of students with varying abilities. J. Learn. Disabil. 39(6), 496–506 (2006)
20. Rellensmann, J., Schukajlow, S., Leopold, C.: Make a drawing. Effects of strategic knowledge, drawing accuracy, and type of drawing on students' mathematical modelling performance. Educ. Stud. Math. 95(1), 53–78 (2016). https://doi.org/10.1007/s10649-016-9736-1
21. Pedrosa, C.M., Barbero, B.R., Miguel, A.R., Pedrosa, C.M., Barbero, B.R., Miguel, A.R.: Spatial visualization learning in engineering: traditional methods vs. a WebBased tool. J. Educ. Technol. Soc. 17(2), 142–157 (2014)
22. Kösa, T., Karakuş, F.: The effects of computer-aided design software on engineering students' spatial visualisation skills. Eur. J. Eng. Educ. 3797 (2018). https://doi.org/10.1080/03043797.2017.1370578
23. Sorby, S.A.: Spatial abilities and their relationship to computer aided design instruction. In: Proceedings of ASEE Annual Conference, pp. 4449–4454 (1999)
24. Hayes, J.C., Kraemer, D.J.M.: Grounded understanding of abstract concepts: the case of STEM learning. Cogn. Res. Principles Implications 2(1), 1–15 (2017). https://doi.org/10.1186/s41235-016-0046-z
25. Martín-Dorta, N., Saorín, J.L., Contero, M.: Development of a fast remedial course to improve the spatial abilities of engineering students. J. Eng. Educ. 97(4), 505–513 (2008). https://doi.org/10.1002/j.2168-9830.2008.tb00996.x
26. Kaufmann, H., Schmalstieg, D.: Mathematics and geometry education with collaborative augmented reality. Comput. Graph. 27(3), 339–345 (2003). https://doi.org/10.1016/S0097-8493(03)00028-1
27. Taçgin, Z., Uluçay, N., Özüağ, E.: Designing and developing an augmented reality application: a sample of chemistry education. Turkiye Kim. Dern. Derg. Kisim C Kim. Egit.1(1), 147–164 (2016)
28. Fidan, M., Tuncel, M.: Integrating augmented reality into problem based learning: the effects on learning achievement and attitude in physics education. Comput. Educ. 142, 103635 (2019). https://doi.org/10.1016/j.compedu.2019.103635
29. Ensafi, M., Thabet, W., Devito, S., Lewis, A.: Field testing of mixed reality (MR) technologies for quality control of as-built models at project handover: a case study. Epic Ser. Built Environ. 2, 246–254 (2021)
30. Vassigh, S., et al.: Teaching building sciences in immersive environments: a prototype design, implementation, and assessment. Int. J. Constr. Educ. Res. 00(00), 1–17 (2018). https://doi.org/10.1080/15578771.2018.1525445
31. Lindgren, R., Johnson-glenberg, M.: Emboldened by embodiment: six precepts for research on embodied learning and mixed reality. Educ. Res. 42(8), 445–452 (2013). https://doi.org/10.3102/0013189X13511661

32. Squire, K., Klopfer, E.: Augmented reality simulations on handheld computers. Learn. Sci. **16**(3), 371–413 (2007). https://doi.org/10.1080/10508400701413435
33. Stieff, M., Lira, M.E., Scopelitis, S.A., Stieff, M., Lira, M.E., Scopelitis, S.A.: Gesture supports spatial thinking in STEM. Cogn. Instr. **34**(2), 80–99 (2016). https://doi.org/10.1080/073 70008.2016.1145122
34. Dünser, A., Steinbügl, K., Kaufmann, H., Glück, J.: Virtual and augmented reality as spatial ability training tools. ACM Int. Conf. Proceeding Ser. **158**, 125–132 (2006). https://doi.org/ 10.1145/1152760.1152776
35. Hohenwarter, M.: GeoGebra (2018). https://www.geogebra.org/?lang=en
36. Martin, J., Saorín, J., Contero, M., Alcaniz, M., Perez-lopez, D.C., Mario, O.: Design and validation of an augmented book for spatial abilities development in engineering students. Comput. Graph. **34**, 77–91 (2010). https://doi.org/10.1016/j.cag.2009.11.003
37. de Ravé, E.G., Jiménez-Hornero, F.J., Ariza-Villaverde, A.B., Taguas-Ruiz, J.: DiedricAR: a mobile augmented reality system designed for the ubiquitous descriptive geometry learning. Multimedia Tools Appl. **75**(16), 9641–9663 (2016). https://doi.org/10.1007/s11042-016-3384-4
38. Khan, M., Trujano, F., Maes, P.: Mathland: constructionist mathematical learning in the real world using immersive mixed reality. In: Beck, D., et al. (eds.) iLRN 2018. CCIS, vol. 840, pp. 133–147. Springer, Cham (2018). https://doi.org/10.1007/978-3-319-93596-6_9
39. Widada, W., Herawaty, D., Nugroho, K.U.Z., Anggoro, A.F.D.: Augmented reality assisted by GeoGebra 3-D for geometry learning. J. Phys. Conf. Ser. **1731**(1), 012034 (2021)
40. Khalil, M., Farooq, R.A., Çakiroglu, E., Khalil, U., Khan, D.M.: The development of mathematical achievement in analytic geometry of grade-12 students through GeoGebra activities. Eurasia J. Math. Sci. Technol. Educ. **14**(4), 1453–1463 (2018). https://doi.org/10.29333/ejm ste/83681
41. Kamariah, A.B., Ahmad Fauzi, M.A., Rohani, A.T.: Exploring the effectiveness of using GeoGebra and e-transformation in teaching and learning mathematics. Adv. Educ. Technol. **2**, 19–23 (2010)
42. Fife, J.H., James, K., Bauer, M.: A learning progression for geometric transformations. ETS Res. Rep. Ser. **2019**(1), 1–16 (2019). https://doi.org/10.1002/ets2.12236
43. Shaghaghian, Z., Burte, H., Song, D., Yan, W.: Learning geometric transformations for parametric design: an augmented reality (AR)-powered approach. In: Gerber, D., Pantazis, E., Bogosian, B., Nahmad, A., Miltiadis, C. (eds.) Computer-Aided Architectural Design. Design Imperatives: The Future is Now. CAAD Futures 2021. Communications in Computer and Information Science, vol. 1465, pp. 515–527. Springer, Singapore (2022). https://doi.org/10. 1007/978-981-19-1280-1_31
44. Shaghaghian, Z., Burte, H., Song, D., Yan, W.: Design and evaluation of an augmented reality application for learning spatial transformations and their mathematical representations. In: IEEE Conference on Virtual Reality and 3D User Interfaces Abstracts and Workshops (VRW) (2022)
45. Bonder, G.M., Guay, R.B.: The Purdue visualization of rotations test. Chem. Educ. **2**(4), 1–17 (1997). https://doi.org/10.1007/s00897970138a
46. Khan Academy. https://www.khanacademy.org/math/geometry-home/transformations
47. Hart, S.: Human Performance Research Group, NASA task load index user manual v. 1.0 (1980). https://humansystems.arc.nasa.gov/groups/TLX/
48. Pintrich, P.R., De Groot, E.V.: Motivational and self-regulated learning components of classroom academic performance. J. Educ. Psychol. **82**(1), 33–40 (1990)
49. Alizadeh, B., Behzadan, A.H.: Flood depth mapping in street photos with image processing and deep neural networks. Comput. Environ. Urban Syst. **8**, 101628 (2021)

50. Razavi, M., Alikhani, H., Janfaza, V., Sadeghi, B., Alikhani, E.: An automatic system to monitor the physical distance and face mask wearing of construction workers in COVID-19 pandemic. SN Comput. Sci. 3(1), 1–8 (2021). https://doi.org/10.1007/s42979-021-00894-0
51. Alizadeh, B., Li, D., Zhang, Z., Behzadan, A.H.: Feasibility study of urban flood mapping using traffic signs for route optimization. EG-ICE 2021 Work. Intell. Comput. Eng. (2021). https://arxiv.org/ftp/arxiv/papers/2109/2109.11712.pdf
52. Johnson, L.: Trigonometry : An Overview of Important Topics. OPUS Open Portal t (2016)
53. Lodico, M.G., Spaulding, D.T., Voegtle, K.H.: Methods in Educational Research: from Theory to Practice. Jossey-Bass, San Francisco, vol. 28 (2010)

Chatbots, Robots and Virtual Teachers

Towards Deep Learning-Powered Chatbot for Translation Learning

Moneerh Aleedy[1,2]([✉]), Eric Atwell[1], and Souham Meshoul[2]

[1] School of Computing, University of Leeds, Leeds LS29JT, UK
scmmale@leeds.ac.uk
[2] Information Technology Department, College of Computer and Information Sciences, Princess Nourah Bint Abdulrahman University, Riyadh, Saudi Arabia

Abstract. As a consequence of the recent advances in artificial intelligence and educational technologies, the education sector is witnessing significant changes and transformations through massive use of intelligent systems with the goal to assist students in their learning experience and teachers in delivering academic knowledge in a better way while reducing burnout and stress. Communication, knowledge acquisition, and learning are now possible anytime and anywhere through modern technologies. However, learning translation is a process that requires continuous effort, enthusiasm, and motivation from both students and instructors. While some universities adopt traditional and outdated approaches to translation instruction, others use more innovative ways. Within this context and in order to foster a student-centered translation learning approach, our work focuses on taking advantage of recent advances in machine learning to develop a chatbot to help language learners, especially translators, develop their skills by having a conversation with a chatbot and getting the appropriate Arabic translations of English sentences under study. A general framework is proposed, and a first prototype is developed using a part of bilingual corpora. Another focus of this study is the preprocessing phase used to create a sentence-based paired dataset to train the machine learning model from bilingual corpora. The preliminary results are promising.

Keywords: Artificial intelligence · Chatbots · Education · Translation learning · Machine learning · Bilingual corpora

1 Introduction

Students pass through several phases during their learning journey, starting from admission, then courses registration, academic advising, learning, exams, feedback, and finally graduation. Artificial intelligence (AI) has shown impressive successes in the field of natural language processing (NLP), and the recent success in machine learning has broadened its use. As a result, AI and NLP researchers have taken upon themselves the task of helping students during their journey. One of the AI technologies that are taking the leads recently is the educational chatbot, which is a conversational agent that responds to student queries based on its design purpose.

© The Author(s), under exclusive license to Springer Nature Switzerland AG 2022
P. Zaphiris and A. Ioannou (Eds.): HCII 2022, LNCS 13329, pp. 131–141, 2022.
https://doi.org/10.1007/978-3-031-05675-8_11

AI educational chatbots serve various purposes, such as responding to students' administrative inquiries about courses, objectives, learning outcomes, academic rules, and regulations. Other education chatbots are used to teach courses, conduct exams, and some chatbots just chat with the student to relieve study pressure.

Language and translation learning also benefit from the power of AI technologies by using chatbots to help learners continue conversations in English, Arabic, or many other languages. Also, improve their vocabulary, grammar, and the four language skills: listening, reading, speaking, and writing.

This paper aims to use AI and NLP techniques to create a chatbot to help the translation students and the instructors and supervisors perform a specific translation task by giving alternative Arabic phrases in a particular context for any English sentence provided.

This paper will be structured as follows: Sect. 2 reviews chatbots in language learning, translation learning and discusses challenges in terms of language and translation. Section 3 provided the research methodology used to create a translation chatbot. Finally, in Sect. 4, the conclusion and future work are given.

2 Related Work

2.1 Chatbots in Language Learning

Chatbot technologies have helped language learners practice conversation, improve their vocabulary and grammar for different languages, receive instant feedback about their achievements and motivate them by getting rewards [1, 2].

An excellent example of such a bot is **Vasya**, a Russian mobile application designed to teach English via text, audio, and video instructions. Vasya is called a chatbot, but it is actually an interactive tutorial based on a semi-communicative approach. It requires the learner to read, listen and pronounce words and phrases in English. Vasya has a good sense of humor and easily explains grammar. It's perfect for beginner-level English learners but not suitable for advanced levels. According to its creators, at more advanced levels, learning becomes very complex and requires a human tutor [2].

A virtual English language tutor known as **Andy** English Bot helps users learn and practice English. It allows its users to chat, study new words, learn grammar and play language games in the form of conversations. With Andy, users can practice daily interactions such as greeting and chatting about the weather. It is also possible to learn how to ask and answer questions. However, Andy fails to remember previous conversations and talks too fast, so; students cannot understand and respond [1, 3].

Duolingo is one of the most popular language-learning chatting platforms. It aims to improve general language skills through games and practice speaking with chatbots. Moreover, virtual language tutors help users to learn a new language comfortably without the embarrassment of miscommunicating with native speakers, and it supports more than 23 different languages [1, 2].

GenieTutorPlus is another example of language-teaching chatbots. It automatically detects and corrects grammatical errors in learners' sentences and improves their ability to speak a foreign language by returning the corrected results and giving better expressions [4].

2.2 Translation Learning

Foreign language learners frequently use translation to facilitate language learning and acquire a new language. Although translation has played different roles in language teaching for students from different social backgrounds, most educators agree that translation is a powerful tool to help students understand foreign words and expressions more confidently and express ideas in the target language [5].

The researchers in [5] explore some strategic use of translation in English learning that enhances English skills, including reading, writing, listening, and speaking. The first strategy is learning by linking the new words to their mother-language equivalent; they found this method more effective than learning vocabulary in context. Moreover, another strategy involves using technology aids such as dictionaries, notes, electronic translation machines, etc. Finally, interaction with other students.

The approaches most frequently used in translation courses are: comparing two translations, familiarizing with collocations, expressions, and terms, conducting group discussions, editing the target text, and using translation tools such as dictionaries and general and specialized encyclopedias [6].

Furthermore, many researches on the use of parallel bilingual or multilingual corpora in classrooms have shown potential benefits for translation students. The teachers can use such combinations in the classroom to introduce students to a set of parallel texts that include cases from both the source and target languages. This can help students increase their awareness and enhance their translation skills by studying and reflecting on how professional translators can achieve different types of translation [7]. Moreover, translation teachers can also use a monolingual target language to introduce students to different styles of the target language and to encourage them to explore and observe how the target language is used authentically by native speakers. This action enhances students' knowledge and helps them to become more professional and independent [8]. The use of corpus methods to assess the quality of students' translations can be linked to other digital tools that are useful to both teachers and researchers in the field of translation. Teachers can implement digital language databases (online collection), online dictionaries based on parallel corpora, or machine translation platforms in their courses. The motivational potential of using these tools, on the part of students, is very high, as in all cases when didactic methods intersect with real-life interests (for example, comparing Google Translate with the target set of texts for classes) [9].

In a study on 47 undergraduate EFL students enrolled in a translation course in two Moroccan Universities, the study measured the students' abilities in English-Arabic and Arabic-English translation. The students' ability in English-Arabic translation is greater than their ability in the Arabic-English version. However, the overall scores that students got in English-Arabic are above average and below average in Arabic-English, suggesting that these acceptable values are not at the expected level of ability in both types of translation [5]. This indicates a strong need to enrich this field with research to develop students' translation levels.

2.3 Challenges

Chatbots are developed for many languages such as English, Arabic, French, etc. However, each language has its own sentence structure, punctuation rules, and the use of spaces, which is a barrier for current chatbots to deal with [10, 11]. For English chat-bots, the authors [10] mentioned several points that affect the efficiency of chatbot conversations; the most important ones include the inability to recognize grammatical errors and similar meanings questions. Moreover, information retrieval from a database is not realistic; two questions may look different in terms of words but have the same meaning, so similarity measures should be used to eliminate differences [10, 12].

On the other hand, the Arabic language chatbots have many linguistic complexities because of the different types of Arabic language: Classical, Modern, and Colloquial. First, classical Arabic, which is used in the Quran, is more complex in grammar and vocabulary. The second type is Modern Arabic, which is considered the official language of the Arab countries and is used in everyday language, education, and media. Finally, in Colloquial Arabic, the third type, the grammar, and vocabulary are less sophisticated. However, different Arab countries have different Colloquial Arabic, and most people use it in their everyday spoken conversations and informally writing [13]. Moreover, Arabic writers make very common mistakes in spelling some problematic letters, such as Alf Hamza and Ta Marbouta. Morphological richness Arabic words are influenced by a large number of features such as gender and numbers. Also, verbs, adjectives, and pronouns are all gender-specific, requiring the chatbot to have two different responses systems for male and female users. As in other languages, Arabic has its own set of unique dialogue expressions, for example, while the English greeting expression "good morning" gets the answer "good morning", the Arabic equivalent greeting " صباح الخير" "Morning of Goodness" gets the answer " صباح النور" "Morning of Light" [14, 15, 16]. Moreover, Arabic is considered a pro-drop language in which the subject of the verb can be identified implicitly in its morphology; the subject is embedded in the verb, unlike in English. For example, the sentence " ذهبت إلى الحديقة" in Arabic can be expressed as "I went to the park". The subject she and the verb went are represented in Arabic by the singular verb " ذهبت" [17]. A collaboration between linguists and computer scientists is required to overcome these challenges.

3   Proposed Framework

The framework we proposed in this paper consists of two main stages offline, and online. In the offline stage, we first understand the main domain of the research. Then we study the data and understand all of its components. After that, we manipulate the data to make it ready to use as conversational data. The last phase in the offline stage is working on the machine learning model, which includes planning, building, and evaluating.

On the other hand, direct communication with the user occurs in the online stage. The user uses the interface to send the question to the chatbot, which is then processed and fed to the trained model to get the appropriate response and send it back to the user. Figure 1 illustrates the general framework.

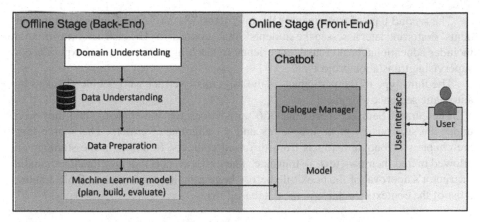

Fig. 1. The general framework

3.1 Domain Understanding

A series of interviews were conducted with a member in the Translation Department at the language college at Princess Nourah bint Abdulrahman University, Riyadh, Saudi Arabia, to identify the needs in the teaching and learning Translation from English to Arabic languages. Moreover, the meetings illustrated the challenges that faculty members face and discussed the best way to use AI technologies to support translation teaching and learning based on the student, teacher, and supervisors' needs. As a result, the following three main problems are identified:

- Give suggestions for alternative phrases translations.
- Highlights common translation mistakes.
- Assessing the students' translation projects based on students' previous translation scores from Saudi Learner Translator Corpus (SauLTC).

This paper will focus on the first problem: giving suggestions for alternative phrases translations.

3.2 Data Understanding

The proposed corpus is the Saudi Learner Translator Corpus (SauLTC) [18], part of the "Design and Build the Saudi Bilingual Blog for Translation Learners" project funded by PNU. It is an English-Arabic translation corpus composed of three sub-corpora and three participants profiles.

The first corpus is English student source text; the second and third corpora include two versions of the translations to the Arabic language: the draft translation, which is the student's first attempt to translate the source text on her own; and secondly, the post-feedback final translation.

The collection of SauLTC involves three types of participants. The first and primary type of the participant is the student who produced the translation. The student profile contains information related to the student translator, the source, and the translated text.

The second type of participant is the instructor, who provided feedback on the students' drafts and later assessed the students' final submission. The instructor information includes educational background, experience in teaching translation, and experience in supervising translation projects.

The third type of the participant is the alignment verifier who double-checked the automatic sentence alignment.

The current SauLTC corpus has 366 translations for 366 students, and they were under the supervision of 48 instructors and 23 alignment verifiers. The source texts are chapters or booklet extracts from different contexts. In addition, the students are allowed to find their own texts to translate. The only caveat is that they had to obtain the instructor's approval of the book title before beginning implementation. Table 1 shows a list of the contexts available in the database [18].

Table 1. SauLTC contexts

Context	Number of texts in the database under each context
Health	109
Psychology	41
Self-help	66
Business	51
Parenting	12
Language	12
Religion	1
Education	28
Biography	1
Autobiography	20
Nutrition	11
Management	1
Fiction	7
Social sciences	1
Sciences	3
History	2
Total	**366**

3.3 Data Preparation

We received the corpus as an SQL dump file, and then we extracted the data in CSV format to make it easier to study and analyze. We used python to extract the data, and as a result, we got 19 tables. As this research focuses on giving alternative phrases in Arabic, we explore the file table in detail, see Table 2.

Table 2. File table details.

Column name	Description
ID	Row sequence number
Type	Type of translation (SOURCE, DRAFT, FINAL)
GroupNumber	Translation file group number
TransID	Translator ID
Version	Translation version
Year	Translation submission year
Text	The English or Arabic text
Genre	The classification of the text

After extracting the file table, we explore the data and select the "Health" context because it has the largest translated texts. The database contains 109 different translation texts under the Health category. In addition, the following steps are performed using python and jupyter Notebook:

- Select Health context texts.
- Remove the unnecessary columns (ID, groupNumber, version, Year).
- Remove the draft text rows since we need the final revised Arabic translation from the English source text.
- Modifying the data to create English-Arabic pairs.
- Split the source and target texts into sentences based on the ".".
- Remove numbers.
- Replace "″″" with "″″" in all texts.
- Expanding English contractions.
- Remove punctuation and New Line(\n).
- Lowercase all English text.
- Manually check and correct the divided sentences.

Table 3 shows a sample of the data after applying preprocessing steps.

Table 3. Sample of the data after applying the preprocessing steps.

	English	Arabic
0	the stress of misunderstanding i have met countless people with autism who misread social situations and behavior and even after someone tries explaining what they had not grasped they still do not understand	الضغوط الناتجة من سوء الفهم لقد التقيت بالعديد من الناس المصابين بالتوحد والذين يفهمون الأوضاع والتصرفات الاجتماعية بشكل خاطئ والذين لن يفهموا مهما حاول الناس الشرح لهم مالم يستطيعوا إدراكه
1	enduring that experience again and again takes its toll	ومرورهم بهذه التجربة مرارا وتكرارا يسبب لهم الحزن
2	knowing i am supposed to understand this but no matter how hard i try i cannot causes frustration unhappiness and anxiety	ومعرفتي بأني مهما بذلت من جهد شديد لأفهم لن أستطيع يسبب لي التعاسة والحزن والقلق
3	many react by shutting down in the face of social encounters or simply avoiding them	ويتعامل العديد من المصابين بالتوحد مع المرض عن طريق الانغلاق عن اللقاءات الاجتماعية أو تجنبها
4	some turn inward and experience depression	والبعض الآخر يعايش الاكتئاب وينغلق على نفسه
5	selfesteem suffers as they ask why do not i understand this what is wrong with me am i stupid social understanding is only one kind of being smart	كما أنهم يعانون من عدم الثقة بالنفس ويتساءلون لماذا أنا وما لا أفهم هذا ؟ ما العيب الذي أعاني منه ؟ هل أنا غبي الذكاء الاجتماعي إلا نوع واحد من أنواع الذكاء
6	you can be brilliant in many other ways and still struggle with grasping facial expressions and other subtle cues in social situations	ومن الممكن أن تكون ذكيا بعدة طرق أخرى ومع ذلك ستعاني من عدم فهم بعض تعابير الوجه والإشارات الدقيقة في المواقف الاجتماعية
7	social understanding requires what howard gardner famous for his theory of multiple intelligences called interpersonal intelligence	ويتطلب الذكاء الاجتماعي ماسماه هاورد قاردنر بالذكاء الشخصي والذي عرف بنظريته عن الذكاءات المتعددة
8	a person with strengths in this area can assess the emotions desires and intentions of others across different social situations	والشخص الذي لديه نقاط قوة في هذا المجال قادر على أن يقيم العواطف ورغبات الآخرين في مختلف المواقف الاجتماعية
9	of course someone who struggles with interpersonal intelligence can demonstrate intelligence in for example music math or solving complex puzzles	وبالطبع الشخص الذي لديه ذكاء شخصي من الممكن أن يظهر لديه عبقرية في الموسيقى والرياضيات أو حل الألغاز الصعبة
10	aware of their difficulty many children apologize for themselves almost habitually—even without understanding what they are apologizing for	و دائما مايعتذر الأطفال المصابين بالتوحد عن أنفسهم وذلك لوعيهم بمشكلتهم – حتى إذا لم يفهموا ما يعتذرون عنه
11	they may understand social rules in extremes of black and white	وقد تبدو القوانين الأجتماعيه لديهم أما بيضاء أو سوداء
12	they are making every effort to get it right and if they suspect they have not said the right thing or acted the right way their instinct is to blurt out sorry sorry no matter how many times parents or teachers reassure them they come to expect that they will make mistakes so they automatically apologize	ويبذل هؤلاء الأطفال ما بجهدهم لجعل الأمور صحيحة حتى إذا شعروا بأنهم لم يتكلمون أو يتصرفون بالطريقة الصحيحة دائما تجبرهم فطرتهم على قول أسف أسف مهما طمئنهم والديهم أو أساتذتهم ودائما مايشعرون بأنهم سيخطئون لذلك يقومون بالاعتذار مسبقا
13	living in a state of constant confusion about even ordinary social interactions can mean that when situations arise that are unanticipated or truly unfamiliar it is likely the child will react in unexpected or extreme ways	في الأحداث ويعيشون في حالة من التشتت حتى الأجتماعية الطبيعية مما يعني أن الطفل عادة عندما يواجه أي حدث غير متوقع أو غريب فمن المتوقع أنه سيتصرف بطريقة غير لائقة أو غير مألوفة

(continued)

Table 3. (*continued*)

14	to an observer the behavior can look rash sudden or inexplicable but it is often the result of frustration and anxiety that has been building in the child for some time	ومن وجهه نظر الملاحظ أن هذا التصرف قد يبدو سريع ومفاجئ و لا يمكن تفسيره ولكن عادة يكون نتيجة الإحباط والقلق الذي تجمع داخل الطفل منذ وقت

3.4 Modeling

The infrastructure used for this experimentation involved using python programming language and jupyter Notebook. Before doing any complex modeling, we need to transform the dataset into a numerical format suitable for training. We apply the word tokenization and lemmatize, and then we use doc2bow to convert a list of words into the Bag of Words (BOW) format. We split all the text in the dataset into an array of tokens (words), then we built a vocabulary dictionary that contains all words in the dataset and their corresponding index value. The array of words is then converted to an array of indexes.

In this experiment, we created a retrieval-based chatbot called "TranslatorBot" that uses TF-IDF to match user English sentences with corpora's most relevant Arabic sentence. It is built from scratch using NLTK and GENSIM Libraries.

3.5 Preliminary Result

To make a conversation with the TranslatorBot, the student starts typing in the textbox. The chatbot responds with a message asking the student to enter the English text he/she wants to find alternatives in the Arabic language. To end the conversation, the student typed "bye". Figure 2 shows a sample conversation with the chatbot.

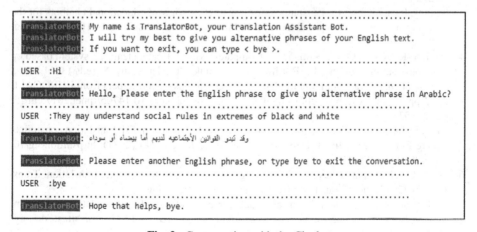

Fig. 2. Conversation with the Chatbot

The preliminary results are promising and give us a clear insight into how the conversation will go through. In addition, TranslatorBot will help students find solutions to their translation problems by quickly reviewing terms and phrases related to the translations they are looking for anytime and anywhere. Moreover, when the chatbot responds with the most relevant Arabic sentences based on the student sentences in English, the students will learn how to translate these sentences, and their translation skills will be improved. The purpose of this chatbot is not to give translations but to show how to translate sentences in different ways.

4   Conclusion and Future Work

This paper highlights two main problems, the first one is creating a chatbot for teaching translation, and the other one is dealing with bilingual corpora. We encourage future researchers to investigate the impact of using deep learning models to solve such problems. Moreover, extracting pair sentences accurately to train the chatbot is very important, as it affects the chatbot performance. For that reason, we also suggest investigating the different methods of creating sentences-based bilingual corpora.

Acknowledgment. I'd like to thank the Deanship of Scientific Research for funding the research project at Princess Nourah bint Abdulrahman University (Grant Reference: 60206/GKD).

References

1. Na-young, K., Cha, Y.J., Kim, H.-S.: Future English learning: Chatbots and artificial intelligence. Multimedia-Assist. Lang. Learn.**22**, 32–53 (2019)
2. Dokukina, I., Gumanova, J.: The rise of chatbots-new personal assistants in foreign language learning. Procedia Comput. Sci. **169**, 542–546 (2020). https://doi.org/10.1016/j.procs.2020.02.212
3. Smutny, P., Schreiberova, P.: Chatbots for learning: a review of educational chatbots for the Facebook messenger. Comput. Educ. **151**, 103862 (2020). https://doi.org/10.1016/j.compedu.2020.103862
4. Choi, S.-K., Kwon, O.-W., Kim, Y.-K.: Computer-assisted English learning system based on free conversation by topic. In: Borthwick, K., Bradley, L., Thouësny, S. (eds.) CALL in a climate of change: adapting to turbulent global conditions – short papers from EUROCALL 2017, pp. 79–85. Research-publishing.net (2017). https://doi.org/10.14705/rpnet.2017.eurocall2017.693
5. Akki, F., Larouz, M.: A comparative study of English-Arabic-English translation constraints among EFL students. Int. J. Linguist. Transl. Stud. **2**(3), 33–45 (2021). https://doi.org/10.36892/IJLTS.V2I3.163
6. Jafari, O.: How approaches to teaching English can be used for teaching translation. Trans. J. **17**(2), (2013). http://translationjournal.net/journal/64teaching.htm
7. Al Hassan, A.: A corpora-driven approach for the Sudanese EFL translation classroom: moving beyond bilingual dictionaries and intuition. ADAB 31–47 (2015). https://doi.org/10.46673/1311-000-035-013
8. Classroom, T.: Moving towards a corpus-driven pedagogy for Omani translation major students. Arab World English J. **12**(1), 40–58 (2021). https://doi.org/10.24093/AWEJ/VOL12NO1.4

9. Mădălina Chitez, L.P.: Digital methods in translation studies: using corpus data to assess trainee translations. B.A.S. British Am. Stud. **26**(26), 241–251 (2020)

10. Nuruzzaman, M., Hussain, O.K.: A survey on Chatbot implementation in customer service industry through deep neural networks. In: Proceedings - 2018 IEEE 15th International Conference on e-Business Engineering, ICEBE 2018, pp. 54–61, December 2018. https://doi.org/10.1109/ICEBE.2018.00019

11. Ayanouz, S., Abdelhakim, B.A., Benhmed, M.: A smart chatbot architecture based NLP and machine learning for health care assistance. ACM Int. Conf. Proc. Ser. (2020). https://doi.org/10.1145/3386723.3387897

12. Niranjan, M., Saipreethy, M.S., Kumar, T.G.: An intelligent question answering conversational agent using Naïve Bayesian classifier (2012). https://doi.org/10.1109/ICTEE.2012.6208614

13. Aljameel, S.S., O'Shea, J.D., Crockett, K.A., Latham, A., Kaleem, M.: Development of an Arabic conversational intelligent tutoring system for education of children with ASD. In: 2017 IEEE International Conference on Computational Intelligence and Virtual Environments for Measurement Systems and Applications, CIVEMSA 2017 - Proceedings, pp. 24–29, July 2017. https://doi.org/10.1109/CIVEMSA.2017.7995296

14. Ali, D.A., Habash, N.: Botta: an Arabic dialect Chatbot, pp. 208–212 (2016)

15. Al-Ghadhban, D., Al-Twairesh, N.: Nabiha: an Arabic dialect chatbot. Int. J. Adv. Comput. Sci. Appl. **11**(3), 452–459 (2020). https://doi.org/10.14569/IJACSA.2020.0110357

16. AlHumoud, S., Al Wazrah, A., Aldamegh, W.: Arabic Chatbots: a survey. Int. J. Adv. Comput. Sci. Appl. **9**(8), 535–541 (2018). https://doi.org/10.14569/IJACSA.2018.090867

17. Alkhatib, M., Shaalan, K.: The key challenges for Arabic machine translation. In: Shaalan, K., Hassanien, A.E., Tolba, F. (eds.) Intelligent Natural Language Processing: Trends and Applications. SCI, vol. 740, pp. 139–156. Springer, Cham (2018). https://doi.org/10.1007/978-3-319-67056-0_8

18. Al-Harthi, M., Al-Saif, A.: The design of the SauLTC application for the English-Arabic learner translation corpus. In: Proceedings of the 3rd Workshop on Arabic Corpus Linguistics, pp. 80–88 (2019). Accessed 8 Dec 2021. https://aclanthology.org/W19-5610

An Educational, Semi-autonomous Telepresence Robot Called Sally

Selene Caro-Via(✉) 🆔, Albert Garangou-Culebras🆔, Alex Falcó-Olmo🆔,
Carlota Parés-Morlans🆔, and Raquel Ros🆔

La Salle - Ramon Llull University, Barcelona 08022, Spain
selene.caro@salle.url.edu

Abstract. Approaching technologies to young users has been broadly tackled in the past years through different methods. From well-known competitions, to commercial kits, students are quickly grasping technology at early stages of life. At La Salle-URL university we have been developing robotics workshops for the past 8 years. Despite the efforts on constantly improving these workshops, we have reached a point where a radical change is required. There is an urgent need to update our workshops programme to offer more challenging content and new methodologies addressing the current students' demands on the one hand. On the other, we also need workshops that integrate in an effective way the inclusion of both on-line and on-site students without being detrimental to either group. In this paper, we propose a new academic methodology for the robotics workshops, along with additional tools. In this sense, we present our robot Sally, a semi-autonomous telepresence robot, that will support the proposed methodology. Students will be introduced to robotic capabilities that are currently being used in research and industry; 3D design; multiple sensors and actuators programming and applications for a voice assistant, among other topics.

Keywords: Educational robotics · Learning methodologies · Telepresence robot

1 Introduction

This project is born as a result of different robotics workshops that are held at La Salle-URL university. The goal of the workshops is to approach robotic technology to young students (aged 16–18-years-old) and more specifically, to young women in order to increase their interest in technological areas. In the workshops, students acquire robotics skills through the design and implementation of a robot. In the past years, we used to cover such competencies by using Lego Mindstorms [2], Arduino [3], 3D Modelling with SketchUp [4] and Tinkercad [5]. However, we have detected that the students attending the workshops already gained initial knowledge related to robotics previously, through one of the many

Supported by La Salle-Ramon Llull University.

existing robotics competitions (such as the First Lego League [1] where they learn block programming and how to build robots, or by developing hands-on projects with other types of hardware, such as Arduino [3]). Moreover, these first experiences with basic technology skills are increasing as the years go by. Many high schools are already offering programming courses (e.g. Python, C, etc.) to students, as these can also participate in many programming competitions addressed to young ages, such as HP CodeWars [7] and International Olympiad in Informatics [8], among others. When they join the workshops at La Salle-URL university, they are in their 2nd year of high school, meaning that their research project could also be related to robotics, increasing their knowledge in Arduino [3] or even Raspberry Pi [6].

On the other hand, we must also take into account the current pandemic situation, where students can only attend the workshop through online platforms. The two pasts programs were held 100% (year 2020) and 8% (year 2021) online. Although we observe a decrease of online access in the past year, we must keep in mind that the pandemic situation can still change from one day to another. In 2020 we had to reduce the number of workshops and adapt the content to the new online methodology, never done before. The previous workshops were strongly focused on hands-on activities, so we had to create new practical approaches mainly oriented to developing software. 2020 s s students worked with a virtual robot and they missed the fact to directly work with a real one. In contrast, 2021 s s students had a chance to work with physical components (e.g. Arduino) within the laboratories. However, the pandemic situation did not allow sharing objects, so only one person in the team could touch the wires and components. Moreover, once the workshop ended, we had to fully clean all components touched (complicating the task since most electronics cannot be cleaned with regular products).

Thus, there is an urgent need to update our workshops programme to offer more challenging content and new methodologies addressing the current students' demands on the one hand. And on the other, we also need workshops that integrate in an effective way the inclusion of both on-line and on-site students without being detrimental to either group.

We therefore propose the creation of a new programme where students learn with a bespoke robot. There are two key requirements that we must take into account when designing the workshop programme: (1) the design of the robot to be used must allow learning advanced aspects in robotics in a novel way tailored to high school students and (2) to allow online access to remote students so they can also actively participate in the tasks developed on-site. Among all the existing types of robots, we have opted for a semi-autonomous telepresence robot because it contains many capabilities used in robots used nowadays. The robot, called Sally, is being created by members of the robotics's club of La Salle.

This paper is structured as follows: We first introduce existing robots for educational purposes. Next, we proposed the methodology to be applied in La Salle's workshops. We then describe the design of our robot Sally, i.e. the tool to achieve the learning goals, and finally, we provide conclusions of our project.

2   State-of-the-Art

Nowadays there are many companies that are focused on introducing technology knowledge to students. As already mentioned, the First Lego League [1] is a well-known robotics competition addressed at students from primary to high schools (children between 4 and 16 years-old). This competition has the participation of 110 countries, which corresponds to more than 679.000 of people. Here in Spain and Andorra 17.500 students participate in such competition. In this competition participants elaborate a research project; design, build and program a robot; and participate in a final tournament that tests their skills and learning. Such research and robot design change the topic each year.

VEX [15] is another well-known robotics competition. It has different categories depending on the age of the students, starting with 4-years-old children. These students learn programming, electronics and mechanical skills while they build and program a robot for such competitions. They can use different languages to program their robots: Scratch [11], Python and C++. The material used to build such robots is plastic or aluminium.

Arduino [3] has also extended its offer towards educational tools for STEAM classes that empower and support students as they progress through middle school (ages between 11 and 14), high school (ages between 14 and 17), and university (students older than 17 years old). For high school students, they have Internet of Things (IoT) kits and some applications and programs to conduct scientific experiments and to guide students through the fundamental concepts of electronics and coding.

There are also companies that offer robots to entertain and teach children. In these cases, the goal is not to build the robot itself (it is already assembled), but to give a basic tool to start learning programming skills. It is the case of Aisoy [9], Robobo [10], and Turtlebot [12]. Moreover, Aisoy and Robobo are used to teach children different kind of subjects such as maths or learning foreign languages.

Aisoy [9] started in Spain in 2009 creating a social robot, Aisoy1. It was revolutionary, emotional and democratic (both robot and child take decisions together). It was a quite innovative robot at that time. With Aisoy1, children from 8 to 12 years old learned to program with Scratch [11]. As it was designed to be a member of the family, it had Artificial Intelligence (AI) and could express feelings. Nowadays they have developed two different models: Aiko (for children from 6 to 99 years old) and KiK Robot ().

- Aiko, for children between 6 and 99-years-old (Fig. 1 (a)), is going to be released this Spring 2022. It is an affective, helpful and cooperative friend. It plays with children and also can be a mentor to learn new languages (English, Spanish). It can develop children's STEAM and socio-emotional skills through play-based activities and conversations.
- KiK, for children between 8 and 12-years-old (Fig. 1 (b)), is fiscally similar to Aisoy1. It is designed to teach coding skills to children. It develops STEM skills while they create a personal assistant, a character, a game, in short, whatever it comes to their minds. All these, by using AI and Scratch.

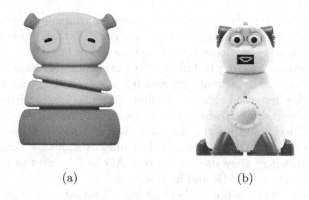

(a)   (b)

Fig. 1. Aisoy robots. (a) Aiko [36]. (b) KiK robot [37].

Robobo [10] (Fig. 2 (a)) is created by MINT; a company from A Coruña (Galicia, Spain). Robobo [10] consists in a mobile base where a smartphone is placed. The base simulates the body of the robot, while the smartphone simulates its brain and face. It has many sensors and capabilities such as tactile sensors, face, colour and shape detection, text to speech, sound recognition and emotion expression. It can be programmed with Scratch [11], Python or ROS (well-know robot framework broadly used in research and industry [20]) adapting to the knowledge of the student.

Turtlebot [12] (Fig. 2 (b)) is a low-cost robot kit with open-source software. It was created in November 2010. Its main idea is that students can add items and accessories to the robot in order to improve it. It works with ROS [20], thus enabling the use of libraries for visualization, planning, and perception, control and error handling. Thus, it has been extensively used in universities where students start to learn ROS [20].

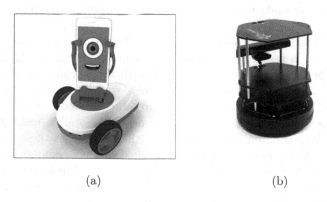

(a)   (b)

Fig. 2. Educational robots. (a) Robobo [38]. (b) Turtlebot 2 [39].

There are other types of projects that focus on introducing technology to children. Jurado et al. [21] used a robot called KIBO to teach technological skills to 5 groups of 15 students aged 4–6 years old during the academic course 2017/2018. Besides acquiring technical skills, students also improved their collaborative, communicative, creativity and behaviour skills. A similar project is DOPPLER [22], where the authors use robotics and activities with subjects such as maths and physics to help students acquire such competencies. In [23], Giang et al. taught 'Media and informatics' and 'Maths' using the Bee-Bot robot in a Primary School using Online Distance Learning. A somehow similar project is Robotikum [24], where they use the robot NAO to develop the computational thinking of students in middle and high school.

At La Salle, we had a robot, called LSMaker [13] that was given to first grade year students. The goal was to give students a basic wheel-based mobile robot that students would use through the different undergraduate years to consolidate the knowledge (e.g. programming, electronics) acquired through lectured sessions. In a similar way, Seng [25] built two robots using Actobotics and goBilda, aluminium-based construction systems, used for undergraduate projects and as research with robots. Lopez-Rodriguez et al. [26] created Andruino-R2, a modular, extensible, open and low-cost robot based on Android and Arduino, which is also compatible with ROS. It is an educational tool used in vocational training labs and classrooms, engineering courses, e-learning and massive open online courses (MOOCs). In [27], Untergasser et al. present an educational framework to train robotics engineers on all the necessary areas involved in robotics (electronics, mechanics and programming). Its goal is to provide different levels of complexity to foster students' individual abilities.

On the other hand, we also want to talk about semi-autonomous telepresence robots, as our final goal is to create one. To start with, we must say that many semi-autonomous telepresence robots have been created for different purposes. OriHime-D [28] is one example of semi-autonomous telepresence robot (Fig. 3 (a)). It weighs 20 kg. and works as a waiter in a Tokyo café. It is 1.20 m high robot that works thanks to the movements ordered from a distance by a disabled person.

Pepper [29] is a social robot created by SoftBank Robotics Corp (Fig. 3 (b)) that can be also a semi-autonomous telepresence robot. It weighs 28 kilos and it is 1.21 m height. Its height is designed with the purpose of facilitating the communication between the robot and the human, whether the human is standing or sitting. It has been used in elder care and child education. In fact, they sold 2000 robots in Japan for educational purposes. Tanaka et al. [30] created a scenario in which children learnt together with the robot at their home environments from a human teacher who gave the lesson from a remote classroom. The teacher appeared in the Pepper's chest display and children could select a program by touching it. Not all semi-autonomous telepresence robots have to have a humanoid appearance, one example of it is Ohmni (Fig. 3 (c)) from Ohmni Labs [31]. It measures 142.2 cm and it has a base of 35.3 × 43.7 cm. It is used in healthcare, education, industries, senior care and for telework.

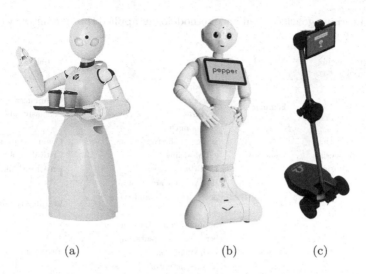

(a)   (b)   (c)

Fig. 3. Semi-autonomous telepresence robots. (a) OriHime-D [40]. (b) Pepper [41]. (c) Ohmni [42].

To summarize this section, we have explained different approaches to introduce technologies, and more specifically robotics, to young students from a broad range of ages. We started reviewing well-known competitions focused on providing first experiences in robotics. However, they do not use yet advanced developments in robotics. Next, we talked about robots used to teach programming skills through robotics (Aisoy and Roboho). Since these are already assembled, students will not acquire mechanical or electronics experience with them. The Turtlebot is a good platform to start with as it has the possibility to add external components, such as cameras to teach vision, or robotic arms, for manipulation. However, this platform does not fulfill our expectations because of its low stability while moving around. Hence, opted for developing our own robot to be used in the workdshops as described in next section.

3   Learning Methodologies

As already introduced, the goal of the robotics workshops is that students acquire notions of robotics, from designing to developing a simple robotic application. To this end, they will use Sally, a semi-autonomous telepresence robot, as it requires capabilities that are key in robotics nowadays. More complex robots rely on these capabilities. Therefore, through simplified examples that students will face while working with Sally, they will be introduced to basic skills in robotics that they will further develop if they opt to studying robotics in the future.

There are 4 robotics workshops at La Salle, lasting 4 h each. Each workshop contains a theoretical and a practical session. Table 1 summarizes the learning goals, content and methodologies applied throughout the workshops. We next describe them in more detail.

Table 1. Learning goals, content and methodologies applied throughout the workshops.

Workshop	Learning objectives	Method	Content	Soft-skills
1	Robotics 3D design 3D printing	Seminar	Introduction History Features Embodiment	Communication skills Persuasive ability
		Hands-on	Design of the robot 3D Modeling 3D Printing bases	Communication skills Critical thinking Creative thinking
2	Electronics Programming	Seminar	How sensors/actuators/ processors work and types AI Manipulation / Locomotion	Learning capabilities
		Hands-on	Scratch implementation with simple examples of sensors/actuators/processors	Teamwork
		Project-based	Sally introduction Program robot behaviour Initial computer vision applications	Flexibility Teamwork Decision-making Problem-solving Leadership
3	Interaction Ethics Programming	Seminar	HRI Social Robotics Verbal & Non-verbal interaction Ethics in robotics	Initiative
		Project-based	Dialog management Non-verbal interaction through facial expressions	Flexibility Teamwork Decision-making Problem-solving Leadership
4	Programming	Seminar	Navigation SLAM	Learning capabilities
		Project-based	Creation of the class map Localization of the robot inside such map Provide a goal to Sally	Flexibility Teamwork Decision-making Problem-solving Leadership

3.1 Workshop 1: What is a Robot?

Understanding and discussing what is a robot, its main features, and its embodiment design (which greatly varies depending on its application). As a practical exercise, the students will design their own social and semi-autonomous telepresence robot, according to a given set of requirements. First, they will draw different designs and, later, they will use 3D modelling tools to implement it. Thus, they will not only apply the learnings of the first part of the session, but they will also learn key aspects to take into account while designing for 3D printing. At the end of the session, each student will have its own 3D printed robot model.

3.2   Workshop 2: Sensing, Acting and Reasoning

This workshop focuses on the three essential capabilities of a robot. How to understand our surrounding world (sensing), how to reach our goal based on that information (reasoning) and how to act on it (actuators). In terms of sensing, we will discover different types of sensors, from simple ones that allow us to model immediate and local information (e.g. light sensors, bumpers...), to complex ones, which enable advanced world models such as object and activity recognition (e.g. lidar, cameras, ...). Regarding the reasoning, we will program different processors that either allow a low level control of components (e.g. Arduino. Raspberry Pico) that can react to local sensed information, to more powerful ones (e.g. Raspberry Pi 4B), that can reason in a deliberated manner to achieve long-term goals. In this sense, we will include basic notions of Artificial Intelligence (AI), its evolution as it has been gaining huge relevance in the past 20 years in the field of robotics becoming now an essential capability in advanced robots. Finally, we will study the different types of actuators robots may need in order to interact with the real world, focusing on manipulation (to allow interaction with objects) and locomotion (to allow the robot to move around the world). With respect to hands-on work, we will first focus on experimenting with less complex components (simple sensors, motors and Arduino) so the students can start from scratch implementing simple examples. The second block of the session will initiate the project-based approach adopted in the remaining workshops, where the students will apply the concepts learnt throughout the sessions by implementing or extending the existing modules of the Sally system. After introducing the robot Sally to the students for the first time, they will focus on programming Sally, to deep into the reasoning component of the system. The robot will already be mounted, so they can focus on the high-processing features of the system, such as the robot behavior (e.g. receptionist robot) and initial computer vision applications. Advance locomotion aspects, i.e. autonomous navigation, will be tackled in the last workshop session.

3.3   Workshop 3: Interaction and Ethics in Robotics

Given the great advances in the robotics field, robots are quickly moving from industrial settings to home/working settings as services systems. As such, the need for designing robots capable of interacting with people has challenged the robotics research community to integrate the human in the loop to whom the robot shall provide a service as part of its functional goal. Thus, the Human-Robot Interaction (HRI) is a young field that emerges to study how robots shall naturally interact with people without forcing the user to have any technical knowledge on how to do so. A sub-field of HRI is that of Social Robotics, which focuses on provided social intelligence to robots. Humans are social entities by nature, and the most simplistic interaction requires basic social skills that allow us to easily communicate with each other. If we expect robots to be part of our everyday lives, these should also be provided with a minimum set of social skills. Such shift on how we foresee the integration of robots in society, inevitably implies seriously considering ethical concerns in this regard. To what extent should robots be "humanized"? What are the implications of introducing robots in our homes? How is our privacy affected? Who will be responsible for any collateral damage either physical, psychological or emotional?

This workshop will then introduce the field of HRI to students, focusing on verbal and non-verbal interaction methods, and raise awareness of the ethical implications on integrating such technology in society. The first block of the workshop will introduce theoretical concepts of HRI and ethics, combining debates on a set of ethical dilemmas (e.g. autonomous-driving cars, or robot-carers) giving space for students to think about the social challenges they will need to face in the future while openly discussing their views. The students will then continue implementing their project. On the one hand, they will integrate in Sally their own dialogue manager system based on the Alexa voice-assistant, covering verbal behavior notions. And on the other hand, they will introduce basic non-verbal behavior through facial expressions displayed in Sally's screen.

3.4   Workshop 4: Autonomous Navigation

Finally, the last workshop addresses a basic skill for mobile robots: navigation, the ability to autonomously travel around the environment to reach a specific location. A general overview of the algorithms developed, i.e. simultaneous localization and mapping (SLAM), will be described, as well as existing tools to achieve such task. The students will then learn to use such tools and configure them. The hands-on project will consist on building a map of the classroom, localizing the robot inside such map and evaluating the navigation capabilities of the robot by providing different goals to reach. To this end, a basic interaction task will have to be developed so the user can indicate the robot's goal.

3.5   Additional Skills

Besides the aforementioned workshops, we foresee the following additional skills students can acquire through the robotics workshop (from low to high complexity):

- Learning to weld electronics components by explaining different 74 LS series chips [16], such as logic gates, standard combinational blocks, and so on. Depending on the knowledge of the students, we could provide them a circuit to weld in a circuit board.
- Learning multitasking programming. Using Arduino or Raspberry Pico, the students will learn how to run several processes in parallel.
- Applying computer vision methods. Using a camera and AI, students will create applications using the MediaPipe library [32] to recognize their faces, hands postures, and so on.

– Learning to use microprocessors and databases. Once the students have a solid base in Arduino [3], they can continue developing their skills by using ESP32 or ESP8266, which are two processors created by ESPRESSIF [17]. These processors can be programmed using the Arduino IDE (nothing new will learn from here) but include wireless connection. Thanks to this connection, they will be able to get access to a date base, such as Firebase [18], so they can also have a first experience with the use of data bases.
– Learning Brain-Computer Interfaces (BCI) with OpenBCI [19]. By analysing brain activity, students can control the robot with their brain.
– Learning the ROS framework (Robot Operating System [20]). Based on the ROS communication system, students can program the robot through the implementation of different nodes that share information to achieve a simple task.

3.6 Application in Other Workshops

The university also offers other types of workshops which could benefit from the use of Sally. Thus, students with other thematic interests, can also have an opportunity to engage with robots through different perspectives. To illustrate, they can develop an app to control a robot in the smartphone applications workshop and, in the robotics workshop, program the movement depending on what the robot receives from the app. The next list these workshops and its respective proposed exercise that relates to Sally:

1. The website workshop, where students can create a web interface to control the robot (similar to the web-based interfaces offered by commercials robots). The main control features are: to visualise the images provided by the robot camera, send written utterances that the robot can then say out loud and finally, control its motion to teleoperate it around the environment.
2. The smartphone applications workshop, where the students can develop an app to control Sally's motors either through the use of buttons or by panning and tilting the smartphone (a similar app has been previously developed at the university to control the LSMaker [14]).
3. The video games and virtual environments workshop, where students can design a virtual environment to play with a virtual Sally, similar to VEX [15]. Therefore, they can create a virtual environment to test their programs to, lately, test it in the real Sally.
4. The cybersecurity and ethical hacking workshop, where they can learn how to protect the robot and website from hacking.

4 Sally Implementation

As previously explained, we have developed a semi-autonomous telepresence robot called Sally, as a tool for acquiring competencies in the robotics field. In this section we are going to explain the design of Sally and the hardware included related to the different workshops.

The design of Sally has been inspired by the TurtleBot 2 [12] and Pepper [29] robots by combining the stackability of the first, and the height usability of the second. Thus, Sally is designed with a stackable base to allow a modular approach so it can be easily adaptable to different applications and learning needs as shown in Fig. 4. You can easily access each shelf in order to add or remove components, or even remove the whole shelf in order to modify it or replace it. It has a main vertical metal frame that joins the different shelves, reaching a comfortable enough height to interact with. The robot's width is designed to fit through doors, elevators, aisle and common spaces. Finally, its weight is low enough to easily manually move it to relocate it when necessary.

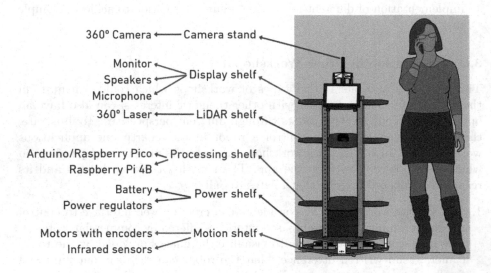

Fig. 4. Design of the robot Sally describing its shelves and main components.

Sally is designed with a minimum set of functionalities which are distributed on different shelves. Such functionalities are the basic ones in order to build a semi-autonomous telepresence robot required for the workshops. We next provide a general description of each shelf and its purpose:

– **Motion shelf**: it includes the wheels, motors and sensors related to motion. In order to explore different locomotion strategies the robot has been provided with four omni-directional wheels to allow its movement in different directions To achieve these movements, each wheel has to be controlled independently. Therefore, Sally includes four motors with encoders to detect how much distance or rotations the wheel has done. Finally, to avoid bumping into steps and falling down, infrared sensors have been placed at each edge to detect distance to the floor. They will avoid movement into a direction where the robot could fall.

As explained in Sect. 3, the content in this shelf is related with session 2 of the robotics workshops. Working with these electronic components students will understand the importance of using simple sensors that allow a reactive response to the complexity of real environments while traveling around.

– **Power shelf**: it contains the battery and voltage regulators for all the robot components. There is no content dedicated to this topic within the workshops sessions presented above. However, it could be used in the future to introduce electronics concepts such as Ohm's law, simple voltage calculations and wiring and soldering.

– **Processing shelf**: it contains Arduino and Raspberry boards. On one hand, a Arduino Mega 2560 R3 or a Raspberry Pi PICO controls the motion and sensors of the motion shelf. The Arduino will enable those students who has no previous experience to learn it. Also, its large number of ports enables us to add more sensors and actuators to the robot if needed in a future. The other option, Raspberry Pi PICO, is a quite new platform, cheaper compared with Arduino boards, and it is not programmed in the common Arduino Language but mainly in different Python flavours and C/C++. Thanks to this feature, advanced students, who have already worked with Arduino, have a change to learn other programming languages widely used in the robotics community, such as Python and other object-oriented languages. The use of microprocessors is addressed in the second session of the workshop series as described in Sect. 3.

On the other hand, a Raspberry Pi 4B with 8GB, the newest Raspberry Pi model with the higher RAM version, controls the robot from a higher point; using ROS. As it is known, the advanced robots use ROS to control and send information to different nodes. Therefore, students will have an introduction to this system and use it in the fourth session of the workshop where, as described in Sect. 3, they will learn navigation.

– **Lidar shelf**: it contains a 360° laser, also called LiDAR. It is used to detect distances to objects in the environment surrounding the sensor. Therefore, we can obtain a 2D distances maps around Sally. This type of sensor is typically used for navigation, where a robot requires a map to travel from one point to another.

We must take into account that the created map is computed from the height where the LiDAR is placed. If we place it close to the floor, it will detect the table legs only, but not the surface of the table. Hence, the map (model of the world) will include a set of columns only. Thus, if Sally tries to navigate around those hypothetical columns, it would end up colliding with the table (since Sally is taller than a table). Therefore, this shelf is placed at a distance of 80 centimetres from the floor, since most tables have such standard height, to detect tables as proper obstacles that need to be avoided accordingly. Notice that no other component should be place in this shelf, to avoid blocking the field of view of the LiDAR.

The content of this topic is addressed in session 4 of the robotics workshops.

– **Display shelf**: it is related to the interaction with humans and, therefore, we can find the 'head' of Sally. To simulate a head, we need a face, microphones to listen to the user and speakers to give a response. For all these reasons and to simplify the building of Sally's head, we decided to use a voice assistant. We have opted for the Amazon Echo Show 8 device, since it has a good sound quality and a screen. The screen facilitates the implementation of facial expressions, focusing on the eyes area. Moreover, we make use of the Alexa skills to provide the dialogue component of the system. This shelf will be introduced in the third workshop.

– **Camera stand**: it includes an extensible support, where a camera is mounted to stream or record videos. We have opted for a 360° field-of-view camera to have full view of the environment around Sally. The captured images are streamed into a web interface designed to process the video and being able to look around as a user.

Since one of the goals of Sally is to interact with users or to be part of the audience, we have to design the appropriate height of the camera to be at a "natural and human" height. If the camera is placed too low, it will capture the bottom of the tables and legs of people around. On the other hand, building a tall robot will make it more unstable and will capture images over the head of people. Thus the final result has an extensible rod with the camera on top to raise it when using the camera and retract it inside the body of the robot when the camera is not needed to avoid shaking. The desired camera height is between 1.4 and 1.5 m. During the workshops, we expect to exploit the camera usage to introduce computer vision notions to students.

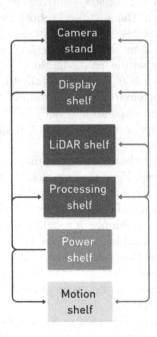

Fig. 5. Block diagram of the relation between the shelves.

In Fig. 5 we can see a block diagram on the relationship among the different shelves. The power shelf provides power to all the other shelves, except for the LiDAR one. The LiDAR gets its power from the Processing shelf since it is directly connected to the processing unit through serial a USB port. On its turn, the Processing shelf has a bidirectional connection to the rest of shelves. This is because it senses the rest of the shelves in order to know the state of the robot and also to send them commands to perform actions.

5   Conclusions and Future Work

In this paper, we have presented a new robot called Sally to be used at La Salle's robotics workshops, where students will learn basic concepts in robotics while adding features to the robot.

As mentioned, Sally includes the necessary hardware and a framework that allows students to learn about sensors and actuators, voice assistants, 3D modeling, and website design amongst others. Besides, students will learn that hardware and software systems are exposed to innacuracies of the real world, and therefore, such imprecision may cause errors in the system performance that they will need to troubleshoot. Hence, students will learn different ways to mitigate those situations such as adding more sensors or programming fault-recovery algorithms.

Students will learn theory and practical skills related to robotics through the four workshops. In the first one, they will be introduced to robotics and start by designing their own robots. In the second workshop they will perform hands on activities to learn about sensors, actuators and processors; they will make Sally to move taking into account the sensors data. The third workshop is related to interaction, where they will develop a chat scene between Sally and a human. Finally, the fourth workshop addresses navigation concepts, where students will create a map of the environment with Sally and navigate through it.

Moreover, when designing Sally we have considered multiple settings where it may prove useful. The robot can be used to teach the basics of navigation systems either remotely or in person, as well as to synchronously stream a university tour to those staying at home. Note that the hardware has been chosen following the current trends in the market, enabling prolonged use. However, we are aware that the hardware included now may become outdated in the future. To this end, Sally's modular design allows an easy replacement of components and materials as new needs may appear.

References

1. First Lego League Homepage. https://www.firstlegoleague.soy/. Accessed 25 Dec 2021
2. Lego Mindstorms EV3 Product page. https://www.lego.com/en-us/product/lego-mindstorms-ev3-31313. Accessed 27 Dec 2021
3. Arduino Homepage. https://www.arduino.cc/. Accessed 25 Dec 2021

4. SketchUp Homepage. https://www.sketchup.com/. Accessed 27 Dec 2021
5. Tinkercad Homepage. https://www.tinkercad.com/. Accessed 27 Dec 2021
6. Raspberry Pi Homepage. https://www.raspberrypi.org/. Accessed 25 Dec 2021
7. HP CodeWars Homepage. http://hpcodewarsbcn.com/. Accessed 25 Dec 2021
8. Olimpiada Informática Española Hompage. https://olimpiada-informatica.org/. Accessed 25 Dec 2021
9. Aisoy Homepage. https://aisoy.com/. Accessed 27 Dec 2021
10. Robobo Homepage. https://theroboboproject.com/. Accessed 27 Dec 2021
11. Scratch Homepage. https://scratch.mit.edu/. Accessed 27 Dec 2021
12. Turtlebot Homepage. https://www.turtlebot.com/. Accessed 28 Dec 2021
13. Albo-Canals, J., Garcia-Casulleras, M., de Cordoba, D., Canaleta, X., Gonzalez-Dachs, E.: The educational robotic platform LSMaker EV1: standardization vs customization. In: 2014 9th Iberian Conference on Information Systems and Technologies (CISTI), pp. 1–5 (2014). https://doi.org/10.1109/CISTI.2014.6877005
14. LSMaker Companion Application in Apple Store. https://apps.apple.com/us/app/lsmaker-companion-la-salle/id1229083709. Accessed 28 Dec 2021
15. VEX Robotics Homepage. https://www.vexrobotics.com/. Accessed 29 Dec 2021
16. 74LS series in Futurlec. https://www.futurlec.com/IC74LS00Series.shtml. Accessed 29 Dec 2021
17. ESPRESSIF Homepage. https://www.espressif.com/. Accessed 29 Dec 2021
18. Firebase Homepage. https://firebase.google.com/. Accessed 29 Dec 2021
19. OpenBCI Homepage. https://openbci.com/. Accessed 29 Dec 2021
20. ROS Homepage. https://www.ros.org/. Accessed 29 Dec 2021
21. Cojo, E.J., Escudero, D.F., Llampallas, X.C.: Acompañamiento a profesores de Infantil para integrar la robótica en el aula: experiencia realizada en cuatro escuelas en Cataluña. V Congreso Internacional sobre Aprendizaje, Innovación y Cooperación. CINAIC 2019, 09 October 2019. https://doi.org/10.26754/CINAIC.2019.0081
22. Anjo, A.B., Amaro, S., Bispo, R., Barbosa, D., Ribeiro, V., Bergano, M.: DOPPLER project: inspiring a new generation in STEM. In: International Conference on Robotics in Education (RiE), RiE 2020, pp. 106–111 (2021). https://doi.org/10.1007/978-3-030-67411-3_10
23. Giang, C., Negrini, L.: Educational robotics in online distance learning: an experience from primary school. In: International Conference on Robotics in Education (RiE), RiE 2021, pp. 34–40 (2021). https://doi.org/10.1007/978-3-030-82544-7_4
24. Zeaiter, S., Heinsch, P.: Robotikum: promoting STEM education in schools using an adaptive learning scenario. In: International Conference on Robotics in Education (RiE), RiE 2020, pp. 3–15 (2021). https://doi.org/10.1007/978-3-030-67411-3_1
25. Seng, J.: Constructing robots for undergraduate projects using commodity aluminum build systems. In: International Conference on Robotics in Education (RiE), RiE 2021, pp. 210–220 (2021). https://doi.org/10.1007/978-3-030-82544-7_20
26. Lopez-Rodriguez, F.M., Cuesta, F.: Andruino-R2: android and Arduino based low-cost ROS-integrated educational robot from scratch. In: International Conference on Robotics in Education (RiE), RiE 2021, pp. 262–273 (2021). https://doi.org/10.1007/978-3-030-67411-3_23
27. Untergasser, S., Hild, M., Panreck, B.: An educational framework for complex robotics projects. In: International Conference on Robotics in Education (RiE), RiE 2021, pp. 94–104 (2021). https://doi.org/10.1007/978-3-030-82544-7_10

28. Takeuchi, K., Yamazaki, Y., Yoshifuji, K.: Avatar work: telework for disabled people unable to go outside by using avatar robots OriHime-D and its verification. In: The 15th annual ACM/IEEE International Conference on Human-Robot Interaction (HRI2020) (2020). https://doi.org/10.1145/3371382.3380737
29. Pandey, A.K., Gelin, R.: A mass-produced sociable humanoid robot: pepper: the first machine of its kind. IEEE Robot. Autom. Mag. 1 (2018). https://doi.org/10.1109/MRA.2018.2833157
30. Tanaka, F., Isshiki, K., Takahashi, F., Uekusa, M., Sei, R., Hayashi, K.: Pepper learns together with children: development of an educational application. In: 2015 IEEE-RAS 15th International Conference on Humanoid Robots (Humanoids) (2015) https://doi.org/10.1109/HUMANOIDS.2015.7363546
31. Ohmni LAbs Homepage. https://ohmnilabs.com/. Accessed 13 Gen 2022
32. MediaPipe Homepage. https://mediapipe.dev/. Accessed 16 Gen 2022
33. Image VEX 123. https://www.vexrobotics.com/media/wysiwyg/VEX_123_3.png
34. Image VEX IQ. https://content.vexrobotics.com/images/vexiq/gen2/vex-iq-gen2-clawbot.png
35. Image VEX V5. https://www.vexrobotics.com/media/catalog/product/cache/d64bdfbef0647162ce6500508a887a85/2/7/276-7040_2.jpg
36. Image Aiko. https://cdn.shopify.com/s/files/1/0228/4703/products/aisoy-robotics-robot-aiko-28140472467594_1200x.png
37. Image KiK Robot. https://s3.eu-central-1.amazonaws.com/robotica-es/uploads/items/ITEM_10801_FOTOPROD.png
38. Image Robobo. http://dream.isir.upmc.fr/UserFiles/Images/robobo_clean2.png
39. Image Turtlebot. https://www.macs.hw.ac.uk/RoboticsLab/wp-content/uploads/2018/11/turtlebot.png
40. Image OriHime-D. https://cdn-xtrend.nikkei.com/atcl/contents/18/00205/00016/01.jpg
41. Image Pepper. https://www.softbankrobotics.com/emea/themes/custom/softbank/images/full-pepper.png
42. Image Ohmni. https://ohmnilabs.com/wp content/uploads/2020/04/Ohmni_Supercam_Robot-e1580413919219.png

The Impact of Avatar Teachers on Student Learning and Engagement in a Virtual Learning Environment for Online STEM Courses

Denise Daniels(✉) and Joon Suk Lee

Virginia State University, St. Petersburg, VA 23806, USA
ddan5700@students.vsu.edu

Abstract. Due to the recent Covid-19 pandemic, we have seen a considerable shift to online education. The pandemic prompted many academic institutions to quickly develop virtual courses and improve pre-existing online courses to deal with the drastic increase of online students. However, the process of creating virtual courses remains largely tedious. With technological advancement, institutions can now offer personalized virtual courses for individual students by automating course content creation. Computer-generated course content can be easily customized to meet individual student needs. This study examines the potential problems associated with virtual learning and evaluates the feasibility of employing computer-generated course content. It also analyzes the influence avatar teachers have on student learning and engagement as a first step in determining the impact of computer-generated courses. The study shows that institutions should ensure video lectures are well designed and utilize an appropriate teacher voice. The study reports mixed feedback from an interview study that explores the impact of human and avatar teachers' physical characteristics on student learning. Some students believed that the avatar teachers were engaging, while some found it distracting. On the other hand, some students did not feel that the teacher's physical characteristics impacted their learning as long as the course material was delivered well.

Keywords: Virtual learning · Avatar teachers · Physical characteristics · Online learning

1 Introduction

The COVID-19 pandemic has created a wide-reaching impact on education. Many schools and universities responded to the pandemic by shutting down non-essential campus operations and blindly shifting away from in-person instructions to teaching remotely. This sudden switch to remote learning has created unequal and negative impacts on students from families of low socioeconomic status [1].

With the advancement of technology in recent years, we have developed solutions to many social and economic issues we face. Given many institutions' abrupt shift to online education, the necessity for a solution to streamline creating online content while also assuring its efficacy in delivery has grown. One potential solution is the use

P. Zaphiris and A. Ioannou (Eds.): HCII 2022, LNCS 13329, pp. 158–175, 2022.
https://doi.org/10.1007/978-3-031-05675-8_13

of technology to generate course content. Today's technology can enable educators to automate the production and customization of online course content. Technologies can be used to generate online lecture videos from pre-written text scripts or tweak existing video lectures' features. For instance, the lecturer's voice, accent, and physical aspects, as well as the language used in the course, can easily be altered. Educators might be able to use such technology to address some of the challenges of online learning.

The goal of this research is twofold. We aim to investigate potential issues associated with virtual learning and experimentally test the possibility of using technology-generated course content.

In a traditional learning environment, social scientists have examined the impact of teacher physical characteristics on students' learning and engagement but have found conflicting results. For example, some studies show that same-race instructors improve students' academic performance [25, 35, 36], while others had mixed results or found no correlations [24, 33, 37]. Similarly, research has identified several factors that can influence learning, including teachers' accents, the language spoken at students' homes, students' socioeconomic status, school quality, religion, teacher-student interactions, and passive instruction [62, 66]. Though these studies show the various ways we might improve learning, implementing these elements into practice in a real classroom environment may be contentious and impracticable. For example, finding lecturers with similar physical characteristics as the students is impractical, if not impossible. Furthermore, dividing students in classrooms based on race and gender to be taught by a specific instructor may result in a slew of discriminatory issues. We also have to consider that there might be other factors that the studies might have failed to take into account. In other words, implementing classroom policies based on the findings of a few studies might yield unintended and irreversible outcomes. Implementing classroom policies should be done cautiously.

However, the online instruction setting provides a unique opportunity to implement and verify the efficacy of such findings. Compared to the traditional setting, changes made to online instruction can relatively easily be undone. For instance, we can examine the effects of teachers' physical characteristics on student learning by providing different versions of online lectures. Such changes can always be undone if the changes do not produce positive results. In addition, there is usually a one-way interaction between the prerecorded teacher and a student in a virtual learning environment, eliminating the many factors and interactions impacting student learning in a traditional setting. When designing virtual courses, we may employ artificial intelligence and machine learning to create computer-generated teachers customized by race, gender, age, and ethnicity. Furthermore, we can utilize computer-generated voices and translate online course videos from one language to another. The ability to easily generate course content may also allow students to choose or customize their own personal teachers. Therefore, as a first step in identifying possible issues with virtual learning and providing technology-generated courses, this study seeks to understand the impact of avatar teachers on student learning and engagement.

2 Literature Review

2.1 Similarity Attraction Theory

According to the similarity attraction theory, people are attracted to others similar to them [11, 14]. Studies have shown that having attribute similarities with a teacher, such as gender, race, ethnicity, and age, boosts a learner's self-efficacy, which leads to better academic performance [6, 67]. With artificial intelligence, machine learning, and other advancements in technology, we can explore similarity-attraction between teacher and student and determine if that improves student learning and engagement in a virtual learning environment, as this may be difficult in a traditional classroom.

"Classrooms are not and can never be neutral sites for the production or reproduction of knowledge. Those of us who step into classrooms as professors and as students do not shed our identities at the door with our coats." (pp. 10, [61])

As Rakow [61] stated, students and educators inevitably bring their identities into the learning process, including gender, ethnicity, and age. Some early studies on classroom interaction have reported incidents of differential faculty behaviors toward a distinctive group of students. For instance, Hall and Sandler [42] argued that female students are disadvantaged in higher education because of professors' differential treatment of students based on their gender. While the study of Hall and Sandler has subsequently and frequently been contested, criticized for being speculative, and counter-argued, it is also true that multiple studies reported gender-biased, differential faculty behaviors. Boersma et al. showed that female instructors provide more extended responses to female students [12]. Constantinople et al. said that instructors, regardless of their gender, are more likely to expand upon male students' comments than that of female students [22]. Jewell and McPherson reported results suggesting that female faculty members are more likely to inflate grades [47]. Dee calls these unintended biases in teachers' expectations of and interaction with students with different gender and ethnicity active teacher effects [26]. Students' perceived accounts of gender-biased faculty behaviors have also been reported. Students see female professors as more often knowing and calling students by their names [24] and encouraging more classroom interactions [7, 24]. In contrast, male professors are perceived to use more offensive humor and make more offensive comments [17, 24].

Furthermore, it is important to note that in addition to the teachers' unintended differential behaviors, which are still consciously remediable, their unchangeable personal traits also impact student learning. The passive teacher effects are triggered by a teacher's personal traits such as gender and ethnicity, not explicit teacher behaviors [26]. Today's educators try their best to be impartial and be value-neutral in their classrooms. Yet, their personal identities spontaneously and unavoidably create differential impacts on students, influencing student learning. For this reason, researchers and educators have long been exploring passive teacher effects. In particular, gender and race interactions in classrooms have been investigated extensively. A number of studies investigated whether demographic similarities between students and instructors influence academic performance (e.g., [16, 36, 44, 65]), retention rates (e.g., [15, 60, 64]) and classroom participation (e.g., [13, 38, 69]).

However, the previous findings on gender, race, and age interactions are often contradictory and inconclusive—for example, several studies exploring gender interactions in the classroom report inconsistent findings. Brooks [13] reported that male students participate more than female students in female-taught classes. Sternglanz and Lyberger-Ficek [69] reported that male students are more likely to dominate discussion in male-taught classes. Fassinger [38], on the other hand, reported that instructor gender does not affect the participation of male students while female students are more likely to participate in female-taught classes.

While retention of female students is found to be higher when their STEM courses are taught by female instructors [60, 64], another study found no evidence that an increase in the number of female faculty members in a department leads to a rise in the number of female majors [15].

The positive same-gender effect on student performance has also been reported multiple times. Lindahl analyzed data on 9th-grade students in Sweden and showed a positive correlation between student test scores and the percentage of teachers of the same gender [56]. Hoffmann and Oreopoulos also reported that same-gender instructors increase the average grade performance of students by 5 percent of its standard deviation [44]. Carrell et al., however, reported that instructor gender has little impact on male students but has a significant effect on female students' academic performance [16]. Robst et al. [64] found that instructor gender has a more significant impact on female students only when their classes have few female students.

Results from studies investigating the same-race effect are also incompatible and inconclusive. For example, Price found evidence that black students are more likely to stay in a STEM major when their STEM courses are taught by black instructors [60]. Evans [35] and Dee [25] reported that the same-race instructors improve students' academic performance. Fairlie et al. reported similar findings that the performance gap between white students and underrepresented minority students falls by 20 to 50 percent when courses are taught by underrepresented minority instructors [36]. Yet, other studies reported mixed results or found no effect at all [33, 34, 37].

It's not surprising that contradictory and inconclusive findings are common, given the numerous other factors that can influence learning in a traditional classroom setting due to teacher-student interaction. It is impossible to identify all the possible factors impacting classroom learning. For instance, the passive teacher effects between a female teacher and a female student in a dominant female classroom would differ from the passive teacher effects between a female teacher and a female student in a male-dominated classroom. The gender and ethnicity of a teacher and the gender and ethnicity of peers can affect student learning. In addition, besides gender and ethnicity, other teacher characteristics can have critical impacts. Compared to an instructor's gender and race, the instructor's instructional skills can have a more significant impact on student learning. Lecture topics and accents of non-native speaking instructional staff are also known to affect student learning [66]. Student learning is further recognized to be influenced by a family's socioeconomic status, family structure, school quality, neighborhood factors, as well as the caste and religious divide between instructors and pupils [62]. Moreover, every utterance and every gesture that instructors make in a classroom and any interactions between an instructor and a student, any interactions amongst the students, and any non-interactions will consequentially impact student learning. Hence, there's always room for another unaccounted factor influencing study results. With a virtual learning environment can eliminate many of these factors affecting a student's learning experience, allowing an effective way to evaluate the similarity-attraction between teacher and student.

2.2 Virtual Learning

Dung [31] defines virtual learning as the use of technology like computers and the internet to connect teachers and students who are physically separated by distance, time, or both. In recent years, many academic institutions started to utilize virtual learning to provide online education to students and eliminate the need to attend classes physically [3, 31, 72]. Virtual courses, according to Dung [31], allowed universities to accept a higher number of students. Dung [31] further reported that virtual courses enable institutions to offer classes to a large number of students minimizing the cost of staffing and travel.

While offering online courses may benefit universities, it often leaves students responsible for securing technology and the internet to attend classes, which may be difficult for many [1]. Several other studies have identified other concerns students have raised with virtual learning. Yang and Cornelius [73] reported that virtual learning facilitated delayed teacher feedback, causing students to grow disengaged and frustrated with a course. Similarly, Young and Norgard [74] found that interactions between instructor and student provided a sense of community. However, when such contact did not occur, students were frequently left doubtful of their knowledge of a topic [74]. Dung's [31] research found that students were also concerned about minimal interaction with other students, which reduced the social aspect of a class that would usually be present if held in person. Other studies found that virtual learning may cause students to feel isolated, unmotivated, and distracted [73, 74]. Dung [31] reported that students complained about the long online class time, which caused exhaustion, boredom, and less engagement.

While some studies have indicated that virtual learning limits interactions [31], other have found that virtual learning is more flexible and allows students to customize their learning experience [27]. Studies reported that students' distance from campus made online learning a convenient option [73, 74]. Students would not need to allow time for travel. Young and Norgard [74] also mentioned that online learning provided students with the flexibility to complete their education despite demanding work and family commitments. Furthermore, compared to a typical classroom environment, where you cannot re-access information taught in real-time, Soffer, Kahan and Nachmas [68] discovered that students frequently re-access learning material more than once when learning virtually, implying that students may choose an order in which to learn.

2.3 Animated Avatars in Education

Pedagogical agents are computer-animated characters designed to help student learning in multimedia learning environments [48]. The possibility of employing pedagogical agents to enhance learning has been explored in recent years [4, 9, 10, 30, 43, 57] because learning is an inherently social process [53, 70]. These studies typically focus on simulating social interactions between animated agents and students to enhance students' engagement and learning [52]. They see pedagogical agents as "social models" and explain that these social models can be used to motivate learners [51].

While early research concerning pedagogical agents was more focused on the development of pedagogical agents [40, 48, 49, 54] and did not examine the pedagogical value of the agents, more recent studies started to look at instructional values of these animated agents. For example, Dunsworth and Atkinson [32] compared a text-based tutoring system with a Clippy-like agent-based system. They showed that the agent-based system is significantly more beneficial for learning than the text-based system [32]. Holmes studied fifth-graders in a virtual science learning environment and reported that students who interacted with an agent could generate deeper explanations than students who did not interact with an agent [45]. Other studies also reported similar findings [57, 63]. Researchers studied different agent roles such as a tutor and a co-learner [17, 39, 41] and the use of static picture agents versus animated agents [19].

However, most previous work on pedagogical agents focused on comparing an agent condition with a non-agent condition. As far as we know, no previous work tried to compare a computer-generated agent with a live person. In addition, most of these agents are characters in 3D modeled world (e.g., SecondLife) or assistive and auxiliary characters added to the main learning contents. Some studies [8, 51] have examined the similarity attraction theory with animated agents. However, no study has investigated how demographic similarities between avatar teachers and students play a role in online video-based learning.

3   Research Methodology

3.1   Participants

Participants were recruited using an inclusion/exclusion criterion from students currently pursuing a STEM-related degree from Virginia State University. This institution is a Historically Black College and University (HBCU) located in Petersburg, Virginia. Twenty-one (21) students participated in this study. Twenty (20) participants identified themselves as Black/African American, and one (1) participant identified as other.

3.2   Procedures

Participants were randomly selected to participate in three teacher conditions. The three conditions are: (1) fixed human teacher, (2) fixed avatar teacher, and (3) user-selectable avatar teacher. Each participant participated in the study virtually via Zoom (https:// zoom.us/), where they watched a STEM course video, completed a survey, and partook in an interview. A video lecture course on IF statements was created with the ability to change the presenter to a human teacher or multiple avatar teachers. The content, design, and teaching voice were consistent throughout all videos. For the fixed human teacher condition, all participants watched the IF statements lecture with the same black human professor. For the fixed avatar teacher condition, all participants watched the IF statements video lecture with the same black avatar teacher. Lastly, for the user-selectable avatar teacher condition, participants chose one avatar teacher to be taught by from five (5) avatar teachers. These included an Asian, black, white, robot, and an alien avatar. After completing the video lecture, each student was asked to complete a survey created using Qualtrics (https://www.qualtrics.com/). On completion of the survey, each participant was interviewed. All interviews were recorded using Zoom's recording feature.

3.3 Data Analysis

The interview data collected from the participants was subjected to a thematic analysis. This analysis was conducted to find notable themes and patterns in the responses of the participants. Each participant's interview recordings were transcribed from speech to text and proofread for accuracy. This study looks to understand students' perceptions of teachers presenting STEM-related material in a virtual learning environment. The study further investigates the usefulness of an avatar teacher on delivering a STEM course in a virtual environment and examines how participants feel about learning virtually.

4 Findings

4.1 Online Learning

In prior years, the conventional method of imparting knowledge to students in an educational setting required both the student and the teacher to be physically present [29]. This traditional way of teaching is still used to this date. However, many institutions have implemented online and hybrid or blended teaching styles in recent years [3]. With an increase in the number of online courses offered by tertiary institutions, we must explore the benefits virtual classes have over face-to-face [74]. Virtual learning provides flexibility that is not attainable with face-to-face learning [74], and we have seen this in the findings.

The Flexibility of Virtual Learning. Virtual learning environments commonly provide more time and location flexibility [68]. Many participants stated that they prefer virtual learning and asserted that it allowed them to learn in their favored environment. Participant #3 said, *"Okay, yeah, I like learning virtual because I feel like I'm more of my own space where I'm comfortable."* Participants also expressed that virtual learning allows them to choose where they attend class. Participant #4 said, *"I like to learn virtually because I could be anywhere and I could actually access the class at the any point while instead of missing a class by being someplace else."* Participant #3 also seemed to agree when they stated, "But if I'm virtual, I get to pick where I want to have my school work done at." Participants further explained that virtual learning helps with scheduling. For instance, participant #22 stated, *"I think I find it kind of easier and easier to work with my schedule."* The information you acquire in a traditional learning environment is usually in a defined order where students are unable to personalize their learning [67]. However, participants indicated that virtual courses would permit them to re-watch lectures at a desired point to comprehend the information presented fully. For example, when asked what they liked about virtual learning, participant #23 stated, *"because if I miss something or miss heard or something, I can easily go back in the video and then* *look at it again."* Virtual learning allows participants to determine the optimal manner to engage in and learn from online courses based on their responses.

Virtual Learning Environment Suitability. On the contrary, some participants expressed that they do not like to learn virtually. They believed that virtual learning could be a distraction. Participant #6 stated, *"Right now, I do not like it because it feels like I'll be easily distracted more than actually learning face to face."* Furthermore, participants were also concerned that virtual courses do not provide a hands-on experience. Participant #11 said, *"I wouldn't be able to get that hands-on experience to be how I am with being inside the class."* Similarly, Participant #21 said, *"I mean, all subjects I say I don't want it to be virtual because I'm a hands-on learner, um, but I'm going to like stick to this topic, so like computer science, programming, math, even science, like regular science, I feel like it shouldn't be um virtual at all because like it's a lot of hands-on, like help that you will definitely need."*

Not all students have access to a learning environment to learn effectively online [1]. Furthermore, being in your own surroundings may need a degree of discipline to avoid being distracted by items or technology that you would not usually see or utilize in a classroom. STEM courses can also be very hands-on. While schools may use numerous incentives to ensure that students receive the hands-on experience they need or require, such courses may make it highly challenging.

Video Lecture Course Structure. Researchers believe that the structure of an online course can affect student learning [29, 74]. Therefore, when asked about their likes and dislikes about the video lecture presented, it was to no surprise that participants expressed thoughts on the elements of the video lecture and indicated improvements that could be made. For instance, when asked about what they liked about the video lecture, participant #5 stated, *"Um, I liked how he explained it and used visuals like the, like the charts and stuff, the flowcharts."* However, participant #5 said, *"I wish he could like maybe slow down a little bit and like really explain each one. But other than that, it's alright."* Similarly, participant #25 stated, *"It was a little fast for me the first time around, but again just watch it again; it not; it is not too big of a deal."* Participants also expressed appreciation towards examples included in the video lecture. For instance, when asked what they liked about the video lecture, participant 11 stated, *"That it showed examples, rather than just it being just a lecture."* Some participants also liked that the video lecture was short. For example, participant #23 stated, *"I like that he kept it short and didn't really drag on too much."* A video lecture for a STEM course can be organized and designed in a variety of ways. Participants appreciated the STEM video lecture's use of examples, graphs, and charts, as well as the video briefness and focus. According to some participants, the video lecture may be slowed down. However, as we'll see in the next section, other participants thought the video was well-paced.

Virtual Teacher's Tone and Pace. A presenter's voice is essential when creating lecture videos, therefore it's no surprise that participants had opinions about the teacher's voice. For instance, Participant #24 stated, *"I liked that um his tone of voice and how it was more paced. Like he wasn't rushing through the video, rushing through the topic. It was more sort of at a slower pace."* Participants also believed that the voice of the teacher made the video lecture engaging. Participant #22 explained, *"Well, he, I, also what kind of engage, engages you to listen to this video is how he sounds like. He doesn't sound like flat like he's just reading information. He kinda sounds like he wants you to be engaged, and it makes you feel engaged."* Participants listened intently to the teacher's voice while they delivered their video lecture, emphasizing the importance of the teacher's tone, enunciations, and pace to students.

4.2 Teacher Physical and Professional Characteristics

Researchers have expressed that race, ethnicity, language, academic credentials, and experience are all factors that can affect students learning in the traditional classroom setting [21, 25, 35, 36, 61, 65]. As mentioned in the methodology, we randomly assigned participants to three conditions. These conditions included (1) a fixed avatar teacher, (2) a user-selectable avatar teacher, and (3) a fixed human teacher. Participants in each condition had differing opinions about the physical and professional characteristics of professors who delivered the course material, as well as how this influenced their learning.

Teacher Credibility. Under the fixed avatar teacher condition, in which all participants were taught by the same avatar instructor, several participants discussed teacher credibility. When asked if a teacher's physical characteristics may influence a student's learning, they stated they were more concerned with the teachers' topic understanding. Participants #1 and #3, for example, stated:

"No, it doesn't really matter, as long as you know what you're teaching and how, it depends on how we teach it. I think that matters most. The other stuff really don't matter to me." - P1.

"Not really. Just as long as you know what you're talking about. I don't care if you're the standard third. As long as I feel like you know your character, your personality, like you actually care about my education; you care about me learning, then I don't care what you are." - P3.

Another participant associated the content delivery to the professor's possible trustworthiness in presenting the course. When asked about what they liked about the video lecture, participant #6 stated, *"What I like about the lecture video, cause it's more understanding because he seems to know what he knows what he's saying. So, it'd be better for me if a professor knows what he's saying, instead of like, just reading the um, just reading what the PowerPoint says."*

Many professors have certifications that allow them to teach a specific STEM subject. As a result, participants valued the teacher's ability to effectively and confidently explain the course material.

Human Teacher Preference. Several participants in the fixed avatar condition voiced concern about the avatar instructor's credibility but did not indicate a wish for a different teacher. After picking an avatar teacher among five (5) avatar instructors, a participant in the user-selectable avatar teacher condition said that they preferred to see the human teacher. For instance, when asked if they believe a teachers' physical characteristics can affect their learning, participant #11 stated, *"not about the characteristics, but it's better to see the teacher so that you could get that feel that they're there, especially if it's virtual."* Participant #11 did not think a teacher's physical characteristics matter; they believed that a human teacher would provide a better connection to learning. On the contrary, participant #12 believe that no matter who the teacher is, the content of the course can be delivered effectively. They stated: *"Well, because there may be an avatar, but it's still teaching facts to a student, like whether or not it's either a real teacher or an avatar teacher."*

Teacher Accents. As previously said, STEM professors may come from a variety of backgrounds, resulting in teachers speaking having in a variety of native languages which influence their accents. When asked if a teacher's physical characteristics could impact a student's learning, participants in the fixed human teacher condition refrained from commenting on the teachers' physical characteristics and instead to spoke on a teacher's accent. For instance, participant #21 and #22 stated:

"The only thing that do affect my learning is when I have a teacher, that like, that, like, like, with no offense, but like when they have, like, they speak a different language, like they, like, I can tell English is not their first language. So, it makes it harder for me to understand. Like I'm still going to try to ask questions, and all that stuff, like that would never change. But it just makes it harder for me to comprehend and understand. That do be the hardest, like if they have, like, a strong accent." - P21.

"I mean, I don't know how to put it, like sometimes it's just hard to um, I guess understand what some professors are saying when they do have stronger accents." P22.

Many students may struggle to understand a teacher with a strong and distinct accent from their own. As a result, t Students may find it difficult to learn and stay focused on watching a video lecture that has this issue.

Teachers and Race. Being unbiased and neutral in a traditional classroom setting can be challenging [61]. Differential impacts on students due to a teacher's personal identities may always occur, affecting student learning and engagement [12, 22, 26, 42, 47]. The ability to customize avatar teachers, as well as the employment of avatar teachers, may be able to eliminate some of these disparities. In all conditions, many participants stated that they prefer to be taught by a teacher with a similar racial and ethnic background. Participants believed that having a teacher from the same racial or ethnic background guaranteed that they understood their life circumstances and gave them the confidence to succeed. For instance, participants said:

"I just feel like, um, I'll be, there'll be able to relate to me more and just really be able to help me and stuff like that, honestly." -P5.

"I feel like a lot of people from similar backgrounds or races, or whatever, I feel like they understand what each other, each other, going through a lot more. Like they'll see it from that point of view a lot easier than somebody from the opposite, you know." -P16.

"Like it's good for like representation to see somebody like yourself doing it. But that won't necessarily be something that would like motivate me to succeed or uh give

me like better proficiency. But it is a good thing like to actually see somebody that looks like you or uh somebody that's like underrepresented, because then it shows that you have a chance of making it.". - P20

On the contrary, many participants reinforced that the credibility and ability of the professor to explain the content matters most:

"It doesn't really matter what the race is, or not, as long as long as they explain it more so that I can actually understand it without me actually have to go back in class to ask for help, that's fine with me." - P6.

"Um, I think that it's just on based off of how you teach, um rather than how you look. Um because if you're, anybody can look a certain type of way, but it's how you present the material to me." - P11.

"Um, it doesn't really matter, as long as they're a professor that can get the information across." - P22.

"Because it's kind of, I mean, it's the same thing, as long they know what they're talking about that's what matters." - P23.

In a traditional classroom setting, students are typically unable to choose their teacher based on their physical preferences characteristics [29]. However, these findings suggest that some students have preferences that may impact how they learn.

4.3 Virtual Learning with Avatar Teachers

Given that students are typically unable to select or customize professors based on physical characteristics, the study aimed to examine the impact of avatar teachers on virtual learning. An avatar teacher taught participants in two different ways: a fixed avatar teacher or a user-selectable avatar teacher. Therefore, participants had an animated character presenting their video lecture. Some participants believed that the avatar teacher was distracting or may be distracting others watching the lecture video. For instance, when asked if they liked the video lecture, participant #1 said, *"I was getting distracted, not even because it was just online. I was just getting distracted with the um the Bitmoji that the instructor was using. It was just; I don't know. It was just distracting. It was just too much going on with him moving."* Likewise, participant #4 stated, *"For me, I could envision what the professor looks like, so I could, and it doesn't bother me, but for some others they might just be bothered by the avatar itself and will just and will be distracted by the avatar, the avatar, instead of paying attention to the lecture."* Furthermore, participant #3 believed that the avatar teacher would distract individuals who would often focus on the professor speaking rather than the slides being presented. They stated, *"But what I think other people would have a downfall is was like with the emoji thing or because, you know, it can be distracting to those who watch the professor talk instead of watching the slides."*

On the contrary, a few participants believed that the avatar teacher made the video lecture more engaging. For instance, participant #12 stated, *"I'm guessing that it helped me. Um, Hang on. I think it made me more engaged."* Some participants further explained that the avatar teacher was something new and different, making the video lecture appealing. For instance, when asked if they believed the avatar teacher had a positive impact on their learning and engagement. Participant 15 stated, *"I guess one of the benefits, it can be more, um, like, I guess enticing, like, I guess it can make people more interested in the course, you know, if you do it right."* They further stated, *"I think it had been positive for me, just in the sense that, like, I don't know, it's just something else to look at too."*

According to the findings, participants in the fixed avatar teacher condition perceived the avatar instructor to be more distracting than those in the avatar teacher choice condition. Furthermore, some participants were worried that the avatar teacher would divert attention away from the video's written material and visuals.

4.4 Virtual Learning with a Human Teacher

Participants found the avatar teachers to be distracting or engaging. However, the study also investigated the impact of human teachers. The majority of participants taught by a human teacher believed that the teacher's physical characteristics did not positively or negatively affect their learning. Participants were more concerned with the course content and delivery than with the physical characteristics of the teacher who was presenting the material. For instance, participant #22 stated, *"Because I didn't really think the appearance mattered. If that makes sense. I wasn't really paying attention. I was trying to pay attention to what they were, the message they were trying to convey."* Similarly, participant #24 said, *"I feel, as you know, it doesn't bother me, so I will learn either way, because I'm not more so concerned on the person's appearance, but on the topic or subject I am being taught on."*

4.5 Choosing Your Teacher

Studies have found that given the opportunity to personalize their learning experience, students are more likely to succeed in a class [68]. Similarly, a few participants believed that having the choice to choose a teacher from would make virtual learning more engaging and likeable. For example, participants stated:

"Um uh in advantage will be, you know, since people would either choose their avatar or anything like that, they may like, you know, it may become like a more likeable thing to them, to which they could potentially learn better." – P14.

"It makes them a little bit more engaging to them. The clients says like, okay, like, who are we gonna have our teacher look like this time or something like that." – P15.

"It might just engage them more, and they might be like, you know, I'm so excited because this person is teaching this or therefore." – P24.

Similarly, many applications that enables users to personalize their experiences. As a result, some participants thought that having avatar teachers would enable them to choose someone who best represented them. Participant #7 mentioned their ability to select from various characters when playing video games. They stated:

"Um, it's just representations, it's seeing your representation. You know, uh, people go out to see movies with people that look like them a lot more. So, somebody might want to learn a little more if they see an avatar that looks like them. I know playing games, I like a game more if they give, if you can have a black character with black characteristics. So, it's just representation. So, I might want to learn more if I see an avatar that looks like me." - P7.

Participants also believe that the choice would satisfy preferences. When asked if they believe having the choice between a human teacher or avatar teacher could improve learning and engagement, Participant #23 stated, *"definitely, yes."* When asked why, they said, *"Because this cause I'm see everyone is going to have different preferences. So, if people like I'd rather have the avatar, then I mean, that's what works for them and then."*

On the contrary, some participants believed that having the choice of choosing their teacher will not improve their learning or engagement and could cause a distraction.

"Um, me personally, no. I think it's kind of the same, but to if, if a person does feel like you know, it might, they might learn better with a different thing. I think if there's a way that you can pick what type of teacher you want, then you know, if that helps you, then so be it." - P3.

"No, it's just really based off of, um, how they present the information and the stuff that they give us, the materials that they give us for us obtain it." - P11.

"I see I don't, because if people were able to choose and make it or whatever, no probably be to call on looking at what they made and like, warn about what it looks like and change it often and causing a distraction" - P4.

5   Discussion and Conclusion

In this study, we examined avatar teachers' effect on student learning and engagement as the first steps in identifying issues associated with virtual learning and the possibility of addressing those issues using computer-generated courses. We divided participants into three groups, where each group participated with a specified teacher condition. These included a fixed human teacher, fixed avatar teacher, and user-selectable avatar teacher. We qualitatively analyzed how students felt about virtual learning and the impacts of a teacher's physical characteristics on student learning and engagement with interviews.

Studies have found that virtual learning provides flexibility for students receiving an education [73, 74]. Similarly, our results showed that virtual learning allowed students to choose their own location to attend class, helped them create their own schedule, and re-visit teaching material at any point and time. These findings reveal that students can personalize their learning experience with virtual learning, which may help students learn at a pace best suited for them.

Many participants liked that the video lecture on IF statements utilized diagrams and examples, was short in length, and well-paced. Participants also liked that the teacher's voice was engaging. On the contrary, some participants believed that the video was too fast. Though there was mostly positive feedback on the video lecture content and structure, the findings showed that students rely on video lectures to be informative, well organized, and well-paced. As a result, while creating video lectures, institutions must take the time to design video lectures that will guarantee students are sufficiently motivated to watch a video lecture in its entirety and can apply what they have learned.

On exploring the impact of teachers' physical characteristics in each condition, we found that a teacher's credibility, accent, and race may impact a student's learning and engagement. Many participants in the fixed avatar teacher condition were not concerned about their teachers' physical characteristics but mainly about their knowledge. Similarly, we found that some participants in the fixed avatar and user-selectable avatar condition preferred to be taught by a human teacher. Results implied that a human teacher provides a sense of connection, instilling trust in the information delivered in the video lecture. Thus, when creating online video lectures, we may want to provide credentials or information assuring the competency of avatar teachers or computer-generated teachers.

Rubin and Smith [66] found that accents can affect student learning. Similarly, participants in the fixed human teacher condition acknowledged difficulty understanding professors with strong accents. Students may become frustrated and unable to absorb content presented in a video if they are unable to understand what the teacher is saying. Therefore, institutions should consider a teacher's voice when creating online video courses.

Moreover, studies found that same-race instructors improve students' academic performance [25, 35, 36]. As a result, it's not surprising that many participants said they would prefer to be taught by someone of their own race. They explained that a teacher of a similar race established representation and provided a sense of likeness. Hence, there is a need to provide students with online courses that can offer similarities between teachers and students.

The study found mixed views on avatar teachers' impact on student learning and engagement. Some participants believed that the avatar teacher made them more engaged, while others found it distracting. Though many participants thought that the avatar teacher was a distraction, some felt that choosing an avatar teacher might help improve their own or other students' learning and engagement. The findings indicated that the avatar teacher took participants' attention away from additional text and visual information presented in the video lecture. Participants were too focused on watching the avatar rather than listening to and reading the information presented. This indicates that it may take time for students to get used to computer-generated courses. On the other hand, the avatar teacher attracted participants in such a way that they were completely concentrated on watching the video lecture, even if they were only looking at the teacher.

With computer-generated courses, we can provide students with the opportunity to be taught by someone of the same racial or ethnic background as them, as it would be easy to customize a teacher's physical traits using artificial intelligence and technology. Similarly, computer-generated courses can easily allow institutions to provide video lectures with different languages and voices best suited for each student to learn. Furthermore, it can allow for easy course design to suit students' needs and address feedback received.

The objective for the future is to expand the study's sample size. A survey will also be utilized to determine the impact of each teacher condition on students' learning and engagement and which condition resulted in greater comprehension of the material taught.

References

1. Adnan, M., Anwar, K.: Online learning amid the COVID-19 pandemic: students' perspectives. Online Submission 2(1), 45–51 (2020)

2. Aguilera-Hermida, A.P., Quiroga-Garza, A., Gómez-Mendoza, S., Del Río Villanueva, C.A., Avolio Alecchi, B., Avci, D.: Comparison of students' use and acceptance of emergency online learning due to COVID-19 in the USA, Mexico, Peru, and Turkey. Educ. Inf. Technol. **26**(6), 6823–6845 (2021)

3. Allen, I.E., Seaman, J.: Changing course: ten years of tracking online education in the United States. Sloan Consortium. PO Box 1238, Newburyport, MA 01950 (2013)

4. Atkinson, R.K.: Optimizing learning from examples using animated pedagogical agents. J. Educ. Psychol. **94**(2), 416–427 (2002)

5. Bahasoan, A.N., Ayuandiani, W., Mukhram, M., Rahmat, A.: Effectiveness of online learning in pandemic COVID-19. Int. J. Sci. Technol. Manag. **1**(2), 100–106 (2020)

6. Bandura, A.: Self-efficacy: The Exercise of Control. W.H. Freeman, New York (1997)

7. Banks, T.L.: Gender bias in the classroom. J. Legal Educ. **38**, 137 (1988)

8. Baylor, A.L., Kim, Y.: Pedagogical agent design: the impact of agent realism, gender, ethnicity, and instructional role. Intelligent Tutoring Systems, Maceió, Alagoas, Brazil (2004)

9. Baylor, A.L.: Expanding preservice teachers' metacognitive awareness of instructional planning through pedagogical agents. Educ. Tech. Res. Dev. **50**(2), 5–22 (2002)

10. Baylor, A.L.: Agent-based learning environments as a research tool for investigating teaching and learning. J. Educ. Comput. Res. **26**(3), 227–248 (2002)

11. Berscheid, E., Walster, E.H.: Interpersonal Attraction. Addison Wesley (1969)

12. Boersma, P.D., Gay, D., Jones, R.A., Morrison, L., Remick, H.: Sex differences in college student-teacher interactions: fact or fantasy? Sex Roles **7**(8), 775–784 (1981)

13. Brooks, V.R.: Sex differences in student dominance behavior in female and male professors' classrooms. Sex Roles **8**(7), 683–690 (1982)

14. Byrne, D., Nelson, D.: Attraction as a linear function of proportion of positive reinforcements. J. Pers. Soc. Psychol. **1**(6), 659 (1965)

15. Canes, B.J., Rosen, H.S.: Following in her footsteps? Faculty gender composition and women's choices of college majors. Ind. Labor Relat. Rev. **48**(3), 486–504 (1995)

16. Carrell, S.E., Page, M.E., West, J.E.: Sex and science: how professor gender perpetuates the gender gap. Q. J. Econ. **125**(3), 1101–1144 (2010)

17. Chan, T., Chou, C.: Exploring the design of computer supports for reciprocal tutoring. Int. J. Artif. Intell. Educ. (IJAIED) **8**, 1–29 (1997)

18. Chu, J.H., Loyalka, P., Chu, J., Qu, Q., Shi, Y., Li, G.: The impact of teacher credentials on student achievement in China. China Econ. Rev. **36**, 14–24 (2015)

19. Clark, R.C., Mayer, R.E., Thalheimer, W.: E-learning and the science of instruction: proven guidelines for consumers and designers of multimedia learning. Perform. Improv. **42**(5), 41–43 (2003)

20. Clarke, A., Milner, H., Killer, T., Dixon, G.: Bridging the digital divide. Adults Learn. **20**(3), 20–22 (2008)

21. Clotfelter, C.T., Ladd, H.F., Vigdor, J.L.: Teacher credentials and student achievement: longitudinal analysis with student fixed effects. Econ. Educ. Rev. **26**(6), 673–682 (2007)

22. Constantinople, A., Cornelius, R., Gray, J.: The chilly climate: fact or artifact? J. High. Educ. **59**(5), 527 (1988)

23. Coyner, S.C., McCann, P.L.: Advantages and challenges of teaching in an electronic environment: the accommodate model. Int. J. Instr. Media **31**, 223–228 (2004)

24. Crawford, M., MacLeod, M.: Gender in the college classroom: an assessment of the "chilly climate" for women. Sex Roles **23**(3–4), 101–122 (1990)

25. Dee, T.S.: Teachers, race, and student achievement in a randomized experiment. Rev. Econ. Stat. **86**(1), 195–210 (2004)

26. Dee, T.S.: A teacher like me: does race, ethnicity, or gender matter? Am. Econ. Rev. **95**(2), 158–165 (2005)

27. Dhawan, S.: Online learning: a panacea in the time of COVID-19 crisis. J. Educ. Technol. Syst. **49**(1), 5–22 (2020)
28. Dillenbourg, P., Schneider, D., Synteta, P.: Virtual learning environments. In: Proceedings of the 3rd Hellenic Conference Information & Communication Technologies in Education, pp. 3–18. Archive Ouverte HAL, Rhodes, September 2002
29. Dimitrios, B., Labros, S., Nikolaos, K., Koutiva, M., Athanasios, K.: Traditional teaching methods vs. teaching through the application of information and communication technologies in the accounting field: Quo Vadis? Eur. Sci. J. **9**(28) (2013)
30. Driscoll, D.M., Craig, S.D., Gholson, B., Ventura, M., Hu, X., Graesser, A.C.: Vicarious learning: effects of overhearing dialog and monologue-like discourse in a virtual tutoring session. J. Educ. Comput. Res. **29**(4), 431–450 (2003)
31. Dung, D.T.H.: The advantages and disadvantages of virtual learning. IOSR J. Res. Method Educ. **10**(3), 45–48 (2020)
32. Dunsworth, Q., Atkinson, R.K.: Fostering multimedia learning of science: exploring the role of an animated agent's image. Comput. Educ. **49**(3), 677–690 (2007)
33. Ehrenberg, R.G., Brewer, D.J.: Did teachers' verbal ability and race matter in the 1960s? Coleman revisited. Econ. Educ. Rev. **14**(1), 1–21 (1995)
34. Ehrenberg, R.G., Goldhaber, D.D., Brewer, D.J.: Do teachers' race, gender, and ethnicity matter? Evidence from the national educational longitudinal study of 1988. Ind. Labor Relat. Rev. **48**(3), 547–561 (1995)
35. Evans, M.O.: An estimate of race and gender role-model effects in teaching high school. J. Econ. Educ. **23**(3), 209–217 (1992)
36. Fairlie, R.W., Hoffmann, F., Oreopoulos, P.: A community college instructor like me: race and ethnicity interactions in the classroom. Am. Econ. Rev. **104**(8), 2567–2591 (2014)
37. Farkas, G., Grobe, R.P., Sheehan, D., Shuan, Y.: Cultural resources and school success: gender, ethnicity, and poverty groups within an urban school district. Am. Sociol. Rev. **55**(1), 127–142 (1990)
38. Fassinger, P.A.: Understanding classroom interaction: students' and professor's contributions to students' silence. J. High. Educ. **66**(1), 82 (1995)
39. Graesser, A.C., Person, N., Harter, D.: Teaching tactics and dialog in AutoTutor. Int. J. Artif. Intell. Educ. **12**(3) (2001)
40. Graesser, A.C., Wiemer-Hastings, K., Wiemer-Hastings, P.M., Kreuz, R.: AutoTutor: a simulation of a human tutor. Cogn. Syst. Res. **1**(1), 35–51 (1999)
41. Gulz, A., Haake, M.: Design of animated pedagogical agents - a look at their look. Int. J. Man Mach. Stud. **64**(4), 322–339 (2006)
42. Hall, R.M., Sandler, B.R.: The Classroom Climate: A Chilly One for Women? (1982)
43. Heidig, S., Clarebout, G.: Do pedagogical agents make a difference to student motivation and learning? Educ. Res. Rev. **6**(1), 27–54 (2011)
44. Hoffmann, F., Oreopoulos, P.: A professor like me the influence of instructor gender on college achievement. J. Hum. Resources **44**(2), 479–494 (2009)
45. Holmes, J.: Designing agents to support learning by explaining. Comput. Educ. **48**(4), 523–547 (2007)
46. Huang, J., Russell, S.: The digital divide and academic achievement. Electron. Library (2006)
47. Jewell, R.T., McPherson, M.A.: Instructor-specific grade inflation: incentives, gender, and ethnicity. Soc. Sci. Q. **93**(1), 95–109 (2012)
48. Johnson, W.L., Rickel, J.W., Lester, J.: Animated pedagogical agents: face-to-face interaction in interactive learning environments. Int. J. Artif. Intell. Educ. **11**, 47–78 (2000)
49. Johnson, W.L., Rickel, J.W., Stiles, R., Munro, A.: Integrating pedagogical agents into virtual environments. Presence **7**(6), 523–546 (1998)
50. Kim, Y., Baylor, A.L.: Pedagogical agents as social models to influence learner attitudes. Educ. Technol., 23–28 (2007)

51. Kim, Y., Baylor, A.L., Shen, E.: Pedagogical agents as learning companions: the impact of agent emotion and gender. J. Comput. Assist. Learn. **23**(3), 220–234 (2007)
52. Kim, Y., Baylor, A.L.: A social-cognitive framework for pedagogical agents as learning companions. Educ. Tech. Res. Dev. **54**(6), 569–596 (2006)
53. Lave, J., Wenger, E.: Situated Learning: Legitimate Peripheral Participation. Cambridge University Press, Cambridge (1991)
54. Lester, J.C., Converse, S.A., Kahler, S.H., Barlow, S.T., Stone, B.A., Bhogal, R.S.: The persona effect: affective impact of animated pedagogical agents. In: CHI, pp. 359–366 (1997)
55. Li, C.S., Irby, B.: An overview of online education: attractiveness, benefits, challenges, concerns, and recommendations. College Stud. J. **42**(2) (2008)
56. Lindahl, E.: Gender and ethnic interactions among teachers and students: evidence from Sweden. Working Paper (No. 2007: 25) (2007)
57. Moreno, R., Mayer, R.E., Spires, H.A., Lester, J.C.: The case for social agency in computer-based teaching: do students learn more deeply when they interact with animated pedagogical agents? Cogn. Instr. **19**(2), 177–213 (2001)
58. Nguyen, T.: The effectiveness of online learning: beyond no significant difference and future horizons. MERLOT J. Online Learn. Teach. **11**(2), 309–319 (2015)
59. Nguyen, T.D., Redding, C.: Changes in the demographics, qualifications, and turnover of American STEM teachers, 1988–2012. AERA Open **4**(3), 2332858418802790 (2018)
60. Price, J.: The effect of instructor race and gender on student persistence in STEM fields. Econ. Educ. Rev. **29**(6), 901–910 (2010)
61. Rakow, L.F.: Gender and race in the classroom: teaching way out of line. Feminist Teach., 10–13 (1991)
62. Rawal, S., Kingdon, G.: Akin to my teacher: does caste, religious or gender distance between student and teacher matter? Some evidence from India (No. 10–18). Quantitative Social Science-UCL Social Research Institute, University College London (2010)
63. Robertson, J., Cross, B., Macleod, H.: Children's interactions with animated agents in an intelligent tutoring system. Intelligent tutoring system. Int. J. Artif. Intell. Ed. **14**(3, 4), 335–357 (2004)
64. Robst, J., Keil, J., Russo, D.: The effect of gender composition of faculty on student retention. Econ. Educ. Rev. **17**(4), 429–439 (1998)
65. Rothstein, D.S.: Do female faculty influence female students' educational and labor market attainments? Ind. Labor Relat. Rev. **48**(3), 515–530 (1995)
66. Rubin, D.L., Smith, K.A.: Effects of accent, ethnicity, and lecture topic on undergraduates' perceptions of nonnative English-speaking teaching assistants. Int. J. Intercult. Relat. **14**(3), 337–353 (1990)
67. Schunk, D.H., Hanson, A.R., Cox, P.D.: Peer-model attributes and children's achievement behaviors. J. Educ. Psychol. **79**(1), 54 (1987)
68. Soffer, T., Kahan, T., Nachmias, R.: Patterns of students' utilization of flexibility in online academic courses and their relation to course achievement. Int. Rev. Res. Open Distrib. Learn. **20**(3) (2019)
69. Sternglanz, S.H., Lyberger-Ficek, S.: Sex differences in student-teacher interactions in the college classroom. Sex Roles **3**(4), 345–352 (1977)
70. Vygotsky, L.S., Cole, M.: Mind in Society: Development of Higher Psychological Processes. Harvard University Press (1978)
71. Wingate, N.: Sexism in the classroom. integrated. Education **22**(1–3), 105–110 (2006)
72. Wladis, C., Hachey, A.C., Conway, K.: An investigation of course-level factors as predictors of online STEM course outcomes. Comput. Educ. **77**, 145–150 (2014)

73. Yang, Y., Cornelius, L.F.: Students' perceptions towards the quality of online education: a qualitative approach. Assoc. Educ. Commun. Technol. (2004)
74. Young, A., Norgard, C.: Assessing the quality of online courses from the students' perspective. Internet High. Educ. **9**(2), 107–115 (2006)

My English Teachers Are Not Human but I Like Them: Research on Virtual Teacher Self-study Learning System in K12

Lixia Deng[1], Yun Zhou[1(✉)], Tianle Cheng[1], Xiao Liu[1], Tao Xu[2], and Xu Wang[2]

[1] Faculty of Education, Shaanxi Normal University, 199, South Chang'an Road, Xi'an 710062, Shaanxi, People's Republic of China
{dlx,zhouyun,20046,chengtl}@snnu.edu.cn
[2] School of Software, Northwestern Polytechnical University, 127 West Youyi Road, Xi'an 710072, Shaanxi, People's Republic of China
xutao@nwpu.edu.cn, wangxu0528@mail.nwpu.edu.cn

Abstract. English is the most used second language in the world. Mastering vocabulary is the prerequisite for learning English well. In middle school, students direct their own studying outside the classroom to facilitate memorizing and understanding. However, the lack of teacher guidance in the self-study process will negatively affect learning. Producing video lecture materials including talking teachers costs time, energy, and money. The development of artificial intelligence makes it possible to create such materials automatically. However, it is still unclear whether a system embedded with AI-generated virtual teachers can facilitate self-study compared with the system with merely the speech in self-study in K12. To address this gap, we conducted a user study with 56 high school students, collecting learning outcomes, user experience, and learning experience. Results showed that the virtual teacher helps to improve the student's English learning performance both in retention and transfer. Participants reported high user and learning experience. Our findings shed light on the use of virtual teachers for self-study students in K12.

Keywords: Virtual teacher · Self-study · Video lecture · Second language learning · K12

1 Introduction

English is the most used second language in the world. Mastering vocabulary is the prerequisite for learning English well. Students often need to spend extra

This work was supported by projects of the National Natural Science Foundation of China (62077036), and the national key research and development program of China under grant No.: 2018AAA0100501.

time outside the classroom to practice the language. Making excellent teaching resources often require much time, financial resources, and energy. Additionally, one of the biggest challenges for learners to self-study is the lack of teacher guidance and companionship, leading to distraction and shallow cognitive processes during learning. The development of artificial intelligence makes it possible to create such materials automatically. However, it is still unclear whether a system embedded with AI-generated virtual teachers can facilitate self-study compared with the system with merely the speech in self-study in K12.

To address this gap, we first propose a self-study vocabulary learning system, providing teaching videos and vocabulary exercises. The videos were automatically generated by the engine [30], only with a photo or a clip and a lecture text. Then, to evaluate whether the virtual teacher and the system can help middle school students improve their learning performance and to investigate students' subjective feelings, we conducted a user study in middle schools and focused on three following questions:

- **RQ1:** Can the virtual teacher promote learning outcomes?
- **RQ2:** What's the learning experience when learners study English with and without the virtual teacher?
- **RQ3:** What's the user experience when learners study English with and without the virtual teacher?

Then we conducted a user study with 56 high school students, collecting learning outcomes, user experience, and learning experience. Results showed that the virtual teacher helps to improve the student's English learning performance both in retention and transfer. Participants reported high user and learning experience.

2   Related Work

In this section, we discuss the work related to pedagogical agents in interactive learning environments. The use of digital learning equipment and resources in an informal setting is as important as learning in a formal education environment [23]. However, learning in an informal environment lacks teacher supervision, and management relies on student self-discipline, so teaching materials need to be carefully designed and organized to enhance learning. In addition, as the COVID-19 pandemic spreads around the world for a long time, face-to-face learning has been hindered. Students need to complete more learning at home, and schools and teachers need to build a large number of digital learning materials suitable for learners to use at home. Providing practical and rich teaching resources is an urgent issue.

2.1   English Learning System

With the development of digital teaching technology, more and more English-assisted teaching tools have been developed to support students' after-school learning. Sandberg [27] developed a mobile English learning APP that supports after-school learning, providing gamification methods such as word spelling, picture-word matching, and judgment questions for elementary school students to review the words they had learned in class. The results indicated that learners who used the mobile app performed better than learners who did not use the app when completing word tests. Chen [7] designed a personalized mobile English word learning system that recommends suitable words for learners based on their vocabulary ability and memory cycle, aiming at improving learners' performance interest in learning. Liu [22] proposed a handheld English language learning organization, in which learners scan a QR code into an augmented reality environment to complete English learning in the company of a virtual companion, and the study results show that the system is helpful for college students to learn English. Sun [28] used WordNet technology to design a word learning system to help students distinguish between the confusing near-synonyms and similar-looking vocabulary (NSSL). The results showed that students using the system could effectively help them identify NSSL words. Cheng [10] developed a campus English learning system(Student Partner) to help students find English practice partners on campus. This system supported learners to communicate using text, pictures, and voice. Their results showed that students believed that such a system would help students learn English well. Hwang [19] developed a mobile game for practicing English listening and presentation skills in which learners construct sentences based on cards and questions and give oral responses. The findings indicated that learners using the app performed better than controls groups on verbal post-test. Still, there was no significant difference between the two groups on the listing post-test. Chen [8] developed a mobile English learning system, which provides timely news and automatically retrieves vocabulary from articles that are new or unfamiliar to learners to enhance learners' English reading skills and vocabulary skills.

Although existing research provides many learning tools for English learning, they mainly focus on the design of the technology and tools. Less consideration is given to the role of teaching agents in teaching tools. Students use digital tools to complete learning freely, lacking supervision and guidance. It is crucial to consider how to design teaching agents in learning tools to promote learner concentration to improve learning effectiveness.

2.2   Social Agency Theory

Social agency theory argues that social cues in multimedia learning are conducive to allowing the learner to feel social companionship and they are communicating with another person [12]. Agents as a social presence can improve the overall attention of the learner and promote the deep cognitive processing of learning materials to obtain better learning results [6]. Teacher-student interaction is one of the most significant contributors to learner satisfaction with the curriculum and perceived learning [15]. Wang [29] conducted an eye-tracking experiment on math instructional videos with or without teachers, and the results showed that when learning materials are relatively simple, teachers can help learners maintain attention and promote their cognitive processing of learning materials.

Mayer [24] studied the effects of teaching agent posture, facial expressions, gaze orientation, and anthropomorphic movements on learning outcomes in multimedia learning. They found that social cues had a positive impact on learning transfer testing. Guo [17] study found that agents speaking in videos caused students to be more engaged with the learning content than without agents. Moreno [25] compared the effectiveness of teaching with and without agents and found no difference in learning retention, but learners who learned with agents performed better on learning transfer tests. Meanwhile, they reported a higher level of interest and motivation.

Nonverbal communication plays a vital role in human-to-human interactions, as it is in online learning and video teaching [1]. The teaching agent is embedded in the learning video as a visual stimulus, providing non-verbal interaction cues, such as expression, gaze, and posture. Teaching agents can provide nonverbal communication to enhance learners' comprehending of the learning content [29]. Chen [9] compared the effects of lecture recording with lecturer and sliders, portrait plus video recording, and voiceover on learners. They found that participants felt significantly lower cognitive load and better learning with teacher pictures compared with the sound-only teaching video. Johnsoncite [20] studied the effects of animated female teaching agents with indicative movements and eye gaze on students' learning of circuit knowledge and found that learners with lower prior knowledge were more likely to benefit from teaching agents.

2.3 Teaching Agent

A teaching agent is an image that appears on a screen to provide teaching support and motivation to learners in the multimedia learning environment [14]. The teaching agents guide learners to focus on meaningful learning content by gaze or gesture. They show the prerequisites, relationships, or results related to the learning content to assist the learner in processing the information [18,21]. Teaching agents can exist in the form of animated or static images, human or non-human [11].

An animated teaching agent is an animated image that appears on a teaching screen to facilitate learning in a computer learning environment [18]. Prior studies have shown that animation pedagogical agents improve learning by stimulating social interaction and increasing engagement. Animation agents with speech are more conducive to learners in terms of learning retention and migration than animation agents that render text [13]. Baylor [3] compared the teaching agent of anthropomorphic animation with the teaching agent of static pictures and found that there was no significant difference in the effects of the two on learning retention. 3D teaching agents use 3D modeling techniques to generate three-dimensional human or other images, often used in virtual reality or augmented reality environments to interact with students on the fly. Ashoori [2] built an augmented reality learning environment for disease knowledge teaching, a virtual animated agent that can be moved is provided, the agent recognizes the learner's need for help or lost clues and volunteers to consult them. The results show that the learner feels a personalized experience when using the agent. Instructional agents also provide navigation guidance to prevent learners from getting lost during exploration in complex virtual reality or augmented reality environments.

Realistic pedagogical agents look natural and more likely to be trusted by learners. Unnatural agent images can distract learners [4]. Most teaching agents appear in cartoon animations or 3D models in existing studies. Cartoon animation renders the outline of the agent without presenting realistic details and is not rich enough in terms of emotional expression. Three-dimensional models can simulate the 3D sense of real people. Still, the 3D model characters in most of the current studies are relatively rough, the movements and expressions are relatively blunt, which is easy to cause a sense of distrust among learners. Well-produced animations and 3D model effects often require a high time, human resources, and financial resources. Therefore, this study uses virtual teacher generation tools to convert character pictures and texts into lecture teacher videos, which is easy to produce and can achieve realistic teaching agent effects. The virtual teacher plays the learning support and motivational role. The study aims to provide a new direction for the teaching agent field under computer-supported teaching.

3   User Study

This user study explores how AI-generated pedagogical agents impact learning performance, usability, user experience, and learning experience in self-study.

3.1   Participants

We recruited 60 participants, who were junior high school first-year students, aged between 12 and 13 (M = 12.3, SD = 0.47). We randomly selected two classes in seventh grade. Four students were excluded because they failed to submit a complete questionnaire. Finally, 56 participants were included in this study (27 males and 29 females).

3.2   Experiment Design

The participants were randomly assigned to two groups: the experimental and the control groups. The experimental group used the application with a pedagogical agent (see Fig. 1 left), while the control group used only the speech version (see Fig. 1 right). We asked the two groups to complete a prior-knowledge test online a week before the experiment to ensure that the two groups had no prior knowledge bias. In the prior knowledge test, participants were asked to give the Chinese meanings of the English words to be learned. As shown in Table 1. We found that there was no significant difference between the experimental group (Mdn = 3) and the control group (Mdn = 3) in the prior knowledge test, U = 261.5, Z = −1.020, p > 0.05, r = −0.08.

Table 1. Prior knowledge test.

Group	Prior knowledge test
	p
Virtual teacher	>0.05
Non-virtual teacher	

Fig. 1. The interface of the English learning system with a virtual teacher (left) and without virtual teacher (right)

3.3 Dependent Measures

The dependent variables included learning effect, user experience, and learning experience, as shown in Table 2. We tested learning retention and transfer as performance. The learning experience questionnaires were from Ramsden [26], and the user experience questionnaires were adapted from Bourgonjon [5].

Table 2. Dependent measures.

Variable	Category	Questions	Type	Min/max
Learning retention	Learning effect	9	Blank filling	
Learning transfer	Learning effect	9	Single choice	A-E
Perceived usefulness	User experience	4	5 point Liket	1–5
Perceived ease of use	User experience	5	5 point Liket	1–5
Perceived usability	User experience	4	5 point Liket	1–5
Use intention	User experience	3	5 point Liket	1–5
Emotion and motivation	Learning experience	3	5 point Liket	1–5
Social presence	Learning experience	4	5 point Liket	1–5
Cognitive load	Learning experience	2	5 point Liket	1–5
Interest and satisfaction	Learning experience	4	5 point Liket	1–5

3.4   Learning Materials

The learning system was developed using Unity2019, including explanation videos and practices. The practices in the applications offer feedback. The talking pedagogical agent was generated by an engine proposed by the work [30]. In this experiment, the image of the pedagogical agent was a famous comedian.

The learning materials were selected from English vocabulary in Grade seven English textbooks. Nine words were used. As shown in Fig. 1, the explanation videos included slides to present words, phonetics, Chinese interpretation, and word examples. The pedagogical agent explains the meaning, the usage, and examples. The application in the control group only offered speech.

3.5   Procedure

The experiment was conducted in a room equipped with computers with the procedure as shown in Fig. 2. We installed and tested the applications in advance. The students were informed of the experimental contents and then learned by themselves. After learning, students completed the tests and filled out questionnaires. The whole experiment was about forty minutes.

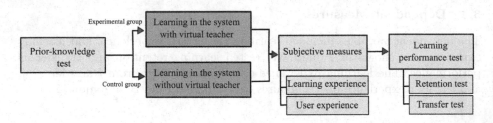

Fig. 2. The experimental procedure.

4   Results

This section reports the data analysis results related to the learning outcome questionnaire (learning retention and learning transfer) and subjective questionnaire (user experience and learning experience). All the data of learning outcomes were tested by the Shapiro-Wilk test. The results showed that the data was non-normal distribution, so the test method used is a non-parametric test. The analysis methods used are the Mann-Whitney U test and the Wilcoxon test. Mann-Whitney U test was used to compare the differences between two independent samples, Wilcoxon was used to testing the difference between two related samples. The learning outcome data were analyzed in SPSS. The boxplot of subjective questionnaire was drawn in Spyder using the seaborn library of Python.

4.1 Learning Outcome

As shown in Table 3, there was a significant difference between the prior knowledge performance (Mdn = 3) and post-test performance (Mdn = 9) in the experimental group, Z = −4.435, p < 0.01. There was also a significant difference between the pre-test performance (Mdn = 3) and post-test performance (Mdn = 7) in the control group, Z = −4.021, p < 0.01. Results showed that the design of learning systems and learning materials helped improve learners' performance.

Table 3. Prior knowledge and retention performance.

Group	Virtual teacher	Non-virtual teacher
	p	p
Prior knowledge test	<0.01	<0.01
Retention test		

As shown in Table 4, there was a significant difference in learning retention between the experimental group (Mdn = 9) and the control group (Mdn = 7), U = 125, Z = −4.492, p < 0.01, r = −0.346. There was significant difference in learning transfer between the experimental group (Mdn = 7) and the control group (Mdn = 4), U = 148, Z = −3.210, p < 0.01, r = −0.248. The results showed that the use of AI-generated pedagogical agents facilitated learning retention and transfer more.

Table 4. Retention and transfer performance.

Group	Retention test	Transfer test
	p	p
Virtual teacher	<0.01	<0.01
Non-virtual teacher		

4.2 Subjective Questionnaire Measurement

As shown in Fig. 3, the learning experience included satisfaction, attention, reliability, social presence, and cognitive load. The box plot results showed that the median of satisfaction, attention, reliability and social presence were all 5, reflecting the high evaluation by learners. The median of the cognitive load was 3.5, showing that the cognitive load was not high.

The utility is used to evaluate whether the functions integrated into a system are available, while usability is used to measure the use effect of these functions when completing specific tasks and the satisfaction brought to users [16]. Ease

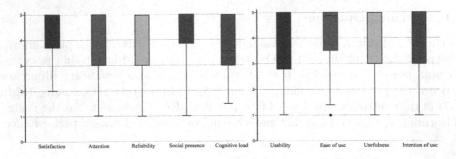

Fig. 3. The boxplot of learning experience (left) and user experience (right)

of use is used to measure the ease of operation of a system, Intention to use indicates whether users are willing to use the system regularly or recommend it to others. These indicators are key indicators to measure the effectiveness of a system. As shown in Fig. 3, the usability, ease of use, usefulness and use intention felt by learners when using the system are investigated. The median of usability, usefulness and use intention is 5, and the median of usability dimension is 4. The results showed that the user experience evaluation of the system is high.

5   Discussion

- **RQ1:** Can the virtual teacher promote learning outcomes? The results indicated that both experimental group students' retention and transfer test significantly outperformed the control group. The presence of teachers in the vocabulary learning system helps promote learners' learning output. This result is consistent with social agency theory, namely, pedagogical agent as a social cue can facilitate students' in-depth understanding and processing of learning materials. Although the learners who did not use virtual teachers also improved their learning performance through learning on the system, the degree of progress was significantly lower than that of the experimental group.
- **RQ2:** What's the learning experience when learners study English with and without the virtual teacher? What's the learning experience when learners studying English with the virtual teacher generated by artificial intelligence? Most learners showed high satisfaction with virtual teachers. They could concentrate on learning content with the help of teachers. The presence of teachers' images makes learners feel the social presence, and the cognitive load is normal. This conclusion is consistent with the previous conclusions on the impact of teachers on learners in video learning, that is, teachers' verbal, nonverbal, and appearance images have an impact on learners' learning input and feelings. The teacher used in this system is a well-known comedian. Its amiable image, smiling expression, and natural mouth shape provide learners with a very friendly figure of teachers and partners to promote learners to participate in learning.

- **RQ3:** What's the user experience when learners study English with and without the virtual teacher? The English vocabulary system designed in this study to support learners' after-school practice has been highly praised by learners in terms of functional integrity, functional effectiveness, and ease of use. Learners showed a strong intention to use the system and were willing to use it as a tool for their daily learning and recommended it to others. The possible reason might be that the system has designed a clear and concise interface, easy-to-use interaction, and teachers' accompanying learning. The selected learning contents were closely related to students' classroom knowledge so that learners felt the practical role of the system.

6 Limitations and Future Work

Although the results of this study proved the effectiveness of our virtual teacher and English learning system, there are still limitations in this study. First, the experimental duration was not long and was only conducted once in middle school. Excellent learning results and experience may be affected by the novelty of students using virtual teachers for the first time. Thus, we will conduct an extensive experiment to study how AI-generated pedagogical agents impact learning over a long period. Second, this study only compared the conditions with and without virtual teachers. We will investigate more conditions about virtual teachers. Finally, the learning system only supports the after-school practice of English vocabulary. In English learning, learners need to practice grammar, listening, reading, and writing simultaneously. As an after-school English learning system, we should consider designing more comprehensive learning content to support English learning in an all-around way.

7 Conclusion

The study explores the impact of AI-generated virtual teachers on secondary school students completing after-school English learning. In this study, we conducted an experiment involving 56 participants. First, we investigated the influence of virtual teachers on learning performance. The results show that virtual teachers exist in teaching videos as social cues can significantly improve learner achievements and promote learners' understanding and application of learning content. Second, we investigated subjective experience. The results showed that the use of virtual teachers made learners feel a high sense of trust, satisfaction, social presence, and an appropriate level of cognitive load. This indicated learners' acceptance of the AI-generated pedagogical agents as the teacher. Finally, we investigated the user experience. Most learners believed that the system was easy to use. The results showed the system's feasibility as an after-school English learning for middle school students. Virtual teachers generated with photos can be used to assist teachers in developing digital teaching resources that are conducive to learning, which significantly saves the time and energy cost of making teaching resources. For students, using such an after-school English learning tool with virtual teacher teaching, simulating the completion of learning under the guidance and supervision of teachers, is beneficial to the learning effect and learning experience.

References

1. Argyle, M.: Bodily communication. Routledge, 2nd edn. (2013). https://doi.org/10.4324/9780203753835
2. Ashoori, M., Shen, Z., Miao, C., Gay, R., Zarrabi, N.: Mentor agent: an intelligent virtual teacher for personalized learning environments. In: Proceedings of the 7th WSEAS International Conference on Distance Learning and Web Engineering (2007)
3. Baylor, A.L., Ryu, J.: The effects of image and animation in enhancing pedagogical agent persona. J. Educ. Comput. Res. **28**(4), 373–394 (2003). https://doi.org/10.2190/V0WQ-NWGN-JB54-FAT4
4. Bercht, M., Viccari, R.: Pedagogical agents with affective and cognitive dimensions. In: V Congreso Iberoamericano de Informática Educativa, pp. 4–6. Citeseer (2000)
5. Bourgonjon, J., Valcke, M., Soetaert, R., Schellens, T.: Students' perceptions about the use of video games in the classroom. Comput. Educ. **54**(4), 1145–1156 (2010). https://doi.org/10.1016/j.compedu.2009.10.022
6. Butcher, K.R.: The Cambridge Handbook of Multimedia Learning, 2nd edn. Cambridge University Press (2014). https://doi.org/10.1017/CBO9781139547369.010
7. Chen, C.M., Chung, C.J.: Personalized mobile English vocabulary learning system based on item response theory and learning memory cycle. Comput. Educ. **51**(2), 624–645 (2008). https://doi.org/10.1016/j.compedu.2007.06.011
8. Chen, C.M., Hsu, S.H., Li, Y.L., Peng, C.J.: Personalized intelligent m-learning system for supporting effective English learning. In: 2006 IEEE International Conference on Systems, Man and Cybernetics. vol. 6, pp. 4898–4903. IEEE, Piscataway (2006). https://doi.org/10.1109/ICSMC.2006.385081
9. Chen, C.M., Wu, C.H.: Effects of different video lecture types on sustained attention, emotion, cognitive load, and learning performance. Comput. Educ. **80**, 108–121 (2015). https://doi.org/10.1016/j.compedu.2014.08.015
10. Cheng, S.C., Hwang, W.Y., Wen, D.W., Wu, S.Y., Hsiehe, C.H., Chen, C.Y.: A mobile and web system with contextual familiarity and its effect on campus English learning. In: 2010 Third IEEE International Conference on Digital Game and Intelligent Toy Enhanced Learning, pp. 222–224. IEEE, Piscataway (2010). https://doi.org/10.1109/DIGITEL.2010.57
11. Clark, R.C., Mayer, R.E.: E-learning and the science of instruction: proven guidelines for consumers and designers of multimedia learning. Wiley (2016). https://doi.org/10.1002/pfi.4930420510
12. Cui, G., Lockee, B., Meng, C.: Building modern online social presence: a review of social presence theory and its instructional design implications for future trends. Educ. Inf. Technol. **18**(4), 661–685 (2013). https://doi.org/10.1007/s10639-012-9192-1
13. Domagk, S.: Do pedagogical agents facilitate learner motivation and learning outcomes? J. Media Psychol. (2010). https://doi.org/10.1027/1864-1105/a000011
14. Erickson, T.: Designing agents as if people mattered. Softw. Agents, 79–96 (1997)
15. Fredericksen, E., Swan, K., Pelz, W., Pickett, A., Shea, P.: Student satisfaction and perceived learning with online courses-principles and examples from the SUNY learning network (1999). https://doi.org/10.24059/olj.v4i2.1899

16. Gulz, A.: Benefits of virtual characters in computer based learning environments: claims and evidence. Int. J. Artif. Intell. Educ. **14**(3, 4), 313–334 (2004)

17. Guo, P.J., Kim, J., Rubin, R.: How video production affects student engagement: an empirical study of MOOC videos. In: Proceedings of the First ACM Conference on Learning@ Scale Conference, pp. 41–50. Association for Computing Machinery, New York (2014). https://doi.org/10.1145/2556325.2566239

18. Heidig, S., Clarebout, G.: Do pedagogical agents make a difference to student motivation and learning? Educ. Res. Rev. **6**(1), 27–54 (2011). https://doi.org/10.1016/j.edurev.2010.07.004

19. Hwang, W.Y., Shih, T.K., Ma, Z.H., Shadiev, R., Chen, S.Y.: Evaluating listening and speaking skills in a mobile game-based learning environment with situational contexts. Comput. Assist. Lang. Learn. **29**(4), 639–657 (2016). https://doi.org/10.1080/09588221.2015.1016438

20. Johnson, A.M., Ozogul, G., Moreno, R., Reisslein, M.: Pedagogical agent signaling of multiple visual engineering representations: the case of the young female agent. J. Eng. Educ. **102**(2), 319–337 (2013). https://doi.org/10.1002/jee.20009

21. Johnson, W.L., Rickel, J.W., Lester, J.C., et al.: Animated pedagogical agents: face-to-face interaction in interactive learning environments. Int. J. Artif. Intell. Educ. **11**(1), 47–78 (2000)

22. Liu, T.Y., Tan, T.H., Chu, Y.L.: 2D barcode and augmented reality supported English learning system. In: 6th IEEE/ACIS International Conference on Computer and Information Science (ICIS 2007), pp. 5–10. IEEE, Piscataway (2007). https://doi.org/10.1109/ICIS.2007.1

23. Mayer, R.E.: The promise of multimedia learning: using the same instructional design methods across different media. Learn. Instr. **13**(2), 125–139 (2003). https://doi.org/10.1016/S0959-4752(02)00016-6

24. Mayer, R.E., DaPra, C.S.: An embodiment effect in computer-based learning with animated pedagogical agents. J. Exp. Psychol. Appl. **18**(3), 239 (2012). https://doi.org/10.1037/a0028616

25. Moreno, R., Mayer, R., Lester, J.: Life-like pedagogical agents in constructivist multimedia environments: cognitive consequences of their interaction. In: EdMedia+ Innovate Learning, pp. 776–781. Association for the Advancement of Computing in Education (AACE) (2000)

26. Ramsden, P.: A performance indicator of teaching quality in higher education: the course experience questionnaire. Stud. High. Educ. **16**(2), 129–150 (1991). https://doi.org/10.1080/03075079112331382944

27. Sandberg, J., Maris, M., De Geus, K.: Mobile English learning: an evidence-based study with fifth graders. Comput. Educ. **57**(1), 1334–1347 (2011). https://doi.org/10.1016/j.compedu.2011.01.015

28. Sun, K.T., Huang, Y.M., Liu, M.C.: A wordnet-based near-synonyms and similar-looking word learning system. J. Educ. Technol. Soc. **14**(1), 121–134 (2011)

29. Wang, J., Antonenko, P.D.: Instructor presence in instructional video: effects on visual attention, recall, and perceived learning. Comput. Hum. Behav. **71**, 79–89 (2017). https://doi.org/10.1016/j.chb.2017.01.049

30. Xu, T., Wang, X., Wang, J., Zhou, Y.: From textbook to teacher: an adaptive intelligent tutoring system based on BCI. In: 2021 43rd Annual International Conference of the IEEE Engineering in Medicine & Biology Society (EMBC), pp. 7621–7624. IEEE, Piscataway (2021). https://doi.org/10.1109/EMBC46164.2021.9629483

Eduino: A Telegram Learning-Based Platform and Chatbot in Higher Education

Mohammad Khalil[✉] and Magnus Rambech

Centre for the Science of Learning & Technology (SLATE), University of Bergen, Christiesgate 13, 5020 Bergen, Norway
mohammad.khalil@uib.no

Abstract. This paper presents Eduino, a chatbot that is built on the popular social media platform 'Telegram' and serves as a learning-based platform conversational agent. Following the methodology of Data Science Research, three iterative stages are carried out for the development. Eduino provides a feature set covering functionality for acquiring lecture notes and course schedules, completion of course related quizzes, and contacting course professors through a conversational messaging interface. The chatbot was evaluated using a usability test and semi-structured interviews. The overall perception from students was positive. Students appreciated the efficiency of acquiring course content in a new novel format and found the experience to be immersive and user friendly.

Keywords: Chatbot · Mobile · Technology-Enhanced Learning · Higher Education · Usability

1 Introduction

In the last two decades, smartphones has become a borderline necessity in many of students' everyday life. This change is seen throughout the usage of digital devices in higher education as a whole, not only for mobile devices, but also for educational institutes which continuously adapt to and take advantage of modern technology as tools to enhance the teaching and, most importantly, the learning experience. This involves the origin of digital learning platforms such as Canvas, where course content is offered to personal devices (e.g., laptops, mobile phones). These solutions offer mobile alternatives to their desktop-oriented counterparts. The streamlining of interactions with these platforms is often done in the form of native applications and websites. As a result, opportunities arise to utilize chatbot technology to further enhance interactions and communication by and with students to allow them to acquire course content in a targeted and effective way using the friendly messaging interface.

Chatbots (also known as conversational agents, smartbots, chatterbots, bots, etc.) are software applications designed to partake in online chat conversations via text, in place of direct conversation with a live human agent (Shawar and Atwell 2007). While this is not the case for all chatbots, some are designed to convince their human counterpart that they are interacting with a human being instead of an automated software simulating

P. Zaphiris and A. Ioannou (Eds.): HCII 2022, LNCS 13329, pp. 188–204, 2022.
https://doi.org/10.1007/978-3-031-05675-8_15

human-like behavior through text messages (e.g., ELIZA (Weizenbaum 1966)). These chatbot systems are developed with the intent of ultimately passing the Turing test (a test of a machine's ability to make itself indistinguishable from a human) by artificially replicating the patterns of human interactions. This is today typically done using machine learning to enhance the chatbot's ability of processing natural language, making them able to work independently from a human operator. However, the ambition of passing the Turing test is not present for all chatbots. The main difference between those who strive to pass the Turing test and those who do not, is that a typical chatbot's knowledge base is limited to its intended field of use, whereas the more ambitious chatbots require a much broader knowledge (Holotescu 2016). This is because the Turing test assumes that the human agent can converse about whichever topic they want with their counterpart (the conversational agent). For the matter of designing a chatbot, this is helpful, as they are not required to have a thorough knowledge and are therefore able to focus on their specific domain of knowledge like assisting users in booking a flight ticket or acquiring course content, for this study.

This study will not discuss chatbots that are designed to pass the Turing test. Instead, the study focuses on chatbots that do not replicate humans but services. Today, this is typically common where many chatbots provide administration services, for example by assisting in customer support or ordering products online. An advantage for such chatbots that developers and designers can utilize is the assumption that the users of these chatbots will typically have a goal they want to complete whilst interacting with their chatbot. This assumption can directly affect the design of interaction patterns, as well as the conversation topics available for the chatbot. As certain patterns of behaviors tend to arise, this can be taken in advantage by the developers (Holotescu 2016).

The concept of the chatbot in this research work is an interpretation of a computer program that communicates with humans through text and provides services in order to achieve a predetermined goal. The study at hand tackles the following research questions.

1.1 Research Question

The primary goal of this work is to create and evaluate a conversational chatbot for higher education content. That is, to demonstrate the content from a university in a novel format. The main research questions are:

RQ1: *Can chatbots improve higher education content accessibility through the usage of mobile devices? and How do the students perceive that?*

RQ2: *How can chatbots as interactive and conversational tools present the learning content of modern learning platforms?*

The paper is organized as follows; Sect. 2 brings in the related work of this study. In Sect. 3, we explained in detail the following methodology to develop the chatbot and its evaluation process. Section 4 shows the results of the development and the usability test. We finally discuss the work with Sect. 5 and conclude with Sect. 6 the main contribution of this work, impact, and limitations.

2   Related Work

The work mainly falls under the umbrella of three areas: Human–Computer Interaction (HCI), Interaction Design and Chatbot Design. We briefly narrate them and together with chatbot history in education.

2.1   Chatbot History

One of the earliest milestones of computer programs utilizing natural language processing was ELIZA, a conversational agent developed from 1964 till 1966 by Joseph Weizenbaum. Using a methodology called pattern matching, ELIZA attempted to mimic conversation by matching user prompts to scripted responses (Weizenbaum 1966). ELIZA became an inspiration for many developers in the field. This in turn resulted in new conversational agents adopting ELIZA's approach to a large extent, further expanding their technologies by introducing lesser additions such as Text-to-speech.

The growth of chatbots has accelerated rapidly early in the twenty-first century. In 2001, ActiveBuddy released SmarterChild, a conversational agent where AOL Instant Messenger and MSN Messenger were used.

By 2011, conversational agent technology gained a significant increase in its sophistication. It was at this time that a new form of conversational agents started to rise, in the form of virtual assistants. Siri, developed by Apple, and Alexa the developed by Amazon, are examples of common virtual assistants that most people are familiar with today. These agents provide the ability to interact with users through natural language processing as well as accomplish tasks for their users such as providing navigational information or weather forecasts. Eventually, Facebook and other companies such as Telegram released their direct messaging applications for smartphone devices in 2014 and 2016, respectively. By introducing these platforms, they allowed for the creation of conversational agents for non-AI services.

2.2   HCI-Human–Computer Interaction and Interaction Design

Today, HCI covers most studies of technology ranging from computers to mobile phones, as well as household appliances and in-car navigation systems, and how it influences human work and activities (Dix 2009). Interaction Design and User-Centered Designs are both terminologies associated with HCI, as they are design disciplines focused on creating computer technology that is intuitively easy and pleasant to use.

In contrast to HCI, interaction design as a term has become more refined. Within all technologies, interaction design is a wider discipline that encompasses design methods, philosophy, and science. One primary goal of interaction design is to provide good *usability*. Usability as a term refers to the efficiency experienced by users when accessing and understanding an interactive product, such as an application with a graphical interface.

For chatbots, HCI forms the structure in how users interact with text-based chatbots. Current works in the field of HCI on chatbots is in considerable interest for improving chatbot designs and evaluating them. There is a lack of design research that shows that there is still not a clear knowledge of design challenges that need to be solved in the chatbot domain (Rapp et al. 2021). The advantage of HCI research illustrates in finding design research techniques that present better chatbots.

2.3 Chatbot in Education

In their study *"When Robots Talk - Improving the Scalability of Practical Assignments in MOOCs Using Chatbots"*, Bollweg et al. (2018) conducted research on the state of the art of chatbots being used as tools in eLearning within higher education. Their aim was to provide insight on how chatbots can assist in overcoming the challenge of limited resources when evaluating practical assignments in Massive Open Online Courses.

Bollweg et al. (2018) study involved conducting a structured literature review on the topic of chatbots and searched for papers and conference proceedings using 'Chatbot(s)', 'eLearning', and 'MOOC' as applied keywords for their search. Their result totaled 47 papers, of which 20 of these were classified as relevant for their study. After a thorough reading of the 20 papers, the final inclusion of papers was only 6 studies. With only 6 relevant studies covering the implementation and evaluation of chatbots in eLearning environments, Bollweg et al. (2018) point out that their literature review revealed a huge knowledge gap in the applicability of chatbots in eLearning.

Similar to the literature review performed by Bollweg et al. (2018), Winkler and Söllner (2018)'s study *"Unleashing the Potential of Chatbots in Education: A State-Of-The-Art Analysis"*, aimed at structuring existing chatbot literature (80 papers) in educational environments. The review verified that chatbots presence in eLearning has increasing usefulness. Winkler and Söllner (2018) express that chatbots have the potential to create individual learning experiences for students and therefore increase learning outcomes and support lecturers by serving as a course-assistant.

More recently, a review article by Hwang and Chang (2021) explored trend of chatbots in education. Hwang and Chang (2021) identified that studies on chatbots in education have been mainly influenced by the United States and South East Asia, raising awareness for other countries on contributing to this area. They also identified other research related gaps with respect to the number of empirical studies and evaluating their usability.

As a result of the mentioned related works, the literature is in desire of more empirical work on chatbots in education. Therefore, this research work contributes specifically to this area by developing a chatbot, called Eduino that offers university content in a novel format for students at the University of Bergen in Norway.

3 Methodology and Chatbot Development

The umbrella methodology followed in this research work is strongly related to HCI research, namely Design Science Research by Hevner and Storey (2021). Within, we followed two main approaches:

- Agile development of the proposed chatbot (Trivedi 2021), entailing one's desire to develop and react to change, according to several inputs during the development process, the method was considered due to flexibility in handling the various thriving technology changes in today's programming.

- Heuristics usability testing by Nielsen (1994). The most casual approach is heuristic assessment, which entails making usability experts judge whether each dialogue feature adheres to usability principles.

3.1 Design Science Research

Hevner and Storey (2021) present a suggestive list of guidelines for researchers to apply to their artifacts. These guidelines are intended to assist in creating a structured workflow by drawing an outline for what role an artifact will play in a given research. In common sense, this entail several iterations of design and improvement of the artifact in addition to the evaluation process.

3.2 Agile Development

Agile as a concept refers to one's desire to develop and react to change (Trivedi 2021). There are two methods within Agile development. The first focuses on planning ahead, setting deadlines, and assigning work to specific tasks, the second strives towards visualizing work while restricting the amount of work in progress. Both focus on several iterations to create artifacts quickly.

3.3 Nielsen's Heuristics and System Usability Scale (SUS)

Heuristic evaluation is showcased by Nielsen (1994) as the most informal method of usability inspection. Nielsen offers a set of ten heuristics that can be used to evaluate a user interface. Although this list is designed to enable a full heuristic evaluation, it can be modified as desired to fit a given field of study. The table below shows the principles we followed to evaluate the chatbot usability (Table 1).

Table 1. Chatbot usability evaluation principles

Nielsen's 10 principles of heuristics (1994)	
1. Visibility of system status	6. Recognition rather than recall
2. Match between system and real world	7. Flexibility and efficiency of use
3. User control	8. Aesthetic
4. Consistency and standards	9. Help users recognize, diagnose, and recover from errors
5. Error prevention	10. Help and documentation

As a part of the user testing procedure for a product, gauging its usability is a vital step. Brooke (1996) purposes his SUS as a reliable usability scale to assess and provides a score for artifacts.

3.4 Telegram Bot API

Telegram is an instant and free messaging application. Telegram has been chosen since it offers a simple Application Programming Interface (API) to create chatbots. Telegram is widely used. In April 2020, Telegram reported a peak of 400,000,000 monthly users worldwide, which is a doubling of users since March 2018 when they reported reaching 200,000,000 monthly users (Durov 2020).

Telegram is available on a variety of devices, including smartphones, tablets, and personal computers, which extends across most Windows, Android and Apple devices. This makes the platform very accessible to students and professors, especially in the Norwegian higher education systems where digitization is mainly centered around Windows-powered devices.

Telegram offers a programming interface (API) called Telegram Bot API11 which is used to link our chatbot to the messaging application Telegram. This API allows the chatbot server running in NodeJS to communicate with the Telegram server. This so that the chatbot is available via the Telegram application.

3.5 Chatbot Configuration

Setting up the development environment was simple in terms of complexity. As soon as the project was created in Visual Studio and uploaded as a repository to GitHub, the chatbot had to be registered to Telegram. This was done using Telegrams' chatbot module called BotFather. By initiating a conversation with BotFather using the "/newbot"-command, the chatbot creating process was triggered. As a part of creating a chatbot, it had to be given a name. The name *Eduino* was introduced at this point and was chosen due to its contraction of the words "Education" and "ino", which is a typical tail for robot related names.

Eduino then received a unique token to access Telegram's HTTP API. This token was integrated in the source code, which made the chatbot accessible through the Telegram application whenever the NodeJS application was running.

3.6 Creating Course Content

The lecture we used in our study is a higher education course from University of Bergen from Norway. The materials were distributed in a folder structure that included PDF files for all of the semester's lectures, the obligatory assignments, as well as the files for the self-assessment weekly quizzes related to the different lectures. In total, this resulted into 12 lecture files, 12 assignment files and 12 quiz files. The content structure is depicted in Fig. 1. We used JavaScript and JSON to structure the course and giving properties representing necessary data such as timestamps for lectures, week numbers, filenames for corresponding lecture notes and quizzes, and finally a short description and the lecturers name for the given lecture.

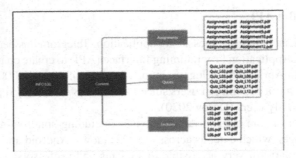

Fig. 1. Content structure used in Eduino Chatbot

4   Results

Through Design Science Research method, we followed 3 iterations to prepare the chatbot and evaluate it.

4.1   The First Iteration

The first iteration focused on identifying expectations among potential users and creating a stable development environment. The questionnaire that was held at the start of the first iteration had five main purposes: 1: To create a profile of the user base, 2: Acquire knowledge about whether students use their mobile phone in everyday life as students, 3: Find out if mobile phone use in everyday life is directly related to courses and studies, 4: Map previous experiences with chatbots, 5: Acquire knowledge of what expectations the students would have of a chatbot related to a university course. The survey consisted of 15 multiple choice questions and open texts.

We used Google forms to dispatch the survey. The questionnaire received 44 responses, of which 37 fully completed it. Provided the page limitation of this paper, we disseminate the main outcomes of the survey results in Table 2.

Table 2. Required services summarized from the survey questionnaire in the first iteration of developing Eduino chatbot

Requirement	Description
Device compatibility	The majority see that the chatbot must be accessible through applications that are compatible with both IOS and Android based smart devices
Skills needed	Many users said that they should not be required to have prior knowledge of the chatbot before use
Free service	An important feature required by the users is that the proposed chatbot should be free-serviced
User friendly	Key requirement is that the chatbot needs to be user friendly and should not oversaturate a chat conversation with large chunks of content at a time
Mimic real conversation	It is beneficial to mimic real conversation to the highest possible. Interacting with the chatbot should resemble a normal conversation between two humans in a chat application, where messages are sent and replied to rapidly

4.2 The Second Iteration

The second iteration was focused on developing Eduino the chatbot to a Minimum Viable Product (MVP) following the Agile methodology. To form the functionalities in the chatbot, we created 4 main features as the following:

- Lecture, with command as /lecture "number"
- Lectures, with command as /lectures
- Quiz, using the command /quiz "number"
- Help, using the command /help

Below is a brief explanation on each command.

Lecture Feature (Singular)
Eduino fetches the available lecture notes corresponding with the parameter number when triggering this command with a parameter included. A message sent by the user containing the text "*/lecture 1*" will return a message with relevant information about the lecture in question, such as date and timestamp, as well as the appropriate file for the first lecture in the semester, as an example. This feature is a more accessible method of obtaining lecture notes. By having this feature as a chatbot command, the efficiency of accomplishing this goal is increased significantly compared to its alternative, both in terms of time requirement and number of interactions needed.

Lectures Feature (Plural)

Figure 2 depicts the command */lectures*. This command causes Eduino to parse the formatted schedule file for upcoming lectures in the semester. The lectures are then put into a descending chronological list which is further returned to the user through a text message. This command requires no parameters and is used by sending a message containing text equal to *"/lectures"*. This command was used as an alternative to navigating through the university's calendar and provides necessary information about the semester schedule on the go.

Fig. 2. Example of "/lectures"

Quiz Feature

The quiz-command fetches a self-assessment quiz linked to the lecture corresponding with the passed parameter, which is a number representing a lecture from first to last, as in the *"/lecture"*-command. This feature allows self-assessment quizzes to be easily available on mobile phones through few interactions and is suitable for students that either want to prepare themselves for an upcoming lecture or review the content of a lecture after it is held.

Help Command

The *"/help"*-command was implemented to allow the user to inspect Eduino functionalities (Fig. 3).

Fig. 3. Example of /help command in Eduino (shown in the Norwegian language)

4.3 The Third Iteration

The third iteration set out to improve Eduino's level of fidelity and improve the quality and usability before doing the evaluation. We expanded the chatbot ability and improved it's features as the following:

Professor Feature
With this ability, the student can chat with the lecturer of the course as seen in the figure below (Fig. 4).

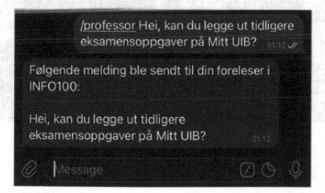

Fig. 4. /professor command example. (Shown in the Norwegian language, the student asks if (s)he can submit the assignment on the learning management system)

Tracking Course Progression
The student with this feature can see what parts of the course they finished. This is implemented through a green checkbox as seen in Fig. 5.

Fig. 5. Tracking course progression feature in Eduino chatbot

Self-assessment Quiz Improved

This functionality further had its usability improved by utilizing Telegram's in-line keyboard for options. This enabled answers to be sent by pressing a button corresponding to the correct letter (A, B, C, D), which further caused self-assessment quizzes to be interactable using one hand. When a quiz is completed, a summary consisting of the student's username, answers and score are generated as shown in Fig. 6.

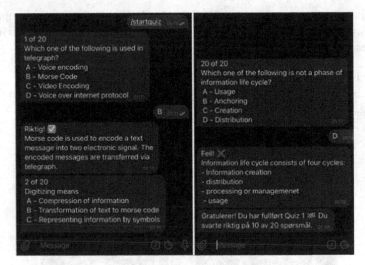

Fig. 6. Improved self-assessment quizzes in Eduino

4.4   Final Design

Below in Fig. 7, we list several screenshots taken from the final design of Eduino chatbot after the followed three iterations of development.

Fig. 7 The final design of Eduino with several functionalities available to the students to select and to chat with the lecturer

4.5 Heuristic and Usability Testing

We were able to do a heuristic usability testing with 5 students with which each spent 15 min interacting with the chatbot followed by another 15 min semi-structured interview and filling out a System Usability Scale (SUS). The participants to test Eduino were given a list of premade tasks to complete as shown in Table 3.

Table 3. Summary of the usability testing of the chatbot

Usability tasks	Results of the usability survey and interview
Task 1: Find Eduino on Telegram	- 4 of 5 completed this task without needing assistance - 1 participant was confused by the Telegram interface and required some guidance
Task 2: Obtain an overview over Eduino's abilities	- 5 of 5 completed this task without mistakes
Task 3: Obtain an overview over all lectures this semester	- 5 of 5 completed this task without mistakes - 1 participant clicked the command from the overview gained in **task 2** - 4 participants typed the command by hand
Task 4: Find lecture notes for the upcoming lecture	- 4 of 5 completed this task without mistakes - 1 participant performed the same action as for task 2 before realizing their mistake. No assistance needed - 1 participant expressed confusion when the notes did not appear immediately - 3 of 5 opened the lectures notes
Task 5: Start and complete the quiz for the next lecture	- 5 of 5 completed this task correctly - Participants showed excitement towards the quiz interaction and was generally aiming to gain a high score
Task 6: Travel 1–5 weeks ahead in time	- 5 of 5 completed this task correctly
Task 7: Find lecture notes for the week you skipped ahead to	- 4 of 5 scrolled back up the overview from **task 2** before doing the task - 1 participant used the */help* command as a reminder on how to complete the task
Task 8: Start the quiz tied to the same lecture (do not complete it)	- 5 of 5 remembered the */startquiz* command from task 5
Task 9: Pause your quiz progression	- 3 of 5 completed this task correctly - 2 of 5 just stopped answering to questions to pause and progressed to **task 10**. 1 participant used the */help* command to find the */pausequiz* command. The other participant scrolled all the way up to the initial list from **task 2**

(continued)

Table 3. (*continued*)

Usability tasks	Results of the usability survey and interview
Task 10: Send a message to the course's professor	- 3 of 5 completed this task correctly - 2 of 5 misunderstood the command-description, and included the angled brackets indicating a parameter in their message **Correct:** */professor Hello World* = "Hello World" **Wrong:** */professor < Hello World >* = " < Hello World > "
Task 11: Resume the quiz from task 9 (completion not necessary)	- 5 of 5 completed this task correctly - 2 of 5 guessed that */resumequiz* would be the correct counterpart to */stopquiz* - 2 of 5 scrolled up to the command list - 1 participant used the */help* command again
Task 12: Obtain an overview over all lectures this semester	- 5 of 5 completed the task - 5 of 5 scrolled to most recent command list - For participants that had not used the /help command at this point, significant time was spent scrolling all the way to the top of the conversation - Participant expressed satisfaction towards the visual representation of lectures that had already been held in correspondence with the number of weeks they skipped ahead in **task 6**
Task 13: Fill out System Usability Scale (SUS)	- 5 of 5 completed the task

Next, we gathered the SUS scores from the participants. Each of which answered separately and answered within a scale score. As mentioned earlier, we used Brooke (1996) method which result in five score in between 0–100. The average of the score is 79 (see Fig. 8), showing a good reception of usability.

5 Discussion

5.1 RQ1: Can Chatbots Improve Higher Education Content Accessibility Through the Usage of Mobile Devices? and How do the Students Perceive That?

The questionnaire conducted in the initial data gathering process showed that there several cases present in which chatbots would be considered as an option for accessing course content by students. The questionnaire shows that a large portion of the potential user group on several occasions has experienced a desire to acquire course content while being outside of university premises, such as when traveling to or from campus.

By utilizing the messaging interface of modern chat-applications, chatbots can allow the users to access content in a natural manner suitable for mobile devices in the form of text-based messages/requests. Although interaction design related to chatbots is more

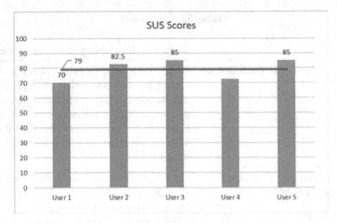

Fig. 8. SUS score

about designing interaction patterns rather than a graphical interface, this study has shown that it is just as feasible to design a good user experience with a predetermined interaction pattern for chatbots compared to native applications or websites. Where a graphical interface will present the user with several possibilities on the same page in the format of clickable elements such as buttons or links, the possibilities for user errors are introduced more clearly than with a chatbot, where all interactions take place at the user's request instead. For mobile devices, where screen size is a legitimate limitation, this becomes a strength in the chatbot's favor, as the possibility of error steps can be limited through a targeted design for interactions. This is not to suggest that native applications or websites are not viable alternatives. These platforms allow for a higher fidelity of features by utilizing a graphical interface for interactions, but this might happen at the cost of efficiency and accessibility compared to chatbots, where simplicity is in focus.

In this research, the concept of trying out the chatbots in education was found to be a powerful strategy for constructing effective interactions for mobile devices aligning with several studies that found chatbots in e-learning platforms satisfying to the students (e.g., Clarizia et al. 2018). The technology allows the design of interaction patterns where the user can make specific requests for what they want to acquire, as opposed to having to navigate through a graphical interface to locate the content they are searching for.

This strength was appreciated by students participating in the usability testing which showed that the ease of access for course content through the chatbot was positively perceived.

5.2 RQ2: How Can Chatbots as Interactive and Conversational Tools Present the Learning Content of Modern Learning Platforms?

One of the challenges identified during development is how the chatbot as a tool could be used to present course content of higher education courses. We found out that converting content structure is necessary. For example, self-assessment quiz files should be rewritten in processable format (JSON) which enables presenting the content of the quizzes dynamically instead of statically through file sharing.

By using Telegram's integrated keyboard (in-line keyboard) for presentation of possible answer options, the need for the user manual input was expelled. As a result, this has led to seamless interaction between the application and the user. In fact, this was desirable since the purpose of the service was to provide an accessible and feasible content outside users' normal working area.

The findings from the user test showed that all users unsolicited completed quizzes by holding the mobile device in their dominant hand. They used their thumb on the same hand to navigate through quizzes and answer questions, which suggests that interacting with the content was not cumbersome for the users. The finding of this study that this has further shown that presenting course content in this format is not only *feasible,* but also efficient through mobile devices meets Tsivitanidou and Ioannou (2020) conclusion points that chatbot can act as remote and novel educational delivery supplier.

Files such as presentations in a form of PDF and PPT requires other supporting applications to be installed on user's device. Presenting the content by linking the user to third party services like websites or native applications is an option to consider, although this functionality would contradict with the design principle that interactions should be limited to the messaging interface to maintain efficiency and immersion.

5.3 Limitations

In order for Eduino chatbot to have a presence within the digital channels of university environment, maintaining the application is vital. The application should be given hosting privileges on a supporting server run by specialists such as the IT-department or be deployed using third-party server hosting services (e.g., Amazon AWS, Microsoft Azure, Heroku). The infrastructure of the application should be utilized to fit the new server, and content should not be stored locally on the application server as static files. By integrating Eduino into university's learning management systems such as Canvas or Moodle, content can be managed and made available dynamically, which would significantly increase in fidelity of the application. Another limitation of this chatbot is the need for human intervention in many of the stages including adding course content and maintenance. Research assistants in this case can be a possible solution to reduce the load on the lecturer/professor.

6 Conclusions

The main contribution of this research is a high-fidelity chatbot application, Eduino. Eduino is dedicated to assisting students at the University of Bergen in Norway by making course content both more accessible and immersive on mobile devices. During development, an agile methodology was used in developing the chatbot. Using JavaScript frameworks together with the Telegram API Node Package, we result in having a server-like infrastructure and environment to offer the service not only to students, but also to teachers.

Using heuristic usability testing, It was found that Eduino chatbot was suitable as a platform for deploying course content that is enjoyable also accessible for students who currently use smartphones in a regular manner.

We finally conclude that while chatbots can be utilized to simplify the administrative workload for lecturers, the implementation of smart chatbots using Artificial Intelligence and NLP should not serve as a mitigation of student-to-lecturer requests, as this might lead to frustration and diminishing trust in this relationship.

References

Bollweg, L., Kurzke, M., Shahriar, K.A., Weber, P.: When robots talk-improving the scalability of practical assignments in MOOCS using chatbots. EdMedia+ Innovate Learn., 1455–1464 (2018)

Brooke, J.: Sus: A "quick and dirty" usability. Usability Eval. Ind. **189**(3) (1996)

Clarizia, F., Colace, F., Lombardi, M., Pascale, F., Santaniello, D.: Chatbot: an education support system for student. In: International Symposium on Cyberspace Safety and Security, pp. 291–302 (2018)

Dix, A.: Human-computer interaction. In: Liu, L., Özsu, M.T. (eds.) Encyclopedia of Database Systems. Springer, Boston (2009). https://doi.org/10.1007/978-0-387-39940-9_192

Durov, P.: 400 Million Users, 20,000 Stickers, Quizzes 2.0 and €400K for Creators of Educational Tests (2020). https://telegram.org/blog/400-million

Hevner, A.R., Storey, V.C.: Externalities of design science research: preparation for project success. In: International Conference on Design Science Research in Information Systems and Technology, pp. 118–130 (2021)

Holotescu, C.: MOOCBuddy: a Chatbot for personalized learning with MOOCs. In: RoCHI, pp. 91–94 (2016)

Hwang, G.-J., Chang, C.-Y.: A review of opportunities and challenges of chatbots in education. Interact. Learn. Environ., 1–14 (2021)

Nielsen, J.: Usability inspection methods. In: Conference Companion on Human Factors in Computing Systems, pp. 413–414 (1994)

Rapp, A., Curti, L., Boldi, A.: The human side of human-chatbot interaction: a systematic literature review of ten years of research on text-based chatbots. Int. J. Hum Comput Stud. **151**, 102630 (2021)

Shawar, B.A., Atwell, E.: Chatbots: are they really useful? LDV Forum **22**(1), 29–49 (2007)

Trivedi, D.: Agile methodologies. VerisonOne. Agil. Made Easier. (2021)

Tsivitanidou, O., Ioannou, A.: Users' needs assessment for chatbots' use in higher education. In: Central European Conference on Information and Intelligent Systems, pp. 55–62 (2020)

Weizenbaum, J.: ELIZA—a computer program for the study of natural language communication between man and machine. Commun. ACM **9**(1), 36–45 (1966)

Winkler, R., Söllner, M.: Unleashing the potential of chatbots in education: a state-of-the-art analysis. Acad. Manag. Ann. Meet. (AOM) (2018)

Exploring the Role of Chatbots and Messaging Applications in Higher Education: A Teacher's Perspective

Juan J. Merelo[1]([✉])[iD], Pedro A. Castillo[1] [iD], Antonio M. Mora[2] [iD],
Francisco Barranco[1], Noorhan Abbas[3] [iD], Alberto Guillén[1] [iD],
and Olia Tsivitanidou[4] [iD]

[1] Department of Computer Architecture and Technology, University of Granada, Granada, Spain
jmerelo@ugr.es
[2] Department of Signal Theory, Telematics and Communications, University of Granada, Granada, Spain
[3] School of Computing, University of Leeds, Leeds, UK
[4] CYENS Centre of Excellence, Nicosia, Cyprus

Abstract. The use of new technologies such as messaging applications and chatbots in higher education is rapidly growing in Western countries. This entails a careful consideration of the potential opportunities and/or challenges of adopting these tools. Hence, a comprehensive examination of the teachers' opinions and needs in this discipline can shed light on the effective ways of enhancing students' learning and boosting their progress. In this contribution, we have surveyed the opinions of instructors based in Spain (mainly) and Spanish-speaking countries. Specifically, we aimed to collect teachers' feedback about their opinions regarding the introduction of the messaging platforms and chatbots in their classes, understand their needs and to collect information about the various educational use cases where these tools are valuable. In addition, an analysis of how and when teachers' opinions towards the use of these tools can vary across gender, experience, and their discipline of specialization is presented. The key findings of this study highlight the factors that can contribute to the advancement of the adoption of messaging platforms and Chabots in higher education institutions to achieve the desired learning outcomes.

Keywords: Educational chatbots · Messaging platforms · Higher education

1 Introduction

The introduction of new technologies in the classroom, to be successful, involves extra teacher training, devising methods for enhancing student engagement with the new technology, and indeed acquiring new skills by students and teachers alike. Some technologies are readily adopted, but others require longer time for full adoption. In most cases, the magnitude of the uptake of the new technology impinges on the collaboration of all the parties using it. Hence, examining the users' opinions is an important first step in boosting this collaboration and reaping the benefits of the technology. Recently, a surge in the use of synchronous instant messaging tools in higher education such as WhatsApp, Telegram and Facebook Messenger took place. Some messaging applications have built-in chatbots to support a synchronous conversation between the different parties [25], while other chatbots are developed as standalone systems and can possibly be attached to a messaging application using an API (Application Program Interface).

A chatbot is a program, sometimes developed using Artificial Intelligence techniques, able to communicate in a similar way as humans do [11], using, in some cases, natural language. Indeed, most of these applications would be, apparently, close to passing a classic Turing test [15], since they are able to answer almost any question fluently, and even pose own questions in their conversations. The recent advancement in this discipline has played an important role in many fields especially in education and online tutoring [24]. These automatic systems facilitate the delivery of personalized learning by adapting to students' pace of learning and providing customized online tutoring outside the classroom. Thus, chatbots can significantly contribute to providing interactive learning experiences as well as improving individual attention [3]. In this sense, chatbot technology offers a great opportunity for the improvement of tutoring systems [3], as not all students are comfortable with face-to-face tutoring with the instructor. In many cases, some students experience stress because of their need to ask a question in front of the entire class and resort to contacting their teachers later via email. Consequently, this can lead to not only a delay in obtaining answers to their questions but can also cause a significant increase in their teachers' workload, especially when factoring in the disproportion between the class size and the number of teachers. Hence, the chatbot technology has a potential to mitigate this problem by providing answers to students' questions and facilitating a dynamic and autonomous learning experience [12, 13]. In addition, using an automated system such as a chatbot, can draw teachers' attention to topics that students struggle to comprehend or need further assistance in understanding.

The majority of studies conducted so far have studied how these messaging applications and/or chatbots are used to deliver personalized learning in classrooms that occurs anytime anywhere, promote collaborative learning experiences, group discussions [19] and boost students' sense of belonging to their institutions [2]. Hence, due to the paucity of research that explores the use of these technologies from the teachers' perspectives, this paper aims to investigate their opinions/needs and the challenges/opportunities of adopting these technologies in classrooms to paint a better picture of how they can positively contribute to enhancing the learning process in higher education institutions.

In this study, we use the key findings of the first phase of this study reported in [16] about students' opinions and preferences of using messaging applications for educational purposes in collecting and comparing teachers' opinions about this matter. In this paper, we aim to answer the following research questions:

RQ1 - Are teachers already using messaging apps in their classes?

RQ2 - Which chatbots' features would teachers find useful in their classes?

RQ3 - Which kind of interaction do teachers prefer with their students?

RQ4 - What kind of interaction media features do teachers value the most?

By answering these questions, we aim to aim to explore best practices and innovative use of chatbots in higher education. The remainder of the paper is organized as follows:

first, an overview of the current research in this field is presented. The methodology used in designing and conducting the surveys is explained in Sect. 3, and the results of the surveys are shown in Sect. 4. Finally, we discuss these results and conclude with a series of recommendations.

2 Background

The widespread and rapid adoption of free Mobile Instant Messaging (MIM) tools/platforms such as WhatsApp, Telegram, WeChat and Facebook Messenger stems from their simplicity, ease of use and multi-modality (i.e. video, audio, text) [26]. Using these tools in higher education can facilitate the delivery of personalized learning that occurs anytime anywhere, promote collaborative learning experiences and group discussions [19]. WhatsApp is, at least in most Western countries, the most popular MIM platform used by educators to provide assignments' feedback to students, support course discussions, and provide learning resources in informal learning settings [19]. Moreover, the use of WhatsApp in higher education could enhance social presence [26] and foster trust relationships between educators and students embedded in the social learning process [10]; however, this last paper also reflects the need for learners to "take ownership of the tool" and the advantages of social learning in general. At the same time, it also mentions different challenges, among which the most important is the blurring of social and academic life; indeed, there are challenges when using MIM tools that occur due to the blurring of boundaries between academic and private life. This can lead to technostress [10], difficulty in managing responsibilities, especially among mature students, and lack of privacy [26]. Students' dropout of the MIM groups, as they can leave groups at any time, can hinder their learning and undermine educators' efforts [17]. In addition, there is a need to set rules and norms for these MIM groups in order to maintain the safety of these online communities for students [2]. However, these rules should not affect students' ownership and control, since it is vital to advance in their learning [10] process. This is why examining the role of MIM in higher education is still a challenge, and why the opinions of the teaching community towards them have to be examined, as we do in this paper.

The use of MIM, although possibly valuable by itself, can be enhanced via the use of chatbots, which, being conversational agents, usually dwell in systems where synchronous conversations take place. The use of conversational agents (chatbots) in higher education is still at its infancy [28]. Nevertheless, recent studies examining their positive impact on students' academic performance [20] and engagement [2, 25] have led to a growing interest in using this technology in the (possibly virtual) classroom. Indeed, the use of chatbots in collecting course feedback from students in higher education improved students' response quality and boosted their enjoyment levels [1]. According to [22], using either tools such as mobile devices or teaching strategies based on gamification [29] can improve student motivation. In this sense, the authors in [21] adopted a quasi-experimental, survey-based approach to report the positive impact of using instant messaging tools in boosting students' knowledge and mitigating their feelings of isolation.

Several higher education chatbots' evaluation studies have been undertaken. For instance, a recent evaluation review study presented by Smutny and Schreiberova [24] examined 47 educational chatbots implemented in Facebook Messenger with the focus to identify characteristics and quality metrics such as language, subject matter and platform, whereas the study undertaken by P´erez and collaborators [20] aimed to categorize educational chatbots, according to their, purpose into service-oriented and teaching-oriented. The first category includes those that provide service support such as the chatbot Ask Holly [8] and Dina [23]; both chatbots respond to students' questions about enrolment and registration. Ask L. U. [14] answers students' frequently asked questions about timetables, grades, tutors and societies. LISA [7] and Differ [25] facilitate breaking the ice between new students by introducing them to each other.

On the other hand, teaching-oriented chatbots are more sophisticated, as they set personalized learning outcomes and monitor learning progress. For instance, [9] reported on "eduAssistant", a virtual teaching assistant chatbot developed on the Telegram messaging platform. In this study, the Tele-gram platform is chosen because it is easy to use, students are familiar with its features, and it enables them to exchange messages in different formats (text, audio and video) [9]. In addition, Telegram could operate on all devices and operating systems. The "eduAssistant" chatbot acts as an automatic agent in teacher-content-student, facilitating real-time feedback loops and providing a personalized learning experience relevant to the students' acquired skills and knowledge. Using this chatbot, educators can create interactive instances in their lectures where they pose questions to their students and the chatbot assists those who need further help by giving them more hints and reporting it to their educator's dashboard [9]. This can help educators locate those students that need more attention and send them more educational resources relevant to their academic attainment. In addition, a recent study has analyzed how the use of chatbots positively affected the learning outcomes of students in a Chinese class [6].

3 Methodology

This study followed a quantitative approach towards addressing its research objective, by collecting rich data about the use of messaging applications and chatbots by educators in both universities and colleges through the use of two online surveys. Both surveys were piloted by the authors of the paper and their colleagues before using it in the study. All the comments collected from this trial were incorporated in the surveys.

For addressing research questions 1–3, an online survey was administered (i.e., Google Form), in Spanish, comprised by six questions focusing on demo-graphic data (i.e., sector, gender, degrees, discipline, age, teaching experience), followed by four multiple choice questions allowing the participants to choose multiple answers in each of those. The multiple-choice questions focused on the use of messaging apps in the teaching practice, the type of chatbot use cases that teachers consider useful to be used in their teaching, and the type of interactions that teachers prefer to have with their students while using messaging apps in their teaching, and the impact of COVID on the teaching practice. This survey was administered to both university and tertiary non-university teachers (i.e., teaching in the vocational sector). The responders were reached out through the use of mailing lists and Telegram groups. The survey was shared among university teachers that teach in Spanish (mainly Andalucía and Galicia) universities, and also Costa Rica and Mexico, and tertiary non-university teachers who are based mainly in Andalucía. Data collection with the use of the survey took place in the first quarter of 2021, post-pandemic and while, at least in Spain, many universities had mandatory virtual teaching. Responses were stored automatically in a Google Drive spreadsheet.

For addressing the 4th research question, a second online survey was administered (i.e., Google Form), in Spanish, comprised by four questions focusing on demographic data (i.e., gender, age, degrees, teaching experience), followed by two multiple choice questions with single answers and one multiple choice question allowing the participants to choose multiple answers. The items of this survey focused on the kind of interaction media features that the teachers value the most. The survey was administered to university teachers teaching at the University of Granada, but also student teachers who attended a teacher formation course (on the use of new technologies in higher education). The responders were reached out using mailing lists, while an invitation to participate in the survey was also promoted in the newsletter of the vice deanship for International Relations of the University of Granada. Responses were stored automatically in a Google Drive spreadsheet.

4 Results and Analysis

Our findings per Research Question (RQ) are given in the sections that follow. For addressing RQs 1–3 data from the first survey was used. A total of 282 teachers responded to this first survey, from which 193 teachers mentioned that they teach at the University (68.4%) and 89 at other tertiary education institutions (31.6%). In relation to their gender, 179 teachers were male (63.5%), 98 females (34.8%) and 5 teachers preferred not to indicate their gender (1.8%). In terms of age, most of the participants (n = 111) in this survey were 45–55 years old (39.4%), while 91 teachers were 35–45 (32.3%), 46 were 25–35 (16.3%) and 34 teachers were older than 55 (12.1%). Last, 84 teachers had a teaching experience of 16–25 years (29.8%), 75 teachers 6–15 years of experience (26.6%), 69 teachers had 0–5 years of experience (24.5%) and finally, 54 teachers had more than 25 years of teaching experience (19.1%).

4.1 RQ1 - Are Teachers Already Using Messaging Apps in Their Classes?

Teachers were queried about whether they use messaging apps in their classes, specifically, Telegram, WhatsApp, Slack (an application used mainly in IT departments and software development), or any other messaging app, and whether they use messaging apps provided by their academic institution (see Table 1). Overall, the majority of the teachers responded that they do use messaging apps in their classrooms, from which apps provided by the academic institution (n = 159, 56%) and WhatsApp (n = 124, 44.0%) were the most common responses. Only 19 teachers (6.7%) replied that they do not use any messaging app in their class.

With respect to specific disciplines, Engineering and Technology teachers are more active in their use, but the number of teachers from Humanities who answered they used these apps in their classes is also remarkable (around 60% use the apps provided

Table 1. Use of messaging apps to assist the learning process

Messaging app	Yes		No	
	Frequency	%	Frequency	%
Telegram	62	22.0	220	78.0
WhatsApp	124	44.0	158	56.0
Slack	15	5.3	267	94.7
Other	60	21.3	222	78.7
Provided by the Academic Institution	159	56.4	123	43.6
None	19	6.7	263	93.3

by their institutions). Although no significant differences were found regarding gender, female teachers answered they use instant messaging apps more than male teachers (about 10% more). Also, teachers in vocational Education use WhatsApp more than university teachers. Regarding the distribution of the use of messaging apps per age, there are no significant differences for WhatsApp and apps provided by their own academic institutions. However, younger teachers also use Telegram with more than 25% responding they do, a percentage that falls to about 10% for teachers that are 55 or older. One interesting result is that about 65% of teachers with more than 25 years of experience use the platforms provided by their institutions while the percentage goes down to less than 50% for teachers with 6–15 years of experience.

Some of the questions in the survey were focused on the impact of the COVID19 pandemic between the 2020 and 2021 academic years in the teachers' attitudes towards the use of instant messaging apps in their class. Our main intention in this case was to assess whether a crisis will bring about some kind of change in the use of tools. Teachers' responses are summarized in Figs. 1, 2, 3 and 4 below, showing that about 77% of teachers already used these tools before the pandemic and kept using them during the pandemic lockdowns that forced students and educators to use remote education schemes. Moreover, approximately 15% of them switched their messaging app for one that offered a safer interaction with their students. According to the responses, an additional 16% started using messaging apps during the pandemic for the first time in their classes.

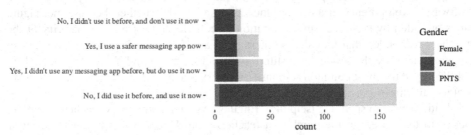

Fig. 1. Total count of responses for the use of messaging apps after the COVID-19 pandemic grouped by gender (PNTS stands for Prefer Not To Say).

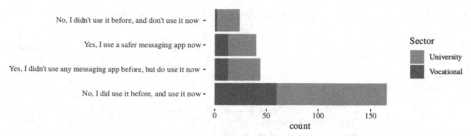

Fig. 2. Total count of responses for the use of messaging apps after the COVID-19 pandemic grouped by sector (PNTS stands for Prefer Not To Say).

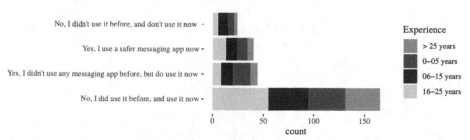

Fig. 3. Total count of responses for the use of messaging apps after the COVID-19 pandemic grouped by years of experience (PNTS stands for Prefer Not To Say).

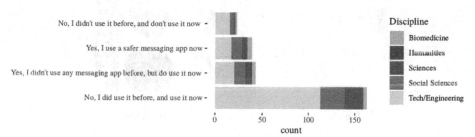

Fig. 4. Total count of responses for the use of messaging apps after the COVID-19 pandemic grouped by discipline.

A chi-square test of independence was performed to examine the relation between instructors' discipline, sector, and gender and any potential changes that occurred to the use of messaging apps due to the covid-19 pandemic. The relation between the latter variable and the instructors' sector was significant, $X^2_{(4, N = 282)} = 9.598$, $p = 0.048$. The frequencies cross tabulated are given in Table 2, Pearson's residuals for the Chi-square test are given in Fig. 5. In effect, this finding indicates that how teachers responded to the use of messaging apps during the pandemic and in particular, whether they changed their habits in the use of apps for teaching purposes, was related to their sector (university vs vocational). The majority of the teachers (n = 165) mentioned that no changes in their habits occurred due to the emergency remote teaching, as the use of messaging apps was part of their teaching practices and remains the same, from which 105 teachers come from the university, and 60 teachers from the vocational sector.

Table 2. Sector * post-covid changes cross tabulation

		Sector		Total
		University (f)	Vocational (f)	
Post-covid changes	Yes, I use a safer messaging app now	27	13	40
	Yes, I didn't use any messaging app before, but do use it now	31	13	44
	No, I did use it before and use it now	105	60	165
	No, I didn't use it before and don't use it now	22	2	24
	Other	8	1	9
Total		193	89	282

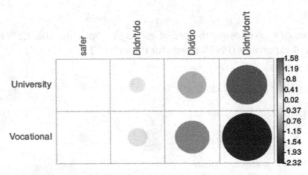

Fig. 5. Analysis for sector and post-covid changes

The relationships between changes in the use of messaging apps, due to the covid-19 pandemic, and the instructors' discipline, $X^2_{(24, N = 282)} = 44.856$, p = 0.006, as well as the gender, $X^2_{(8, N = 282)} = 16.249$, p = 0.039 were also significant. This finding indicates that how teachers responded to the use of messaging apps during the pandemic was also related to their gender and discipline. In fact, from the majority of the teachers who did not change their habits in this respect (n = 165), most of them are males (n = 114) and come from the technology (n = 60) and engineering (n = 53) disciplines (see Tables 3, 4) (Figs. 6 7).

4.2   RQ2 - What Kind of Chatbots Would Teachers Find Useful in Their Classes?

For answering RQ2, teachers were provided with a list of different potential chatbot functionalities (use cases) and were requested to respond on whether each given use case would be useful in their classes. The findings are summarized in Table 5.

Table 3. Gender * post-covid changes cross tabulation

		Gender			Total
		Male	Female	Prefer not to say	
Post-covid changes	Yes, I use a safer messaging app now	20	20	0	40
	Yes, I didn't use any messaging app before, but do use it now	20	23	1	44
	No, I did use it before and use it now	114	47	4	165
	No, I didn't use it before and don't use it now	18	6	0	24
	Other	7	2	0	9
Total		179	98	5	282

Table 4. Discipline * post-covid changes cross tabulation

		Discipline							Total
		Engineering	Social Sciences	Sciences	Biomedicine	Humanities	Technology	Other	
Post-covid changes	Yes, I use a safer messaging app now	7	11	5	5	1	10	1	40
	Yes, I didn't use any messaging app before, but do use it now	13	12	5	4	2	7	1	44
	No, I did use it before and use it now	60	26	20	4	0	53	2	165
	No, I didn't use it before and don't use it now	14	4	1	2	1	1	1	24
	Other	5	0	1	1	1	1	0	9
Total		99	53	32	16	5	72	5	282

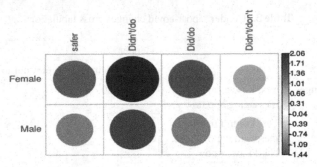

Fig. 6. Analysis for gender and post-covid changes

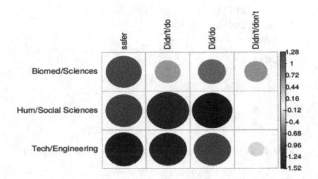

Fig. 7.

Table 5. Perceived useful chatbot use cases

Chatbot use cases	Yes		No	
	Frequency	%	Frequency	%
Answering to students' FAQs	148	52.5	134	47.5
Assigning student grades	113	40.1	169	59.9
Facilitating agenda formation	171	60.6	111	39.4
Sharing class material	136	48.2	146	51.8
Other use case	25	8.9	257	91.1

From the findings it occurs that the most favorable use case for chatbots in Higher Education and vocational training is their use for the facilitation of an agenda formation (171 positive response, 60.6%), followed by the FAQs use case (148 positive responses, 52.5%) and the sharing class material use case (136; 48.2%). Answers to these questions are plotted in Figs. 8, 9, 10, 11, grouped by gender, sector, years of experience in education, and discipline respectively.

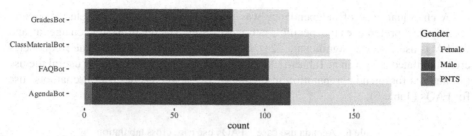

Fig. 8. Count of types of chatbots for class perceived as the most useful for teachers grouped by gender (PNTS stands for Prefer Not To Say).

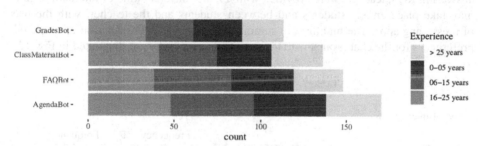

Fig. 9. Count of types of chatbots for class perceived as the most useful for teachers grouped by sector.

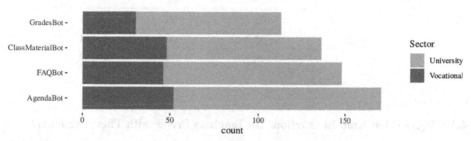

Fig. 10. Count of types of chatbots for class perceived as the most useful for teachers grouped by years of teaching experience.

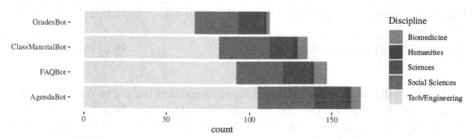

Fig. 11. Count of types of chatbots for class perceived as the most useful for teachers grouped by discipline.

A chi-square test of independence was performed to examine the relation among participants' preferences for specific chatbot use cases. The relation between agenda and the FAQs use case was significant, $X2_{(1, N = 282)} = 10.467, p = 0.001$. The frequencies cross tabulated are given in Table 4. Out of the 171 teachers who consider useful the use of chatbots for agenda preparation in the class, 103 also consider useful chatbots' use for FAQs (Table 6).

Table 6. Agenda use case * FAQs use case cross tabulation

		FAQs		Total
		Yes	No	
Agenda	Yes	103	68	171
	No	45	66	111
Total		148	134	282

4.3 RQ3 - What Kind Interactions Do Teachers Prefer with Their Students?

Since chatbots are intended to mediate or help in this interaction, it is essential to understand the kind of interaction teachers prefer. In order to find out these modes, and thus answering RQ3, teachers were provided with a list of different kind of interactions that may take place among students and between students and the teacher, with the use of messaging apps. The findings are summarized in Table 7. Distribution of teachers' preferences for the chat groups with their students per gender are illustrated in Fig. 12.

Table 7. Type of interactions preferred

Kind of interactions	Yes		No	
	Frequency	%	Frequency	%
Chat interactions among students in the same course	171	60.6	110	39.0
Chat interactions among students, teachers, and the faculty	13	4.6	269	95.4
Chat interactions among students of the same study year and teachers	51	18.1	231	81.9
Teacher not being part of the interaction	113	40.1	169	59.9

Regarding the social factor of chat groups that teachers use in class, it appears that the vast majority prefer small groups only with the students from the same course. Thus, teachers do not want to participate in a chat group with students; either they want to simply leave the students alone in their own chat group, or otherwise they prefer not to be part of that interaction. Chat interactions among students, teachers, and the faculty were less preferred by the teachers.

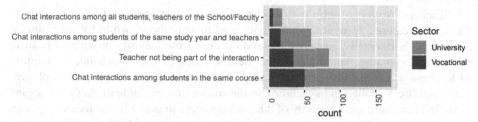

Fig. 12. Distribution of teachers' preferences for the chat groups with their students: from groups only with their students from a specific course to groups with greater social interaction with all students in their School or Faculty.

4.4 RQ4 - What Kind of Interaction Media Features Do Teachers Value the Most?

For addressing RQ 4, data from the second survey was used. A total of 205 teachers responded to this survey, from which 187 were graduate teachers (91.2%) and 18 student teachers (8.8%). From those, 124 were (60.5%), 65 female (31.7%) and 16 teachers preferred not to indicate their gender (7.8%). In terms of age, the majority of the participants (n = 70) was again, as in the first survey, 45–55 years old (34.1%), while 67 teachers were 35–45 (32.7%), 42 were 25–35 (20.5%) and 26 teachers were older than 55 (12.7%). In terms of teaching experience, 59 teachers had a teaching experience of 16–25 years (28.8%), 51 teachers had 6–15 years (24.9\%) and 0–5 years of experience (24.9%), and 44 teachers more than 25 years of teaching experience (21.5%). The teachers were asked about what kind of interaction media features they value the most; the frequencies and percentages of their responses are given in Table 8.

Table 8. Interaction media features valued by teachers

Interaction features	Yes		No	
	Frequency	%	Frequency	%
Analytics	108	52.7	97	47.3
Connectivity	119	58.0	86	42.0
Familiarity	121	59.0	84	41.0
Hidden Phone	113	55.1	92	44.9
Horizontally	134	65.4	71	34.6
Official formation	42	20.5	163	79.5
Pluggability	65	31.7	140	68.3
Sustainability	157	76.6	48	23.4
Unidirectionality	27	13.2	178	86.8
Officiality	150	73.2	55	26.8
Synchronous communication	45	22.0	160	78.0
Other	5	2.4	200	97.6

Teachers' responses are distributed between positive and negative in relation to the media features: analytics, connectivity, and hidden phone, while for the features: familiarity, horizontally, sustainability and officiality the majority provided a positive response, designating their preference to these features. On the other hand, the majority of teachers seems to consider not valuable the presence of official formation, pluggability, unidirectionality and synchrony in the interaction media features of messaging apps. In other words, the majority of the teachers seem to prefer to use messaging apps to which they are already familiar, and which have been granted by their academic institution, normally also accompanied with technical support by the university's staff and which do not require any actions on the behalf of the teachers for maintenance. In addition, the majority of the teachers value more the messaging apps in which there is no hierarchy in the communication level among the different users (i.e., teachers, students), and when the use of the app does not require or reveal their personal phone number. Last, most of the teachers value the most messaging apps that provide analytics in a form of a dashboard. A chi-square test of independence was performed to examine the potential relationship among the various features. The statistically significant correlations are given in the table that follows.

As indicated from the chi square results, the presence of the analytics feature in messaging apps, has been found to be positively correlated with the presence of features such as, connectivity, familiarity, official formation, pluggability and sustainability. That means, that teachers who prefer to use an app (or tool) that provides analytics about students' actions and/or performance, most probably also prefer this app to be able to be connected to other applications, offer different plugins to the teachers and be an app with which the teachers are already familiar, while receiving some training from the university about its use and do not have to worry about its maintenance. In addition, the hidden phone feature was found to be correlated with the features: official formation (i.e., the university offers some training courses or talks about the tool/app) and unidirectionality (i.e., only the teacher can publish information in the channel). This can be expected, as teachers might prefer not to reveal personal data, such as their personal phone number, when the tool is being introduced by the university and when the level of communication is one-way (i.e., from the teacher to the students). Furthermore, pluggability has been found to be correlated with official formation, implying that teachers who prefer pluggability as a feature in a messaging app/tool, they should also prefer to having this tool/app being properly and officially introduced by the university and offer some training about its usage (Table 9).

Table 9. Chi-square analyses

	Connectivity	Familiarity	Horizontality	Official formation	Pluggability	Sustainability	Unidirectionality	Officiality
Analytics	12.172***	4.855**	Ns	4.144*	12.490***	4.314*	ns	ns
Connectivity	–	Ns	5.971***	ns	16.286***	ns	ns	ns
Hidden phone			Ns	5.678*	4.683*	ns	4.515*	ns
Horizontality		–	Ns	ns	ns	ns	ns	5.453*
Official formation				–	8.163**	ns	ns	ns

***p < 0.001, **p < 0.01, *p < 0.05.

5 Discussion

This study sheds the light on educators' growing usage of messaging applications in classrooms even before COVID19. Recent research [19] examining the use of messaging applications in higher education claimed that WhatsApp is widely used by educators. However, in this study, although 44% of educators reported using WhatsApp in their classrooms, more than half of the survey responses (nearly 56%) claim using technologies supported by their institutions. One possible explanation for this finding could be that educators wanted to ensure that their institutions can oversee their efforts in supporting their students during the learning process. Another reason could be attributed to institutions mandating the use of specific technologies that they support. Hence, this finding probes more queries about the actual reasons contributing to this shift in technology preference among educators and its implications on the students/educators' interaction and learning.

In addition, as recent research examining students' usage of messaging applications with their peers in higher education [2] argue that students prefer to use the non-institution messaging applications to form informal discussion groups with their peers, further research should aim to investigate this wide spectrum of usage of these applications and their impact on the learning process. The question examining the use of messaging applications during the pandemic (COVID19) reflects the big challenge of having to change habits during a major crisis.

The survey responses reveal some gender differences in this respect as 31% of female educators reported moving to using messaging applications to cope with the new virtual mode of learning during the pandemic compared to only 17% of male educators. Moreover, the survey responses to the question that lists the different functionalities that a chatbot can be used for indicating that nearly 60% of educators favored using chatbots in grading and 47.5% in answering students' FAQs.

The survey results, when grouping by experience, confirm the previous observation that experienced teachers are willing to accept new technological challenges, at least, similar to younger teachers. Younger educators are also willing to use chatbots for other uses. Therefore, as in many other methods of technology acceptance, answers to the survey suggest that the introduction of simple, and institution-supported, instant messaging and chatbot technologies would increase the perceived usefulness (which is one of the key metrics in technology acceptance models). Since most institutions already have some 'virtual campus' or learning management system, adding some easy automation, or connection to personal instant messaging tools, could really help on board the learning community on these new technologies.

As it appears in the responses presented above, teachers' responses are equally distributed between positive and negative in relation to the media features: analytics, connectivity, and hidden phone number; that is, none of them is a prevailing factor on choosing one technology over another. However, for the features: familiarity, horizontally, sustainability and officially the majority provided a positive response, designating their preference to these features. On the other hand, the majority of teachers seems to consider not valuable the presence of official formation, pluggability, unidirectionality and synchrony in the interaction media features of messaging apps.

Our survey results suggest that there is no precise timings to introduce chatbot technologies in classes. However, responses to questions related to change of behavior during and after the first stay at home stage of the pandemic does not suggest that major (or minor) crisis could be an opportunity to introduce new technologies, since it does not bring major changes in attitudes. A minor crisis would be, for instance, rollout of a new higher education law, or introduction of new degrees. Although external changes do offer the chance of piloting new technologies, they do not seem to bring changes in attitudes in the teaching staff (which, after all, is bound to be the same). In absence of a clear answer in this direction, the right moment to introduce new technologies is always when the IT and managing staff is ready to support it (since, as we have seen before "official" support is one of the factors that is most valued by teachers).

Survey questions related to the messaging applications being used by tertiary education teachers, opens a new line of inquiry about what they perceive as such, and about how it is used. Namely, the responses indicated that the teachers perceived as messaging application not only what is usually called a chat or instant messaging app such as WhatsApp or Microsoft Teams, but also the means provided by the university for communicating with the student, such as a feature of grading applications that will email the grade to the student. This implies that there is a need by teachers, communication with students, also mostly unidirectional, and that it does not matter so much how that need is covered. How- ever, this will need careful consideration, including how it ties with the automation of the learning experience that the chatbots bring. There are several future lines of work informed by our results of this survey. For instance, the rollout of extensive videoconferencing and virtual teaching solutions that the COVID pandemic has brought has also taught us a series of lessons. It increases isolation, for instance, and decreases the amount of synchronous contact that happens in the fringes of the classroom: teaching staff offices, before and after class. A future line of work would be focused on exactly this, and what kind of needs could be covered by chatbot technology. We will create a series of international surveys that will investigate this.

6 Conclusions

The key findings of this study shed the light on educators' preference to use messaging applications that their institutions support. Technology adoption literature often focuses on users' perceptions of the technology's usefulness and ease of use as important prerequisites for successful adoption and utilization. Nevertheless, in higher education, institutions' role in integrating these tools to their educational systems can improve the uptake of these applications and shape the social and educational experiences of their students. To accomplish this fruitful integration, institutions must ensure that these messaging applications not only are GDPR (General Data Protection Regulation) compliant to keep students' data secure, but also should provide IT support to all stakeholders who use the applications.

Comparing these results with those obtained in student surveys in [16], we have understood better the differences between the teachers' points of view and/or intentions and that of their students when using the messaging applications in higher education. Teachers tend to adopt technologies supported by their institutions. The fact they do so could be caused by a desire to ensure that their universities can oversee their efforts in supporting their students during the learning process. Another reason could be their familiarity with the technology provided by their institutions. On the other hand, students use the non-institution messaging applications to form informal discussion groups with their peers. It is worth noting that peer support and collaboration is inseparable from learning [27] and correlates positively with higher retention in higher education [18]. Therefore, both perspectives are complementary and play different roles in promoting the learning process.

As in many other methodologies that try to assess technology acceptance, answers to the survey suggest that the introduction of simple, and institution-supported, instant messaging and chatbot technologies would increase the perceived usefulness (which is one of the key metrics in technology acceptance models). Since most institutions already have some virtual campus or learning management system, adding some easy automation, or connection to personal instant messaging tools, could really help onboard the learning community on these new technologies.

What we are going to propose next is a possible process of technology introduction that is compatible with the conclusions of this study, but that would have to be piloted in order to check its value, and its relationship with better learning outcomes, as well as higher teacher satisfaction. Once that initial introduction of institutional messaging automation tools is done, teachers (and students as well) will probably prefer the kind of bots that alleviate bureaucratic or repetitive tasks, such as answering frequent questions or answers on class or assignment deadlines, as indicated by their answers to the respective questions. These will help the introduction of more complex chatbots that will affect more directly learning outcomes, such as chatbots that help students integrate in the class or are able to identify (and address) learning problems in students or in groups of them. These should also be accompanied by analytics on student interaction, as well as possibly some natural language processing that will help assess the general mood of the class, and how different material (or external factors) affect it.

Acknowledgements. This work is part of the project EDUBOTS, which is funded under the scheme Erasmus + KA2: Cooperation for innovation and the exchange of good practices - Knowledge Alliances (grant agreement no: 612446).

References

1. Abbas, N., Pickard, T., Atwell, E., Walker, A.: University student surveys using chatbots: artificial intelligence conversational agents. In: Zaphiris, P., Ioannou, A. (eds.) HCII 2021, pp. 155–169. Springer, Cham (2021). https://doi.org/10.1007/978-3-030-77943-6_10
2. Abbas, N., Whitfield, J., Atwell, E., Bowman, H., Pickard, T., Walker, A.: Online chat and chatbots to enhance mature student engagement in higher education. Manuscript submitted for publication (2021b)
3. Agarwal, R., Wadhwa, M.: Review of state-of-the-art design techniques for chatbots. SN Comput. Sci. 1(246) (2020)
4. Agresti, A.: Categorical Data Analysis, 3rd edn. Willey, Hoboken (2013)

5. Bernier, J., Barchéin, M., Cañas, A., Gómez-Valenzuela, C., Merelo, J.: The services a university website should offer. Inf. Soc. Educ. Monit. Revolution. Serie Sociedad de la Educación **9**, 1746–1750 (2002)
6. Chen, H.-L., Widarso, G.V., Sutrisno, H.: A chatbot for learning Chinese: learning achievement and technology acceptance. J. Educ. Comput. Res. **58**(6), 1161–1189 (2020)
7. Dibitonto, M., Leszczynska, K., Tazzi, F., Medaglia, C.M.: Chatbot in a campus environment: design of LiSA, a virtual assistant to help students in their university life. In: Kurosu, M. (ed.) HCI 2018, pp. 103–116. Springer, Cham (2018). https://doi.org/10.1007/978-3-319-91250-9_9
8. Durham University: Meet holly (2021)
9. Fernoagă, V., Stelea, G.-A., Gavrilă, C., Sandu, F.: Intelligent education assistant powered by chatbots. In: The International Scientific Conference eLearning and Software for Education, vol. 2, pp. 376–383. "Carol I" National Defense University (2018)
10. Gachago, D., Strydom, S., Hanekom, P., Simons, S., Walters, S.: Crossing boundaries: lectures' perspectives on the use of whatsapp to support teaching and learning in higher education. Progressio **37**(1), 172–187 (2015)
11. Gong, L.: How social is social responses to computers? The function of the degree of anthropomorphism in computer representations. Comput. Hum. Behav. **24**(4), 1494–1509 (2008)
12. Griol, D., Molina, J., de Miguel, A.: The geranium system: multimodal conversational agents for e-learning. In: 11th International Conference Distributed Computing and Artificial Intelligence, vol. 290, pp. 219–226 (2014)
13. Kim, H.Y.: More than tools: emergence of meaning through technology enriched interactions in classrooms. Int. J. Educ. Res. **100**(101543) (2020)
14. Lancaster University: Lancaster University launch pioneering chatbot companion for students (2019)
15. Moor, J.: The Turing Test: The Elusive Standard of Artificial Intelligence, vol. 30. Springer, Dordrecht (2003). https://doi.org/10.1007/978-94-010-0105-2
16. Mora, A.M., Guillén, A., Barranco, F., Castillo, P.A., Merelo, J.J.: Studying how to apply chatbots technology in higher-education: first results and future strategies. In: Zaphiris, P., Ioannou, A. (eds.) HCII 2021, pp. 185–198. Springer, Cham (2021). https://doi.org/10.1007/978-3-030-77943-6_12
17. Mwakapina, J.W., Mhandeni, A.S., Nyinondi, O.S.: Whatsapp mobile tool in second language learning: opportunities, potentials and challenges in higher education settings in tanzania. Technical report, Macrothink Institute (2016)
18. O'Boyle, N.: Front row friendships: relational dialectics and identity negotiations by mature students at university. Commun. Educ. **63**(3), 169–191 (2014)
19. Panah, E., Babar, M.Y.: A survey of WhatsApp as a tool for instructor-learner dialogue, learner-content dialogue, and learner-learner dialogue. Int. J. Educ. Pedagogical Sci. **14**(12), 1198–1205 (2020)
20. Pérez, J.Q., Daradoumis, T., Puig, J.M.M.: Rediscovering the use of chatbots in education: a systematic literature review. Comput. Appl. Eng. Educ. **28**(6), 1549–1565 (2020)
21. Pimmer, C., Bruhlmann, F., Odetola, T.D., Oluwasola, D.O., Dipeolu, O., Ajuwon, J.: Facilitating professional mobile learning communities with instant messaging. Comput. Educ. **128**, 102–112 (2019)
22. Roblyer, M., McDaniel, M., Webb, M., Herman, J., Witty, J.V.: Findings on facebook in higher education: a comparison of college faculty and student uses and perceptions of social networking sites. Internet High. Educ. **13**(3), 134–140 (2010)
23. Santoso, H.A., et al.: Dinus intelligent assistance (DINA) chatbot for university admission services. In: 2018 International Seminar on Application for Technology of Information and Communication, pp. 417–423. IEEE (2018)

24. Smutny, P., Schreiberova, P.: Chatbots for learning: a review of educational chatbots for the Facebook messenger. Comput. Educ. **151**, 103862 (2020)
25. Studente, S., Ellis, S., Garivaldis, S.F.: Exploring the potential of chatbots in higher education: a preliminary study. Int. J. Educ. Pedagogical Sci. **14**(9), 768–771 (2020)
26. Tang, Y., Hew, K.F.: Is mobile instant messaging (MIM) useful in education? Examining its technological, pedagogical, and social affordances. Educ. Res. Rev. **21**, 85–104 (2017)
27. Timmis, S.: Constant companions: instant messaging conversations as sustainable supportive study structures amongst undergraduate peers. Comput. Educ. **59**(1), 3–18 (2012)
28. Yang, S., Evans, C.: Opportunities and challenges in using ai chatbots in higher education. In: Proceedings of the 2019 3rd International Conference on Education and E-Learning, pp. 79–83 (2019)
29. Yildirim, I.: The effects of gamification-based teaching practices on student achievement and students' attitudes toward lessons. Internet High. Educ. **33**, 86–92 (2017)

An Interactive Robot Lecture System Embedding Lecture Behavior Model

Toshiyuki Shimazaki[✉], Ayumu Sugawara, Mitsuhiro Goto, and Akihiro Kashihara

The University of Electro-Communications, 1-5-1 Chofugaoka, Chofu, Tokyo, Japan
shimazaki@uec.ac.jp

Abstract. In lectures, lecturers need to control the attention of learners to make them interested and to maintain their attention while monitoring their situation. Our previous work suggests that a robot as lecturer properly conducts non-verbal lecture behavior to have better learner engagement and attention control advantages over human lecturers. However, it is difficult to maintain learners' interests in a longer lecture, although attention control would be possible in shorter lectures. This causes them to miss following the contents of lectures. In this work, we have developed an interactive robot lecture system in which the robot interacts with learners by means of non-verbal behavior for keeping their attention when they miss the lecture. Towards attracting their attention, the system first estimates their states of understanding and attention from their posture based on a presentation scenario, which represents the lecture sequence. Next, the system attempts to keep the learners' attention with interactive lecture behavior by re-constructing the presentation scenario with their estimated states. The reconstruction is done with the lecture behavior model designed in this work. The interactive behavior is implemented using NAO, a humanoid robot, by combining pause, repeat, and skip behavior with paralanguage. We conducted a case study with 10 participants whose purpose was to evaluate the impressions of interactive behavior generated by our system. The results suggest that it is effective in keeping attention.

Keywords: Human-robot interaction · Robot lecture · Robot presentation · Lecture Behavior Model

1 Introduction

In lectures with presentation slides such as an e-learning lecture on video and a university lecture, it is important for lecturers to control the attention of learners to attract their interests and to keep their engagement. This requires lecturers to properly use their non-verbal behavior involving gaze, gesture, and paralanguage. In a longer lecture, in particular, lecturers should interact with learners by means of non-verbal behavior according to their states of taking the lecture. Such interactive non-verbal behavior allows lecturers to maintain learners' engagement in lectures.

On the other hand, it is not easy even for experienced human lecturers to make an appropriate use of non-verbal actions during the lecture or to keep the track of learners'

P. Zaphiris and A. Ioannou (Eds.): HCII 2022, LNCS 13329, pp. 224–236, 2022.
https://doi.org/10.1007/978-3-031-05675-8_17

states. For example, an unskilled lecturer may not utilize gestures or may always look at the laptop PC in hand while lecturing. In e-Learning lectures, in addition, it is not always possible to monitor the states of learners. It is accordingly difficult for learners to understand what they need to pay attention to, which allows them to miss some parts of the lecture. They may not be able to follow the lecture, and not be able to understand the lecture contents.

In our previous work, we focused on non-verbal behavior for lectures and developed a robot lecture system in which a robot gives a presentation using appropriate non-verbal behavior instead of a human lecturer in an e-Learning lecture [1]. We conducted a case study, in which we compared three types of lectures: a video lecture given by a human lecturer, a robot lecture that reproduced the lecturer's behavior, and a robot lecture that reconstructed the lecturer's behavior. The results suggest that the robot lecture with reconstruction is more significantly effective in improving learners' attention, and understanding of the lecture contents. In our previous work, on the other hand, we did not consider learners' states of taking the lecture and interactive lecture behavior. Some problems could not be solved when learners miss the lecture or when they lose attention on and understanding of the lecture [2, 3].

In this work, we have developed an interactive robot lecture system that supports the maintenance of learners' attention by reconstructing the sequence of presentation slides and oral explanation, and also by generating interactive behavior by means of the estimation of learners' comprehension and attention states, and by encouraging learners to pay attention. In this work, a presentation scenario is defined as the content of slides, associated non-verbal behavior, verbal explanation, and the order of slide presentation (slide sequence) that the lecturer considers when designing a lecture.

This paper is organized as follows. Section 2 outlines related work and shows the Lecture Behavior Model. The Interactive Robot Lecture System is described in Section 3. Section 4 outlines a case study using the system and discusses it. Conclusions and suggestions for future work are presented in Sect. 5.

2 Robot Lecture

2.1 Related Work

In this section, we describe related work on learning support using robots and compare with this work. Kidd et al. [4] and Köse et al. [5] suggest that robots can positively in-fluence learners' engagement with a task through interaction. Bainbredge et al. [6] and Li [7] suggest that physically present robots elicit more engagement with the task through interaction than doing screened robots. Leyzberg et al. [8] and Schodde et al. [9] have also found that the physical presence of a robot providing learners with interactive instruction can positively increase their learning gains. In addition, practical work on learning support using robots is being conducted. You et al. [10] utilize a robot as a teaching assistant. It has been shown that robots as teaching assistants are effective in maintaining learners' attention and increasing their motivation.

These results from related work suggest that interactive robot lectures could work in helping learners maintain their attention.

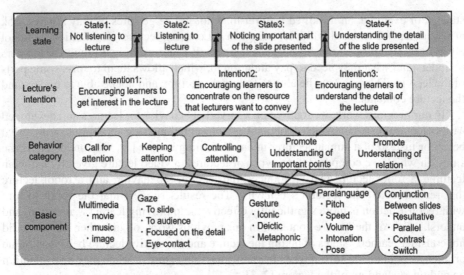

Fig. 1. Lecture behavior model.

On the other hand, this work aims to develop an interactive robot lecture that responds to the learner's state. These can be achieved by using the system developed in this work, which is described below, as a method to grasp learners' states of taking a lecture. By understanding the learner's state of attendance, it is possible to reconstruct presentation scenarios according to the situation. The presentation scenario can be reconstructed according to the situation, and attention maintenance can be achieved interactively. These approaches are the novelty of this work.

2.2 Lecture Behavior Model

In the previous work, it was necessary to clarify the nonverbal behavior in robot lecturer in response to lecture intentions. Therefore, we designed a Lecture Behavior Model to derive appropriate nonverbal behaviors from lecture intentions, as shown in Fig. 1. The model consists of three-layers consisting of lecture intention, behavior category, and basic components of behavior.

When lecturers have the intention 2, for example, the model suggests the necessity of non-verbal behavior for keeping attention, controlling attention, or promoting understanding of important points as behavior category. If they use non-verbal behavior for controlling attention, the model induces them to select and combine the corresponding basic components to conduct behavior such as facing to the slide with deictic pointing gesture.

3   Interactive Robot Lecture System

3.1   Framework

Figure 2 shows the framework of interactive robot lecture system. In this work, we use NAO, a humanoid robot manufactured by SoftBank Robotics. The system conducts interactive robot lecture with three functions: estimation of learner's states, presentation scenario reconstruction, and interaction with a learner.

NAO first gives a lecture presentation based on a presentation scenario created in advance. At the same time, the system monitors learners to acquire their skeleton data and face tracking data using Kinect. Using these data, the system estimates their states to compare with states assumed in the presentation scenario.

If the estimated states are consistent with the assumed ones, the lecture presentation is conducted according to the presentation scenario. If not, the system reconstructs the presentation scenario, which involves changing the slide sequence by following the scenario control model.

Following the reconstructed scenario, second, the system gives an interactive lecture to deliver the lecture contents to learners. The scenario includes the timing for switching slides, non-verbal behavior to be conducted, and audio files to be played. Learners can respond to interactive actions from NAO through the browser displaying the slides. For example, when the system detects their states inconsistent with assumed ones, NAO will ask if it should repeat a slide, and a learner could enter YES or NO.

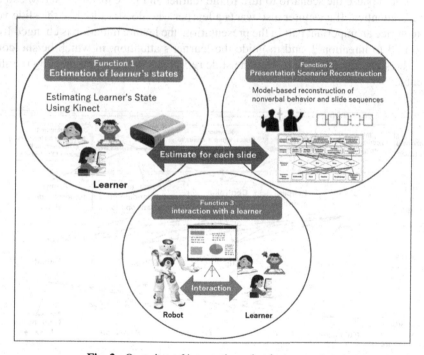

Fig. 2. Overview of interactive robot lecture system.

3.2 Scenario Control Model

To maintain learners' attention to lecture, it is necessary to change the presentation scenario interactively according to their states of taking the lecture. As shown in Fig. 3, we have accordingly designed a scenario control model based on the lecture behavior model, which derives an appropriate reconstruction of the presentation scenario from changes in lecture intention [11, 12]. This model consists of three layers: changes in lecture intention, scenarios control category, slide sequence control, and basic scenario components.

The model demonstrates how the presentation scenario is reconstructed from changes in the lecture intention. A change in the lecture intention means a change in the lecturer's intention to respond to the current state of the learner when there is a discrepancy between the current state of the learner and the state of the learner assumed in the pre-designed presentation scenario. The scenario control category represents the purpose for which the presentation scenario is to be reconstructed, and links the slide sequence control required for the reconstruction with the combination of the scenario basic components to conduct it.

Slide sequence control is performed with a pause, skip, and repeat as shown in Fig. 4. For example, if a lecturer wants a learner who is looking away and not concentrating to focus on a slide, the lecture intention is changed from intention 2 to intention 1, in which he/she could pause the scenario to turn to the learner and raise his/her voice to call the learner's attention. If a lecturer also wants a learner who does not look at the slide very well to notice an important part in the presentation, the lecture intention is changed from intention 3 to intention 2, and to guide the learner's attention, in which he/she could repeat the scenario and explain the same slide repeatedly while supplementing the slide contents.

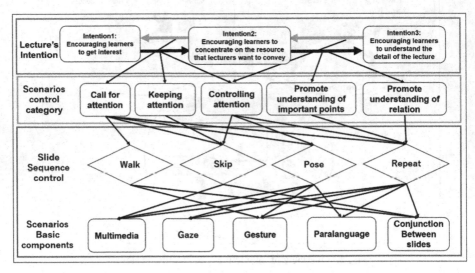

Fig. 3. Scenario control model.

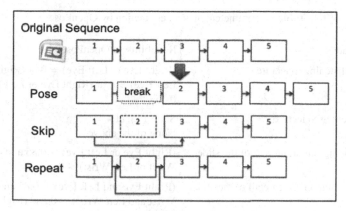

Fig. 4. Controlling slide sequence.

3.3 Reconstructing Lecture Behavior

In this work, presentation scenario reconstruction involves reconstructing lecture behavior in robot lecture. Figure 5 shows an overview of reconstructing lecture behavior in the system. The system conducts the reconstruction with four functions: lecture recording, learning state estimation, interactive behavior with NAO [13], and slide display browser.

In the lecture recording, the system generates the presentation scenario from a lecture with Kinect [14] or a lecture video of human lecturer. The data to be recorded are lecture intention, gestures (pointing and facing), speech contents, and paralanguage (voice volume and pitch). The size and color of the text on slides are also captured.

The lecture intention is entered by clicking on an object in PowerPoint or Google Slide to attach intentions (1) to (4) in the lecture behavior model. We extract the coordinate data of the face-facing and pointing gestures in each frame using OpenPose [15]. Then, the extracted OpenPose coordinate data is converted to indirect coordinates driven by NAO to reproduce the gestures. The speech contents are transcribed using Google Speech To Text as the speech recognition function. The paralanguage is converted into NAO speech using Praat [16], which extracts the pitch and volume frequencies of the speech.

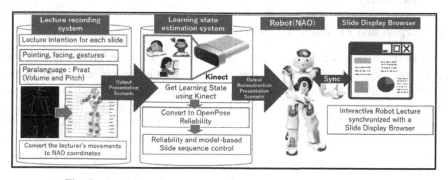

Fig. 5. Overview of reconstructing lecture behavior using system.

Table 1. Parameters of state estimation by OpenPose.

Learning state	Reliability of OpenPose
State1: Not listening to lecture	(Right Eye or Left Eye) = 0 or (Right Eye or Left Eye) = 0 or (Right Eye or Left Eye) < 0.25
State2: Listening to lecture	State 1, 3, or 4 None of the above
State3: Noticing important part of the slide presented	(Right Eye or Left Eye) > 0.85 and (Right Wrist or Left Wrist) > 0
State4: Understanding the detail of the slide presented	(Right Eye and Left Eye) > 0.85 and (Right Wrist and Left Wrist) > 0 and (Right Ear and Left Ear) > 0.4

In the learning state estimation, the system uses Microsoft's Kinect and OpenPose to estimate learners' states based on the lecture behavior model. Table 1 shows the parameters for estimating learner's states using OpenPose. The degree of learner's attention is estimated by combining the confidence of each coordinate of OpenPose as a result of preliminary experiments conducted by the authors. For example, learning state 1 in the lecture behavior model, where a learner is not listening to the lecture, is considered to be a case where the learner is looking away. Therefore, if the confidence of the right ear or the confidence of the left ear in the OpenPose coordinate data is set to zero, it can be assumed that the learner is looking away. Based on the scenario control model, the system determines lecture intention, scenario control category, and sequence control based on the learner's state estimated.

NAO then gives an interactive lecture based on the data collected from the lecture recording and the estimation results of the learning states.

The slide display browser synchronizes with NAO's interactive lecture and presents the slides to the learner in the slide display browser. The learner can also input YES/NO as for whether the interaction by NAO is necessary or not.

4   Case Study

4.1   Purpose and Experimental Design

In this work, we conducted a case study whose purpose was to ascertain whether interactive robot lecture could be more effective for controlling learners' attention and more beneficial for understanding the lecture contents. By comparing robot lecture involving interactive scenario reconstruction and the one involving simple reproduction, it is possible to confirm the validity of scenario reconstruction using the lecture behavior model.

Participants were 10 graduate and undergraduate students. We prepared two videos of robot lecture whose topic was numerical calculation taken for second-year undergraduate students. One was a video in which NAO conducted interactive robot lecture with reconstruction presentation scenario reconstruction (IL-condition), and the other was the one in which NAO conducted robot lecture without the reconstruction (NL-condition). These videos were for about 30 min. Participants were required to view the two videos to compare and evaluate the robot lectures in the videos.

As a within-participant design, each participant viewed the two videos under the two conditions. In order to counterbalance the order effects of the conditions, we randomly assigned 10 participants to two groups as shown in Table 2. For example, IL-NL group first viewed the video under IL-condition, then viewed the video under NL condition.

Figure 5 shows a screenshot of the robot lecture video. As shown in this figure, one learner and the lecture slides used by NAO appeared on the video. The learner in the video intentionally changed his posture as the lecture progressed, so that the participants could see the changes in his/her learning states.

After viewing the videos all participants were required to take an understanding test about numerical calculation, and then to answer a 7 Likert scale questionnaire including the 18 questions shown in Table 3 (Q1–Q18). Finally, they were required to answer a two-way questionnaire that asked the 10 questions shown in Table 3 (Q19–Q28) (Fig. 6).

Table 2. Procedure for video viewing.

Group	Robot lectures videos	
IL-NL group	IL-condition	NL-condition
NL-IL group	NL-condition	IL-condition

Fig. 6. Screenshot of the robot lecture video.

Table 3. Details of question items.

Q1: pose, Q4: repeat, Q7: skip, and Q10: walk: How well was the timing of the lecture behavior (pose, repeat, skip, and walk)?

Q2: pose, Q5: repeat, Q8: skip, and Q11: walk: How much did the robot prevent the learner from missing the lecture contents with the lecture behavior?

Q3: pose, Q6: repeat, Q9: skip, and Q12: walk: How much did the robot promote the learner's understanding of the lecture with the lecture behavior?

Q13: How much did the learner attend the lecture?

Q14: How appropriate were the robot's speaking, face orientation, and movement?

Q15: How much did the learner have eye contact with the robot?

Q16: How much did the robot have the lecture interactively?

Q17: How much did the robot conduct the lecture according to the learner's states?

Q18: How well did the robot estimate the learner's states?

Q19: Which robot lecture did you find easy to understand?

Q20: In which robot lecture did you feel easy to pay attention to the slides?

Q21: In which robot lecture did you feel easy to understand where you should focus on?

Q22: Which robot lecture did you find easy to listen to?

Q23: In which robot lecture did you feel the robot was talking to the learner?

Q24: In which robot lecture did you feel appropriate for the robot to face or point at?

Q25: In which robot lecture did you feel the robot and the learner have eye contact?

Q26: In which robot lecture did you feel you could attend for a longer time?

Q27: Which robot lecture did you want to attend?

Q28: Which robot lecture did you feel you could concentrate on?

4.2 Results and Discussion

Figure 7 and Fig. 8 show the results of the questionnaires as for interactive robot behavior (pause, skip, repeat, walk) in the IL-NL group and the NL-IL group. In the questionnaire, for each behavior, the participants were asked whether they felt that the timing of the robot behavior was appropriate (Q1, 4, 7, 10), whether they felt that it could prevent the learner from missing the lecture (Q2, 5, 8, 11), and whether they felt that it could help him/her understand the lecture (Q3, 6, 9, 12).

Figure 7 shows that the mean values of Q2, Q3, Q8, and Q11 were above 6, suggesting the effectiveness of pause, repeat, and walk. Figure 8 shows that the mean values in NL-IL group were higher than those in IL-NL group. NL-IL group had a higher mean value for walk-related movements than IL-NL group, possibly because they watched the video under IL condition after watching the one under NL condition to have a stronger impression of IL condition. In both groups, the mean values of all questionnaire items were 3.5 or higher. From these results, we can conclude that the interactive robot behavior was generally evaluated as appropriate one.

In both groups, in addition, only the walk behavior had a mean higher than 5. The mean value of skip was lower than 5 only in both groups. In particular, NL-IL group had the highest standard deviation of Q5 (SD = 1.52). The reason for this may be that the participants does not consider it appropriate to skip the lecture itself, or that the appropriate timing of skipping varies depending on the participants.

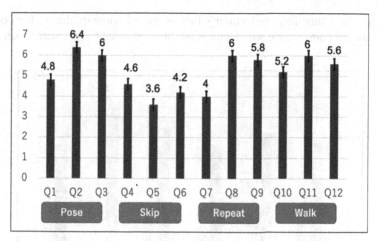

Fig. 7. Average scores of the effectiveness of pause, repeat, and walk (IL-NL Group).

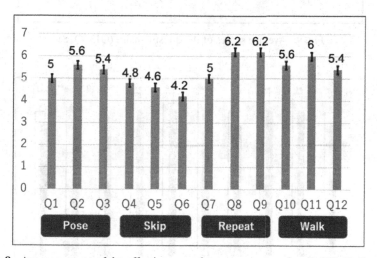

Fig. 8. Average scores of the effectiveness of pause, repeat, and walk (NL-IL Group).

Figure 9 shows the average scores of questionnaire (Q13 to Q18) after viewing the videos between the two conditions. The results of the two-tailed t-test showed that IL condition was higher for all the questions, and there was a significant difference between IL condition and NL condition (*p < .05).

Figure 10 shows the results of the impression questionnaire conducted after watching the robot lecture in the two conditions. Fisher's direct probability test was used to analyze the independence of IL and NL conditions, and a significant difference was found for all questions (*p < .05, **p < .01).

As a result, IL condition outperformed NL condition, suggesting that interactive robot lecture may be more effective than robot lecture. The reason why the participants chose NL condition for some of the questions may be that they are not comfortable with lectures in which they feel the lecturer's face or gaze frequently during the course, or that they are not comfortable with lectures being interrupted by interactive behavior.

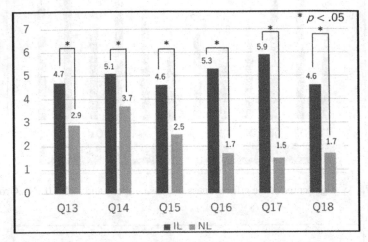

Fig. 9. Average scores of the questionnaire (Q13–Q18).

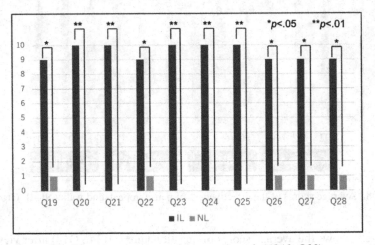

Fig. 10. Average scores of the questionnaire (Q19–Q28).

In addition, there were some comments suggesting the effectiveness of the robot's interactive behavior for attention maintenance, such as "I thought it was nice that the robot praised me for concentrating" and "I thought that the unnatural feeling of the walk, which was different from that of a human lecturer, may have conversely encouraged learners to pay their attention.

On the other hand, there were some comments suggesting the necessity for improving the robot lecture, such as "the robot's intonation bothered me," "it was difficult to understand where the robot was pointing," and "I felt that it required attention to listen to the robot's voice for 30 min," but there were no negative comments about the robot's behavior or interaction.

These results suggest that IL condition was more effective in supporting attention maintenance than NL condition.

5 Conclusion

In this work, we have developed an interactive robot lecture system that reconstructs a presentation scenario by estimating and grasping the learner's states to support the learner's attention maintenance during lecture. The results of the case study with 10 participants suggested that the interactive robot lecture system was effective in supporting learners' attention maintenance, and also suggested the effectiveness of using walk behavior by a humanoid robot to draw learner's attention.

In future, we plan to conduct another case studies with more participants, in which they take a 30-min interactive robot lecture with and without lecture scenario reconstruction. In particular, we will conduct an objective evaluation of the interactive robot lecture by using the understanding test after the lecture, the number of interactions between the learner and the robot, the estimated rate of learning states, and the learner's gaze as evaluation indicators, and will ascertain whether it is effective in supporting attention maintenance.

Acknowledgment. This work is supported in part by JSPS KAKENHI Grant numbers No. 18K19836 and 20H04294.

References

1. Ishino, T., Goto, M., Kashihara, A.: A robot for reconstructing presentation behavior in lecture. In: 6th International Conference on Human-Agent Interaction (HAI), pp. 67–75, Southampton, UK (2018)
2. Kashihara, A., Ishino, T., Goto, M.: Robot lecture for enhancing non-verbal behavior in lecture. In: Isotani, S., Millán, E., Ogan, A., Hastings, P., McLaren, B., Luckin, R. (eds.) AIED 2019. LNCS (LNAI), vol. 11626, pp. 128–132. Springer, Cham (2019). https://doi.org/10.1007/978-3-030-23207-8_24
3. Ishino, T., Goto, M., Kashihara, A.: Robot lecture for enhancing presentation in lecture. Res. Pract. Technol. Enhanc. Learn. (RPTEL) 17(1) (2022)
4. Kidd, C.D., Breazeal, C.: Effect of a robot on user perceptions. In: IEEE/RSJ International Conference on Intelligent Robots and Systems (IROS), vol. 4, pp. 3559–3564 (2004)
5. Köse, H., Uluer, P., Akalın, N., Yorgancı, R., Özkul, A., Ince, G.: The effect of embodiment in sign language tutoring with assistive humanoid robots. Int. J. Soc. Robot. 7(4), 537–548 (2015)
6. Bainbridge, W.A., Hart, J.W., Kim, E.S., Scassellati, B.: The benefits of interactions with physically present robots over video-displayed agents. Int. J. Soc. Robot. 3(1), 41–52 (2011)
7. Li, J.: The benefit of being physically present: a survey of experimental works comparing copresent robots, telepresent robots, and virtual agents. Int. J. Hum Comput Stud. 77, 23–37 (2015)

8. Leyzberg, D., Spaulding, S., Scassellati, B.: Personalizing robot tutors to individuals' learning differences. In: 9thACM/IEEE International Conference on Human-Robot Interaction (HRI), pp. 423–430 (2014)
9. Schodde, T., Bergmann, K., Kopp, S.: Adaptive robot language tutoring based on Bayesian knowledge tracing and predictive decision-making. In: Proceedings of the ACM/IEEE International Conference on Human-Robot Interaction (HRI), pp. 128–136 (2017)
10. You, Z.J., Shen, C.Y., Chang, C.W., Liu, B.J., Chen, G.D.: A robot as a teaching assistant in an English class. In: IEEE International Conference on Advanced Learning Technologies (ICALT 2006), pp. 87–91 (2006)
11. Sugawara, A., Kashihara, A.: Evaluating interactive robot lecture. In: Human-Agent Interaction Symposium 2021, P-4 (2021). (in Japanese)
12. Kashihara, A., Sugawara, A.: An adaptive lecture scenario for interactive robot lecture. Japan. Soc. Inf. Syst. Educ. Res. Rep. **35**(6), 19–26 (2021). (in Japanese)
13. SoftBank Robotics NAO. https://www.softbankrobotics.com/jp/product/nao. Accessed 9 Feb 2022
14. Microsoft Kinect. https://azure.microsoft.com/en-us/services/kinect-dk. Accessed 9 Feb 2022
15. OpenPose. https://github.com/CMU-Perceptual-Computing-Lab/openpose. Accessed 9 Feb 2022
16. Praat. https://www.fon.hum.uva.nl/praat. Accessed 9 Feb 2022

Learning by Teaching Partner Robot in Collaborative Reading

Takahito Sudo[✉] and Akihiro Kashihara

The University of Electro-Communications, 1-5-1 Chofugaoka, Chofu, Tokyo, Japan
t.sudo@uec.ac.jp

Abstract. Collaborative reading is an important activity for second language learners to practice communication. However, it is not easy for Japanese learners to read English sentences with a partner due to their embarrassment and lack of confidence. Our previous work has suggested that collaborative reading with a partner robot can reduce learners' psychological reluctance. On the other hand, there was a problem that some learners focused on reading English sentences in collaborative reading. In other words, learners did not care what the partner robot reads. In this work, we have developed a learning environment where a robot reads English sentences with incorrect grammar in collaborative reading, and learners teach the robot the grammatical mistakes. We also conducted a case study with 9 participants whose purpose was to evaluate learners' prosociality against the partner robot and the effectiveness of learning-by-teaching. The results suggest the possibility that learners improve their prosociality via teaching activity, and that teaching activity promotes reflection on their grammatical knowledge.

Keywords: Learning by teaching · Second language learning · Partner robot

1 Introduction

It is important for second language learners to communicate in a group. Collaborative reading as group work is often conducted in English education. However, there are cases where learners hesitate to participate in reading activities due to their difficulty in interpersonal relationships, embarrassment about reading English, or lack of confidence [1]. We accordingly proposed a partner robot for promoting collaborative reading and developed a system that supports collaborative reading with the robot [2]. It is suggested that the system can reduce learners' psychological reluctance to read English sentences and help them communicate in English effectively. On the other hand, the system has an issue where learners tend not to communicate with the robot but to read the given English sentences. This means they do not often care what the partner speaks, in which they could not obtain any communication experience in English.

In this work, we propose a learning-by-teaching partner robot that reads sentences in incorrect English grammar. The robot expects learners to listen carefully to its speech to correct mistakes made by the robot and teach the incorrect grammar. This teaching activity would promote their prosociality, and also helps them obtain effects of learning-by-teaching, which involves reflection on their own knowledge about the grammer [3].

In addition, we have also developed the learning-by-teaching system, which gives learners opportunities to teach the robot how to read in correct English grammar. In this paper, we describe the system and report a case study, in which we compared collaborative reading containing teaching activity and collaborative reading without teaching activity. The results suggest that teaching activity promotes learners' prosociality in the subjective evaluation and also their reflection on their grammatical knowledge.

2 Collaborative Reading with a Robot

2.1 Collaborative Reading

In English classes of Japanese primary and secondary education, pair-work and group-work are essential. Collaborative reading that is a reading activity using textbooks is often conducted to gain experience of communication in English. Obara pointed out that the pair-work promotes communication among learners and their willingness to participate in the learning activities. However, learner's reluctance to use English as second language makes it hard to conduct learning activities effectively [1, 4]. According to [1], the reason why learners are inactive to communicate is uncomfortableness in speaking English. This could decrease their self-efficacy. Yashima stated that willingness to communicate (WTC), and motivation for learning English are important for ESL (English as Second Language) learners. In addition, low self-efficacy and psychological reluctance due to anxiety and embarrassment have a negative impact on WTC [5]. These factors often interfere with conversation and interactive learning activities in English. How to avoid it to promote collaborative reading in English is the main issue in this work.

2.2 Related Work

Our previous work proposed a learning system to support collaborative reading in English with a partner robot [2]. Learners read English sentences with the robot. The robot has a voice recognition function, which is used to recognize their speech and to point out their wrong speech based on the recognition results.

The reason why we use a robot as a partner for collaborative reading is to reduce psychological reluctance and give learners a sense of communication. According to [6], human often anthropomorphizes robots and tend to view them as if they were human. We accordingly presume that communication with robots provides an interpersonal context similar to communication with human. Furthermore, other studies found that people who are not good at communication could actively talk to robots, and people who suffer from disorder of social anxiety play through interaction with robots [7]. Besides, an evaluation experiment in our previous work [2] suggested that collaborative reading with a partner robot reduced psychological resistance such as embarrassment and awkwardness compared to with a human, and moreover improved learners' motivation and self-efficacy.

2.3 Purpose

In collaborative reading in English, learners tend to read sentences without care about what their partner reads, which is different from the intention of training communication skills in English.

In this work, we aim to enhance the prosociality of learners toward the robot to make learners careful what the robot reads in collaborative reading. Towards this aim, we have developed a learning-by-teaching partner robot system. The system makes the robot read grammatically incorrect sentences and allows learners to teach the mistakes. We expect that the grammatical mistakes attract the learners' attention to what the partner robot reads, which motivates them to teach and promote their prosociality. We also expect that learners can gain learning effects from learning-by-teaching, in which they can reflect on their grammatical knowledge.

3 Learning-by-Teaching Partner Robot

3.1 Framework

Figure 1 shows the framework of the learning-by-teaching system. This system uses two NAOs, humanoid robots manufactured by SoftBank Robotics, as a teacher robot and a learner robot. The learner robot speaks English sentences slowly to play a role as a learner.

This system takes the following steps to help a learner do learning by teaching the partner robot.

1. Collaborative reading between the teacher robot and the learner robot
2. The teacher robot teaches the learner robot how to speak when it makes a mistake.
3. Collaborative reading between a learner and the learner robot
4. The learner teaches the learner robot how to speak when it makes a mistake.
5. Feedback on the teaching activity the learner did

We describe the details of each step and the expected learning effects. In step 1, the teacher robot and the learner robot collaboratively read sentences according to a script prepared. The learner robot makes a grammatical mistake. In step 2, the teacher robot teaches the learner robot the mistake and how to speak the sentence correctly. In the previous steps, we expect the learner to understand how to teach the learner robot, and at the same time, to be motivated to teach. In step 3, the learner and the learner robot collaboratively read sentences. The learner robot makes the same mistakes as in step 1, in which it corrects some of the mistakes made in step 1. We assume that the learner listens carefully to what the learner robot reads to teach its mistakes. In step 4, the learner teaches the sentences that he/she feels the learner robot has spoken with incorrect grammar. The robot asks the learner if it was wrong about each sentence the robot reads. If there is a mistake, the learner then presents the robot with the correct utterance. We expect that the teaching activity allows the learner to notice the wrong grammatical knowledge and the mistakes that he/she might make. In step 5, the teacher

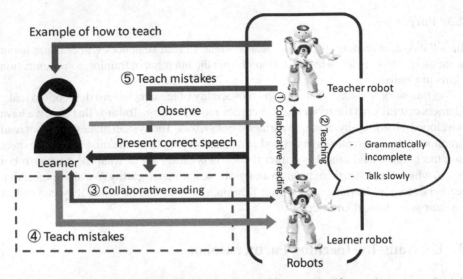

Fig. 1. Framework for learning-by-teaching partner robot system

robot teaches the learner the correct grammar when the learner teaches the learner robot incorrectly or misses grammatical mistakes the learner robot makes.

There are two main reasons to use two robots in this system. The first one is to show a learner an example of how to teach a learner robot. After the robots do the collaborative reading (Step 1), the teacher robot teaches the learner robot who made a mistake in speech (Step 2). The learner can use these activities as a reference to identify sentences the learner robot is supposed to make mistakes and to consider how to teach the learner robot. The second reason is to provide the learner with the correct utterance of the sentences. Depending on the learner, some sentences may appear in the script that they he/she does not know how to read. In this case, the learner cannot notice the mistake even if the learner robot incorrectly reads the sentence. The proposed system aims to provide learners with a teaching experience to enhance their learning effect. Thus, the two robots collaboratively read sentences in advance to avoid the situation.

3.2 Functions

Figure 2 shows the functions of the proposed system. This system provides an environment where the learner robot makes grammatical mistakes in reading activities, and the learner can teach about them. The system has the scripts used for collaborative reading, which includes some sentences. The learner robot is designed to make some mistakes in these sentences. The system displays the sentences and the contents the teacher robot teaches on the monitor. The speeches of the robots are controlled based on the scripts.

The system synchronizes the talk of the learner and the robots in collaborative reading. The system converts the learner's speech and teaching contents into audio data through the microphone, then converts it into string data using Google's Speech-to-Text API. The recognition results returned from the API are used not only to record how the

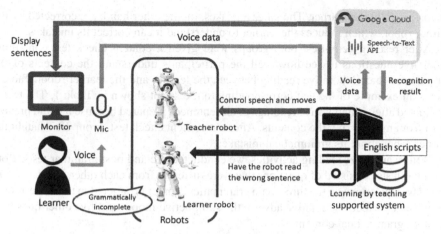

Fig. 2. Functions of learning-by-teaching supported system

learner reads the sentences and what the learner teaches the learner robot but also to decide which sentences the learner teaches.

4 Case Study

4.1 Purpose and Experimental Design

We had a case study whose purpose was to ascertain whether the robot who reads sentences containing wrong grammar would promote learners' prosociality, and whether the teaching interaction would give learners some learning effects from learning-by-teaching. The participants were 9 graduate and undergraduate students in informatics and engineering. We set two conditions: collaborative reading containing teaching interaction (LbT condition), and collaborative reading without teaching interaction (CR condition). As a between-subject design, we divided the participants into two groups called group LbT and group CR. We surveyed their TOEIC scores in advance and assigned 5 of them to group LbT and others to group CR so that English skills of both groups were almost equal.

Figure 3 shows the procedure of the experiment. Group LbT involved collaborative reading with teaching activities. On the other hand, group CR involved collaborative reading without teaching activities, hence the learner robot did not make grammatical mistakes. In this case study, the learner and the teacher robot read the same sentences. We prepared 3 English scripts, each containing one main grammatical content: the present perfect, the relative adverb, and the subjective mood. Learners conducted collaborative reading three times in total with the scripts. Table 1 shows an example of the English scripts and the mistake patterns of the learner robot. In collaborative reading between robots, the learner robot makes mistakes in the main grammatical contents contained in each script and in the other grammatical contents. The former mistakes are not corrected in collaborative reading between a learner and the learner robot, which are expected to be corrected by the learner. The latter mistakes, on the other hand, are corrected by the learner robot, which induces the learner to understand it can correct its mistakes.

After reading activities, both groups were given a content check test containing about five questions to see how well the participants understand the contents of the scripts used in collaborative reading between the learner and the learner robot. Table 2 shows an example of the test corresponding to the script shown in Table 1. The test is conducted after collaborative readings of all sentences prepared because it could prevent them from memorizing the contents. After the content check test, group LbT taught the learner robot about its grammatical mistakes.

Before and after reading activities, we conducted pre and post grammar tests. Both grammar tests consisted of questions that were different from each other. The tests contained five questions on the three main grammatical contents targeted in this experiment: the present perfect, the relative adverb, the subjunctive mood, and five other questions on other grammatical contents.

We then conducted a post-questionnaire that included 17 questions with a 5 Likert scale at the end of the experiment. Table 3 shows the contents of the questionnaire consisted of questions about collaborative reading with robots, impressions of the robot, and motivation. In addition, group LbT was asked additional 4 questions with a 5 Likert scale and 2 descriptive questions about teaching activity of the teacher robot, impression of their teaching activities, and what they noticed through their teaching.

Figure 4 shows the system used in the case study. We placed a monitor displaying English sentences in front of a participant, with the teacher robot on the left and the learner robot on the right. In addition, the microphones were placed out of sight of the participant. The monitor displayed one sentence that the participant and the robots read at a time.

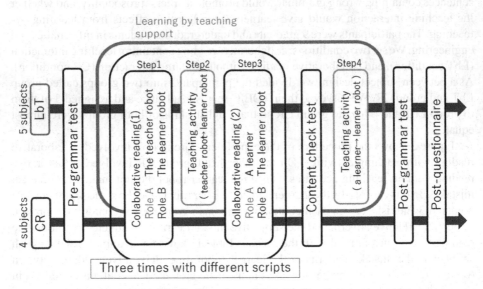

Fig. 3. Procedure of the experiment

Table 1. Correct sentences, mistakes of the learner robot and teaching contents

Correct sentences	Mistakes of the learner robot (shaded area is where learners read, * indicates mistakes appear both collaborative readings)	Teaching content by the teacher robot
Have you been interested in Japan for a long time?	* Have you are interested in Japan for a long time?	Use the past participle in the present perfect tense.
Yes, I have. I often bought manga since I was 10 years old.		
Wow! Why did you like manga so much?	Wow! Why do you like manga so much?	It was not in the past tense.
Some characters were cool, and others wore such cute clothes.		
I see. How long have you been a dress designer?	* I see. How long do you been a dress designer?	Use "have" in the present perfect tense.
Since 2008.		

Table 2. Examples of the content check test

Questions	Answer
Which countries are you interested in?	Japan
What job do you have?	A dress designer
When did you start buying comics?	10 years old
Why did you say you like comics?	Some characters were cool, and others wore such cute clothes

4.2 Results and Discussions

Figure 5 shows the average scores from the results of the pre/post grammar test. The test contains 5 questions for each grammatical content: the present perfect, the relative adverb, the subjective mood, other grammar. From the one-sided t-test, there were significant differences between the average scores in pre/post grammar tests of the LbT Group for the relative adverb and the subjective mood (relative adverb: $t(4) = 2.99$, p $< .05$, subjective mood: $t(4) = 2.14$, p $< .05$), and there was a tendency of significant difference between the average scores in pre/post grammar tests of the LbT Group for the present perfect ($t(4) = 1.83$, p $< .10$). Moreover, there was a significant difference between the average scores in pre/post grammar tests of the CR Group for the relative adverb ($t(3) = 7.0$, p $< .01$). These suggest that teaching grammatical mistakes to the learner robot could promote reflection on their grammatical knowledge and enables effective learning.

Table 3. Post-questionnaire

Q1: How much did the collaborative reading between robots help you?
Q2: How much did you concentrate on the collaborative reading with the learner robot?
Q3: How much did you care what the learner robot said?
Q4: How much easy did you feel the collaborative reading was?
Q5: How well motivated did you feel to participate in the collaborative reading?
Q6: How much did you do the collaborative reading?
Q7: How much did you want to get good at collaborative reading?
Q8: How well anxiety did you feel in the collaborative reading?
Q9: How well embarrassed did you feel in the collaborative reading?
Q10: How much did you enjoy the collaborative reading?
Q11: How many English skills did you feel that you have more than the learner robot?
Q12: How many English skills did you feel that the learner robot has more than you?
Q13: Did your impression of robots change after collaborative reading?
Q14: How much confidence did you gain in speaking English through the system?
Q15: How much would you like to communicate with a foreigner?
Q16: How much did you want to study with this system?
= = = = = = only group LbT = = = = = = = =
Q17: How helpful was the teaching activity from the teacher robot to the learner robot
Q18: How much did you want to teach the learner robot?
Q19: How much resistance did you feel to teach the learner robot?
Q20: How well do you think you've been teaching without mistakes?
Q21: Are there any mistakes that you missed teaching? (descriptive)
Q22: What did you find anything through teaching activity? (descriptive)

Fig. 4. Learning by teaching supported system in use

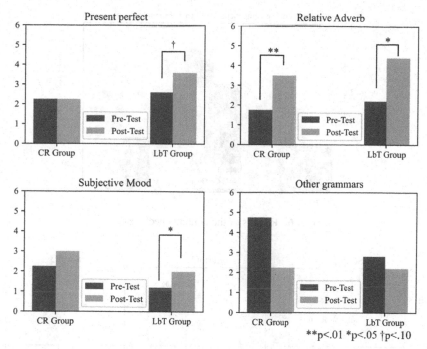

Fig. 5. Results of the pre/post grammar tests

Figure 6 shows the average scores from the results of the content check test. From the two-sided t-test, there were no significant differences between all the average scores although the CR group got higher scores than the LbT group in all tests about these scripts. Figure 7 shows the correlation between the scores of the content check test and the number of times the participants of the LbT group taught regardless of whether it was correct or incorrect. From these results, it is considered that the more the participants teach the learner robot, the less they care what the robot was reading.

Figure 8 shows the results of the post questionnaire. From the two-sided t-test, there were tendencies of significant differences between the average scores of the LbT group and CR group in some questions: Q1, Q4, Q7 (Q1: $t(7) = -2.06$, $p < .10$, Q4: $t(7) = 2.18$, $p < .10$, Q7: $t(7) = -2.16$, $p < .10$). The question of Q1 asked whether the collaborative reading between the two robots was helpful. According to the result, it is considered that the grammar mistakes of the learner robot made collaborative reading confusing for LbT group. The question of Q4 asked if the participants felt it was easy to read with a robot. According to the result, it is considered that teaching activity in collaborative reading promoted learners' self-efficacy and made them feel that collaborative reading seemed easy. The question of Q7 asked if the participants wanted to get good at collaborative reading. According to the result, it is considered that the learner robot's behavior of making mistakes allowed them to feel that there was no problem not to be able to read perfectly. Furthermore, from the two-sided t-test, there were significant differences between the average scores of the LbT group and the CR group in Q11, Q12 (Q11: $t(7) = 3.33$, $p < .05$, Q12: $t(7) = -3.44$, $p < .05$). The question of Q11 asked whether the

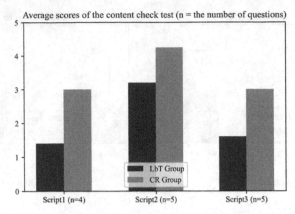

Fig. 6. Results of the content check tests

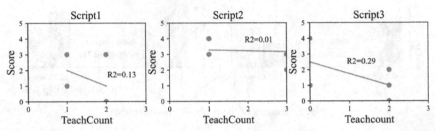

Fig. 7. Correlation between the scores of the content check test and the number of times the learner taught the robot

participants thought that they had better than the learner robot in collaborative reading, and Q12 was the opposite question of Q11. It is suggested that teaching activity could make learners feel that their English was better than the learner robot.

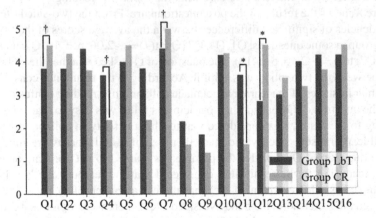

Fig. 8. Average scores of the post questionnaire (Q1–Q16).

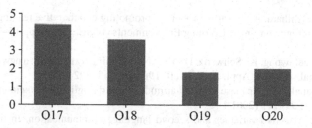

Fig. 9. Average scores of the post questionnaire for the LbT group (Q17–Q20).

Figure 9 shows the average scores of the post questionnaire that asked only the LbT group. The results indicated that some of them wanted to teach, others hesitated so that they have anxiety about their English skills. Moreover, some of them were reminded of grammatical contents and tried to care grammar when they read English.

These results suggest that teaching grammar mistakes promote learners' reflection on their grammatical knowledge. Besides, behavior in which the learner robot read with incorrect grammar motivates learners to teach, and gives them confidence. On the other hand, learners tend to find where the learner robot makes mistakes although they may not care what the robot reads about.

5   Conclusion

In this work, we have proposed and developed a learning by teaching partner robot system for promoting prosociality and learning effects. The results of the case study suggest that the teaching activities promote the prosociality of learners and give learners confidence in their English skills. On the other hand, teaching activity helps learners find where the partner robot makes mistakes, although it doesn't help them remember what their partner read. In addition, it is suggested that teaching grammar contents gives learners an effect from learning-by-teaching.

In future, we plan to conduct another case study with more participants. We will refine the system, and consider some criteria for objectively measuring learners' prosociality. In addition, some of the participants in the case study pointed out that the English sentences and grammar tests were too difficult. Thus, we will reconsider the English sentences used in another case study.

Acknowledgement. This work is supported in part by JSPS KAKENHI Grant numbers 18K19836 and 20H04294.

References

1. Obara, Y.: The effect of oral reading instructions focused on pair work —using the results of proficiency test and questionnaires—, Kansai English Language Education, vol. 39, pp. 37–56 (2016)

2. Adachi, Y., Kashihara, A.: A partner robot for promoting collaborative reading. In: The International Conference on Smart Learning Environments (ICSLE 2019), pp.15–24, Texas, USA (2019)
3. Biswas, G., Leelawong, K., Schwartz, D., Vye, N.: Learning by teaching: a new agent paradigm for educational software. Appl. Artif. Intell. **19**(3–4), 363–392 (2005)
4. Suarez, A., Tanaka, Y.: Japanese learners' attitudes toward English pronunciation. Bull. Niigata Seiryo Univ. **1**, 99–111 (2001)
5. Yashima, T.: Affective variables and second language communication. Institute of Foreign Language Education and Research Kansai University, vol. 5, pp. 81–93 (2003)
6. Kiesler, S., Powers, A., Fussell, S.R., Torrey, C.: Anthropomorphic interactions with a robot and robot-like agent social cognition. Soc. Cogn. **26**, 169–181 (2008)
7. Kawashima, K.: A trial of case-study classification and extraction of therapeutic effects of robot-therapy: literature review with descriptive-analysis. Reports from the Faculty of Clinical Psychology, Kyoto Bunkyo University, vol. 28, no. 2, pp. 1–12 (2014)

Collaboration Technology

Applying Natural Language Processing to Teamwork – A New Dashboard for CTMTC Methodology

Miguel Á. Conde[1]([⊠]) [iD], Adrián Andrés-Gómez[2], Francisco J. Rodríguez-Sedano[3] [iD], and Camino Fernández-Llamas[1] [iD]

[1] Department of Mechanics, Computer Science and Aerospace Engineering, Robotics Group, Universidad de León, Campus de Vegazana S/N, 24071 León, Spain
{mcong,cferll}@unileon.es

[2] School of Mechanical, Computer Science and Aerospace Engineering, Universidad de León, Campus de Vegazana SN, 24071 León, Spain
aandrg01@estudiantes.unileon.es

[3] Department of Electric, Systems and Automatics Engineering, Robotics Group, Universidad de León, Campus de Vegazana S/N, 24071 León, Spain
francisco.sedano@unileon.es

Abstract. In our current society the acquisition of competences such as teamwork is essential. However, the evaluation of how this competence is developed is not easy and requires methodologies and tools to support the assessment process. In this sense several Learning Analytics tools have been developed. They explore students' interactions in different types of tools such as forums or instant messaging apps. However those tools are especially focused on the quantitative evaluation of the interaction and are not very usable. This work presents a new dashboard that analyzes students' Telegram interactions while they work as a team to address a project. The innovation of this tool lies in the functionalities included to explore not only numbers about messages, replies, type of messages, characters, etc., but the content of the texts. To do so natural language processing and sentiment analysis libraries were used. The tool has been tested successfully with 4 subject editions in which it is possible to appreciate an evolution in students' interactions.

Keywords: Natural language processing · Learning analytics · Teamwork · Telegram · Dashboard

1 Introduction

Teamwork competence acquisition is very important in our current socioeconomic context. Both the industry and the academy see this competence acquisition as something critical [1–4]. However, as shown in different works the evaluation of such process is hard and especially time-consuming [5]. Something with a very important impact in contexts where teachers should evaluate an important number of students or groups.

© The Author(s), under exclusive license to Springer Nature Switzerland AG 2022
P. Zaphiris and A. Ioannou (Eds.): HCII 2022, LNCS 13329, pp. 251–261, 2022.
https://doi.org/10.1007/978-3-031-05675-8_19

In order to deal with this Fidalgo et al. proposed CTMTC methodology [6, 7]. It facilitates the development of teamwork competence through the development of projects following stages adapted from the International Project Management Association (e.g.: storming, norming, performing, delivery and documentation) [8]. When using CTMTC the students addressed the projects as a team, using different technologies and producing project outputs. These results and the students' interactions shreds of evidence can be analyzed to carry out both summative and formative evaluations by using different rubrics [9]. With them, the teachers could know not only how the group has developed the project but also how each of the members has acquired the TWC. It has been applied in very different contexts with very positive results that show the flexibility of the methodology [6, 9–14].

The evaluation carried out requires of exploring several issues which need of the support of a Learning Analytics tool. In this way the time to evaluate a group could be affordable for the teacher. First versions of this LA tool have been focused mainly on the evaluation of the students' interaction shreds of evidence and mainly from a quantitative perspective [12]. In a second version of the LA tool, it was adapted taking into account students requests about the communication/interaction tool. Students were not happy using the LMS Forums and prefer to use a more realistic communication way such as the instant messaging tools. This led to the development of a LA Tool that explores WhatsApp conversations [15] and others that analyze Telegram [16]. However, in both cases the teachers require an improvement in the tool, both in the usability and in the functionality.

One of the main problems to deal with is how to show as much information as possible in a single screen and how to show useful data representations [17]. In addition, it is necessary not only to consider quantitative data about students' interactions but to go deeper on this analysis considering issues such as teamwork behavior, leadership, sentimental analysis. This makes it necessary to redesign the existing LA tool for CTMTC to explore, by using techniques such as Natural Language Processing (NLP), the evidence and present the results in a simple but comprehensive way.

This work presents the tool defined and the initial validation. It is structured as follows. First the theoretical context of the work is presented. Section 3 describes the tool architecture and main functionalities. In Sect. 4 the authors present the tool with the data of one of the subjects in which it is applied and also the main perceptions of teachers involved as experts in the development. Finally, some conclusions are posed.

2   Theoretical Context

In this section we are not going to delve into some terms discussed enough in the literature such as Learning Analytics [18, 19] or the idea of using dashboards to facilitate decision making [20, 21]. However, it is necessary to understand why we need to go beyond the existing learning analytics tools for CTMTC and the existing initiatives of using NLP for educational and assessment purposes.

Regarding the first issue and as commented above, a LA tool was defined to facilitate the evaluation of students' interactions in forums, and later was adapted to consider instant messaging tools. However, in both cases the results explored were merely quantitatively, with some exceptions such as the possibility to see who has begun the first conversation, the last message and when they have been posted. This was not enough, it was necessary to know not only what the students have said during their interaction, but the meaning of the messages, the students' sentiments and intentions when writing and so on. In this way it would be possible to explore issues such as leadership [22] or teamwork behavior [23]. In order to do so it is necessary to apply NLP techniques in a very heterogeneous context such as the instant messaging texts.

NLP is described as Chowdhury as "an area of research and application that explores how computers can be used to understand and manipulate natural language text or speech to do useful things" [24]. In the case of Learning Analytics, the idea is to be able to analyze what the students can say or write during the educational process. Possible applications are described in Macnamara et al. work [25] such as writing assessment [26], intelligent tutoring systems [27], MOOC applications [28] or discourse generated in Computer Support Collaborative Learning [29, 30].

This discourse analysis is what can be more relevant for the present research, as the student dialog between them when completing the projects by following CTMTC methodology. On these topics several authors have explore three issues that can be interesting for the LA tool to develop:

- Sentiment analysis related with students feedback [31, 32] which is something to take into account when dialoguing.
- Dialog act analysis, understood as "the intention behind an utterance in conversation to achieve a conversational goal" [33]. In this sense works such as [33] show a possible way to model the conversations, others pose automatic recognition of different ways dialogs act [34], or the possibility to assess quality of texts [35].
- Discourse similarity analysis to explore students' behaviors, collaboration patterns, learning patterns or competence development [36, 37].

But, on the other hand, this dialog analysis should consider the type of language used, that is, how students write on instant messaging tools, which is not the common way. In this sense, works such as [37, 38] can be taken into account.

Given this context the tool is going to explore the students' interactions in a Telegram group taking into account the similarity of the discourse with leaders' speeches, the classification of the type of interactions and the sentimental analysis.

3 The LA Tool

The new release of the LA tool has changed not only because we have included a dashboard instead of a simple visualization context to study students' pieces of evidence, it has been also updated in some of the components as Telegram has also updated their API libraries.

Regarding the tool presented in [16] we have changed some of the components. Figure 1 shows in white those that have not changed, in light yellow those with simple updates and in light blue those that are new or that have been almost completely changed.

It is possible to see that the bot has been changed because some new commands were included, but most of the components in the server are new such as the information

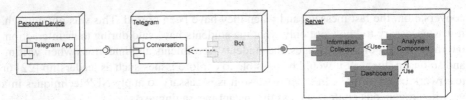

Fig. 1. LA tool deployment diagram

collector, the analysis component, and the dashboard. In the next sections we briefly described the components and the server side.

3.1 The Bot

The bot component has been the one that includes less changes since the past release of the LA tool. The aim is the same, to have a component that allows gathering students' messages from the group conversation. Those messages will be sent to the Information Collector through an API.

To do this the bot should be included by the students into their conversation group and they should set it up. This requires that each student use a command to define their personal ID and other to specify their group name. The group is necessary for further analysis of the messages of the group. The personal ID because we are not going to gather any students' personal data such as their mobile telephone numbers, but we need to know who has written each message, so we link the student telegram_id with a personal_id which is known by the teacher. In addition, the bot will facilitate information about the name of the activity which can be extracted from the conversation group name. Finally for this release and after the problems that some students had setting up the group, we have included a help command which shows the individual settings (personal_id and group) of each student that use it.

3.2 The Connection API

For this version of the tool the technology employed for the communication among the information collector and the bot is an API provided by the library *python_telegram_bot*. In this case the delivery of the messages between the collector and the bot is not based on webhooks as in the previous version but in the use of an API that requires a token to facilitate access to the information.

The information is mainly manipulated by using an updater object. It is going to facilitate the polling of updates in the conversation. This is complemented with several command handlers (to develop the functionality of the above mentioned commands) and dispatcher handlers that allows management of each type of messages. This enlarge the options of analysis as we are able not to take into account only messages but gifs, stickers, audios, emojis and so on. Many of these types of interactions were not considered in the previous version.

3.3 The Server

In the server side we have several components:

- The information collector. This component is going to use the API methods to gather the messages from the conversation. The communication of the messages is done in JSON and the data obtained stored in a database that is going to consider the information of the student and the group he/she belong to, the messages (attending to issues such as author, dates, type, etc.) and the activity to which the group and the conversations are linked.
- The Analysis Component: The gathered information is obtained through the API, processed in a way that later can fit with the dashboard needs and stored in a database. In this component different analyses were carried out both form a quantitative and from a qualitative perspective but all of them based on the students' interactions into the conversation. The information can be presented in an aggregated way and individually so different calculations are required.

    Regarding quantitative information it is possible to see the number of messages of the students or groups, average number of messages, dates of each of the message, messages counting by types, number of replies, conversation beginning and so on.
- Regarding the qualitative analysis this is a more complex task. In this case we aim to process the natural language of the messages and to do so we employ two main libraries:

    - Sentiment-Spanish. This is an open source library that employs convolutional neural networks to predict the sentiment of Spanish sentences, it is based The model was trained using keras and tensorflow with over *800000* reviews of users of the pages *eltenedor, decathlon, tripadvisor, filmaffinity and ebay* [39].
    - NLTK (Natural Language Toolkit). This platform facilitates text analysis in python, with functions for text classification, tokenization, stemming, tagging, parsing, and semantic reasoning. In order to obtain results linked to CTMTC the idea is to look for similarities with own defined dictionaries related with teamwork and leadership [40].

- The Dashboard. One of the key elements in this new release of the LA is the dashboard. The idea is to implement a new visualization that allows us to obtain more knowledge about what the students have done at a glance. The dashboard is implemented by using python plotly library [41] and distributes the information in two tabs, one for general information and the other for the information related with the group.

Figure 2 shows the general information tab. On it is possible to see several graphs and general quantitative information. This info includes the data shown by the previous tool release but also other information such as the numbers related with documents, stickers, gifs, videos, audios and pools used in the conversations. That information will provide the teachers with feedback about how the students have collaborated in their chats. On the left side it is possible to see different bar graphs, the first one compares the groups by number of messages, the second shows the temporal distribution during the days the task is carried out and the third the distribution in hours. These two graphs will allow the teacher to know when and how the students have work or are working in the methodology and to make decisions about how to motivate them, if necessary to make a continuous work. On the bottom right side there is a steam graph that shows the evolution of the most used conversation words over time, which helps to look for the most common worries of students involved in the discussions. We should point out that all the graphs are interactive and provide extended information when moving the mouse pointer over them.

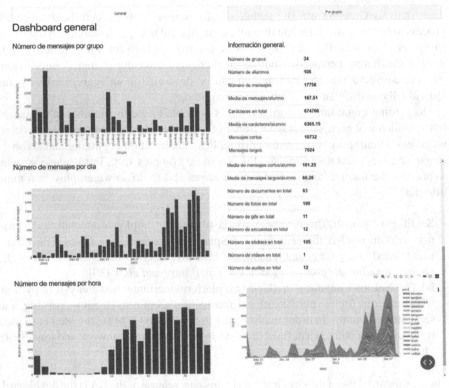

Fig. 2. General LA tool tab.

Figure 3 shows the tab for the group information for a specific group. It includes aggregated information for the group such as the number of messages, the short and the long ones depending on if they are shorter than 35 characters. In addition, we have the individual information for each of the team members. However, this was not enough for the teachers to have an idea about what the students have done, so several functionalities were included: 1) an interactive graph to show the distribution of the different type of the group text messages over the days or the hours of a day; 2) a polar graph with the distribution of those messages that were not of text type; and 3) The same steam graph than in the general tab but with the specific data of the group. Regarding the individual information it was enriched with the number of emojis, mentions and a representation of the similarity of the text with the teamwork dictionary and with positive messages attending to the sentimental analysis library (this type of positive assertions can provide an idea to the teacher of how students are working together).

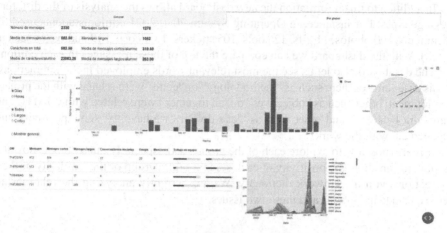

Fig. 3. Group lab tool

4 Tool Evaluation

To evaluate the tool, we have employed two approaches. The first one is currently being completed and consists of an expert validation based on a cognitive walkthrough method. The test has not ended yet, so they are not presented in this paper. The other approach consists of applying the dashboard to the data gathered in the different subjects in which this tool is used. More specifically the tool has been applied in two editions of a second course and one edition of the Computer Science Degree (Operating Systems) and on an edition of a fourth course subject (Accessibility). In both CTMTC is applied to evaluate the individual development of teamwork competence when the students addressed some subject projects. These projects have an important percentage of the subject grade (for more information a description of the subjects is available in [5]). Table 1 shows the distribution of students and messages per student of each of the subjects.

Table 1. Distribution by subject of students and average message number

	Accessibility 2019/2020	Accessibility 2020/2021	Operating systems 2020/2021	Operating systems 2021/2022
N. of students	42	63	106	69
Messages Num.	5.120	8.901	17.756	16909
Avg. messages	121,90	141,29	167,51	245.06

It is possible to see a difference in the message number per student in each subject. It is lower in the first edition of both subjects when the students were beginning to adapt to the system and there is an increment for the second use. We can see that with the new bot version better results are shown in Operating Systems during 2021/22 edition.

In addition to this information the new dashboard allows the analysis of the different message types. For instance, in Operating System 2020/2021 edition students used 63 documents, 190 photos, 11 gifs, 12 pools, 105 stickers, 1 video and 12 audios (as seen in Fig. 2). With the dashboard we can compare the use of these messages in each edition.

The dashboard also let us see the most relevant words employed in the interactions, in this case some of them such as "methodology" or "code" were related with the project development; other such as "objectives" or "all together" were related with CTMTC and teamwork behavior; and other such as "let's do" or "we have to" show positivity and engagement with the work.

It is also possible to explore each of the groups and especially interesting is how the dashboard can show the positivity of each student of the group or the similarity of their interactions with a teamwork dictionary. We are currently analyzing the relationship between students' grades and these two issues.

5   Conclusions

The implementation of a Dashboard that allows a better analysis of what the students have done when working as a group is something necessary in the context of the application of CTMTC methodology. In this way it is possible to facilitate the evaluation of students and to attend not only to quantitative issues but to those which a more qualitative nature, analyzing not only the number of messages but their content.

In this work we have presented a new dashboard that addressed the analysis of students' interactions when using Telegram for project development. The tool has been tested with the data of several students with satisfactory results however there is still a lot of work to do. First it is necessary to complete an expert testing to have a powerful tool that really accomplishes the teachers' needs. It is also necessary to explore their opinion about using the tool once it is finished and how they can use the information provided by the dashboard to facilitate students' acquisition of other competences. From a technological point of view, it is also possible to improve the system by including other representation ways, by building dictionaries with words related with other topics and including other libraries in the analysis component.

In any case, the dashboard and how it is applied is not finished yet but it can be considered as a first step of the analytics of textual students' interactions in instant messaging tools with natural language processing approaches.

References

1. Colomo-Palacios, R., Casado-Lumbreras, C., Soto-Acosta, P., García-Peñalvo, F.J., Tovar-Caro, E.: Competence gaps in software personnel: a multi-organizational study. Comput. Hum. Behav. **29**, 456–461 (2013)

2. Leidner, D.E., Jarvenpaa, S.L.: The use of information technology to enhance management school education: a theoretical view. MIS Q. **19**, 265–291 (1995)
3. Vogel, D.R., Davison, R.M., Shroff, R.H.: Sociocultural learning: a perspective on GSS-enabled global education. Commun. Assoc. Inf. Syst. **7**, 9 (2001)
4. Alonso de Castro, M.G., García-Peñalvo, F.J.: Metodologías educativas de éxito: proyectos Erasmus+ relacionados con e-learning o TIC. Campus Virtuales **11**, 95–114 (2022)
5. Conde, M.A., Rodriguez-Sedano, F.J., Hernandez-Garcia, A., GutiérrezFernández, A., Guerrero-Higueras, A.M.: Your teammate just sent you a new message! The effects of using telegram on individual acquisition of teamwork competence. Int. J. Interact. Multimedia Artif. Intell. **6**, 225–233 (2021)
6. Fidalgo, A., Leris, D., Sein-Echaluce, M.L., García-Peñalvo, F.J.: Indicadores para el seguimiento de evaluación de la competencia de trabajo en equipo a través del método CTMT. Congreso Internacional sobre Aprendizaje Innovación y Competitividad - CINAIC 2013, Madrid, Spain (2013)
7. Fidalgo-Blanco, Á., Lerís, D., Sein-Echaluce, M.L., García-Peñalvo, F.J.: Monitoring indicators for CTMTC: comprehensive training model of the teamwork competence in engineering domain. Int. J. Eng. Educ. (IJEE) **31**, 829–838 (2015)
8. NCB: Bases para la competencia en dirección de proyectos. http://www.lpzconsulting.com/images/CP-_Trabajo_en_Equipo.pdf. Accessed 28 Feb 2014
9. Conde, M.A., Colomo-Palacios, R., García-Peñalvo, F.J., Larrucea, X.: Teamwork assessment in the educational web of data: a learning analytics approach towards ISO 10018. Telematics Inform. **35**, 551–563 (2018)
10. Conde, M.Á., Rodríguez-Sedano, F.J., Sánchez-González, L., Fernández-Llamas, C., Rodríguez-Lera, F.J., Matellán-Olivera, V.: Evaluation of teamwork competence acquisition by using CTMTC methodology and learning analytics techniques. In: Proceedings of the Fourth International Conference on Technological Ecosystems for Enhancing Multiculturality, pp. 787–794. ACM, Salamanca (2016)
11. Sein-Echaluce, M.L., Fidalgo Blanco, Á., García-Peñalvo, F.J., Conde, M.Á.: A knowledge management system to classify social educational resources within a subject using teamwork techniques. In: Zaphiris, P., Ioannou, A. (eds.) LCT 2015. LNCS, vol. 9192, pp. 510–519. Springer, Cham (2015). https://doi.org/10.1007/978-3-319-20609-7_48
12. Fidalgo-Blanco, Á., Sein-Echaluce, M.L., García-Peñalvo, F.J., Conde, M.Á.: Using learning analytics to improve teamwork assessment. Comput. Hum. Behav. **47**, 149–156 (2015)
13. Sein-Echaluce, M.L., Fidalgo-Blanco, Á., García-Peñalvo, F.J.: Students' knowledge sharing to improve learning in engineering academic courses. Int. J. Eng. Educ. (IJEE) **32**, 1024–1035 (2016)
14. Conde, M.Á., Hernández-García, Á., García-Peñalvo, F.J., Fidalgo-Blanco, Á., Sein-Echaluce, M.: Evaluation of the CTMTC methodology for assessment of teamwork competence development and acquisition in higher education. In: Zaphiris, P., Ioannou, A. (eds.) LCT 2016. LNCS, vol. 9753, pp. 201–212. Springer, Cham (2016). https://doi.org/10.1007/978-3-319-39483-1_19
15. Conde, M.Á., Rodríguez-Sedano, F.J., Rodríguez-Lera, F.J., Gutiérrez-Fernández, A., Guerrero-Higueras, Á.M.: Assessing the individual acquisition of teamwork competence by exploring students' instant messaging tools use: the WhatsApp case study. Univ. Access Inf. Soc. **20**(3), 441–450 (2020). https://doi.org/10.1007/s10209-020-00772-1
16. Conde, M.Á., Rodríguez-Sedano, F.J., Fernández, C., Gutiérrez-Fernández, A., Fernández-Robles, L., Limas, M.C.: A learning analytics tool for the analysis of students' telegram messages in the context of teamwork virtual activities. In: Eighth International Conference on Technological Ecosystems for Enhancing Multiculturality, pp. 719–724. Association for Computing Machinery, Salamanca (2020). https://doi.org/10.1145/3434780.3436601

17. Álvarez-Arana, A., Villamañe-Gironés, M., Larrañaga-Olagaray, M.: Improving assessment using visual learning analytics. Educ. Knowl. Soc. **21**, 1–9 (2020)
18. Ferguson, R.: Learning analytics: drivers, developments and challenges. Int. J. Technol. Enhanced Learn. **4**, 304–317 (2012)
19. Siemens, G.: Learning analytics the emergence of a discipline. Am. Behav. Sci. **57**, 1380–1400 (2013)
20. Few, S.: Information Dashboard Design: Displaying Data for At-a-Glance Monitoring. Analytics Press (2013)
21. Vázquez-Ingelmo, A., Garcia-Peñalvo, F.J., Therón, R.: Information dashboards and tailoring capabilities - a systematic literature review. IEEE Access **7**, 109673–109688 (2019)
22. Sein-Echaluce, M.L., Fidalgo-Blanco, Á., Esteban-Escaño, J., García-Peñalvo, F.J., Conde, M.Á.: Using learning analytics to detect authentic leadership characteristics at engineering degrees. I. Int. J. Eng. Educ. **34**, 851–864 (2018)
23. Tasa, K., Taggar, S., Seijts, G.H.: The development of collective efficacy in teams: a multilevel and longitudinal perspective. J. Appl. Psychol. **92**, 17–27 (2007)
24. Chowdhury, G.: Natural language processing. Ann. Rev. Inf. Sci. Technol., 51–89 (2003)
25. McNamara, D.S., Allen, L., Crossley, S., Dascalu, M., Perret, C.A.: Natural language processing and learning analytics. In: Handbook of Learning Analytics, vol. 93 (2017)
26. Allen, L.K., Jacovina, M.E., McNamara, D.S.: Computer-Based Writing Instruction. Grantee Submission (2016)
27. Graesser, A.C., et al.: AutoTutor: a tutor with dialogue in natural language. Behav. Res. Methods Instrum. Comput. **36**, 180–192 (2004)
28. Koller, D., Ng, A., Chen, Z.: Retention and intention in massive open online courses: in depth. EDUCAUSE Review (2013). https://er.educause.edu/articles/2013/6/retention-and-int ention-in-massive-open-online-courses-in-depth
29. Stahl, G.: Group Cognition: Computer Support for Building Collaborative Knowledge (Acting with Technology). The MIT Press (2006)
30. Dong, A.: The latent semantic approach to studying design team communication. Des. Stud. **26**, 445–461 (2005)
31. Alblawi, A.S., Alhamed, A.A.: Big data and learning analytics in higher education: demystifying variety, acquisition, storage, NLP and analytics. In: Conference Big Data and Learning Analytics in Higher Education: Demystifying Variety, Acquisition, Storage, NLP and Analytics, pp. 124–129. IEEE (2018)
32. Aung, K.Z., Myo, N.N.: Sentiment analysis of students' comment using lexicon based approach. In: Conference Sentiment Analysis of Students' Comment Using Lexicon Based Approach, pp. 149–154. IEEE (2017)
33. Austin, J.L., Austin, J.L., Urmson, J.O., Urmson, J.O., Sbisà, M.: How to Do Things with Words, 2nd edn. Harvard University Press (1975)
34. Erkens, G., Janssen, J.: Automatic coding of dialogue acts in collaboration protocols. Int. J. Comput.-Support. Collab. Learn. **3**, 447–470 (2008)
35. Nistor, N., et al.: Finding student-centered open learning environments on the internet: automated dialogue assessment in academic virtual communities of practice. Comput. Hum. Behav. **47**, 119–127 (2015)
36. Liddo, A.D., Shum, S.B., Quinto, I., Bachler, M., Cannavacciuolo, L.: Discourse-centric learning analytics. In: Proceedings of the 1st International Conference on Learning Analytics and Knowledge, pp. 23–33. Association for Computing Machinery, Banff (2011). https://doi. org/10.1145/2090116.2090120
37. Praharaj, S., Scheffel, M., Schmitz, M., Specht, M., Drachsler, H.: Towards automatic collaboration analytics for group speech data using learning analytics. Sensors **21**, 3156 (2021)

38. Misra, A., Walker, M.: Topic independent identification of agreement and disagreement in social media dialogue. arXiv preprint arXiv:1709.00661 (2017)
39. sentiment-analysis-Spanish 0.0.25 Python Software Foundation. https://pypi.org/project/sentiment-analysis-spanish/. Accessed 17 Feb 2022
40. Natural Language Toolkit 3.7. https://www.nltk.org/. Accessed 17 Feb 2022
41. Dash Enterprise. https://plotly.com/. Accessed 17 Feb 2022

Fostering Decision-Making Processes in Health Ecosystems Through Visual Analytics and Machine Learning

Francisco José García-Peñalvo, Andrea Vázquez-Ingelmo[✉],
and Alicia García-Holgado

Grupo de Investigación GRIAL, Departamento de Informática y Automática, Instituto
Universitario de Ciencias de La Educación, Universidad de Salamanca, Salamanca, Spain
{fgarcia,andreavazquez,aliciagh}@usal.es
https://ror.org/02f40zc51

Abstract. Data-intensive contexts, such as health, use information systems to merge, synthesize, represent, and visualize data by using interfaces to ease decision-making processes. All data management processes play an essential role in exploiting data's strategic value from acquisition to visualization. Technological ecosystems allow the deployment of highly complex services while supporting their evolutionary nature. However, there is a challenge regarding the design of high-level interfaces that adapt to the evolving nature of data. The AVisSA project is focused on tackling the development of an automatic dashboard generation system (meta-dashboard) using Domain Engineering and Artificial Intelligence techniques. This approach makes it possible to obtain dashboards from data flows in technological ecosystems adapted to specific domains. The implementation of the meta-dashboard will make intensive use of user experience testing throughout its development, which will allow the involvement of other actors in the ecosystem as stakeholders (public administration, health managers, etc.). These actors will be able to use the data for decision-making and design improvements in health provision.

Keywords: Domain engineering · SPL · Meta-modeling · Information dashboards · Information systems · Healthcare · Health domain

1 Introduction

Information systems have become a critical factor in several contexts. They allow the unification, formatting, processing, and visualization of data through user-friendly interfaces [1]. Moreover, COVID-19 has accelerated the digital transformation in all the business domains such as education [2–6], political decision-making [7, 8], tourism [9, 10], and health systems [11, 12], among others.

Some data-intensive contexts, like the health context [13], present more complexities in their decision-making processes due to the heterogeneity of the data sources

P. Zaphiris and A. Ioannou (Eds.): HCII 2022, LNCS 13329, pp. 262–273, 2022.
https://doi.org/10.1007/978-3-031-05675-8_20

and the different formats involved (structured data, echocardiograms, magnetic resonances, etc. [14–17]). For these reasons, it is necessary to tackle these issues with robust methodologies that enable the development and collaboration of complex services.

This work presents a project focused on tackling data and knowledge management issues in complex contexts. The approach leverages meta-modeling, domain engineering, and artificial intelligence to generate information dashboards that assist decision-making processes.

The rest of this paper is organized as follows. Section 2 provides background for the project proposal. Section 3 outlines the objectives of AVisSA. Section 4 details the methodology followed, and Sect. 5 discusses the project's expected outcomes. Finally, Sect. 6 presents the conclusions derived from the work.

2 Background

Since 2012, the GRIAL Research Group [18] has been developing information technology (IT) solutions for the health sector in collaboration with outstanding partners such as Intras Foundation, which provides support for qualitative data analysis and the usability of solutions built around psychiatric care aspects, Salamanca University Hospital, which develops various software systems, and ArSoft, which researches medical image segmentation. Furthermore, the GRIAL Group is affiliated with the Institute of Biomedical Research of Salamanca (IBSAL).

Technological ecosystems are the natural evolution of IT systems. These ecosystems enable the development of highly complex services while maintaining their evolutionary nature. The main goal of the previous R&D project, the DEFINES project (A Digital Ecosystem Framework for an Interoperable NEtwork-based Society, ref.: TIN2016-80172-R), funded by the Spanish National Research Plan (that ended on June 2021), was to develop a framework of a technological environment as support of services for the management of corporate knowledge, dubbed technological ecosystem [19]. In the context of the TE-CUIDA project, this framework was established in a technological ecosystem for the care domain to provide comprehensive and distant assistance for the needs of official and informal care providers (e.g., family members) of dependent older people (TEchnological ecosystem for support for caregivers, ref.: SA061P17) [20].

In terms of technology, the significant outcomes of both projects allow for the solution of the problem through the design and development of a technological ecosystem that is in line with current software architectures. In this approach, we've proposed a generic framework with a solid evolutionary component, whose architecture can be used in various situations and allows for integrating other software tools and developing new services that add value to the ecosystem.

As an example of the strategy's relevance, it's clear that technological ecosystems in the field of health have sparked much interest in recent years, as evidenced by the several European-funded projects that use a similar approach [21].

However, during the previous projects' review of state of the art, a common lack was discovered [22]: despite their immense potential, technological ecosystems in the health sector face challenges when deployed in real contexts, resulting in the majority of concepts never progress beyond pilot testing.

Comparing the health field with other fields in which technological ecosystems are a reality, it was concluded that proposals in the health sector tend to ignore the evolutionary characteristic of the ecosystem. This capacity to incorporate new tools and services means that the data exchanged, and the knowledge generated in this type of solution has a high added value for other potential users of the ecosystem, beyond the users who are the primary objective of the solution. Besides, the challenge remains at the high-level interfaces to create control panels or dashboards that adapt to the evolving and changing nature of data.

In this light, the current project aims to create a fundamental pillar not only for the success of the ecosystem framework proposed in DEFINES and implemented in TE-CUIDA but also for the development of a solid ecosystem architecture that can be extrapolated with guarantees of success when implementing new services and incorporating new actors that contribute to the ecosystem's evolution. This pillar focuses on using information dashboards [23], which are tools for the graphic representation of the leading indicators involved in achieving the objectives within an ecosystem (e.g., degree of success in providing a service) designed to assist in decision-making processes. The goal is to encourage the extraction of knowledge inherent within the information flows between the ecosystem's components and actors by presenting tailored data for each type of user using visual metaphors.

Dashboards are powerful visualization tools capable of combining various heterogeneous data sources from the components of the ecosystem. Still, their development and configuration have a high degree of complexity due to the heterogeneity of the data, the particular needs of the final users of the dashboard itself, and the evolutionary nature of the technological ecosystems that causes the software components to change, be removed or added to meet the changing needs of the ecosystem itself [24, 25]. These characteristics directly impact manually-developed dashboards [26], which need to address the problem from a software perspective and consider the user experience and application (and data) domain.

This project, AVisSA, aims to develop an automatic dashboard generation system for decision-making in Health ecosystems.

3 Objectives

AVisSA will address the development of an automatic dashboard generation system that adapts to data analysis and knowledge management needs in heterogeneous contexts such as the health sector to improve these processes within the health system, impacting decision-making processes.

The automatic generation of these tools will be based on domain engineering and artificial intelligence techniques to obtain customized products with lower development costs.

Identifying the primitive elements of a dashboard and visualization (such as the scales, axes, visual marks, etc.) allows for greater flexibility when setting up an automatic dashboard generation. It determines the influence and usefulness of the various visual elements according to the context.

On the other hand, branches of artificial intelligence as Machine Learning approaches [27–29] can be applied in conjunction with this paradigm to obtain tailored tools. These tools are fed by the particularities of the user, offering the most suitable components to gain insights and for the achievement of their particular objectives [30].

To achieve the main objective of the project, a set of specific goals are proposed:

- O1. Establishing automatic mechanisms for collecting and analyzing knowledge in the technological ecosystem.
- O2. Developing methods for the storage and anonymized (or pseudo-anonymized) treatment of data. Since medical data may be combined with data related to platform usage, best practices will be established to ensure compliance with privacy regulations and legislation.
- O3. Automatic generation of indicators, metrics, and tools that facilitate decision-making for different types of users in the technology ecosystem (e.g., health professionals, managers, and administration members).
- O4. Using artificial intelligence techniques for automatic customization of data visualization forms to suit the application domain and the preferences and characteristics of each user.
- O5. Providing simulation spaces for training or diagnosis processes based on automatically generated dashboards, including machine learning capabilities with the presented data and learning analytics of the educational actions.
- O6. Evaluating dashboard usability and satisfaction (in terms of the capacity of software to be understood, learned, used, and appealed to the user).
- O7. Evaluating the evolutionary and adaptive capacity of the architecture through its implementation in two sufficiently differentiated case studies: the healthcare field and the monitoring of medical tests based on images.

Achieving these objectives will provide the following benefits:

- Providing tools that allow decision-making based on the visualization of heterogeneous data, regardless of the application domain (e.g., medical data, treatment adherence, patient behavioral trends, etc.).
- Attracting new actors to the ecosystem, providing new services, and adding value to the existing solution (public administration, companies in the health sector, etc.).
- Establishing new synergies with other areas of the health sector (e.g., research networks interested in available data).
- Opening new business channels that allow the commercialization of the solution.

4 Methodology

4.1 Coordination

It is essential to define and plan the tasks adequately, to correctly manage the complexity of the project's objectives and its interdisciplinarity and multidisciplinarity. Six activities are proposed in a 48-month window.

Activity 1 is devoted to the project coordination based on the PRINCE2 (PRojects IN Controlled Environments) project management methodology [31].

4.2 Systematic Literature Review

Activities 2 and 3 represent technological innovation. They will start with in-depth research in the recent advances within the particular context of the automatic generation of dashboards in healthcare environments through SLRs (Systematic Literature Reviews) [32, 33]. Also, the categorization of the data to be extracted, KPIs, and metrics suitable for the different ecosystem actors and users will be addressed in this stage. Based on the best practices and challenges, action-research cycles [34] using SCRUM [35] will be applied. These activities will result in a meta-dashboard implemented and tested in a controlled context, also considering the data life cycle.

4.3 Dashboard Generator

For the conceptualization of the dashboard generator, a meta-modeling approach will be used, allowing extraction of the characteristics of the dashboards domain to obtain a dashboard meta-model that contains the abstract and generic features of these tools. Also, the meta-model will focus not only on the dashboards' technical characteristics and functionalities but also on the human factor.

This allows establishing both a practical framework when developing dashboards and a theoretical work on the technical and end user-related elements that should be considered when designing these tools. Among the details related to the end-user, there exist many determining factors for the correct interpretation of the information displayed: level of data domain knowledge, visual literacy, or even potential biases. Although these factors may seem abstract, it is possible to categorize them to obtain user profiles to build visual tools that allow effective visualization and understanding levels.

The Software Product Lines (SPL) paradigm will be used to develop the meta-model. This paradigm offers a development framework of reusable components based on a previous domain analysis (domain engineering phase) to combine them to obtain customized products adapted to different contexts. Two significant benefits can be attained using this paradigm in conjunction with meta-modeling. The first one is the decrease in the development time of these visual tools since they are generated through the composition of previously developed software assets. The second is the flexibility in the generation process.

Specifically, identifying the primitive elements of the dashboards allows improving their scalability. Once the software assets are designed, it is only necessary to assemble them to obtain any dashboard with any number and type of displays. Besides, because the elements identified are generic, the data domain is not a determining factor when generating dashboards. The high-level layer provided by the meta-model allows to abstract more specific aspects of the information to be displayed, allowing this solution to be adapted to any data set. Finally, thanks to this abstraction of information, it is possible to establish connection mechanisms between the dashboard and the elements of any ecosystem [36].

4.4 Evaluation

During activity 4, a mixed approach (quantitative-qualitative) was chosen for the evaluations because not all observations are susceptible to quantitative measurement when working in terms of the user experience. Therefore, results analysis requires differentiation not only in terms of quantity (quantitative) but also in terms of quality (qualitative). A priori, neither quantitative nor qualitative research is superior to its counterpart and responds to the same inferential logic: both can be equally systematic and provide similarly helpful information [37]. Moreover, if both types of data are integrated and converge, the validity of the obtained generalizations is reinforced.

Activity 5 is devoted to using the meta-dashboard created in activity 4 to generate simulators for training and diagnosis processes, including machine learning capabilities to help students or professionals analyze the medical data they are visualizing and learning analytics functionalities to have comprehensive information about the simulator usage.

Regarding the experimental phases (activities 4 and 5), this research work will make intensive use of the usability laboratory funded by the network of Networked Infrastructures of Castilla y León (INFRARED - ref. USAL05), of which the GRIAL group is a collaborating member.

The user experience studies will be of an ex-post nature, and within this modality of designs, we will opt to carry out a descriptive study of exploratory nature. On the one hand, combined methods such as Conductor and Thinking Aloud will be employed to test the developed tools' use. Besides, a descriptive study using surveys will be carried out and analyzed using correlation techniques. Thus, the research questions will be answered in descriptive terms and in terms of the relationship between variables and after a systematic information collection. This will ensure the rigor and validity of the obtained information.

For the survey-based research, three phases will be established [38]:

1. Theoretical-conceptual: setting out objectives and research hypotheses
2. Methodological: selecting the sample and the variables under study; formulating and preparing the experimental environment.
3. Conceptual statistics: codification and data analysis to obtain results from which generalizations can be made. Furthermore, integrate the conclusions drawn into the initial theoretical framework.

Finally, and thanks to the specific facilities of the usability laboratory, a logging process of the users' interactions with the system will be carried out. These loggings will be correlated with the results obtained in the other investigation and survey stages. The relevance of the results will be verified, on the one hand, from the point of view of usability by experts of the GRIAL design research team, and on the other hand, from a socio-health point of view by members of the research team with experience in this field.

Activity 6 is oriented to disseminating results and exploiting the developed meta-dashboard.

4.5   Team

The team comprises 16 members (7 in the research team, 9 in the work team). 71.43% of the research team members are males, 28.57% of the members are females. 87.71%

of the members of the research team have a Ph.D. degree. 44.44% of the work team members are males, 55.56% of the members are females. 66.67% of the members of the work team have a Ph.D. degree. From the global perspective (16 members, including both research and work teams), 56.25% are males, 43.75% are females, and 75% have a Ph.D. degree. The roles of software engineer, medicine, and neuropsychology mean interdisciplinarity, an expert in educational technologies, and academic researcher suggest multidisciplinary. Finally, manager and data manager roles are the technician profiles for supporting research.

5 Expected Results

5.1 Scientific and Technical Impact

The achievement of the objectives of the present proposal will have a substantial impact on the promotion and generation of frontier knowledge. Specifically, in the following areas:

- Scientific impact and international leadership in the field. The automatic development of dashboards, through a meta-model, allows obtaining visual analysis tools adapted to any domain, facilitating the exploitation of data. Due to the flexibility and adaptability of the dashboards generated using artificial intelligence techniques, the best configuration and design according to the context can be attained. The proposal is at the frontier of state of the art, not only in the health field.
- The innovation of the ideas on which it is based. The systematic studies show no such solution in healthy ecosystems, and meta-dashboards are just developing in other fields. Different techniques have been proposed in the literature to create and adapt dashboards (among them, meta-modeling). Still, most of their applications have not been produced or evaluated in authentic contexts.
- Interdisciplinary and multidisciplinary scientific approach. The approach of the project requires the collaboration of various areas of knowledge. Different experts are involved in domain engineering-based software development, in human-computer interaction for the evaluation of the user experience in the usability lab, and technical staff with expertise in socio-sanitary technologies given the scope of the ecosystem.

More specifically, it is worth noting that the challenges faced by the currently available solutions in the province of dashboards are more accentuated in the field of the health sector. Technological ecosystems and, more specifically, dashboards are a domain that is still in the early stages of development, especially in Spain. With the current health information systems, the static characteristics of performance reporting in the health care sector have resulted in inconsistent, incomparable, time-consuming, and static performance reports that can transparently reflect a round picture of performance and effectively support healthcare managers' decision-making processes. So, the healthcare sector needs interactive performance management tools such as performance dashboards to measure, monitor, and manage performance more effectively.

Software solutions such as dashboards have been commonly related to Business Intelligence (BI) [39]. They allow their users to better manage their data by providing data analysis, information presentation, and integration with other business development environments through metadata management.

To understand the value that this proposal brings by integrating processes and services available in the BI solutions market, it is essential first to identify the challenges that arise within the activities carried out to deploy this type of solution. In general terms, the current BI type solutions, and more specifically, dashboard development, present the following challenges for their deployment:

- Data collection guarantees data quality and consistency among different actors, lines, or processes, including mechanisms to restrict access to information.
- KPIs and Metrics.
- The visual component extrapolates the visualization structure to different processes, lines, or business models.
- To achieve the definition of the dashboard itself, the post-deployment activities are associated with the analysis of the information flows that are established between the ecosystem components and users.

The challenges mentioned above are accentuated when attempting to deploy dashboards in technological ecosystems since they have characteristics that are not present within the areas that traditional BI solutions focus on:

- Its evolutionary component, so that the ecosystem must adapt to changes, both in the context where the ecosystem is deployed and to the changing requirements of users.
- The human component is a fundamental part of the ecosystem at the same level as the software components.

For the above reasons, the success of the current proposal involves a series of improvements over existing solutions:

- The development of a meta-dashboard that can be incorporated into any technological ecosystem so that the definition of the dashboard itself is associated with the analysis of the information flows that are established between the different components of the ecosystem. As well as the interaction of users with the ecosystem technologies.
- The possibility of implementing it in the health environment that has differentiated needs and will improve the knowledge transfer.
- The above will open the market and promote interest in this type of solution from organizations that are part of technological ecosystems or technological solutions in the health sector and have not considered BI a key to their business or activity.
- Provide unified mechanisms to seek the integrity and quality of data from different sources and with varying quality criteria.

5.2 Socio-Economic Impact

The AVisSA technological ecosystems sought to satisfy the aging and care provision challenge, with the particularity of considering the differential characteristics of the Spanish population consisting of the geographical dispersion. Innovative solutions are needed in active aging, especially to allow for an autonomous life in their home environment for as long as possible. Besides, the implementation of the meta-dashboard will enable the incorporation of other actors as stakeholders (public administration, health managers, etc.) who will be able to access the data generated within the ecosystem for decision making and design improvements in health provision.

The exploitation of the data will make it possible to promote the ecosystem between primary users (doctors, caregivers, and patients) and secondary and tertiary users (managers, public administration, research networks), significantly increasing the viability of the initial proposal. Healthcare dashboards can be used for various purposes, including strategy analysis and execution, performance reviews, performance improvement, data comprehension, and scope opportunity.

On the other hand, from an economic perspective, the dashboard market has evolved from being a resource generally used by large companies to monitor their commercial departments to being used in diverse contexts. Each metric can be broken down, analyzed, and correlated with other information.

The main factor driving the growth of the dashboard software market is the increasing appearance of a large amount of structured and unstructured data that different organizations and companies must manage. One of the fundamental causes of this paradigm shift is that data generated by the interaction of users with companies through digital channels is experiencing a faster growth rate than conventional business data. This, together with the high competition between companies due to an increasingly globalized market, is one of the main factors driving the growth of the global dashboard market. Dashboards allow to show in real-time the trends of the different indicators of interest and offer information that can be used in strategic decisions of businesses and all types of organizations.

6 Conclusions

This work describes the AVisSA project, which will address the development of an automatic dashboard generation system (meta-dashboard) based on the data flow in technological ecosystems.

The meta-dashboard will automatically adapt to the needs of analysis and knowledge management in heterogeneous contexts such as the health sector, to improve these processes within the health system, with special impact on decision-making processes. The implementation of the meta-dashboard will make intensive use of user experience testing throughout its development, which will allow the incorporation of other actors in the ecosystem as new stakeholders (public administration, health managers, etc.).

These actors will be able to make use of the data for decision-making and improve the health provision. The exploitation of the data will make it possible to promote the ecosystem from its primary focus on primary users (caregivers and patients) to secondary and tertiary users (managers, public administration, research networks), significantly increasing the viability of the initial proposal. Thus, these tools that support decision-making will improve both the quality of the services provided and their economic efficiency.

Acknowledgments. This research work has been supported by the Spanish *Ministry of Education and Vocational Training* under an FPU fellowship (FPU17/03276). This research was partially funded by the Spanish Government Ministry of Science and Innovation through the AVisSA project grant number (PID2020-118345RB-I00).

References

1. Álvarez-Arana, A., Villamañe-Gironés, M., Larrañaga-Olagaray, M.: Improving assessment using visual learning analytics. Educ. Knowl. Soc. **21** (2020)
2. García-Morales, V.J., Garrido-Moreno, A., Martín-Rojas, R.: The transformation of higher education after the COVID disruption: emerging challenges in an online learning scenario. Front. Psychol. **12** (2021)
3. García-Peñalvo, F.J.: Avoiding the dark side of digital transformation in teaching. An institutional reference framework for eLearning in higher education. Sustainability **13** (2021)
4. García-Peñalvo, F.J.: Digital transformation in the universities: implications of the COVID-19 pandemic. Educ. Knowl. Soc. **22** (2021)
5. García-Peñalvo, F.J., Corell, A., Abella-García, V., Grande-de-Prado, M.: Recommendations for mandatory online assessment in higher education during the COVID-19 pandemic. In: Burgos, D., Tlili, A., Tabacco, A. (eds.) Radical Solutions for Education in a Crisis Context. COVID-19 as an Opportunity for Global Learning, pp. 85–98. Springer, Singapore (2021). https://doi.org/10.1007/978-981-15-7869-4_6
6. García-Peñalvo, F.J., Corell, A.: The COVID-19: the enzyme of the digital transformation of teaching or the reflection of a methodological and competence crisis in higher education? Campus Virtuales **9**, 83–98 (2020)
7. Hai, T.N., Van, Q.N., Thi Tuyet, M.N.: Digital transformation: opportunities and challenges for leaders in the emerging countries in response to Covid-19 pandemic. Emerging Sci. J. **5**, 21–36 (2021)
8. Barrutia, J.M., Echebarria, C.: Effect of the COVID-19 pandemic on public managers' attitudes toward digital transformation. Technol. Soc. **67**, 101776 (2021)
9. Almeida, F., Santos, J.D., Monteiro, J.A.: The challenges and opportunities in the digitalization of companies in a post-COVID-19 World. IEEE Eng. Manage. Rev. **48**, 97–103 (2020)
10. Infante-Moro, A., Infante-Moro, J.C., Gallardo-Pérez, J.: The employment possibilities of the internet of things in the hotel sector and its training needs. Educ. Knowl. Soc. **21** (2020)
11. do Nascimento, M.G., et al.: Covid-19: a digital transformation approach to a public primary healthcare environment. In: Proceedings of the 2020 IEEE Symposium on Computers and Communications (ISCC), Rennes, France, 7–10 July 2020. IEEE (2020)
12. Furtner, D., Shinde, S.P., Singh, M., Wong, C.H., Setia, S.: Digital transformation in medical affairs sparked by the pandemic: insights and learnings from COVID-19 era and beyond. Pharmaceutical Medicine (2021, in Press)
13. Rajkomar, A., Dean, J., Kohane, I.: Machine learning in medicine. N. Engl. J. Med. **380**, 1347–1358 (2019)
14. Litjens, G., et al.: A survey on deep learning in medical image analysis. Med. Image Anal. **42**, 60–88 (2017)
15. González Izard, S., Sánchez Torres, R., Alonso Plaza, Ó., Juanes Méndez, J.A., García-Peñalvo, F.J.: Nextmed: automatic imaging segmentation, 3D reconstruction, and 3D model visualization platform using augmented and virtual reality. Sensors (Basel) **20**, 2962 (2020)
16. Izard, S.G., Juanes, J.A., García Peñalvo, F.J., Estella, J.M.G., Ledesma, M.J.S., Ruisoto, P.: Virtual reality as an educational and training tool for medicine. J. Med. Syst. **42**(3), 1–5 (2018). https://doi.org/10.1007/s10916-018-0900-2

17. García-Peñalvo, F.J., et al.: Application of artificial intelligence algorithms within the medical context for non-specialized users: the CARTIER-IA platform. Int. J. Interact. Multimedia Artif. Intell. **6**, 46–53 (2021)
18. García-Peñalvo, F.J., Rodríguez-Conde, M.J., Therón, R., García-Holgado, A., Martínez-Abad, F., Benito-Santos, A.: Grupo GRIAL. IE Comunicaciones. Revista Iberoamericana de Informática Educativa, 33–48 (2019)
19. García-Holgado, A., García-Peñalvo, F.J.: Validation of the learning ecosystem metamodel using transformation rules. Futur. Gener. Comput. Syst. **91**, 300–310 (2019)
20. García-Peñalvo, F.J., Franco-Martín, M.: Sensor technologies for caring people with disabilities. Sensors **19** (2019)
21. García-Holgado, A., Marcos-Pablos, S., Therón, R., García-Peñalvo, F.J.: Technological ecosystems in the health sector: a mapping study of European research projects. J. Med. Syst. **43**, 1–11 (2019)
22. Marcos-Pablos, S., García-Peñalvo, F.J.: Technological ecosystems in care and assistance: a systematic literature review. Sensors **19**, 708 (2019)
23. Sarikaya, A., Correll, M., Bartram, L., Tory, M., Fisher, D.: What do we talk about when we talk about dashboards? IEEE Trans. Visual. Comput. Graph. **25**, 682–692 (2018)
24. Few, S.: Information Dashboard Design. O'Reilly Media, Sebastopol (2006)
25. Berinato, S.: Good Charts: The HBR Guide to Making Smarter, More Persuasive Data Visualizations. Harvard Business Review Press, Brighton (2016)
26. Vartak, M., Huang, S., Siddiqui, T., Madden, S., Parameswaran, A.: Towards visualization recommendation systems. ACM SIGMOD Rec. **45**, 34–39 (2017)
27. Hu, K., Bakker, M.A., Li, S., Kraska, T., Hidalgo, C.: VizML: a machine learning approach to visualization recommendation. In: Proceedings of the 2019 CHI Conference on Human Factors in Computing Systems, Glasgow, Scotland, UK, May 2019. ACM, New York (2019)
28. Dibia, V., Demiralp, Ç.: Data2Vis: automatic generation of data visualizations using sequence to sequence recurrent neural networks. IEEE Comput. Graph. Appl. **39**, 33–46 (2019)
29. Vázquez-Ingelmo, A., García-Holgado, A., García-Peñalvo, F.J., Therón, R.: Proof-of-concept of an information visualization classification approach based on their fine-grained features. Expert Syst., e12872 (2021, in Press)
30. Vázquez-Ingelmo, A., García-Peñalvo, F.J., Therón, R., Amo-Filvà, D., Fonseca-Escudero, D.: Connecting domain-specific features to source code: towards the automatization of dashboard generation. Cluster Comput. J. Netw. Softw. Tools Appl. **23**, 1803–1816 (2020)
31. Office of Government Commerce: An introduction to PRINCE2: Managing and directing successful projects. The Stationery Office, Belfast, Ireland (2009)
32. Kitchenham, B., Brereton, O.P., Budgen, D., Turner, M., Bailey, J., Linkman, S.: Systematic literature reviews in software engineering – a systematic literature review. Inf. Softw. Technol. **51**, 7–15 (2009)
33. García-Holgado, A., Marcos-Pablos, S., García-Peñalvo, F.J.: Guidelines for performing systematic research projects reviews. Int. J. Interact. Multimedia Artif. Intell. **6**, 136–144 (2020)
34. Baskerville, R.L.: Investigating information systems with action research. Commun. AIS **2**, 19 (1999)
35. Schwaber, K., Beedle, M.: Agile Software Development with Scrum. Prentice Hall PTR, Upper Saddle River (2001)
36. Vázquez-Ingelmo, A., García-Peñalvo, F.J., Therón, R.: Taking advantage of the software product line paradigm to generate customized user interfaces for decision-making processes: a case study on university employability. PeerJ Comput. Sci. **5**, e203 (2019)
37. King, G., Keohane, R.O., Verba, S.: Designing Social Inquiry: Scientific Inference in Qualitative Research. Princeton University Press, Princeton (1994)

38. Buendía, L., Colás, P., Hernández, F.: Métodos de investigación en psicopcdagogía. McGraw-Hill, Madrid (1998)
39. Marcos-Pablos, S., García-Holgado, A., García-Peñalvo, F.J.: Modelling the business structure of a digital health ecosystem. In: Conde-González, M.Á., Rodríguez-Sedano, F.J., Fernández-Llamas, C., García-Peñalvo, F.J. (eds.) TEEM'19 Proceedings of the Seventh International Conference on Technological Ecosystems for Enhancing Multiculturality, Leon, Spain, 16th–18th October 2019, pp. 838–845. ACM, New York (2019)

Agile CTMTC: Adapting Stages for a Shorter Application of the Teamwork Method

María Luisa Sein-Echaluce[1]([✉]) [iD], Ángel Fidalgo-Blanco[2] [iD],
and Francisco José García-Peñalvo[3] [iD]

[1] Departamento de Matemática Aplicada, Escuela de Ingeniería y Arquitectura,
Universidad de Zaragoza, Zaragoza, Spain
mlsein@unizar.es
[2] LITI Laboratorio, Unversidad Politécnica de Madrid, Madrid, Spain
angel.fidalgo@upm.es
[3] Grupo de Investigación GRIAL, Departamento de Informática y Automática,
Instituto Universitario de Ciencias de La Educación, Universidad de Salamanca, Salamanca,
Spain
fgarcia@usal.es
https://ror.org/012a91z28, https://ror.org/03n6nwv02,
https://ror.org/02f40zc51

Abstract. The CTMTC method, to develop teamwork competency, includes a set
of phases and, for each of them, a set of processes and evidence that allow knowing
if the team has acquired the group and individual competencies. However, in many
cases, this structure is too complicated to apply with all its phases when it is a
question of carrying out work that must be cooperative but of short duration,
for example. For these cases, the "Agile CTMTC" method is proposed to reduce
the teamwork processes and allow its application in an agile and simple way
in any cooperative situation, but maintaining the acquisition of individual agile
competencies. Employing a case study, it is concluded that this method allows that
the professional and the members of the work team, under the rules by which each
team is governed, can know, in real-time and transparently, the evolution of the
tasks of both the team and its members, as well as contrast the expected workload
with the real one.

Keywords: Agile competences · Cooperative competences · Teamwork ·
CTMTC

1 Introduction

Teamwork is a skill highly required by entities that demand the employment of university
students [1]. Even in many studies, it is beginning to be considered a decisive factor
compared to other academic characteristics [2]. International reports also indicate the
high demand for teamwork in industry and society [3, 4]. Likewise, this competence is
being associated with the need to educate in values [5]. For example, it is not enough to
train people who master teamwork competence, but they must value ethics in all their

P. Zaphiris and A. Ioannou (Eds.): HCII 2022, LNCS 13329, pp. 274–286, 2022.
https://doi.org/10.1007/978-3-031-05675-8_21

actions [6, 7]. This issue has been underlined in the students' assessment during the COVID-19 pandemic [8, 9].

The main objective of the academic teamwork carried out by students is the acquisition of specific competencies to be applied once they have completed their university studies. One of the most widely implemented international teamwork methods is the model of IPMA (International Project Management Accreditation Agency). This agency has defined two lines for accrediting teamwork competencies: group competencies [10] and individual competencies [11].

Group competencies are based on the Tuckman model [12, 13] and they were designed for small groups. In this model, teamwork is based on the following phases: Forming, Storming, Norming and Performing [14]. Tuckman's model was improved by IPMA itself [10] and by some university institutions [15] by adding a new phase: "Delivering and documentation".

An evolution of the IPMA model appeared with the inclusion of the following competencies that team members should acquire individually:

- Select and build the team.
- Promote cooperation and networking between team members.
- Support, facilitate and review the development of the team and its members.
- Empower teams by delegating tasks and responsibilities.
- Recognize errors to facilitate learning from mistakes.

These competencies are developed from agile methodologies [16] and are applied during all the phases corresponding to the group competencies of the teamwork development already mentioned [17].

Previous research works have developed a method called Comprehensive Training Model of the Teamwork Competence (CTMTC) [18] that supports individual and group competences and has been applied in different universities [19–21].

CTMTC method makes intensive use of Information and Communication Technologies (ICT) to capture evidence of learner interaction and to monitor individual responsibilities and involvements. This method has been successfully tested and validated in several scientific publications [22–24].

Nevertheless, experience shows that to apply this CTMTC method or any other method that works with all the phases of teamwork, the work must be developed for sufficient time to consolidate learning. There are many teams with short duration or require only cooperative competencies due to the training objectives established by the teacher, and in those cases, they do not need the development of all the group phases of the teamwork development.

This work aims to adapt the CTMTC model to all those situations where the work is cooperative or short duration. This adaptation will preserve the acquisition of the same individual and group competencies as the full teamwork development and make intensive use of ICT. From now, we will call "team" to any group of students, even when only cooperative work is involved, and no specific teamwork method is applied.

The proposed model adapts the Norming, Storming, and Performing phases, keeping the remaining ones used in any cooperative work regardless of its duration. Therefore, the objectives of this work are:

- Design a model that preserves the individual and group competencies of a teamwork applicable to cooperative short-term work.
- To identify the tools and procedures applicable to any type and area of academic knowledge.
- To know the students' perception.

The phases mentioned above of CTMTC give rise to the processes of elaboration of the normative and the map of responsibilities and the execution of the work. The common feature of the three processes in the proposed model is that first, the online discussion is done to propose and select, then the discussion is shared, and finally, the results are made explicit in varying degrees of detail, all in a cooperative and online way [25]. Thus, the individual competencies of cooperation and networking are used.

Through a practical case with university students, each process generates results. They are used as evidence to identify the categories of the operating rules proposed by the teams, the types of tasks and the assignment of responsibilities with them, and the monitoring of the development of individual and group tasks transparently and visibly to the team [26]. Thus, the competency on transparency in developing individual and group work is used.

A questionnaire is also carried out to determine the degree of cooperation and decision-making used in each process and the degree of compliance with both regulations and individual responsibilities.

The following sections include the proposed Agile CTMTC model, the context of the application of the method, the results, and the conclusions of this work.

2   Agile CTMTC Model

The CTMTC method consists of a set of processes associated with each of the group phases of "Forming", "Storming", "Norming", "Performing" and "Delivering and documentation" [21]. Each phase produces a concrete group result: formation of the team, the election of the coordinator, norming, mission and objectives, map of responsibilities, planning, execution, delivery of results, and additional documentation [27]. He completion of all phases defines that the team has achieved group competencies. However, separately the phases do not indicate either the individual workload or the acquisition of individual competencies [18].

Agile methodologies have a set of individual competencies associated with the development of teamwork, including cooperation, networking, task delegation, transparency, and monitoring of both the members and the team [16]. These competencies apply to any teamwork, even those requiring short implementation times.

The "AGIL CTMTC" model simplifies the phases of teamwork, as well as the group evidence, to achieve, on the one hand, the application of individual agile competencies and, on the other hand, to be able to evaluate and train in the acquisition of the competency as the teamwork develops.

The group evidence is organized around three processes: 1- cooperative development of the standards, 2- mapping of responsibilities of each individual, and 3- execution of the teamwork. This last process is used to monitor teamwork transparently, ensuring that regulations are complied with and that each individual has assumed the assigned responsibilities. The "Agile CTMTC" model allows to:

- Make and share the operating rules that the members of each team have to accomplish and the consequences of not complying with them.
- Make and share the distribution of the workload foreseen for each team member (individual).
- Know the actual individual workload during the development of the teamwork.
- Contrast the planned and actual workload for each member to be able to make decisions in case the workload is not homogeneous or to foresee which members voluntarily avoid their responsibilities.
- Obtain evidence to know the degree of acquisition of teamwork members.

The model consists of the methodological layer (with the processes) and the technological layer (with the technologies), see Fig. 1.

The technology layer consists of an online message exchange space and an online storage space. All teams use the same technological tools; each team works in private spaces, and the faculty staff can access all spaces.

- The online message exchange space (Fig. 1) is used in all processes and is a system that allows threads of conversation between team members. Separate threads are used for each process. The Execution process additionally has an individual thread where each member includes his or her "diary" with activities performed, incidents, and even reflections and requests for help. These threads are private to the team but accessible to the faculty.
- The online storage space is composed of two subsystems: online file storage (Fig. 1) and a web system, page, or wiki, where conclusions can be posted in a summarized and organized way (Fig. 1).

This technological layer is integrated into the methodological layer formed by the processes described below and shown in Fig. 1: the creation of the operating rules in the "Norming" phase, the creation of the map of responsibilities in the "Storming" phase, and the execution of the "Performing" phase.

Norming (Fig. 1). Phase in which the teams regulate their organization and functioning and establish their members' code of conduct. Some operating rules are external, imposed by the teaching staff, such as the date of completion of the work and, in some subjects, the formation of the team and its work objective. Other rules are internal, created by the members themselves and regulate the behavior of team members and the consequences of non-compliance.

Map of Responsibilities (Fig. 1). The map contains the tasks foreseen for each team member and makes it possible to check that the workload is homogeneous within the team.

Execution (Fig. 1). During this process, each team member writes a personal work diary (report) detailing their progress in completing the work and updates it each time a new task is performed. The team also creates weekly a tracking table that includes a summary of the individual tasks and the total work progress. In this process, the actual workload is checked in order to compare it with what is included in the map of responsibilities.

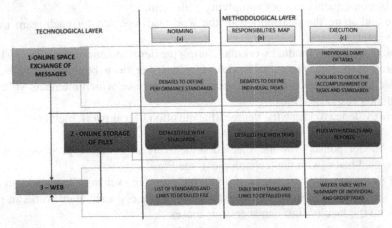

Fig. 1. Agile CTMTC model

The interaction between the members of each team provides evidence of the distribution of the workload in real-time for each member and the acquisition of individual competencies.

The individual competencies to be worked with are those provided by the IPMA model [11], specifically: "Cooperation and Networking", "Review the development of the team and its members", and "Delegating tasks and responsibilities". Developing these competencies is necessary to carry out all the processes, and the evidence will show the degree of individual compliance.

Likewise, we work with another competency, "Recognize errors to facilitate learning", that the teachers promote within the learning method, carrying out formative evaluations by identifying the usual errors of the teams and the way to solve them.

In this work, research-based on a case study is carried out, the model is developed with the methodological and technological layers, it is explained to the students, and they use it during the development of the work. Evidence generated individually is collected through the messages exchanged and the results generated in each process. At the end of the work, a survey is carried out to know the degree of compliance with the regulations, tasks, types of responsibilities, and cooperation and decision-making.

3   Context

The Agile CTMTC model has been applied in the "Programming Fundamentals" subject, corresponding to the first year of the Biotechnology Degree at the Technical University of Madrid, Spain.

The 77 students enrolled in an academic group were distributed in 13 work teams with an average of 6 members per team. The technological layer was the e-learning platform Moodle. The online space for message exchange was the Moodle forum, which each team uses privately and allows to open multiple threads, thus fulfilling the functionality specified in the model. The online storage system was the Moodle wiki, which works similarly to a web page but can be used with separate groups to preserve the privacy of each team. Google Drive was also used to store the files and link them from the wiki.

The students themselves voluntarily chose to be part of a team (maximum with 6 members) through Moodle's "Group selection" tool. The topic of each teamwork could be chosen by the students from three categories, each corresponding to an evaluable block of the subject.

4   Results

The first subsection shows the results related to the evidence generated by the students both individually and collectively in each of the processes. The following subsection will show the students' perception of the processes and the general functioning of the work team.

4.1   Evidence of Processes

Norming Process. To elaborate the norming, all teams used a single thread within the Moodle forum to propose and discuss the proposals and finally elaborate the list of operating rules. Table 1 shows the categories (protocols) of operating rules (access to online exchange system, breach of responsibilities, the inclusion of new rules, results in the organization, incidents reporting, exchange of messages, decision-making, task distribution, and work follow-up), as well as the percentage of teams that included rules for each category in their norming.

Table 1. Categories of operating rules defined by the teams

Categories	%
Access to online exchange system	100.00
Breach of responsibilities	92.31
Inclusion of new rules	84.62
Results organization	76.92
Incidents reporting	76.92
Exchange of messages	61.54
Decision-making	53.85
Task distribution	46.15
Work follow-up	30.77

Map of Responsibilities Process. To draw up the map of responsibilities, all the teams (100%) used a single forum thread which, similar to the previous process, gave rise to a discussion on the distribution of tasks. The responsibilities have been grouped into three categories:

- *Technological responsibilities:* implies commitments in the use of the tools of the technological layer. An initial detection is made of the member or members with more technical knowledge and the member or members with lesser knowledge to establish tasks for learning and using these tools subsequently.
- *Leadership responsibilities:* assignment of tasks to each member of the team on monitoring the development of teamwork, compliance with regulations, team spokesperson in the face of questions from teachers in class, checking the development of the work, and checking compliance with the assigned tasks.
- *Responsibilities on the final result:* these are necessary tasks for elaborating the final work. It is usually based on a work content vision that must be elaborated by each member of the team and which later, in the Execution process, they collaboratively unite to create the final work.

Execution Process. An individual thread has been used for each team member as a work diary and one thread for sharing and generating the tracking table (except two teams that used five threads for pooling, one per week).

Table 2 shows the evidence in the exchange space. The first column includes the team number, in the second column the average number of messages that each team member has posted in their individual thread, and the third column the corresponding standard deviation. It can be seen that the average number of messages per thread is very heterogeneous among the teams.

Table 2. Individual messages in forum threads for the work diary

Team	Mean	Sd
E1	10.33	5.28
E2	22.17	3.82
E3	19.83	4.88
E4	11.83	3.54
E5	9.00	2.10
E6	19.33	4.97
E7	36.33	4.37
E8	40.17	7.05
E9	25.17	11.13
E10	16.80	10.76
E11	47.50	5.47
E12	20.50	4.18
E13	10.60	2.97

All the teams have created a table tracking the execution process. Each row of this table corresponds to a week of the implementation period, and the columns include the following:

- First column: exact dates for each week.
- Second column: list of tasks with the team member who has performed each one.
- Third column: incidences and unforeseen events.

4.2 Students' Perception About the Proposed Processes

At the end of the course and before the final exams of the course, a student satisfaction survey was conducted to find out their perception of the Agile CTMTC method. The following is an analysis of the processes and the acquisition of competencies. Of the students who participated in the teams, 54 answered the survey, representing a sample of 70.13% of the total number of students involved in the research.

The following are results on three aspects that we believe are relevant to the study on the acquisition of individual competencies:

- Degree of cooperation in the teams.
- Degree of cooperation and leadership.
- Division of tasks and decision making.

Degree of Cooperation During the Processes. The survey asked about the degree of cooperation and decision-making required during each process and the organization of results through the two technological tools used: the online storage and the wiki. The question was evaluated on a Likert scale where 1 is associated with "not at all" and 5 with "very much".

Table 3 shows the answers given, where the first column identifies the process, the second column the mean, and the third column the standard deviation.

Table 3. Cooperation during the processes and with technological tools

Indicates the degree of cooperation and decision making necessary during each process	Mean	Sd
Norming	3.54	1.08
Responsibilities map	4.20	0.74
Execution	4.20	0.94
Online storage - files	2.96	1.15
Wiki	3.07	1.21

Degree of Cooperation and Leadership During the Teamwork. To determine the degree of cooperation and leadership during the development of teamwork, four multiple-choice questions with only one option were included in the survey. Table 4 shows in the first column the questions, in the second column the possible options, and in the third column the distribution of frequencies for each option.

Table 4. Cooperation and leadership during the teamwork

Question	Answers	%
The rules that you yourselves created have been complied with?	1- Yes 2- No	100 0
Are there members of your team who have tried to avoid their responsibilities?	1- Yes 2- No	11.11 88.89
Most of the team members have cooperated in leadership tasks?	1- Yes, on their own initiative 2- Yes, but I had to ask him to do it 3- No, I never asked them 4- No because that was my mission	88.89 5.56 3.70 1.85
How have decisions been made in your work team?	1- The leader proposed them, and they were agreed upon the rest 2- Cooperatively among all team members 3- Cooperatively among the most committed members of the team 4- Imposed by the leader	0 88.89 11.11 0

Division of Leadership Tasks and Incident Resolution. One of the aspects to be highlighted in the collective and individual evidence is the division of leadership tasks among the team members. To determine whether the division of tasks has been carried out, whether they have assumed shared leadership and whether there has been cooperation in problem-solving, a question was used to analyze the involvement of the team members when one person assumed leadership. A Likert 5 scale question was used, where 1 is "Never" and 5 is "Always".

Table 5 shows the question in the first column, the mean of answers in the second column, and the third column includes their standard deviation.

Table 5. Degree of leadership tasks execution

Question "Answer de 1-never to 5-always to the sentence: The team members…	Mean	Sd
… have done their tasks assigned in the responsibilities map	4.63	0.62
… have done their assigned tasks on time	4.22	0.79
… have followed my instructions	4.22	0.96
… have accepted my leadership	3.69	1.54
… have contributed to solve the problems	4.74	0.52

5   Conclusions

We include the conclusions for each of the processes that make up the proposed "AGIL CTMC" model, the agile competencies developed by the model, and the future work.

In the norming process, the operating rules established by the teams can be grouped into nine categories (Table 1). The most used are the rules for communicating online among the team members, the consequences of not complying with the rules, including new rules during the teamwork development, organizing the results, reporting the incidents, and decision-making. The least common rules (less than 50% of the teams) correspond to distributing tasks and monitoring teamwork protocols. Understandably, these rules are not used in all work teams since there are two processes in which the criteria are established and analyzed in detail, both the distribution of tasks (responsibilities) and their follow-up. On the other hand, Table 3 shows a high perception (3.54 out of 5) of cooperation and decision-making for establishing regulations. However, of the three processes (regulations, map of responsibilities, and execution), this process (norming) is the one that requires minor cooperation. Table 4 shows that 100% of the teams have complied with their own operating rules.

During the responsibilities map process, the teams have established three types of tasks: technological, leadership, and teamwork development. Likewise, the responsibility map assigns responsibility for the different tasks to each team member, and each team member is assigned tasks in each category. Table 3 shows that establishing tasks and assigning responsibilities requires a high percentage of cooperation and decision-making (4.2 out of 5). Table 5 also shows that the perception of the performance of the tasks assigned to each team member is high: 4.63 out of 5.

The execution process serves to know the actual compliance with the rules and the performance of the tasks assigned to each person. Table 2 shows the average number of messages each member has posted to describe the tasks he or she is performing. Exploring this thread, both team members and teachers, checking what each member has done is possible. The average number of messages per team is very different. There are teams with an average of 9 messages per person and others with an average of 47 messages per person. This does not mean they have not performed the tasks, but they have put minor or more detail in performing them. A tracking table is built from the personal threads, where the performed tasks, incidents, etc., are indicated weekly. The teams that have posted fewer messages have minor detail in the table, for example, no incidents, while the teams that have posted more messages have much more detail.

In some cases, there is a high value for the standard deviation, which means that within the same team, there are people who have posted more details in the personal thread than others. Table 3 shows that this Execution process has required a high percentage of cooperation and decision making (4.2 out of 5). Table 5 shows that the team members have carried out the responsibilities shown in the responsibility map (4.22 out of 5).

Regarding the individual agile competencies, in all processes (Table 3), it has been indicated that there has been a high level of cooperation and decision-making. The cooperation has been online. Therefore, networking has also been performed. These agile competencies are necessary to obtain the results that have been obtained. The competence in distributing tasks has also been fulfilled (map of responsibilities) and the visualization of the entire development process (execution table). Likewise, in Table 4, the team members say they have primarily cooperated in leadership tasks 94.45% (sum of answers 1 and 2), and in decision-making 100% (sum of answers 2 and 3). Only 11.11% of the students think that there have been people who have tried to work less than they were assigned in their team. Table 5 shows that leadership tasks have been performed and executed by the different members of the team (4.22 out of 5), that the members have accepted the person who was performing these leadership tasks (3.69 out of 5), and that if problems have arisen, they have contributed to solving them (4.74 out of 5). It was also necessary to have a training session before starting teamwork to explain the processes and the analysis of individual and group competence.

Future work is based on analyzing the number of messages of each process to establish alarms on the evolution of individual and group competencies as support to predict the final marks of the work and the team members. This analysis is pushed by several facts such as the difference in the messages associated with each individual thread, inside the teams and between them, and the opinions about people who have tried to work less or who have not cooperated.

Acknowledgements. This research was partially funded by the Spanish Government Ministry of Economy and Competitiveness through the AVisSA project grant number (PID2020-118345RB-I00) and by the Technical University of Madrid through the educational innovation project IE22.0602. The authors would like to thank the research groups EtnoEdu of the University of Zaragoza, GRIAL of the University of Salamanca and LITI of the Technical University of Madrid for their support.

References

1. Observatorio de Empleo y Empleabilidad Universitarios. https://oeeu.org/. Accessed 11 Feb 2022
2. Michavila, F., Martínez, J.M., Martín-González, M., García-Peñalvo, F.J., Cruz-Benito, J.: Empleabilidad de los titulados universitarios en España. Proyecto OEEU. Educ. Knowl. Soc. **19**, 21–39 (2018). https://doi.org/10.14201/eks20181912139
3. Kruse, K.: Evidence-based strategies for better teamwork. https://www.forbes.com/sites/kevinkruse/2020/10/08/evidence-based-strategies-for-better-teamwork/?sh=6d68ad8d16ca. Accessed 11 Feb 2022
4. Khalili, F., Swilem, S.: The efficiency of a group counseling program based on psychodrama in enhancing self-awareness and reducing tension among tenth grade students in Qalqilia City. Educ. Knowl. Soc. **22** (2021). https://doi.org/10.14201/EKS.23921
5. OECD: The future of education and skills Education 2030. OECD Publishing, Paris, France (2018)
6. Agredo-Delgado, V., Ruiz Melenje, P.H., Collazos, C.A., Moreira, F., Fardoune, H.M.: Methodological guidelines catalog to support the collaborative learning process. Educ. Knowl. Soc. **21** (2020). https://doi.org/10.14201/EKS.22616
7. Knopik, T., Oszwa, U.: E-cooperative problem solving as a strategy for learning mathematics during the COVID-19 pandemic. Educ. Knowl. Soc. **22** (2021). https://doi.org/10.14201/eks.25176
8. García-Peñalvo, F.J., Corell, A., Abella-García, V., Grande-de-Prado, M.: Online assessment in higher education in the time of COVID-19. Educ. Knowl. Soc. **21** (2020). https://doi.org/10.14201/eks.23013

9. García-Peñalvo, F.J., Corell, A., Abella-García, V., Grande-de-Prado, M.: Recommendations for mandatory online assessment in higher education during the COVID-19 pandemic. In: Burgos, D., Tlil, A., Tabacco, A. (eds.) Radical Solutions for Education in a Crisis Context. COVID-19 as an Opportunity for Global Learning, pp. 85–98. Lecture Notes in Educational Technology. Springer, Singapore (2021). https://doi.org/10.1007/978-981-15-7869-4_6
10. IPMA: ICB -IPMA Competence Baseline Version 3.0. International Project Management Association, Nijkerk (NL) (2006)
11. IPMA: Individual Competence Baseline for Project, Programme & Portfolio Management. Version 4.0. International Project Management Association, Zurich (2015)
12. Tuckman, B.W.: Classics for group facilitators developmental sequence in small groups'. Psychol. Bull. **63**, 384–399 (1965)
13. Tuckman, B.W., Jensen, M.A.C.: Stages of small-group development revisited. Group Organ. Stud. **2**, 419–427 (1977). https://doi.org/10.1177/105960117700200404
14. Cresswell-Yeager, T.: Forming, storming, norming, and performing: using a semester-long problem-based learning project to apply small-group communication principles. Commun. Teach. **35**, 155–165 (2021). https://doi.org/10.1080/17404622.2020.1842476
15. Stein, J.: Using the Stages of Team Development | MIT Human Resources. https://hr.mit.edu/learning-topics/teams/articles/stages-development. Accessed 11 Feb 2022
16. IPMA: IPMA Reference Guide ICB4 in an Agile World. International Project Management Association, Zurich (2018)
17. González-Blázquez, J.L., García-Holgado, A., García-Peñalvo, F.J.: Open approach of scaled agile for organizations and communities dedicated to the development of Open-Source projects. In: Proceedings of the 9th International Conference on Technological Ecosystems for Enhancing Multiculturality (TEEM 2021), Barcelona, Spain, 27–29 October 2021, pp. 752–757. ACM, New York (2021)
18. Fidalgo-Blanco, Á., Léris, D., Sein-Echaluce, M.L., García-Peñalvo, F.J.: Monitoring indicators for CTMTC: comprehensive training model of the teamwork competence in engineering domain. Int. J. Eng. Educ. **31**, 829–838 (2015)
19. Barreiro García, J., Martínez Pellitero, S., González Alonso, M.I.: Aplicación de la metodología CTMTC para evaluación formativa del trabajo grupal en ingeniería de fabricación. Revista Infancia, Educación y Aprendizaje **3**, 499–504 (2017). https://doi.org/10.22370/IEYA.2017.3.2.770
20. Conde-González, M.A., Colomo-Palacios, R., García-Peñalvo, F.J., Larrucea, X.: Teamwork assessment in the educational web of data: a learning analytics approach towards ISO 10018. Telematics Inform. **35**, 551–563 (2018). https://doi.org/10.1016/j.tele.2017.02.001
21. Conde, M.Á., Hernández-García, Á., García-Peñalvo, F.J., Fidalgo-Blanco, Á., Sein-Echaluce, M.: Evaluation of the CTMTC methodology for assessment of teamwork competence development and acquisition in higher education. In: Zaphiris, P., Ioannou, A. (eds.) LCT 2016. LNCS, vol. 9753, pp. 201–212. Springer, Cham (2016). https://doi.org/10.1007/978-3-319-39483-1_19
22. Fidalgo-Blanco, Á., Conde, M.A., Sein-Echaluce, M.L., Garcia-Peñalvo, F.J.: Design and development of a learning analytics system to evaluate group work competence. In: 9th Iberian Conference on Information Systems and Technologies (CISTI), pp. 1–6. IEEE (2014). https://doi.org/10.1109/CISTI.2014.6877099
23. Sein-Echaluce, M.L., Fidalgo-Blanco, Á., Esteban-Escaño, J., García-Peñalvo, F.J., Conde, M.A.: Using learning analytics to detect authentic leadership characteristics in engineering students. Int. J. Eng. Educ. **34**, 851–864 (2018)
24. Fidalgo-Blanco, Á., Sein-Echaluce, M.L., García-Peñalvo, F.J., Conde, M.A.: Using learning analytics to improve teamwork assessment. Comput. Hum. Behav. **47**, 149–156 (2015). https://doi.org/10.1016/J.CHB.2014.11.050

25. Fidalgo-Blanco, Á., Sein-Echaluce, M.L., García-Peñalvo, F.J., Sánchez-Canales, M.: Validation of a semantic search engine for academic resources on engineering teamwork. Int. J. Eng. Educ. **36**, 341–351 (2020)
26. Sein-Echaluce, M.L., Fidalgo-Blanco, Á., García-Peñalvo, F.J., Fonseca, D.: Impact of transparency in the teamwork development through cloud computing. Appl. Sci. **11** (2021). Article 3887. https://doi.org/10.3390/app11093887
27. Sein-Echaluce, M.L., Fidalgo-Blanco, A., Esteban-Escaño, J., García, F.: The learning improvement of engineering students using peer-created complementary resources. Int. J. Eng. Educ. **927**(33), 927–937 (2017)

T-Game: A Team Formation Game for Enhancing Cross-Disciplinary Cooperation

Pei-Yun Wu[iD], Teng-Wen Chang[✉][iD], and Cheng-Chun Hung[iD]

National Yunlin University of Science and Technology, Yunlin, Taiwan
tengwen@gemail.yuntech.edu.tw

Abstract. The advance of technology has communication and knowledge acquisition become more convenient. The ability of participants in single professional field can no longer solve complicated problems. The establishment of cross-disciplinary teams aims to collaboratively solve problems and accomplish tasks which cannot be achieved by a single participant or in a single field. Among factors in facilitating the creativity in the cooperation of designers and technical participants in a cross-disciplinary team, technical participants need suitable communication skills and technical skills and avoid proposing action programs which is technologically practicable but does not conform to designers' intention. Designers, on the other hand, should acquire relevant professional knowledge and be able to reflect and learn from other experts.

From prior research and evaluation, it was discovered that most problems in cross-disciplinary team cooperation appeared on the team formation stage. For instance, uncertain personal positioning and contribution in the team or not understanding other team members' work procedure resulted in conflict among team members and difficulty in achieving the consensus. Due to different professional fields, what was normal in an individual field might not be understood by participants from different fields. The solution should be realized by team members. The cognitive diversity formed by the cross-disciplinary team members from different fields is the key factor in increasing creativity and thoughts; however, how to smoothly integrate such ideas should be considered by team members. Playing characters with different specialties allows members in engineering and design putting themselves in someone's shoes to precede communication and coordination in the process, observe other participants to understand the difference between engineering and design members, and find out solutions to accomplish the goals in short period.

Keywords: Team formation · Empathy · Co-design · Gamification

1 Background

The advance of technology has communication and knowledge acquisition become more convenient. The ability of participants in single professional field can no longer solve complicated problems. The formation of cross-disciplinary team aims to collaboratively solve problems and accomplish events which cannot be achieved by a single participant or

P. Zaphiris and A. Ioannou (Eds.): HCII 2022, LNCS 13329, pp. 287–300, 2022.
https://doi.org/10.1007/978-3-031-05675-8_22

in a single field. Among factors in facilitating the creativity in the cooperation of designers between technical participants in the cross-disciplinary team, technical participants should present suitable communication skills and technical skills and avoid proposing action programs which are technically practicable but do not conform to designers' intention. Designers, on the other hand, require relevant professional knowledge and are able to reflect and learn from other experts (Candy and Edmonds 2002).

1.1 Problems in Cross-Disciplinary Team Formation

From prior research and evaluation, it was discovered that the problems in the cross-disciplinary team cooperation often appeared on the team formation stage, e.g. uncertain personal positioning and contribution in the team or not understanding other team members' work procedures to result in conflict among team members and difficulty in achieving the consensus (Chang et al. 2018). Due to different professional fields, what was normal in individual field might not be understood by participants in the other field. The solution should be realized by team members. Cognitive diversity formed by members from different fields was the major factor in the increase in creativity and thoughts in the cross-disciplinary team. How to smoothly integrate such ideas required team members' considerations. Playing characters different from the specialty allows members in engineering and design putting themselves in someone's shoes, preceding communication and coordination in the process, and observing other participants to understand the difference of engineering and design members at work, find out solutions for problems, and accomplish the goal in short period.

1.2 Research Procedure and Step

In order to comprehend and efficiently achieve cross-disciplinary team formation, a team formation game with the teamwork in design and engineering fields is provided in this study. Aiming at the primary development team in design and engineering, i.e. junior college students with professional knowledge but lack of cross-disciplinary experience, the procedure is designed with experiment. It is expected to have engineers and designers without cross-disciplinary cooperation experiences put themselves in someone's shoes, through the cross-disciplinary game, to comprehend and increase the experience required for cross-disciplinary cooperation and exchange with participants from different fields in the cooperation to enhance the cognition of professional fields and thinking styles of both parties and understand how to solve problems. The interesting game with presence allows the team accomplishing tasks and solving problems in short period.

The research is experimented through the students in the cross-disciplinary course, which combines theory and practice. The game aims to guide students in design and engineering fields to form the cross-disciplinary team and precede game tasks with the professional knowledge. Each student has to apply the professional knowledge to the cooperation and accomplish specified tasks in short period. With participant observation, the research participants precede observation and analysis as well as understand the problems in the process for successive discussion. Due to the effect of the epidemic, the concept for game tasks is developed with Miro and the discussion is preceded through Discord. The relevant procedures and steps are described as below.

1. Stage 1-find a partner: 3–4 participants in each group are provided different task cards, and the participants are grouped according to the specialty.
2. Stage 2-choose roles: The game is preceded twice, playing characters according to specialties for the first time and exchanging characters with different specialties for the second time. Each team should contain at least each of three characters of designer, engineer, and decision maker.
3. Stage 3-solve the specified task: According to tasks provided, engineering and design characters have to provide ideas starting from the characters.
4. Stage 4-reflect problems: Reflect problems at Stage 3 or think of the problems which might appear, propose problems, and discuss solutions. When a team does not have any problems, problems would be randomly given for the team's discussion and solution.
5. Stage 5-accomplish tasks. Teams would briefly report the discussion result for all participants to see and think of the interest and contribution. Personal opinions could be proposed or revised in various theme outcomes, and the favorite outcome is voted. The team with the most votes is the winner.

2 Literature Review

In order to comprehend cross disciplinary team formation for the team formation game design, cross-disciplinary cocreation, empathy, and game case are applied to comprehend cross-disciplinary team formation in this study. In this chapter, past related research is organized, starting from cross-disciplinary cocreation to combine games for comprehending empathy. The interests in and motivation of the game could help explore the design direction of cross-disciplinary team formation game and interaction with team members.

2.1 Team Formation and Co-creation

Along with working styles gradually change into cross-disciplinary cooperation, effective cooperation among different fields was essential for maximizing the potential profits of cross-discipline in current business activities and academic research (Chang et al. 2018). Cross discipline was required in current society and integrated various factors into a brand-new ability. The research result revealed that design thinking training could comprehensively promote students' innovation ability and fully dig out the potential to change the world (Li et al. 2019).

Cross-disciplinary cocreation stressed on team communication between two different fields, formed team consensus, preceded teamwork in professional fields, exchanged among team members in different fields, and formed teamwork decisions in short period. Participants with challenging characteristics in teamwork would be willing to share the ideas and assist in team affairs. Participants good at integration might not be good at expression but would integrate team ideas; such participants presented the characteristics as a leader. There were also participants who would work hard after receiving tasks. Participants with above characteristics in a team would smoothen teamwork (Liao 2016).

2.2   Team Formation and Empathy

Devanshi Sha had students in an engineering-centered private university precede team-work for given problems in the design course. The participants were engineering members without the prior background of design or teamwork. This course stressed on having students better comprehend design process and product development. Devanshi Sha provided design tasks for students participating in the design course, expected the participants to be aware of the function of empathy in design, and improved their empathy. The students also preceded reflection in the process to discuss the observed problems in the design. The research results revealed that the students were aware of the importance of empathy in the course, as tasks could be used for identifying empathy, but the empathy was not enhanced. Nevertheless, they realized the importance of empathy in the entire design process through reflection (Shah et al. 2020).

Building empathy could improve some participants' misunderstanding, which might assist in finding out their potential contribution. The experiment discovered that story-telling could appear consonance among participants and allowed participants putting themselves in someone's shoes to explore problems from different points of view for building empathy (Lam et al. 2017).

2.3   Gamification Case

To analyze people's behaviors through games, it was discovered that interaction was indeed more convenient for users expressing their ideas, reduced communication problems, and facilitated users' judgment and thinking (Lu et al. 2020).

Europe 2045. Europe 2045, an online multi-participant strategy game specifically developed for sociology course in senior high schools, aimed to have the students familiarize political, economic, and social issues in contemporary Europe. In addition to learning current events, the players could develop key competencies of discussion ability, negotiation, teamwork, and group decision making. During the test of Europe 2045, some findings in early research were emphasized and further fined in the course (Šisler and Brom 2008).

EMP-UP. EMP-UP was a game allowing German participants and Syrian participants building empathy. In order to understand the ideas of participants from different culture, the research team, through questionnaire, investigated the experience of participants from different countries in dealing with participants from various places in the world. The participants explained in the questionnaire why they considered it being difficult to build empathy with participants from different cultural background. Racial issues and personal profits of local participants were the priority for solutions. Besides, the situation of refugees was so complicated that it could not have all participants comprehend in short period; it might disperse the discussion. In this case, the research team decided to set young participants as the major target group to explore with the game. The culture of both parties was integrated with storyplay to shorten the culture divide. The game environment was identical to the real world that players could link the virtual environment in the game to the real world (Neuenhaus and Aly 2017).

LEAGUÊ Ideation Toolkit. LEAGUÊ toolkit provided a board with script, five design activities with idea sheets, a log table, and six key GBL dimension cards. The toolkit contained the following cards.

- Primary card: presenting 28 GBL design ideas with problems or tasks (divided into six GBL dimensions).
- Trigger card: providing prompts and examples for GBL design ideas.
- Custom card: Blank cards allow proposing personal design ideas or making solutions.
- Finally, 7 reflection cards provide key lenses or evaluation standards to reflect the design idea and further perfect them.
- Game teams could take turns to select main cards through collaborative discussion and use trigger or custom cards to develop the ideas for the learning game design. In this case, such cards were extremely useful for the integrity of learning game design ideas (Tahir et al. 2021) (Fig. 1).

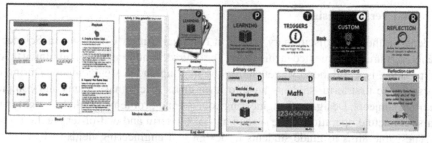

Fig. 1. LEAGUÊ toolkit item (left) and four types of cards (right)

2.4 Summary

According to 2–1, it was discovered that forming a team with people with various characteristics would smoothen the teamwork, and the design thinking training could comprehensively promote students' innovation ability. In 2–2, building empathy by putting oneself in someone's shoes could help improve misunderstanding in the cooperation, and tasks and reflection allowed users realizing the importance of empathy in the entire cooperation process. Regarding three cases in 2–3, key competencies of discussion ability, negotiation, teamwork, and group decision making were developed through learning current events. Storyplay integrated the culture of both parties and shortened the culture divide. The story and card game allowed users connecting game environment to daily life.

In sum, five stages are proposed in the discussion of cross-disciplinary team formation game in this study, including (1) find a partner, (2) choose roles, (3) solve the specified task, (4) reflect problem, and (5) complete tasks, for game design planning. The game design allows team members in engineering and design fields playing different characters and comprehending the type of both parties, has the users finding out problems in the team through professional themes, integrating specialties of both parties through storyplay, and reducing the gap in professional problems. Reflection helps them comprehend and identify different specialties from one's own to achieve the primary consensus; it would be helpful for further division of work.

3 Two Games

According to the summary, the first version design is made to comprehend each other between engineering and design fields, through empathy, and realize the difference in distinct design after the game for iterative correction.

3.1 First Version Design

Students in the cross-disciplinary course in National Yunlin University of Science & Technology are experimented in this study. The course, simultaneously combining theory and practice, is a collaborative course for engineering and design students. During the course in the first term, students have to form cross-disciplinary teams and complete specified subjects. Design and engineering courses and problems would be taught in the course for actual operation in the second half of the term and end-of-term exhibition.

The game aims to guide students in design and engineering fields to form cross-disciplinary teams in the beginning and precede game tasks with the professional knowledge. Each student in the game should cooperate with the professional knowledge and complete specified tasks in short period. The researchers precede observation and analysis with participant observation and understand the problems in the process for successive discussion.

Game Design. The pre-test was preceded on September 2nd, 2021. With physical game for about 50–60 min, students were divided into three groups, and each group had students in engineering and design fields. The game content was revised according to the experimental feedback for the second-time experiment. The toolkit used in the game contained scene card, character card, theme card, obstruction card, reward card, blank poster, sticky note, pen, and sticker. Team members were selected through drawing cards, and the cooperation situation in the game was evaluated at the end to understand team members' thinking styles for further cooperation.

The characters in the game include engineer, designer, helper (engineering), helper (design), and leader (group leader). It is necessary to complete tasks with unacquainted participants. Four task options are provided in the story scenario.

- Technology company (engineering oriented)
- Design company (design oriented)
- Internet company (engineering oriented)
- Game company (design oriented)

The interactive mode is divided into five stages of grouping, deciding characters, solving tasks, resolving obstruction, and accomplishing tasks. 3–4 participants in each team are provided 3–4 specialties or themes related subjects in the course for participants selecting scenarios and themes. Users with the same selection would familiarize with each other in the beginning and are split to different groups to meet different participants. The characters played in the team are selected by drawing a card, including designer, engineer, and decision maker. Each group has at least one of each character. The process allows the participants experiencing different characters to think of affairs with the drawn characters.

At task solving stage, the character of a team leader in each team should lead the team for discussion to develop design ideas according to the drawn theme and scene, e.g. ideas related to chairs in a technology company. With KJ method, characters of engineer and designer have to provide ideas based on the characters and stick sticky notes on the poster. Each participant is given several smaller stickers to stick on ideas which they consider the most important. The preliminary consensus could be formed after this stage.

Problems would appear in the cooperation process, where team members have to collaboratively solve problems. Obstruction cards are provided in the game. Problems encountered by participants with experience in teamwork are organized to become the contents of obstruction cards and help cards, Table 1. Each team should draw obstruction cards, the character of a team leader should lead the team to resolve obstruction. For problems which cannot be resolved, assistance from help cards or helpers could be selected. Helpers are normally instructors and teaching assistants. It is necessary to comprehend the cards and selections of engineers and designer in prior teams used for the problems encountered in the cooperation.

A conclusion is made in the end, where all participants could see the discussion results of other groups, reflect the interests and ability for contribution, and accept other participants' opinions (Fig. 2).

Summary. In the gaming process, it is discovered that the developed task coverage is too huge to clarify the tasks and goal as well as lack empathy and participation intention in the story scenario and task. The story scenario and task are therefore revised to design the second version.

Table 1. Problems and solutions in teamwork

Cross-disciplinary team setting up problems (obstruction card)	Solution (help card)
Engineers prefer quantified answers, while designers hardly have the quantitative adjectives	Discussing the method acceptable by both parties
Designers often draw something which engineers cannot make	For designers understanding what degree an engineer could do
In different fields, it is easy to jump to the conclusion by imagination because of not understanding the difficulty in the other field	It is not always so simple to solve a problem through imagination. It is necessary to understand the fields of the opposite party before making judgment
Different standing basic knowledge and vocabulary. Participants might not contact with or is not aware of common words in the different field	Shortening the cognition difference by mutually understanding professional knowledge in the opposite party's field
Some participants in the management level do not understand web pages or aesthetics but would like to use significant words and expect web designers to make one. It would become abstract and hard to understand	Try to have the opposite party speak out specific outcome, with examples
Designers would do the best to design an object with unknown appearance, fashion style, and details, while engineers would make sure of the required engine system, suspension system, and brake system, find out the maximal value to seek for the balance, and then stuff such hardware into the shape required by "designers". Designers and engineers would start arguing about which is better, design or function	Finding out the method accepted by both parties. When the consensus is not achieved, the group leader or the company direct would make the decision (affected by scene card)
Designers would try to reinforce the convenience and simplify the process direction, while engineers care about effectiveness/efficiency. Both parties pay attention to different points to achieve the effectiveness	Finding out the method accepted by both parties. When the consensus is not achieved, the group leader or the company direct would make the decision (affected by scene card)
Sometimes, designers' design layout does not comprehend the actual execution and the problems of load bearing coefficient and safety factor that the design is gorgeous but is the imagination without understanding the safety or other problems	Having designers understand relevant engineering knowledge and have actual experience

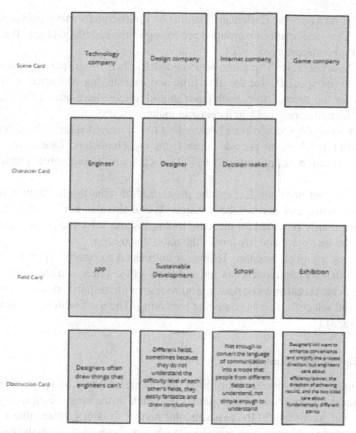

Fig. 2. First version design of scene card, character card, field card, and obstruction card

3.2 Second Version Design

The second experiment was preceded in the cross-disciplinary course on September 24, 2021, with the participation of 22 students, 2 TA, and an instructor. The students were from Department of electrical engineering, Department of computer science & information engineering, Department of industrial management, Department of international business administration, Department of industrial design, and Department of digital media design. Due to the effect of epidemic, online teaching was adopted for the course. Miro is used in the game for the development in the task, and Discord is utilized for the discussion. The experiment was preceded for 4 h, with 2 runs.

The Background of the Story in the Game. One day, you receive a ticket for museum exhibition and feel to visit with the free ticket. In the exhibition, you meet participants from different fields, who also visit with free tickets. With a sudden dizziness, you are in a different era after getting conscious, and there are other participants met in the exhibition. You have to complete tasks together in the era to return the present.

Stage 1-find a partner: Each team contains 3–4 participants and is provided different task cards. The participants are grouped according to the specialty. Due to the epidemic, the grouping is pre-arranged by TA.

Stage 2-choose role: The game is preceded for two times, playing the characters according to the specialty for this first time and exchanging characters with different specialties for the second time. Each team should at least have one of the characters in design field, engineering field, and decision maker.

Stage 3-solve the specified task: According to the provided task, characters of engineer and designer have to provide ideas from the characters. Due to the epidemic, the task distribution is pre-arranged by TA; each team would solve a task at a time (Table 2).

Stage 4-reflect problem: Reflect the problems, or what might happen, in Stage 3, propose problems, and discuss the solution. When there is not a problem, problems would be randomly provided for the team to discuss and solve the problems. Due to the epidemic, the instructor and TA join in the team discussion.

Stage 5-accomplish mission: Teams are requested to briefly report the discussion outcome so that all participants can see and think of the interest in and ability of contribution. Participants can provide personal opinions for theme outcomes, or revise personal opinions, and select the favorite outcome for voting. The team with the most votes is the winner (Fig. 3).

3.3 Review and Evaluation

A questionnaire survey is established after the research activity, and participatory observation is used for understanding students' feedback in the cross-disciplinary team formation game. According to the experimental results, it is discovered that students are extremely interested in putting themselves in someone's shoes through the game. During the game, participants could mutually exchange and understand the thinking styles and specialties of both parties. After completing tasks, they could find out the interests in the team and make contributions. The preliminary experience and consensus achieved by teamwork are listed in Table 3. In the gaming process, each team has distinct cooperation styles. For instance, Team 5 shows enthusiastic discussion in the development process and could rapidly solve problems to achieve the consensus. Some teams would quietly complete the tasks. Some members in Team 1 do not participate in discussions.

In Stage 2-choose role, 37.5% students consider putting themselves in someone's shoes in the cross-disciplinary cooperation is helpful, 50% students regard it not making many differences, and 12.5% do not consider it helpful.

In Stage 3-solve the specified task, 37.5% students consider putting themselves in someone's shoes in the cross-disciplinary cooperation is helpful, 62.5% students regard it not making many differences, and there is not a participant considering it helpless. Moreover, 62.5% students are interested in the task content, and 68.7% students are interested in the task developing stage.

In Stage 4-reflect problem, 37.5% students regard problem thinking being helpful, 50% students do not think of the difference, and 12.5% participants consider it helpless. Regarding problem solving, 50% students consider it helpful, 43.7% students do not think of the difference, and 6.3% students regard it helpless.

Table 2. Game task content

Game task	Task content
Game task 1 Why can birds fly, but not people?	Space-time: the renaissance-Italy Task publisher: Leonardo da Vinci (art, invention, and engineering) Themed task: Leonardo da Vinci, fascinated by flying, is doing the research on bird flying and making the flight vehicle design. You may help collect data and design a flight vehicle conforming to the space-time background and presenting aesthetics and practice
Game task 2 Stargazing is also artistic	Space-time: the renaissance-Italy task publisher: Galileo Galilei (physics and astronomy) Themed task: The first practical telescope is just invented. Galileo Galilei would like to modify the telescope for observing the celestial body. You may help seek for suitable lenses and design a telescope conforming to the space-time background and presenting aesthetics and practice
Game task3 Time travelling is every person's dream	Space-time: the 19th century-Germany task publisher: Albert Einstein (photo-electric and mechanics) Themed task: You meet Albert Einstein in the street. Einstein is very interested in you from the future and expect that you can help design an aesthetic and practical time machine with modern thinking. (possibly referring to Back to the Future and MIB (Men in Black))
game task4 Appearance is as important as function	Space-time: Industrial Revolution-England Task publisher: James Watt (inventor and mechanical engineer) Themed task: You become an employee of James Watt. Please help Watt modify the steam engine and design an aesthetic and practical steam engine related product
Game task5 Enjoy oneself even in the space	Space-time: the 20th century-America Task publisher: Neil Alden Armstrong Themed task: NASA is going to precede Project Apollo. Please use modern thinking to help design aesthetic and practical lunar module and necessity

Fig. 3. Five-stage process

Table 3. Students could find out the interests or present contribution

Field	Students could find out the interests or present contribution
Design A	Software/hardware technology
Engineering A	Discussion
Design B	Problem solving
Design C	Planning
Engineering B	Pulling back divergent ideas or adding new ideas for the team
Engineering C	Technological application, applying network resources to look for practicability
Engineering D	Picking flaws, proving data
Design D	Imagination and introduction method
Engineering E	It is interesting to think of equipment required for the topic; in addition to proposing personal ideas, ideas of which one does not think could be heard
Engineering F	Imaging modeling
Engineering G	Better understanding mechanical structure
Design E	It is interested to think of functionality and modeling
Engineering H	Creative development. Sometimes there are imaginative ideas. Some solutions are proposed in professional field (information engineering)

In Stage 5-accomplish mission, 56.3% students could find out the interests in and ability of making contribution, 43.7% students do not think of any differences, and no participant regard it helpless.

In the experiment, 56.2% students consider the entire game being helpful for putting themselves in someone's shoes, 37.5% participants do not think of the difference, but 87.5% participants regard the game being helpful for forming the team. In regard to the overall gaming processing, 74.9% participants are interested, 18.7% participants do not think of any differences. After completing the entire gaming process, 68.7% participants consider achieving the preliminary consensus with participants with different specialties, 25% participants do not think of many differences, and 6.3% participants consider that they do not achieve the consensus.

There are some problems in the entire gaming feedback of students. (1) Student A from Department of international business administration (engineering), for the first time playing such type of game, considers that it is novel to exchange with different fields; however, due to the setting of space-time background, the imagination and ability are limited. (2) Student B from Department of computer science & information engineering (engineering) considers that KJ method and new program or web page should be introduced in detailed. For instance, the basic function and how to use MIRO, e.g. drawing pictures and adjusting text blocks, should be introduced in advance. Help for task theme is required. For instance, the appearance of the modified telescope could be decorated with the renaissance characteristics and the place to start the function. (3) Students C and D from Department of electrical engineering (engineering) regard the time arrangement being a bit rush. Time goes so fast during thinking and discussion that it is expected to prolong the time or have more time for preliminary interaction and mutual understanding. (4) Since online discussion is adopted for this experiment, no team member speaks out to respond to student E from Department of industrial design (design); it is expected to have some communication. According to students' feedback, the game design would be revised.

4   Conclusion and Future Development

In this research, the cross-disciplinary forming game allows engineers and designers without experience in cross-disciplinary cooperation thinking by putting themselves in someone's shoes in the gaming process. Engineers could comprehend designers through empathy and, after completing the game, understand the different in distinct design, as well as comprehend and increase the experience required for cross-disciplinary cooperation. The research findings show that more than a half students consider the game helpful for putting oneself in someone's shoes and achieving preliminary consensus. More students consider the game helpful for forming a team. Most students could find out the interest or contribution in the game and find out personal positioning in the successive teamwork. Some problems are also discovered in the research. For instance, few students are not good at publicizing personal ideas on online discussion that the rest team members could not smoothly precede discussions. It could be improved in the future. Time could be adjusted to increase discussion time, systematic evaluation could be applied to evaluate team members in the beginning of team formation game, and preliminary grouping before the game could enhance the efficiency.

References

Candy, L., Edmonds E.: Modeling co-creativity in art and technology. Paper presented at the Proceedings of the 4th Conference on Creativity & Cognition (2002)

Chang, T.-W., Lee, Y., Huang, H.-Y.: Visualizing design process by using lean UX to improve interdisciplinary team's effectiveness–a case study. Paper presented at the 2018 22nd International Conference Information Visualisation (IV), London (2018)

Lam, B., Zamenopoulos, T., Kelemen, M., Hoo Na, J.: Unearth hidden assets through community co-design and co-production. Des. J. 20(sup1), S3601–S3610 (2017)

Li, R., Qian, Z.C., Chen, Y.V., Zhang, L.: Design thinking driven interdisciplinary entrepreneurship. a case study of college students business plan competition. Des. J. 22(sup1), 99–110 (2019)

Liao, M.-N.: Co-creation - exploration and research on the joint decision-making mode of interdisciplinary cooperation. Master of Design, National Yunlin University of Science and Technology, Douliou, Yunlin, Taiwan (2016). https://hdl.handle.net/11296/4e3v2g

Lu, J.-R., Chang, T.-W., Wu, Y.-S., Chen, C.-Y.: Multimodal coexistence environment design to assist user testing and iterative design of HiGame emotional interaction design for elderly. In: Gao, Q., Zhou, J. (eds.) HCII 2020. LNCS, vol. 12207, pp. 197–209. Springer, Cham (2020). https://doi.org/10.1007/978-3-030-50252-2_15

Neuenhaus, M., Aly, M.: Empathy up. Paper presented at the Proceedings of the 2017 CHI Conference Extended Abstracts on Human Factors in Computing Systems (2017)

Shah, D., Morkos, B., Yang, X.: Can empathy be taught? The results of an assignment targeted at improving empathy in engineering design. Paper presented at the 2020 ASEE Virtual Annual Conference Content Access (2020)

Šisler, Vít., Brom, C.: Designing an educational game: case study of 'Europe 2045.' In: Pan, Z., Cheok, A. D., Müller, W., El Rhalibi, A. (eds.) Transactions on edutainment I. LNCS, vol. 5080, pp. 1–16. Springer, Heidelberg (2008). https://doi.org/10.1007/978-3-540-69744-2_1

Tahir, R., Wang, A.I.: Completeness and collaboration in the early design phase of learning games: do ideation cards provide scaffolding? In: Zaphiris, P., Ioannou, A. (eds.) HCII 2021. LNCS, vol. 12785, pp. 94–114. Springer, Cham (2021). https://doi.org/10.1007/978-3-030-77943-6_7

Virtual Team Collaboration: How the Empathy Tendency Influences User Experience?

Yifan Yang[1,2] ⓘ, Ying Jing[3](✉) ⓘ, Xu Sun[2,4](✉) ⓘ, Xiaotong Sun[1,2],
Tongfeng Yang[5], Sheng Zhang[1], Qingchao Xia[1], Wei Yang[1], Qijun Li[1],
and Canjun Yang[1]

[1] Ningbo Research Institute, Zhejiang University, Ningbo, China
`Yifan.Yang@nottingham.edu.cn`
[2] Faculty of Science and Engineering, University of Nottingham Ningbo China, Ningbo, China
`Xu.Sun@nottingham.edu.cn`
[3] Business School, NingboTech University, Ningbo, China
`y.crystal@nit.zju.edu.cn`
[4] Nottingham Ningbo China, Beacons of Excellence Research and Innovation Institute,
University of Nottingham Ningbo China, Ningbo, China
[5] Shandong University of Political Science and Law, Jinan, China

Abstract. The subjective experiences and satisfaction of using technology to collaborate remotely may differ due to the individual differences of personal characteristics. The present study aims to investigate the influence of empathy tendency on user experience. Twelve groups of three participants completed a decision-making task in the virtual environment. The results revealed a significant correlation between personal traits (i.e., empathy and the big five personalities), user experience (i.e., social presence), and satisfaction. The level of cognitive empathy has a positive effect on the feeling of social presence, social immersion, and outcome satisfaction in the virtual environment, while is not associated with media satisfaction. The findings of this study suggest that the cognitive ability of empathy, namely the ability to identify with and understand the views of others may increase one's experience and satisfaction in remote collaboration. This study provides an empirical exploration of team interactions in virtual environments and advances user research by identifying the relationship between user's traits (empathy), user experience, and satisfaction.

Keywords: Personality · Empathy · User experience · User satisfaction

1 Introduction

Distributed workforce, dispersed team members and remote collaboration is a recent trend, especially under the circumstance of pandemic covid-19. Digital media is considered an essential medium for remote collaboration, which allows users to communicate and share information across distance [1]. The goal of communication through digital media is to generate an environment that is similar to or even better than face-to-face communication. And better user experience will lead to higher task performance in terms of consensus, satisfaction, and cohesion [2].

© The Author(s), under exclusive license to Springer Nature Switzerland AG 2022
P. Zaphiris and A. Ioannou (Eds.): HCII 2022, LNCS 13329, pp. 301–312, 2022.
https://doi.org/10.1007/978-3-031-05675-8_23

Previous studies have pointed out the importance of personality characteristics in the context of user experience, such as the big five personality traits [3]. However, it remains unclear whether empathy tendency influences user experience and satisfaction during remote collaboration. The ability of empathy is considered to be a core ability of communication and collaboration for social workers, and it has been found to be an important characteristic influencing user experience [4, 5]. The subjective experience of presence and immersion are important features in evaluating user experience [6]. In terms of the social dimension, social presence refers to the sense of being with another person in the mediated environment [7]. Thus it is both theoretically and practically important to explore the relationship between empathy tendency and user experience in a social context.

To address this issue, the aim of this study is to examine the relationship between empathy tendency, user experience, and satisfaction of remote collaboration in mediated environments. The research questions include: How does the tendency of empathy influence the collaborative process and user experience during remote collaboration? How does the empathy influence the perception of presence of other people (i.e. social presence) and interaction with others (social immersion)? We hypothesized that a higher level of empathy tendency would enhance user experience and satisfaction in remote collaboration.

2 Related Background

2.1 User Experience of Social Presence and Immersion

The notion of user experience is increasing in the human-computer interaction literature with the emergence of digital technology. User experience is defined as "the user's perceptions and responses resulting from the use of a system or a service [...]" where presence and immersion are the most widely used components of user experience focused by the literature [8].

Presence, a widely used construct to describe one's user experience, could be defined as "the perceptual illusion of non-mediation a mediated perception of an environment [9]". Presence is a multidimensional construct that could be further divided into two separate dimensions: spatial presence (or telepresence) and social presence (or co-presence). Since these two dimensions of presence refer to the different aspects of experience, they should be considered and measured separately [10]. Spatial presence, strongly related to the spatial properties in the mediated environment, refers to "the extent to which one feels present in the mediated environment [11]" while social presence, focusing on social dimension in an experience, refers to the "sense of being with another [7]". Social presence is considered to be an important part of virtual environments, which offers mediation between people, whether they are avatars controlled by human beings or artificial entities [12]. Studies have also shown that a higher level of social presence would lead to more positive communication outcomes, better experience, such as enjoyment and perceived usefulness [13].

Immersion is another construct of user experience. When compared to the psychological experiences of presence, immersion is usually described as technological quantities and manipulations [12]. However, recent researchers began to argue immersion as a state of mental involvement which could be measured subjectively [14]. Immersion could be characterized as a lack of awareness of time, loss of awareness of the real world, and a sense of being in the task environment [15]. The social influence on the sense of immersion has assigned a marginal role, however, prior studies have proved that social interactions could positively influence the immersive experience [16]. In this study, we use social immersion to empathize the social dimension of immersion.

2.2 Empathy

Empathy is considered an important interpersonal quality and plays a central role in human behavior [17]. Empathy generally refers to the sensitivity to, and understanding of, the mental states of others [17], which involves two major human abilities, affective empathy and cognitive empathy. Affective empathy, the emotional component of empathy, refers to the tendency to experience and care for the feelings of others, while cognitive empathy reflects the ability to identify with and understand the views of others [18]. Cognitive empathy and affective empathy are found to be strongly correlated, however, differences could also be found existing in the composition of cognitive and affective empathy, which can be considered and measured separately [19].

2.3 Personal Traits and User Experience

Understanding the type of users and the characteristics of users are important approaches to predicting user's experience and user satisfaction since previous studies have pointed out the important impact of personality factors on user experience, including the five personalities [3], age, and gender [10], immersive tendencies [5], etc. The relation between empathy and user experience has also been extensively studied and empathy seems to become one of the most promising predictors for presence [6]. Empathy has been found to have a positive effect on the level of presence experience in the virtual environment. It is found that individuals who are more empathic by nature seem to experience a greater level of presence [6]. Nicovich [20] proposed that presence and empathy use the same projective "tool set", since both indicate the connection between individual and individual, individual and environment, and is a reflection of psychological and emotional perception of others. However, it lacks research focusing on the relationship between the different dimensions of empathy and user experience.

When considering different aspects of presence (spatial presence and social presence) and empathy, most studies explored the relationship between spatial presence and empathy [21]. Felnhofer [10] has found that fantasy, one dimension of empathy, is associated with the physical presence, while the other components did not show significant influence on presence. However, little is known about the effects of empathy on social presence when human beings collaborate in virtual environments. The impact of empathy tendency on perceived immersion is also ignored in this process.

As for satisfaction, a positive relationship between empathy and satisfaction has been found in different fields, such as in video games [22], or medical treatment [23]. Empathy tendency was found to be positively associated with social interaction and social functioning, including prosocial behavior and satisfaction [22]. People who are high in empathy may be more prosocial, cooperative, and attentive in remote collaboration and communication, which will lead to a higher level of satisfaction with the process. Thus we hypothesize that the personality trait of empathy would influence user satisfaction, including media satisfaction and outcome satisfaction.

3   Methods

3.1   Participants

An experiment was conducted in which twelve groups of three participants (N = 36, 25 females, and 11 males) took part in and worked on a decision-making task. The group members predominantly consisted of participants from various universities who joined the youth researcher leadership summit and who were recruited from University from Nottingham Ningbo through social media. The age of participants ranged from 18 to 35 and participants were randomly distributed within the groups.

3.2   Tasks and Set up

The task was based on the one used by Schulz-Hardt [24], in which team members were role-played as student representatives of the class deciding the class monitor, or the tourist destination. According to the hidden-profile paradigm, information is asymmetrically distributed among group members, where parts of the information were available to all group members (12 information), while others were not (18 information). Group members have to exchange all the information to reach the objectively best decision.

The team interacted using a video and in a 3D virtual room. In the video condition, group members interacted using a video conference in Tecent meeting, while in the virtual reality (VR) condition, participants wore a headset and join a virtual meeting room on Mozilla Hubs (see Fig. 1). In all conditions, participants were identified by a participation number. After each experiment, questionnaires were distributed to all group members.

Fig. 1. A) Avatars used in the experiment. B) Participants interacted with VR. C) The virtual room environment.

3.3 Procedure

After distributing the participation information sheet and signing the consent form, all participants filled out a demographic survey and personality questionnaires about empathy tendency and big five personalities in the waiting room. After completion of questionnaires, a brief explanation about the experience was given and then participants were brought to the separate laboratory room. To eliminate the effect of the order, we employed a counter-balanced design for the experiment, which enhances experimental control by controlling all treatments in a randomized order [25]. Thus the order experimental conditions (Face-to-face, Video, or VR) and tasks were randomized.

Before the discussion, the materials of the candidate were distributed. Five minutes were given for participants to read the task and materials. Then participants were instructed to reach a joint decision based on the information. Before the VR discussion, a teaching phase was conducted, where participants learned how to use the controller and could take time to explore the room. After the group members reached a consensus, participants were asked to fill out a questionnaire about their experience.

3.4 Measures

The scales used for this study were adapted from previous scales when possible. All the scales were five-point Likert scales, from strongly disagree to strongly agree. Higher values represent a higher agreement with the description.

Empathy. The Basic Empathy Scale (BES) was used to measure empathy [19]. This scale consists of 20 questions, in which 9 for cognitive empathy (i.e., I can often understand how people are feeling even before they tell me.) and 11 for affective empathy (i.e., After being with a friend who is sad about something, I usually feel sad.). In this study, the scale has an internal consistency reliability (Cronbach' s alpha) around 0.71, for cognitive empathy (a = 0.83) and affective empathy (a = 0.62).

The Big Five Personalities. The Big Five factors of personality, including Extraversion, Agreeableness, Conscientiousness, Emotional stability, Openness to experience, cover most aspects of the personality as commonly understood [3]. Extraverts can be described as sociable and outgoing. People who score high on conscientiousness are hardworking, effective, and reliable. Agreeableness refers to someone trusting and helpful in social situations. Emotional Stability, opposite to neuroticism, indicates the extent to which someone is calm, confident, not anxious, and distressful. Open to experience is associated with creativity, adventure, and liberalism. Higher scores represent higher receptive to new ideas. In the present study, the ten-item personality inventory (TIPI) developed by Gosling [26] was used. This scale can stand as a proxy for longer Big-Five instruments and is widely used in psychology to classify personality traits [27].

Social Presence. Baileson's five-item Social Presence Survey (SPS) [28] is a widely used scale in assessing the level of social presence. However, this scale mainly measures the interaction to a virtual character controlled by a computer algorithm. Thus we cut the questions such as "I perceive the person as being only a computerized image, not as a real person." Combining with the questionnaire from Haines [29], finally, three questions were left to measure social presence: 1) I perceive that I am in the presence of another person in the room with me. 2) I feel that the person is watching me and is aware of my presence. 3) I felt like to be connected to the other people on this team. In the present study, the questionnaire's reliability was acceptable with a Cronbach's Alpha coefficient around 0.87.

Social Immersion. The social immersion questionnaire is adapted from Jennett's immersion scales [15], which is widely used to test subjectively immersion, including 1) I am completely involved in the collaboration with partners. 2) When I collaborate with my partners, time flies quickly. 3) I was fully occupied with the collaboration. 4) Collaboration seems to go on naturally and automatically (Cronbach's Alpha = 0.83).

Satisfaction. Satisfaction is an important measure of performance and user experience. It is defined as a psychological effect that is captured as a positive (satisfied), apathetic, or negative (dissatisfied) feeling [30] and it could be described from different dimensions, including satisfaction with the collaborative outcomes (solution satisfaction or outcome satisfaction) [31], and satisfaction with the media (media satisfaction). Outcome satisfaction refers to the overall satisfaction with the task outcomes and performance, whether team members felt committed to and agree with the decision made [32]. The questionnaires were adapted from previous studies [31, 33, 34], where four questions were included 1) I am satisfied with the result of our group decision. 2) I feel I have committed to the group solution. 3) The team was successful in accomplishing the goals of the task. 4) I have the feeling that my group chose the best candidate/best place

(Cronbach's Alpha = 0.90). And media satisfaction refers to whether users are satisfied and comfortable with the media used, which includes two questions 1) I feel satisfied with using this platform. 2) I feel comfortable with using this platform (Cronbach's Alpha = 0.75).

4   Results

4.1   Correlation Analysis Between Personality Traits, User Experience and Satisfaction

Correlation analysis were applied to examine the relationship between personality variables and the subjective experience in remote collaboration, including user experience (i.e., social presence, and social immersion) and satisfaction (i.e., outcome satisfaction, and media satisfaction) (see Table 1).

The assumption that there would be a significant positive correlation between empathy and user experience was confirmed by the analysis, which means users with higher empathy tendencies are more likely to experience a higher level of social presence, social immersion, and outcome satisfaction.

The Big five personality traits were included in the analysis. No relationship could be found between extraversion and user experience. Hence, being sociable and outgoing may not lead to a better user experience and satisfaction in a social situation. Agreeableness is associated with the sense of social presence, conscientiousness could be related to social immersion, and outcome satisfaction, while emotional stability and openness to experiences are related to most of the user experience and satisfaction measured. The positive correlation indicates that the one who is more open to new experiences, relaxed, calm, and self-confident, he or she may experience a higher quality of experience and be more satisfied. Details could be found in Table 1.

Table 1. Spearman's correlation between personality traits, user experience and satisfaction.

		Empathy	Extraversion	Agreeableness	Conscientiousness	Emotional stability	Openness to experiences
User experience	Social presence	0.317*	n.s	0.294*	n.s	0.284*	n.s
	Social immersion	0.317*	n.s	n.s	0.414**	0.380**	0.247*
Satisfaction	Outcome satisfaction	0.404**	n.s	n.s	0.252*	0.334**	0.292*
	Media satisfaction	n.s	n.s	n.s	n.s	n.s	0.303*

Note: $^{**}p < 0.01$, $^{*}p < 0.05$, n.s. not significance.

4.2 Regression Analysis for Relationship Between Empathy and Social Presence

To investigate the effect of empathy on user experience further, we employed a stepwise multiple regression analysis for user experience contrast, which is found to be significant in the correlation analysis (i.e., social presence, social immersion, and outcome satisfaction). All measured personality variables (i.e., demography, empathy tendency, and big five personalities) were entered in the regression analysis as possible predictors of social presence. The results of the stepwise regression analysis are shown in Table 2.

Table 2. Results of the stepwise regression analysis.

Predictor variables		R	R^2	F	p	B	β	t	p	Dependent variable
All demographic and control variables	Gender, age, education, condition and task	0.38	0.15	1.46	0.20				n.s	Social presence
Big five personality	Extraversion	0.53	0.28	1.72	0.88	0.06	0.10	0.72	0.47	
	Agreeableness					0.10	0.19	1.42	0.16	
	Conscientiousness					0.07	0.15	0.95	0.35	
	Emotional stability					0.07	0.18	1.09	0.28	
	Openness to experiences					−0.04	−0.07	−0.41	0.68	
Empathy	Cognitive empathy	0.59	0.35	2.00	0.37*	0.05	0.30	2.34	0.02*	
	Affective empathy					0.01	0.07	0.53	0.60	

Note: $^{**}p < 0.01$, $^*p < 0.05$, n.s. not significance.

The regression model for social presence was significant ($p < 0.05$). The stepwise regression analysis revealed that cognitive empathy was the only variable that made a significant contribution to predicting social presence. Similarly, the regression model of cognitive empathy on outcome satisfaction and social immersion was also significant (respectively $t = 3.07$, $p < 0.01$; $t = 2.86$, $p < 0.01$), showing the significant contribution of cognitive empathy towards user experience and satisfaction.

5 Discussion

The findings confirmed previous research results that the user's experience in a virtual environment is strongly dependent on the user's trait and personality [3, 35]. Prior studies have found the relationship in this area especially between presence and personality, presence and the big five personalities, while this study focuses on the influence of user traits on user experience and satisfaction in a social context. The main finding in this study showed that cognitive empathy could positively contribute to user experience (i.e., social presence and social immersion) and outcome satisfaction. The big five personality traits are positively correlated with user experience and satisfaction, while not significant in predicting social presence in the regression analysis.

The correlation analysis revealed that social presence is more related to agreeableness and emotional stability, while social immersion is associated with conscientiousness, emotional stability, and openness to experiences. This indicated that social presence and social immersion measure different dimensions of user experience, where the person who is more trusting, generous, sympathetic, and cooperative are more likely to experience a higher level of social presence, and the person who is more hard-working, self-disciplined, curious and open-minded are more likely to experience a higher level of social immersion.

The most interesting finding in this study is the positive correlations between empathy and user experience (i.e., social presence and social immersion). Previous studies have already found the relationship between empathy and presence, however, this research was conducted in the social context, where the social presence and spatial presence measure different dimensions of user experience [36]. Our results also confirm shin's idea that both social presence and social immersion are cognitive processes, which are created and modified by the user's personality traits [35].

Besides, the results in this study showed that cognitive empathy played an important role in influencing one's perception in the collaborative process, while affective empathy has few effects on user experience and satisfaction. Thus the ability to identify with and understand the views of others may increase one's experience and satisfaction in remote collaboration. Compare to prior studies, this finding is similar to the positive relationship between presence and fantasy, a subscale of empathy that measures the tendency to identify with characters in movies and fictional situations [5, 20, 35]. However, the results may also attribute to the task, since participants conducted a decision-making task in this experiment, where information and view exchange is vital in this context. Since prior studies have shown that the media form is more relevant in determining the sense of presence in non-emotional virtual environments, and personality characteristics play a more influential role in emotional environments [37, 38].

Our results also show that cognitive empathy is strongly related to outcome satisfaction, which means participants with high empathy tendency tend to be more satisfied with the group decision results and be more confident in the decision performance. This indicates that personality traits are associated with the satisfaction and confidence of performance. No significant correlations between empathy and media satisfaction were found in this study since media satisfaction seems to be a more technologically influenced concept. Thus media form may play a more important role in deciding one's level of media satisfaction than personality traits, which will be discussed in the related paper.

The methodology of this study has some limitations. First, it has been found that different measures to assess the same construct (i.e. presence) will lead to different results [6], since the questionnaires, rating subjectively, may measure different dimensions of the construct based on different theoretical backgrounds. Thus the measures bias should be considered in the experiment. Future studies should consider different measures of a construct, and objective measures could be implemented to verify the measures. Second, personality is a complex construct. Both the demographical characteristic (i.e., gender and age, etc.) and psychological features (i.e., immersion tendency, absorption, spatial intelligence, etc.) may contribute to the sense of user experience in a virtual environment, which is difficult to control all the potential influencing variables [37, 38]. In this experiment, we only controlled the demography and the big five personality traits, the influence of other personal characteristics were not included in the estimation. Finally, the sample size is relatively limited and most of the participants are students. Thus the findings need to be interpreted with caution. Future studies should be conducted with a larger sample to replicate these findings.

Nevertheless, this study contributes to resolving the issues in ongoing research in two aspects. First, this study provides an empirical exploration of team interactions in virtual environments and advances user research by identifying the relationship between user's traits (i.e., empathy) and user experience. This study focuses on social experience between group members rather than solitary experience. By answering the research question and investigating how empathy tendency affect team collaboration and team members' perception of social presence and social immersion, this study clarifies the social perception of users during remote collaboration, i.e., how their empathy was triggered through digital technologies, how the empathy tendency influence user experience and performance, which enrich the theoretical framework of user experience.

Second, this study guides practical implications that support remote collaboration and decision-making. The theoretical framework can be applied in the platform and feature design. Personalized functions of interaction and interface design for remote collaboration platforms according to user's traits (i.e., empathy) could be considered. The findings of this study could also be useful for team managers to control remote collaborative processes.

6 Conclusion

The aim of this study was to investigate the human factors that may lead to high degree of user experience in remote collaboration through digital media. The results revealed a significant correlation between personal traits (i.e., empathy tendency and the big five personalities), user experience, and satisfaction. The level of cognitive empathy has a positive effect on the feeling of social presence, social immersion, outcome satisfaction in the virtual environment. No relationship was found between empathy tendency and media satisfaction. This study provides an empirical exploration of user experience of team interactions in virtual environment and try to explain why different individuals experience differently when confronted with the same virtual environments.

References

1. Oprean, D., Simpson, M., Klippel, A.: Collaborating remotely: an evaluation of immersive capabilities on spatial experiences and team membership. Int. J. Digit. Earth 11(4), 420–436 (2018)
2. Schouten, A.P., van den Hooff, B., Feldberg, F.: Virtual team work: group decision making in 3D virtual environments. Commun. Res. 43(2), 180–210 (2016)
3. Weibel, D., Wissmath, B., Mast, F.W.: Immersion in mediated environments: the role of personality traits. Cyberpsychol. Behav. Soc. Netw. 13(3), 251–256 (2010)
4. Walther, J., Miller, S.E., Kellam, N.N.: Exploring the role of empathy in engineering communication through a transdisciplinary dialogue. In: Proceedings of the 2012 ASEE Annual Conference & Exposition, pp. 25.622.1–25.622.11 (2012)
5. Wallach, H.S., Safir, M.P., Samana, R.: Personality variables and presence. Virtual Reality 14(1), 3–13 (2010)

6. Kober, S.E., Neuper, C.: Personality and presence in virtual reality: does their relationship depend on the used presence measure? Int. J. Hum.-Comput. Interact. **29**(1), 13–25 (2013)
7. Biocca, F., Harms, C.: Defining and measuring social presence: contribution to the networked minds theory and measure. Proc. Presence **2002**, 1–36 (2002)
8. Tcha-Tokey, K., Christmann, O., Loup-Escande, E., Loup, G., Richir, S.: Towards a model of user experience in immersive virtual environments. In: Advances in Human-Computer Interaction 2018 (2018)
9. Lombard, M., Bolmarcich, T.: At the heart of it all: the concept of presence. J. Comput. Mediated Commun. **3** (1997)
10. Felnhofer, A., Kothgassner, O.D., Hauk, N., Beutl, L., Hlavacs, H., Kryspin-Exner, I.: Physical and social presence in collaborative virtual environments: exploring age and gender differences with respect to empathy. Comput. Hum. Behav. **31**, 272–279 (2014)
11. Steuer, J.: Defining virtual reality: dimensions determining telepresence. J. Commun. **42**(4), 73–93 (1992)
12. Oh, C.S., Bailenson, J.N., Welch, G.F.: A systematic review of social presence: definition, antecedents, and implications. Frontiers Rob. AI **5**, 114 (2018)
13. Hassanein, K., Head, M.: Manipulating perceived social presence through the web interface and its impact on attitude towards online shopping. Int. J. Hum Comput Stud. **65**(8), 689–708 (2007)
14. Agrawal, S., Simon, A., Bech, S., Brentsen, K., Forchhammer, S.: Defining immersion: literature review and implications for research on immersive audiovisual experiences. J. Audio Eng. Soc. **68**, 404–417 (2019)
15. Jennett, C., Cox, A., Dhoparee, S., Epps, A., Tijs, T., Walton, A.: Measuring and defining the experience of the immersion in games. Int. J. Hum Comput Stud. **66**, 641–661 (2008)
16. Cox, A., Day, M., Martin, H., Perryman, T.: Who but not where: the effect of social play on immersion in digital games. Int. J. Hum Comput Stud. **71**, 1069–1077 (2013)
17. Smith, A.: Cognitive empathy and emotional empathy in human behavior and evolution. Psychol. Rec. **56**(1), 3–21 (2006)
18. Gini, G., Albiero, P., Benelli, B., Altoe, G.: Does empathy predict adolescents' bullying and defending behavior? Aggressive Behav. Official J. Int. Soc. Res. Aggression **33**(5), 467–476 (2007)
19. Jolliffe, D., Farrington, D.P.: Development and validation of the basic empathy scale. J. Adolesc. **29**(4), 589–611 (2006)
20. Nicovich, S.G., Boller, G.W., Cornwell, T.B.: Experienced presence within computer-mediated communications: initial explorations on the effects of gender with respect to empathy and immersion. J. Comput.-Med. Commun. **10**(2), JCMC1023 (2005)
21. Sas, C.: Individual differences in virtual environments. In: Bubak, M., van Albada, G.D., Sloot, P.M.A., Dongarra, J. (eds.) ICCS 2004. LNCS, vol. 3038, pp. 1017–1024. Springer, Heidelberg (2004). https://doi.org/10.1007/978-3-540-24688-6_131
22. Shoshani, A., Braverman, S., Meirow, G.: Video games and close relations: attachment and empathy as predictors of children's and adolescents' video game social play and socio-emotional functioning. Comput. Hum. Behav. **114**, 106578 (2021)
23. Wang, H., et al.: Association between emergency physician self-reported empathy and patient satisfaction. PLoS ONE **13**(9), e0204113 (2018)
24. Schulz-Hardt, S., Brodbeck, F.C., Mojzisch, A., Kerschreiter, R., Frey, D.: Group decision making in hidden profile situations: dissent as a facilitator for decision quality. J. Pers. Soc. Psychol. **91**(6), 1080 (2006)
25. Campbell, D.T., Stanley, J.C.: Experimental and Quasi-Experimental Designs for Research. Ravenio Books (2015)
26. Gosling, S.D., Rentfrow, P.J., Swann Jr., W.B.: A very brief measure of the Big-Five personality domains. J. Res. Pers. **37**(6), 504–528 (2003)

27. Correa, T., Hinsley, A.W., De Zuniga, H.G.: Who interacts on the Web?: The intersection of users' personality and social media use. Comput. Hum. Behav. **26**(2), 247–253 (2010)
28. Bailenson, J.N., Blascovich, J., Beall, A.C., Loomis, J.M.: Interpersonal distance in immersive virtual environments. Pers. Soc. Psychol. Bull. **29**(7), 819–833 (2003)
29. Haines, R.: Activity awareness, social presence, and motivation in distributed virtual teams. Inf. Manag. **58**(2), 103425 (2021)
30. Shin, D.: How do users experience the interaction with an immersive screen? Comput. Hum. Behav. **98**, 302–310 (2019)
31. Coffeng, T., Van Steenbergen, E.F., De Vries, F., Ellemers, N.: Quality of group decisions by board members: a hidden-profile experiment. Manag. Decis. (2021)
32. Chidambaram, L.: Relational development in computer-supported groups. MIS Q., 143–165 (1996)
33. Savchenko, K., Medema, H., Boring, R., Ulrich, T.: Measuring Mutual Awareness for Digital Human-Machine Interfaces: A Questionnaire for Simulator Studies. In: Boring, R. L. (ed.) AHFE 2018. AISC, vol. 778, pp. 36–46. Springer, Cham (2019). https://doi.org/10.1007/978-3-319-94391-6_4
34. Green, S.G., Taber, T.D.: The effects of three social decision schemes on decision group process. Organ. Behav. Hum. Perform. **25**(1), 97–106 (1980)
35. Shin, D.: Empathy and embodied experience in virtual environment: to what extent can virtual reality stimulate empathy and embodied experience? Comput. Hum. Behav. **78**, 64–73 (2018)
36. Grinberg, A., Serrano-Careaga, J., Mehl, M., O'Connor, M.-F.: Social engagement and user immersion in a socially based virtual world. Comput. Hum. Behav. **36**, 479–486 (2014)
37. Baños, R., Botella, C., Liaño, V., Guerrero, B., Rey, B., Alcañiz, M.: Sense of presence in emotional virtual environments. Proc. Presence, 156–159 (2004)
38. Alsina-Jurnet, I., Gutiérrez-Maldonado, J.: Influence of personality and individual abilities on the sense of presence experienced in anxiety triggering virtual environments. Int. J. Hum Comput Stud. **68**(10), 788–801 (2010)

How to Apply Bloom's Taxonomy to Operator Education in the Way of Human-Machine Cooperation?

Guanghui Yang[1,2], Zhijiang Shao[1,2(✉)], and Zuhua Xu[1,2]

[1] State Key Lab of Industrial Control Technology, Department of Control Science and Engineering, Zhejiang University, Hangzhou 310027, China
{11932063,szj,zhxu}@zju.edu.cn
[2] Alibaba Group, Alibaba-Zhejiang University Joint Research Institute of Frontier Technologies, Hangzhou 310027, China

Abstract. Operator education is essential in the process industry to avoid catastrophic accidents caused by human error. The operators of modern industrial plants not only need professional operation skills, more importantly, understand the behavior of advanced machine algorithms, which has played a critical role in daily industrial practice. In this research, a novel operator education paradigm is proposed. First, a model-based industrial intelligence, called shadow operator, is developed, which combines the two-layer industrial model predictive control framework and human-machine cooperation principles. Second, a hierarchical human-machine cooperation model for process operator training based on Bloom's taxonomy is presented, in which Bloom's taxonomy is an educational psychology model. Finally, five identities of shadow operator, namely task performer, cooperation partner, operation advisor, safety supervisor, and trouble maker, based on the proposed hierarchical model are designed to provide dynamic interaction with human operators. An application case in the industrial gas industry is provided to illustrate the effectiveness of the paradigm.

Keywords: Operator education · Human-machine cooperation · Bloom's taxonomy · Shadow operator · Two-layer model predictive control

1 Introduction

In the complex process industry, the role of operators is now more demanding and critical than ever before. The last three decades have witnessed a significant increase in the sophisticated automation, multivariable process control, and real-time optimization strategy of process industrial plants [1]. These increased complexities pose additional challenges for modern process industrial plants operators and enhance the chances for potential errors [2]. Accident investigation reveals that most of the abnormal situations in the process industry, which arise in a plant, are less due to the failure of equipment or machine algorithm but are more due to human error caused by process operators [3]. Their erroneous interpretation or assumption of process state and a series of terrible

© The Author(s), under exclusive license to Springer Nature Switzerland AG 2022
P. Zaphiris and A. Ioannou (Eds.): HCII 2022, LNCS 13329, pp. 313–325, 2022.
https://doi.org/10.1007/978-3-031-05675-8_24

decisions usually transform a minor problem into a severe accident [4]. Blanc et al. identified four types of human error during accidents: no action (40%), appropriate but late action (31%), aggravating action (24%), and inefficient action (5%) [5]. Lack of adequate and proper training has been identified as one of the primary reasons for human error [6].

Given the safety and integrity of operations, operator training simulators (OTS) for use in chemical and allied process industries have gained increasing popularity in recent years. Ahmad et al. developed an OTS for homogeneously catalyzed two-step biodiesel production from waste cooking oil using Aspen Plus Dynamics & OTS Framework (Aspen Technology, Inc.) [7]. Balaton et al. developed an OTS for a batch processing unit using UniSim software (Honeywell International Inc.) [8]. Sangaran and Haron developed an OTS for an Ethylene Crackers Plant, and the simulation model is built in DYNSIM software (Invensys Inc.) [9]. Pereira et al. presented PETROBRAS' Oil & Gas Production Process and Utilities Simulator Environment, and the software for process modeling is HYSYS (Hyprotech, Ltd./AEA Engineering Software–now Aspen Technology, Inc.) [10]. Yang et al. developed an OTS for air separation process using linear parameter varying system identification model [11]. Up to now, OTS development work has accumulated many articles. We refer readers to [12] for more OTS development details.

The above work provides a practical skill training platform for the central control room operators. To our best knowledge, few literatures focus on training methods. More specifically, researchers pay more attention to developing an OTS with reasonable simulation accuracy but ignore how operators use the OTS for skill training. The typical operator training paradigm in the process industry is shown in Fig. 1. In Fig. 1, an experienced operator acts as a human teacher and offers operation instructions for the trainee. The trainee adjusts his/her operation actions according to the final evaluation feedback. On the one hand, due to factors reported, such as subjectivity and randomness of the default training method, the novice operators are mostly in the trial-and-error state, which deteriorates the training effectiveness. On the other hand, the machine algorithm, an essential element between the operator and the process equipment, is almost wholly ignored in the training method. Benefitting from advances in computers and control algorithms, the role of the human operator has evolved over the last three decades from being predominantly manual (physically "doing" a task) to being predominantly cognitive (requiring "thinking"). The machine algorithm has played a crucial role in modern industrial plants, and the operator directly interacts with it in daily practice. The operator supervises and thinks about the operation of the automated algorithm so that they can intervene in time when the algorithm fails. Therefore, the nature of human errors that affect the system's safety has evolved. According to the survey, the operator's misunderstanding and distrust or over-trust of the machine algorithm's decision-making results often turn minor problems into severe disasters [4, 13]. Consequently, it calls for innovative training tools and approaches for process operators that match the pace of technological development.

In this paper, a novel operator training paradigm is discussed. Based on the two-layer model predictive control framework and the human-machine cooperation principles, a model-based industrial intelligence, called shadow operator, is proposed as a virtual

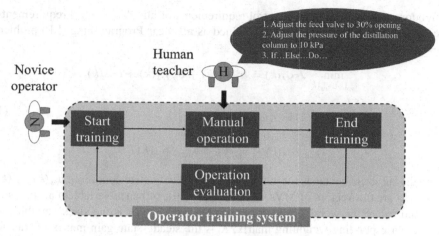

Fig. 1. The typical operator training paradigm in the process industry.

teacher to train novice operators. We present a hierarchical operator training model and design five identities of shadow operator based upon it. The purpose of shadow operator is to provide scientific interaction with the human operators and reproduce the human-machine interaction scenarios encountered in practical operation.

The rest of this work is organized as follows. Section 2 introduces the two-layer industrial model predictive control framework. The hierarchical training model for process operators and the five identities of shadow operator are proposed in Sect. 3. Section 4 introduces the application in the industrial gas industry. Section 5 presents the conclusion.

2 The Two-Layer Industrial Model Predictive Control Framework

Model predictive control (MPC), a receding horizon control strategy, has been widely used in the process industry because of its ability to handle multivariable constrained control problems [14]. In recent years, with the development of theory and technology of predictive control, two-layer MPC has been the mainstream technology in industrial MPC [15]. Two-layer industrial MPC contains steady-state optimization (SSO) in the upper layer and dynamic predictive control (DPC) in the lower layer. The purpose of the SSO module is to quickly provide the optimal operating point for the DPC controller when the operation task is changed. The purpose of the DPC module is to drive the process smoothly and rapidly to the optimal operating point calculated by the SSO module on the premise of satisfying all safety constraints of manipulated variable (MV) and controlled variable (CV).

2.1 Steady-State Optimization Module

The degree of freedom/feasibility analysis in the SSO module needs to be performed first. If there is not enough freedom, priorities, and weightings of CVs will be used to resolve the conflict. Economic optimization will be performed when there are degrees of freedom left after satisfying control requirements of all CVs' control requirements. The steady-state optimization can be defined as a Linear Programming (LP) problem based on an economic index:

$$\min_{u_{ss}^*(k), y_{ss}^*(k)} J_{SSO}(k) = b_1^T u_{ss}(k) + b_2^T y_{ss}(k) + c^T s(k)$$

s.t.

$$y_{ss}(k) = K u_{ss}(k) + d_{ss}(k)$$

$$u_{min} \leq u_{ss}(k) \leq u_{max}$$

$$y_{min} - s(k) \leq y_{ss}(k) \leq y_{max} + s(k)$$

$$(1)$$

where the subscript ss stands for the system is in a steady-state condition; $u_{ss}(k)$, $y_{ss}(k)$, and $d_{ss}(k)$ are the vectors of MVs, CVs, and DVs (disturbance variables) at time step k; b_1 and b_2 are the weighting matrices of MVs and CVs; s is the slack variable and c is the corresponding weighting matrix; K is the steady-state gain matrix of transfer function model $G(q)$ obtained by multivariable system identification. $G(q)$ is expressed as follows:

$$G(q) = \begin{bmatrix} G_{1,1}(q) & \cdots & G_{1,j}(q) & \cdots & G_{1,N_{mv}}(q) \\ \vdots & \ddots & \vdots & \ddots & \vdots \\ G_{i,1}(q) & \cdots & G_{i,j}(q) & \cdots & G_{i,N_{mv}}(q) \\ \vdots & \ddots & \vdots & \ddots & \vdots \\ G_{N_{cv},1}(q) & \cdots & G_{N_{cv},j}(q) & \cdots & G_{N_{cv},N_{mv}}(q) \end{bmatrix}$$

$$(2)$$

where q is the forward shift operator; N_{CV} is the number of CVs and N_{MV} is the number of MVs; $G_{i,j}(q)$ is the transfer function corresponding to the i_{th} CV and the j_{th} MV.

The optimal operation results optimized by SSO ($u_{ss}^*(k)$ and $y_{ss}^*(k)$) are used as the tracking targets of MVs and CVs in the DPC module.

2.2 Dynamic Predictive Control Module

The DPC module solves the tracking problem. In this paper, the MPC algorithm based on step response model is considered. To drive the process to the optimal steady-state operating point calculated by SSO module without violating process constraints, the objective function of the DPC module is defined as:

$$\min_{\Delta u_M^*(k)} J_{DPC}(k) = \sum_{j=1}^{P} \left\| y^{ref}(k+j) - \tilde{y}_{PM}(k+j|k) \right\|_Q^2 + \sum_{j=1}^{P} \left\| \varepsilon(k) \right\|_S^2$$

$$+ \sum_{j=0}^{M-1} \left\| \Delta u_M(k+j) \right\|_R^2 + \sum_{j=0}^{M-1} \left\| u_{ss}^*(k) - u_M(k+j) \right\|_V^2$$

s.t.

$$(3)$$

$$\tilde{y}_{PM}(k+1|k) = \tilde{y}_{P0}(k+1|k) + A\Delta u_M(k)$$

$$y^{ref}(k+j) = y(k) + (y_{ss}^*(k) - y(k))(1 - e^{-T/\tau}), j = 1, \ldots, P$$

$$y_{min} - \varepsilon(k+j) \leq \tilde{y}_{PM}(k+j|k) \leq y_{max} + \varepsilon(k+j), j = 1, \ldots, P$$

$$u_{min} \leq u_M(k+j) \leq u_{max}, j = 0, \ldots, M-1$$

$$\Delta u_{min} \leq \Delta u_M(k+j) \leq \Delta u_{max}, j = 0, \ldots, M-1$$

where $u_{ss}^*(k)$ and $y_{ss}^*(k)$ are the desired tracking targets determined by SSO module; P and M denote the prediction horizon and control horizon, respectively; $y(k)$ is the process output; $\tilde{y}_{P0}(k+1|k)$ and $\tilde{y}_{PM}(k+1|k)$ denote the open-loop prediction and closed-loop prediction of CVs, respectively; $y^{ref}(k+j)$ is the expected reference trajectory of CVs; T is the sampling time, and τ is the time constant of reference trajectory; ε stands for the relax variable of CVs in the DPC module;

Δu_{min} and Δu_{max} denote the lower and upper boundaries of increments of MVs; u_{min} and u_{max} denote the lower and upper boundaries of MVs; $u_M(k)$ and $\Delta u_M(k)$ denote the trajectories of MVs and increments of MVs respectively over the control horizon M; A stands for the dynamic matrix of the system. The relative importance of the objective function contributions is controlled by weighting matrices Q, S, R, and V.

For the nonlinear optimization problem (3), the optimal control move increment $\Delta u_M^*(k)$ can be effectively solved by Quadratic-Programming (QP) algorithm such as Active Set method and Interior Point method.

The industrial two-layer model predictive algorithm is encapsulated as an API: $ITL\_MPC(k)$, and its pseudo-code is as follows (Algorithm 1):

Algorithm 1 Industrial two-layer model predictive control algorithm.

1: function $ITL\_MPC(k)$

2:   Read the current process state in memory

3:   Solve LP problem of SSO module:

4:   $(u_{ss}^*(k), y_{ss}^*(k)) = \underset{u_{ss}(k)}{\arg\min} J_{SSO}(k)$

6:   Update expected trajectory of CVs:

7:   $y^{ref}(k+j) = y(k) + (y_{ss}^*(k) - y(k))(1 - e^{-T/\tau})$

8:   Solve QP problem of DPC module:

9:   $\Delta u_M^*(k) = \underset{\Delta u_M(k)}{\arg\min} J_{DPC}(k)$

10:   return $\Delta u_M^*(k)$

The industrial MPC algorithm has been successfully implemented in the physical plant considered in our project (see Reference [14]), and the operator interacts with it in daily practice. Here, the industrial MPC is introduced into the operator training task and is the foundation of the shadow operator.

3 A Hierarchical Human-Machine Cooperation Model for Operator Training Based on Bloom's Taxonomy

Many training systems have been deployed in different sectors of the process industry, but due to the lack of effective interaction between human and machine algorithms, the training effect is greatly reduced. The realistic demand is that the operator needs to have proficient manual operation skills, understand the machine algorithm's operation behavior, and learn to cooperate and compete with it for the incompetency of the machine algorithm in the face of some emergencies.

The generic principles of human-machine cooperation have been proposed to identify all kinds of interactions between one or several human operators and one or several machine assistance systems [16]. Here, we present a hierarchical human-machine cooperation model for process operator skill acquisition and improvement, as shown in Fig. 2. Figure 2 presents the five cognitive levels of human operators: remember, understand, apply, analyze, and evaluate, which are mentioned in Bloom's taxonomy [17]. (Bloom's taxonomy is an educational psychology model for classifying statements about what students are expected or intended to learn from specific training). The five cognitive levels of human operators in Fig. 2 are organized in a pyramid from the easiest at the bottom to the most difficult at the top to master.

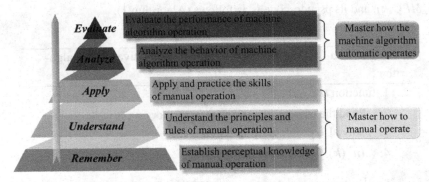

Fig. 2. The hierarchical human-machine cooperation model for process operator skill acquisition and improvement.

Table 1. The relationship between the shadow operator's five identities and the human operator's five cognitive levels.

Training level	Identity of the shadow operator	Functions of the shadow operator	Cognitive level of the operator	How the operator learns
L5	Trouble maker	Make trouble	Analyze, evaluate, apply	Learn from practice
L4	Safety supervisor	Rescue	Apply, understand	Learn from practice & demonstration
L3	Operation advisor	Answer	Apply, understand	
L2	Cooperation partner	Assist	Understand, remember	
L1	Task performer	Show	Remember	Learn from demonstration

   Further, five identities of the shadow operator based on the above hierarchical training model are designed. The five identities are task performer, cooperation partner, operation advisor, safety supervisor, and trouble maker. The shadow operator's five identities correspond to five functional levels of show, assist, answer, rescue, and make trouble.

   In Table 1, we show the corresponding relationship between the five identities of the shadow operator and the five cognitive levels of the human operator. Table 1 is explained from bottom to top as follows:

- **L1:** The function of showing corresponds to the identity of the task performer; that is, the shadow operator will show how to operate the process tasks that need training in advance. The operator needs to remember how to operate in his/her mind.
- **L2:** The function of assisting corresponds to the identity of the cooperation partner; that is, the shadow operator will actively undertake part of the MVs like a partner and gradually reduce the number of MVs undertaken. The operator needs to understand the function and change of each MV. In the above two functions of the shadow operator, the operator does not need or only needs to be responsible for part of the MVs. In the following three functions, the operator needs to be independently responsible for all MVs.
- **L3:** The function of answering corresponds to the identity of the operation advisor; that is, the shadow operator will give operation suggestions when the operator sends out a help request, including how to operate next and the corresponding process operation results. The operator needs to apply the skills learned and further understand how to operate.
- **L4:** The function of rescuing corresponds to the identity of the safety supervisor; that is, the shadow operator will deprive the operator of the control authority when the process is dangerous and operate by itself until the process returns to the safe state, and then return the control authority to the operator. As with the previous level, operators need to apply operation skills and understand the operation method in scary scenes.
- **L5:** The last function of making trouble corresponds to the identity of the trouble maker; that is, the shadow operator will deliberately make biased or even wrong decisions, which need to be identified and intervened by the operator. The operator needs to have the ability to analyze and evaluate the operation of the shadow operator and apply the learned operation skills. The last one is challenging for the operator because the operator needs to have basic operation skills, more importantly, to timely identify and accurately analyze the kind of wrong decisions the shadow operator makes, which needs to understand the behavior of the shadow operator. The last function is crucial for the training of operators because the machine algorithm will make completely wrong decisions due to instrument measurement deviations in practice.

   The idea and conception of the five functions/identities of the shadow operator have been explained, and each identity can be easily implemented through algorithm design. The following content will introduce the algorithm implementation details of the cooperation partner (L2) due to space constraints.

   As the name implies, the cooperation partner will cooperate with the novice operator to complete the operation task. However, it is a gradual and guiding form of cooperation different from the existing fixed cooperation. The virtual cooperation partner will gradually "let go" (reduce the number of MVs it is responsible for), while the novice operator will gradually "take over" (increase the number of MVs he/she is responsible for). The working process of the cooperation partner is shown in Fig. 3.

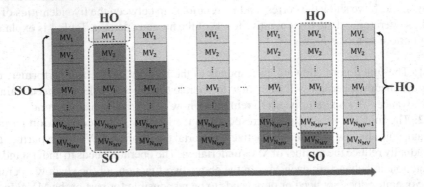

Fig. 3. The working process of the cooperation partner.

In Fig. 3, the MVs covered by pale blue are operated by the shadow operator (SO: cooperation partner, at L2), and the MVs covered by pale gold are operated by the human operator (HO). The task operation progress bar is displayed at the bottom of the Figure. During the operation, the human operator can freely select the MVs he/she is responsible for, and the cooperation partner is responsible for the remaining MVs.

Define MV^{SO} and MV^{HO} as MVs responsible for the shadow operator and the human operator respectively, and then $G(q)$ in Formula (2) is re-expressed as $G(q, MV^{SO})$:

$$G(q, MV^{SO}) = \begin{bmatrix} G_{1,1}(q, MV^{SO}) & \cdots & G_{1,j}(q, MV^{SO}) & \cdots & G_{1,N_{mv}}(q, MV^{SO}) \\ \vdots & \ddots & \vdots & \ddots & \vdots \\ G_{i,1}(q, MV^{SO}) & \cdots & G_{i,j}(q, MV^{SO}) & \cdots & G_{i,N_{mv}}(q, MV^{SO}) \\ \vdots & \ddots & \vdots & \ddots & \vdots \\ G_{N_{cv},1}(q, MV^{SO}) & \cdots & G_{N_{cv},j}(q, MV^{SO}) & \cdots & G_{N_{cv},N_{mv}}(q, MV^{SO}) \end{bmatrix}$$

(4)

where changes with the MV responsible for the shadow operator (MV^{SO}). More specifically, if the MV_i is not contained in MV^{SO}:

$$G_{x,i}(q, MV^{SO}) = 0, x = 1, ..., N_{CV}$$

(5)

Similarly, the gain matrix of $G(q, MV^{SO})$ is re-expressed as $K(MV^{SO})$. Note that the time step corresponding to the current state is k_2, the pseudo-code of the cooperation partner algorithm is explicated as follows (Algorithm 2):

Algorithm 2 Cooperation partner algorithm.

1: **for** every time step $k = k_2, k_2 + 1, k_2 + 2, \ldots$ **do**

2:   Read the current $MV^{SO}(k)$

3:   **if** $MV^{SO}(k)$ is not equal to $MV^{SO}(k-1)$:

4:     Update $G(q, MV^{SO})$ and $K(MV^{SO})$

5:   **end**

6:   Match variables in Formula (1) and (2):

7:   $G(q) = G(q, MV^{SO})$ and $K = K(MV^{SO})$

8:   Call $ITL\_MPC(k)$ and solve $\Delta u_M^*(k)$:

9:   $\Delta u_M^*(k) = ITL\_MPC(k)$

10: **end for**

Based on Algorithm 2, the shadow operator calculates the value of the MV^{SO}. The operator enters the adjustment of the MV^{HO} according to the learned experience and knowledge.

This interactive method reduces the operating pressure of the operator since the operator is gradually taking over all MVs, and provides the operator with a transition process from learning from demonstration to learning from practice.

4 Application in the Industrial Gas Industry

In this work, a cryogenic air separation unit (ASU) with a nominal capacity of 20,000 Nm³/h gaseous oxygen at the Gas Supply Company of Nanjing Iron Steel United Co. Ltd. in China is considered. The ASU adopts the JX300XP distributed control system (DCS) developed by the Zhejiang Supcon Technology Co., Ltd. All equipment of the ASU is provided by the Hangzhou Oxygen Plant Group Co., Ltd. Our previous work has developed an ASU OTS using virtual distributed process unit (DPU) technology and a nonlinear dynamic model (see Reference [11]). This work expands our previous OTS work in the field of human-machine cooperation.

Table 2 lists the MVs of the ASU. In Table 2, HPC and LPC denote high-pressure and low-pressure columns, and CAC-I denotes crude argon column I. We developed a platform for the human-machine cooperative operation, and the cooperation partner's user interface (UI) is shown in Fig. 4.

Table 2. The MVs of the ASU.

Tag	Symbol	Description
MV1	CCSSV_Q	The set value of total air feed flow
MV2	HIC102	The control valve position of product gaseous oxygen flow
MV3	FIC103	The control valve position of product gaseous nitrogen flow
MV4	HIC3	The control valve position of pure liquid nitrogen of high-pressure column (HPC)
MV5	HIC705	The control valve position of crude gaseous argon flow
MV6	PIC104	The control valve position of waste nitrogen pressure of low-pressure column (LPC)
MV7	PICS_3302	The control valve position of oxygen compressor
MV8	LIC701	The control valve position of condenser liquid level of crude argon column I CAC-I
MV9	HC8	The control valve position of product liquid nitrogen
MV10	FIC1	The control valve position of expansion air bypass flow

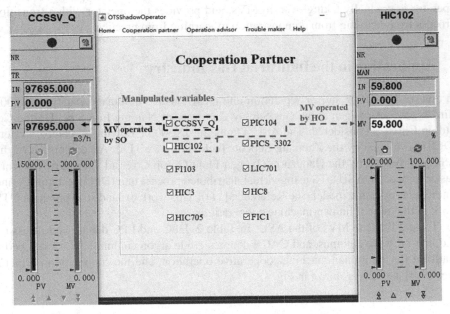

Fig. 4. The UI of the cooperation partner.

In Fig. 4, ☑and ☐denote the MVs responsible for the SO (cooperation partner in this case) and the human operator (HO), respectively. During the operation, the operator can freely choose the MVs he/she is responsible for, and the SO is responsible for the rest.

We applied the SO to the load change operation task of the ASU (the product oxygen flow FI102 increases from 18,000 Nm^3/h to 19,000 Nm^3/h). The shadow operator runs Algorithm 2 every 30 s and solves the optimization problems (1) and (2) to obtain the value of the MVs it is responsible for. A novice operator was selected to complete the task with the SO.

Figure 5 shows the result of the human-machine cooperative operation in this task. In Fig. 5, FI101, FI102 and FI103 are CVs and represent the flow of feed air, product oxygen, and product nitrogen. AI701 represents argon content at the feed of CAC-I, which is a crucial indicator reflecting the working conditions. The smaller the AI701 fluctuation, the better the working conditions, and vice versa. As shown from Fig. 5, at 17:14:24, the novice operator chooses to operate HIC102, an MV that directly controls FI102 manually, and the SO is still responsible for the remaining MVs (see Fig. 4).

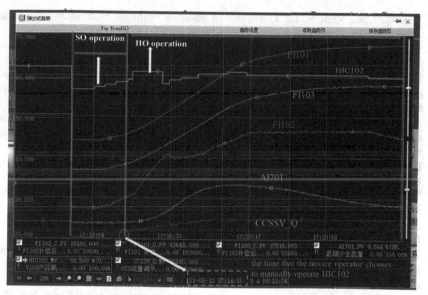

Fig. 5. The result of the human-machine cooperative operation.

After the novice operator took over the HIC102, the SO cooperated with the operator to complete the load change operation task. However, due to the poor operation of the novice operator, the FI102 could not coordinate the changes with other CVs, resulting in large fluctuations in AI701, which is a normal phenomenon because the selected novice operator has not had the opportunity to carry out practical operation training. The novice operator needs a period of training to master complex manual operation skills (responsible for 10 MVs simultaneously), and in this case, the SO can provide help as a partner.

5 Conclusion

In this paper, a novel operator training paradigm is proposed, in which the machine algorithm acts as a virtual trainer to interact with human operators. In the paradigm, a model-based industrial intelligence, called shadow operator, is developed. The shadow operator combines the two-layer industrial model predictive control algorithm and human-machine cooperation principles. Inspired by Bloom's taxonomy, a concept in educational psychology, a hierarchical human-machine model for process operator skill acquisition and improvement is presented. Furthermore, five identities of the shadow operator, namely task performer, cooperation partner, operation advisor, safety supervisor, and trouble maker are designed. The implementation algorithm of the cooperation partner is introduced in detail. An application in the industrial gas industry is provided to show the effectiveness of the cooperation partner.

References

1. Naderpour, M., Nazir, S., Lu, J.: The role of situation awareness in accidents of large-scale technological systems. Process Saf. Environ. Protect. **97**, 13–24 (2015)
2. Salmon, P.M., et al.: Measuring situation awareness in complex systems: comparison of measures study. Int. J. Ind. Ergon. **39**(3), 490–500 (2009)
3. Srinivasan, R., Srinivasan, B., Iqbal, M.U., Nemet, A., Kravanja, Z.: Recent developments towards enhancing process safety: inherent safety and cognitive engineering. Comput. Chem. Eng. **128**, 364–383 (2019)
4. Patle, D.S., Manca, D., Nazir, S., Sharma, S.: Operator training simulators in virtual reality environment for process operators: a review. Virtual Reality **23**(3), 293–311 (2018). https://doi.org/10.1007/s10055-018-0354-3
5. Blanc, P., et al.: Inventaire 2015 des accidents technologiques, Ministère de l'Écologie, du Développement durable et de l'Énergie, Direction générale de la prévention des risques (2015)
6. Nazir, S., Øvergård, K.I., Yang, Z.: Towards effective training for process and maritime industries. Procedia Manuf. **3**, 1519–1526 (2015)
7. Ahmad, Z., Patle, D.S., Rangaiah, G.P.: Operator training simulator for biodiesel synthesis from waste cooking oil. Process Saf. Environ. Protect. **99**, 55–68 (2016)
8. Balaton, M.G., Nagy, L., Szeifert, F.: Operator training simulator process model implementation of a batch processing unit in a packaged simulation software. Comput. Chem. Eng. **48**, 335–344 (2013)
9. Sangaran, S., Haron, S.: Operator training simulator for ethylene plant. Chem. Eng. Trans. **56**, 1621–1626 (2017)
10. Pereira, A.C., Riera, A., Padilla, G., Musulin, E., Nakamura, N.J.: Operator trainer system for the petrobras p-26 semi-submersible oil and gas production unit. Comput. Aided. Chem. Eng. **27**, 1959–1964 (2009)
11. Yang, G., Shao, Z., Xu, Z., Zhang, D., Lou, H., Wang, K.: Development of a novel type operator training simulator framework for air separation process. In: 2021 Chinese Automation Congress, Accepted, Beijing, November 2021
12. Patle, D.S., Ahmad, Z., Rangaiah, G.P.: Operator training simulators in the chemical industry: review, issues, and future directions. Rev. Chem. Eng. **30**(2), 199–216 (2014)
13. Bhavsar, P., Srinivasan, B., Srinivasan, R.: Quantifying situation awareness of control room operators using eye-gaze behavior. Comput. Chem. Eng. **106**, 191–201 (2017)

14. Mayne, D.Q.: Model predictive control: recent developments and future promise. Automatica **50**(12), 2967–2986 (2014)
15. Xu, Z., et al.: Automatic load change system of cryogenic air separation process. Sep. Purif. Technol. **81**(3), 451–465 (2011)
16. Millot, P., Hoc, J.M.: Human-machine cooperation: metaphor or possible reality. In: European Conference on Cognitive Sciences, Manchester, April 1997
17. Krathwohl, D.R.: A revision of Bloom's taxonomy: an overview. Theory Pract. **41**(4), 212–218 (2002)

Correction to: Developing a VR Tool to Support Repeat Pattern Design Learning

Francisco Queiroz⬤, Maria dos Santos Lonsdale⬤,
and Phillip Henry⬤

Correction to:
Chapter "Developing a VR Tool to Support Repeat Pattern Design Learning" in: P. Zaphiris and A. Ioannou (Eds.): *Learning and Collaboration Technologies. Novel Technological Environments*, LNCS 13329, https://doi.org/10.1007/978-3-031-05675-8_9

Chapter ["Developing a VR Tool to Support Repeat Pattern Design Learning"] was previously published non-open access. It has now been changed to open access under a CC BY 4.0 license and the copyright holder updated to 'The Author(s)'. The book has also been updated with this change.

The updated original version of this chapter can be found at
https://doi.org/10.1007/978-3-031-05675-8_9

© The Author(s) 2022
P. Zaphiris and A. Ioannou (Eds.): HCII 2022, LNCS 13329, p. C1, 2022.
https://doi.org/10.1007/978-3-031-05675-8_25

Author Index

Printed in the United States
by Baker & Taylor Publisher Services